David Yallop is a highly r[...]
has over-turned opinion w[...]
As a crime investigator, he has explored the truth behind
Fatty Arbuckle's murder conviction in *The Day the
Laughter Stopped*, campaigned for a royal pardon for
Craig Bentley in *To Encourage the Others*, as well as
chasing the Yorkshire Ripper and Carlos the Jackal. He is
also the author of the groundbreaking and controversial *In
God's Name*, which exposed the corruption within the
Vatican and the murder of John Paul I. This was followed
by *The Power and Glory*, an in-depth exploration of the
papacy of John Paul II and *Beyond Belief*, a searing
indictment of the cover-up of child abuse by the Catholic
Church. He lives in England.

Also by David Yallop

To Encourage the Others
The Day the Laughter Stopped
Beyond Reasonable Doubt
Deliver Us From Evil
In God's Name
To the Ends of the Earth
Unholy Alliance
How They Stole the Game
The Power and the Glory

How They Stole the Game

David Yallop

CONSTABLE • LONDON

Constable & Robinson Ltd
55–56 Russell Square
London WC1B 4HP
www.constablerobinson.com

First published in the UK by Poetic Publishing,
a division of Poetic Products Ltd, 1999

This edition published by Constable,
an imprint of Constable & Robinson Ltd, 2011

A copy of the British Library Cataloguing in
Publication Data is available from the British Library

ISBN: 978-1-78033-401-1

Printed and bound in the UK

1 3 5 7 9 10 8 6 4 2

To Lucy, who shares Pelé's view that 'it's only a game',
and to Fletcher, who agrees with the late Bill Shankly that
'it's more important than life or death'.

Contents

Acknowledgements

As with every other investigation I have undertaken, the list of acknowledgements that follows is but a partial indication of the variety of sources that I have drawn on. As in the past, many would only undertake to assist this investigation in exchange for the promise of anonymity and, as in the past, I respect that wish, although I would observe that for law-abiding individuals to be fearful of retribution when one is dealing with this particular search for truth is an appalling indictment on a state of affairs that exists within international football. I would like to thank those anonymous informants and the following:

His Excellency Rubens Antonio Barbosa, Brazilian Ambassador to the UK, and his Embassy Staff; Monique Berlioux; Wolfgang Berner; Sepp Blatter; Marcio Braga; Bryon Butler; His Excellency Fernando Henrique Cardosa, President of Brazil; Marco Casanova; Dr Mong Joon Chung; Steve Clarke, Mars UK; Richard Denton, Canon; Teddi Domann, McDonald's; Eric Drossart; George Drummond; Mustapha Fahmy; Paul Farrelly; Bureau Chief of the Federal Bureau of Invesigation, Washington, DC; staff of FIFA, Zurich, particularly Keith Cooper, Andreas Herren, Michel Zen-Ruffinen; Barie Gill; Brian Glanville; Celso Grellet; Dr João Havelange; Mava Heffler,

Mastercard; Marc Héraud, Fuji; Bruce Hudson, Anheuser-Busch; Director General and staff of Interpol; Andrew Jennings; UEFA President Lennart Johansson; Jota Jota; Tom Kemmere, Philips; Juca Kfouri; Jim Latham, General Motors; Dr Haddock Lobo; Peter McCormick; John McKnight; Ivan G. Pinheiro Machado, L & P M Editores, Brazil; Sergio A. C. Machado, Distribuidora Record de Servicos, Brazil; Faouzi Mahjoub; His Excellency Roy Chaderton Matos, Venezuelan Ambassador to the UK, and his Embassy staff; UEFA Vice President Dr Antonio Matarrese; Warren Mersereau, Adidas AG; Edson Arantes do Nascimento – Pelé; Jochen H. Pferdmenges; Judith Ravin; Simon Rooks and other staff at the BBC Sound Archives; Claude Ruibal, Coca-Cola; John Salthouse; Laura Sandys; Hiroyuki Sakamoto, JVC; Tim Schramm, Gilette; Karl Schiltz; Secretariat and staff at UEFA; Margaret Shanks; Andrew Sheldon; Vyv Simson; Giulite Soutinho; Roberto Pereira de Souza; staff of Dentsu; staff of the House of Commons Library; staff of ISL; staff of the Olympic Village, Rio; staff of the Press Association Archives; State Prosecutors for Rio, Brazil, Dr Maria Emilia Arauto and Professor Rogerio Mascarenhas and their colleagues; John Sugden; Rogan Taylor; Guido Tognoni; Professor Alan Tomlinson; Brian Tora; Fernanda Verissimo; Derek Wyatt, MP.

Prologue to the 2011 Edition

The book in your hands has not been altered or amended over the past decade. This is the same version that the President of FIFA tried to have banned – the same version that exposed the bribes, the cheating and the corruption. An updated epilogue that covers the bribes, the cheating and the corruption over the past year has been added.

David A. Yallop
London
September 2011

Prologue

During the first week of December 1997 the court of the Sun King came to Marseilles.

The court acolytes, the secretaries, assistants, press attachés, security officers, scurried everywhere. There was always among members of the court an underlying anxiety when 'Le Grand Monarque' was near, particularly when he was giving a public audience. On this occasion the world's media who had gathered were even more deferential than usual. None of them wanted to risk being denied access to the tournament the Sun King had planned for the following summer.

He saw himself as the most powerful man in the world. He was in charge of the world's greatest religion and the coming summer's ceremonies would be watched on television by a cumulative audience of forty billion people. More than six times the population of the world.

An aide hurried forward and muttered in the ear of His Majesty. The aide had to reach on tiptoe to reach the royal ear. In his eighty-second year, the Sun King still stood six feet tall. The athletic muscle tone of his youth had softened slightly but though his weight was now some ten kilos more than in his prime, he remained an imposing figure. His face, which usually resembled a well-kept grave, hovered on a smile, then reverted to a baleful stare, but it was still obvious that he was savouring the moment.

'Do excuse me, ladies and gentlemen. I have to take a phone call from President Chirac.'

Presidents. Kings and Queens. Heads of State. Prime Ministers. He has met every world leader. His Holiness the Pope has been granted a number of audiences. The Sun King has a very clear view of his place in the world order.

'Do you consider yourself the most powerful man in the world?'

Most men asked such a question would demur. Would dismiss it with a laugh. Dr João Havelange, President of Fédération Internationale de Football Association – FIFA – did not demur and he certainly did not laugh.

'I've been to Russia twice, invited by President Yeltsin. I've been to Poland with their President. In the 1990 World Cup in Italy I saw Pope John Paul II three times. When I go to Saudi Arabia, King Fahd welcomes me in splendid fashion. In Belgium I had a one-and-a-half-hour meeting with King Albert. Do you think a Head of State will spare that much time to just anyone? That's respect. That's the strength of FIFA. I can talk to any President, but they'll be talking to a President too on an equal basis. They've got their power, and I've got mine: the power of football, which is the greatest power there is.'

That's the Havelange version of 'yes'.

On face value it is an outrageous claim, but the latterday Sun King offers an array of facts and figures to justify his opinion of himself. The Pope may well preside over one of the world's major faiths, but Havelange rules over a religion that is devoutly followed by more than one fifth of the planet.

'The World Cup 94 in the United States was watched by a cumulative audience of thirty-one billion people. More than five times the population of Earth. The annual turnover of football is $255 billion. It offers direct and indirect employment to more than four hundred and fifty million people. There are national associations affiliated to FIFA in one hundred and ninety-eight countries. More countries are affiliated to my organisation than are members of the United Nations.'

Not so much a case of 'I am the State' as 'I am the world'. João Havelange, like many a ruler throughout history, has strengthened his grasp on his throne by relentlessly increasingly his empire. On 11 July 1974, when he came to power after plotting and conspiring over the previous three years, the number of affiliates was one hundred and thirty-eight. That same year in Germany only sixteen countries contested the final stages of the World Cup. In 1998 in France there were thirty-two countries. This may or may not be for the 'good of the game'. It most certainly had been for the good of Dr Havelange, ensuring, as it had, six continuous terms of office. The increase in the number of international competitions from two to eight had also been a vote winner among the delegates. The FIFA Coca-Cola Cup. The FIFA Futsal World Championship. The FIFA World Championship for women. The Under-17 World Championship for the FIFA/JVC Cup. As British sports writer Brian Glanville remarked to me:

'Havelange has only two ambitions left to fulfil. The first is to become the first posthumous President of FIFA. The second is to organise a World Cup tournament for embryos.'

In less than three minutes, hardly time to boil an egg, the Sun King had returned from his conversation with the President of France. Cordial regrets from Chirac that he would not be able to attend the junketing in Marseilles. The relationship had not always been so cordial.

In 1985, during an International Olympic Committee meeting in Berlin, Chirac, who was then leading the bid from Paris, became enraged as he watched Havelange wheeling and dealing to ensure that the Olympic Games for 1992 went to Barcelona.

The French team had gone to Berlin prepared to rest their case on the merits and virtues of Paris. Havelange, wearing his Olympic Committee member hat, was busily organising the Spanish-speaking members of the Committee behind the Barcelona campaign. The Havelange style of organising such an exercise involves lavish receptions, all-expenses-paid trips for committee members, gifts that began with Rolexes and ended with whatever value the committee member put on his or her vote. Just to make sure the vote stayed committed to Barcelona's cause, members were wined and dined by Prime Minister Gonzalez and key members of his Cabinet and then entertained by the King and Queen of Spain. Chirac exploded.

'If you don't stop this bribery, Dr Havelange, I'll start using my influence in Africa. Not to get the Olympic Games but to stop you getting re-elected as President of FIFA.'

It made no difference. Barcelona got the Games and Havelange has continued unopposed, presiding over the world's most popular religion.

During his brief absence from the press conference, Sepp Blatter, the General Secretary of FIFA, had unwisely allowed questions from the press. The Sun King does not like the press, even less does he like questions from reporters. He turned a basilisk glance in the direction of one questioner.

'Why hasn't Pelé been invited to take part in the draw?'

Mute messages passed between the two men. Blatter, small, rotund, one half of a very curious double act. Havelange, tall and, even now in his eighties, still exhibiting the physique of an Olympic swimmer. Blatter responded.

'We do not have a problem with Mr Pelé.'

There was muffled laughter. Everyone in the room knew that they did indeed have a problem with Pelé.

'So why has he not been invited to take part in the draw along with the other great footballers?'

'We have no problem with Mr Pelé,' Blatter responded. 'But ...'

'We have no problem with Mr Pelé,' Blatter said yet again but this time with a note of finality. The General Secretary had been very well trained over the years by the latterday Sun King and the modern Cardinal Richelieu – Horst Dassler of Adidas. The ladies and gentlemen of the press came a great deal cheaper than an Olympic Committee member. If their potential accreditation to World Cup 98 did not fully concentrate their collective minds, there were always the freebies. The one thousand one hundred and eighty-one journalists milled around for their handouts. Chocolate bars from Snickers, razors from Gillette, filofaxes from Canon. They collected their caps, badges and watches. They slipped on a jacket, put a free football in a bag, took handfuls of stickers, key rings and pens and notebooks, put out their hands for free calculators that obligingly converted a range of foreign currencies automatically.

Small wonder that the tickets to attend this affair were every bit as hot as the tickets for the actual football matches. The scene for the main festivities was the massively and expensively refurbished Stade Vélodrome. It was quite a party.

There were the thirty-eight thousand ordinary guests. There were the one thousand five hundred special guests. If the former contained many children and teenagers, the latter represented the really major players of the game. Not the football stars, though they too were in attendance, but the power brokers, the wheelers and dealers, FIFA delegates who might carry many a vote in their back pockets. Sponsors whose millions paid for much more than the five days of junketing at Marseilles. At a cost of £5 million that represented just a little petty cash. The financial commitment of the sponsors since the mid-1970s had dramatically contributed to the financial feeding frenzy that football has become.

The location might be Marseilles, but a stranger would have been excused for thinking that they had wandered into a rehearsal for a modern-dress play about Louis XIV. The subjects being discussed by small groups huddling conspiratorially had such timeless themes. Money, power, possessions.

One group was preoccupied with the coming struggle for the throne. Would Blatter announce that he was going to run? Would Beckenbauer make a late challenge? What of Platini? Or Grondona or …?

Another group was deep in discussion on marketing and television rights for 2002 and 2006. Talking telephone numbers had been updated. These people talked 'one point four' or 'two point six'. Billions, of course.

In one corner Graham Kelly and Sir Bert Millichip were arguing the merits of pay-TV. 'Just move all the games to Saturday night or Sunday. Revenues in the first year? Oh, on top of the one hundred and sixty million already being paid by Sky, got to be an additional forty million. Growth potential is … Sky High!' They exploded into laughter.

Moving like patrolling barracudas through the room are the players' agents. Not many have managed to get in, just a favoured few with good connections in Zurich. They want a piece of the action. They lust after a share of the wealth that is washing through the game in the last years of the century. Eighteen-year-old Michael Owen on ten thousand a week in 1998 set the benchmark for teenage footballers. By the end of that year, after a sensational World Cup debut, Owen was destined to receive a pay rise. His weekly wage packet with his sponsorship deals added to it would be £50,000. Some of the lads in their twenties

and thirties are pulling in a bit more. David Beckham on
£8.1 million this year just edges out Alan Shearer, but is still
a long way below the top earner, Luiz Nazário de Lima of
Brazil, better known as Ronaldo. He has a contract with
Internazionale of Milan that brings in £100,000 per week,
then there is his share of the $200 million sponsor deal with
Nike that is paid to the Brazilian national squad for World
Cup endorsements. Ronaldo's earnings this year will be
£20.5 million. Just under £400,000 per week. Ronaldo is
twenty-one years of age.

Looking after the needs of the guests were one thousand
staff, a further five hundred security officers and two
squadrons of gendarmes. Ensuring that the festivities ran
smoothly were a further one thousand four hundred and
fifty stage and television technicians. Fourteen articulated
lorries had brought in various items of equipment.

But above all there were the sponsors. World Cup 98 is
not primarily about football. It is first and foremost about
product. The product varies depending on who is making
the pitch.

At Marseilles in early December 1997 there was so much
to do. Always assuming you had the right accreditation,
the right labels, the proper badges and four different kinds
of ID.

One could breakfast with McDonald's and chat to
Ronaldo or Beckenbauer or Carlos Alberto Parreira.
Lunch with the incomparable Pelé, courtesy of MasterCard,
take afternoon tea with foreign ambassadors who were
being paid to be pleasant by Adidas; have a glass of
champagne with Newcastle's Alan Shearer thanks to
Umbro, who produced the England captain as if he were
an extremely large rabbit and had him sign a fifteen-year
deal worth – depending on his performance on the pitch
rather than the cocktail bar – between ten and twenty
million pounds. Shearer's health is market-sensitive. Five

months before the gathering in Marseilles Shearer had sustained a serious injury to ankle ligaments. Overnight £11 million was knocked off Newcastle's shares. If the Umbro campaign had given the guest the taste for more, one could move on to canapés and more champagne, this time from Hewlett Packard. Finally, courtesy of FIFA there was a nine-course dinner with the Mayors of the ten cities where the various football matches would be played and, of course, yet more champagne, while five thousand children marched past the window of the restaurant in torch-light procession. All this and not one football kicked in earnest during the entire five days, the match between a Europe team versus the Rest of the World providing a perfect example of the great difficulty that trained athletes experience when attempting to run on a full wallet.

All of this to celebrate the draw for the first round of the World Cup 98. Picking thirty-two slips of paper from a glass bowl. God only knows what the Sun King had up his sleeve for when the going got serious and we actually had the matches in June. Resplendent throughout the entire proceedings was Dr João Havelange. Never less than immaculately attired. Heaven help any FIFA official who ever comes within his area of vision with a top shirt button undone or a tie loosened. An enduring image of the opening ceremony for the World Cup Finals in the United States in 1994 was the Sun King. On an afternoon in Chicago when the temperature was in the high eighties, with President Clinton perspiring freely, Havelange sat wearing his dark double-breasted suit buttoned up throughout the game. He never betrayed a moment's distress, but then he never betrayed any other emotion either. Marseilles was the same. By comparison with the Sun King, the Sphinx suffers from chronic hyperactivity.

There were moments, however, that gave possible indications that FIFA's President was perhaps reflecting on

things past, on times remembered. A glance into the middle
distance, a failure to respond to a companion's conversation,
an aide telling him where to stand, moments where it
seemed that perhaps for the first time he was accepting that
his long reign was indeed drawing to a close. On 8 June
1998, in Paris, the twenty-four-year reign of President
Havelange would come to an end and the crown would
pass to one of the pretenders to the throne.

If Havelange was indeed indulging in some nostalgic
reflections during the events in Marseilles, there was much
for him to meditate upon. This man, who is very much the
master of all he surveys within the world of football, has
had honours showered upon him.

Those honours include the Cavalier of the Légion
d'Honneur (France), the Order of Special Merit in Sports
(Brazil), the Commander of the Orden Infante Dome
Henrique (Portugal), the Cavalier of Vasa Orden (Sweden)
and the Grand Cross of Elizabeth the Catholic (Spain). The
full list of the honours awarded to the man totals over
three hundred. In 1989 he was nominated for the Nobel
Peace Prize.

All of this and a great deal more besides reflects a man
who should be held in the very highest esteem in any
country where football is played. He told me that when he
took over the FIFA presidency in 1974 the coffers were
empty. Officials were at that time forced to live a hand-to-
mouth existence, this at least is the view of Havelange. He
bowed out in the summer of 1998 leaving FIFA with
property assets worth in excess of $100 million and a
guaranteed income over the next ten years of more than $4
billion.

During his twenty-four-year reign football has been
transformed. Spectators now sit in all-seater modern
stadiums and in many countries have the opportunity to
applaud twenty-two multi-millionaires onto the pitch.

Many leading clubs now have fewer paying spectators than investing shareholders. Performance on the pitch is now matched by movement on the Stock Exchange. Promotion to the Premier League from the First Division in England is worth a minimum of an extra £5 million pounds revenue to a club. The price of relegation? Financial oblivion. During those twenty-four years, despite the excess of commercialism that engulfs football, the game has strengthened its grip on man's imagination. A recent survey established that in Britain 95 per cent of men aged between twenty and thirty-four years of age would rather watch World Cup soccer than make love to the woman of their dreams. Michelle Pfeiffer, Claudia Schiffer and the others relegated to a waiting room until after the penalty shoot-out.

So go out and get your twelve-pack, a crate of Cloudy Bay and your World Cup baseball cap, your World Cup key ring and notepad plus your World Cup sunglasses, your World Cup Adidas clothes and footwear, your World Cup 98 Coca-Cola, your World Cup Canon fax machine, pay for it all with your World Cup 98 MasterCard and settle down in front of your television set. Don't try to get a ticket for any of the matches: with a 20 per cent allocation to sponsors and corporate guests in contrast to 8 per cent per team for their fans you will be unlucky, unless of course you happen to know one of the FIFA executives who are peddling them on the black market. Settle down and raise a can or a glass to the Sun King. More than any other person he is the one individual responsible for the happy state of affairs described above. Even more, he has promised each of the nearly two hundred federations a million-dollar gift per year for the next four years. To each of the six International Confederations he has promised a massive annual gift of ten million dollars for the same period. All of this to 'improve the sport in their regions'. These vast amounts of money would also powerfully concentrate the minds of the delegates some seven months hence when they came to vote for Havelange's successor in Paris.

Dr João Havelange has swum a very long way since competing in the Olympic Pool in Berlin in 1936 and the water has not always been clean. According to the man himself, the world of football owes Havelange much. Why then is he so despised and reviled by so many people, both in and out of the game? Is there any truth in the allegations of corruption? Of illicit arms dealing? Of bribes given and received? Any validity in the allegations that among his friends are numbered some of the worst dregs of society, certainly people that no self-respecting Cavalier of the Légion d'Honneur should be consorting with?

FIFA has as its motto the slogan 'For the Good of the Game'. What follows is an attempt to establish exactly how good for the game have been the life and times of João Havelange.

Part One

His father Joseph Faustin Godefroid died in 1933 when Havelange was just eighteen years of age, his mother Juliette in 1945. Yet even today the now eighty-two-year-old still declares his father to have been his best male friend and his mother to have been one of his best female friends. What fortunate parents.

Born in Rio de Janeiro, Brazil, on 8 May 1916, he was baptised into the Roman Catholic faith as Jean Marie (João) Faustin Godefroid Havelange. His parents ensured that in the classic sense the future President of FIFA had quite a few names to live up to.

His father graduated as a mining engineer from the University of Liège before leaving in 1902 to take a teaching post at the University of San Marcos in Lima, Peru. Ten years later he returned to Liège and married his childhood sweetheart. Before embarking on a career change which would take him to Brazil, he returned to Lima to work out the end of his contract. For this return journey he decided to travel on the ship that was being described as unsinkable – the *Titanic* – but by the time he arrived at Southampton, the ship had departed, thus saving his life and making the presence of Havelange on this earth a future possibility.

The young couple then moved to Rio, where Joseph was to work as a representative of United States Steel. A versatile man, he soon took on further representations for a variety of companies, but the one that would have resonance as far as his son's career is concerned – resonance, that is, for some of João Havelange's critics – was the work that Joseph did for La Société Française des Munitions. If the father is remembered at all outside of the Havelange family today, it is as an arms dealer.

It was a comfortable childhood for João, his brother Jules and his sister Helena. Though not wealthy, the family enjoyed a good quality of life in the Brazilian capital. Wherever the key lay to explain the future achievements of Havelange, it cannot be found in formative years spent in extreme poverty. From his parents he was taught precisely the kind of values that one would expect from practising Roman Catholics.

'My parents always stressed during my upbringing the value of friends. That friendship was something to be respected and maintained ... Respect was yet another principle that I learned during my early years. Whether that of the most important people at the top of the ladder or those at the bottom who need help with their problems. I have the greatest respect for the whole of mankind. Honesty was another principle instilled in me during my education and by my parents from birth onwards, and one which I have respected throughout my life in managing several businesses. I have also followed this principle in carrying out my mandate as head of FIFA.'

One of the inherent dangers in publicly stating the various principles that guide one's life is the possibility that they will come back to haunt you.

Havelange's multi-racial environment in Rio during his early years has undoubtedly proved to be an invaluable asset in later years. A society that covers the full racial spectrum, or at least a considerable part of it as Brazil's does, should with appropriate exposure ensure a freedom from prejudice and a balanced view of the one hundred and ninety-eight countries that currently comprise the FIFA membership, yet over the more than two decades that he ruled supreme over football, one recurring prejudice has emerged. He may be tolerance itself when it comes to blacks, Arabs and Jews. He may welcome with embraces those from India, Japan and Korea. But when it comes to the Old World he has frequently displayed anti-European sentiments. Indeed it was just such views that were fashioned into a winning election platform in 1974. For a man brought up in a household where only French was spoken and the native Portuguese language was very much relegated to minimum use, who then spent part of his school years in France, the Sun King is surprisingly hostile towards Europe. He is first and foremost a Brazilian, who has imposed on world football an infrastructure that is quintessentially South American.

The cronyism, the wheeling and dealing, the secret dubious deals, the nepotism, the lack of democracy and the abundance of dictatorial leadership – aspects that have been such a feature of the Havelange presidency – demonstrate other early influences apart from his parents at work during his formative years. To listen to Havelange – and many have discovered that to interview him is to listen to him – he is the definitive example of the self-made man. Again and again he pays tribute to just one person, to one individual. Himself.

One of the many characteristics that are evident when talking to the President of the world's most widely followed religion is his obsessiveness. It manifests utself in a bizarre recital of his achievements. A recital that can range from the significant to the trivial.

'My period in office represents 8,760 days and I was away from home for 7,200 of them, fulfilling my obligations. But it shows that I have been devoted to the task of developing the importance of football throughout the world ... From 1974 to 1998 I have worked three hundred days a year for FIFA. I have taken part in 720 meetings of FIFA standing committees. I missed only five. I visited 192 countries at least three times. I couldn't go to Afghanistan, the Samoan Islands or four former Soviet republics. I have over that time spent 800 hours per year on planes. That makes a total of about twenty thousand hours ... I flew from Rio to Zurich twelve times a year which makes a total of 288 Rio–Zurich return flights.'

If Trivial Pursuit ever becomes an Olympic event, my money – notwithstanding his age – is on Havelange. He is able to describe every trip he has made in detail, the time he arrived at the airport, the departure times, how long the stopovers were. He'll tell you how he spent every living, waking minute of the twenty-four years. Perhaps not every minute. There are hours, days, weeks that Havelange prefers to draw a veil over, but again and again he will powerfully demonstrate an obsessive personality.

It was one of the particular aspects of João Havelange's personality that I discussed with Dr Haddock Lobo. He and the Sun King had a falling-out in the 1970s but prior to that they had been close friends for nearly fifty years. Lobo recalled the thirteen-year-old Havelange. In view of the fact that his father Joseph had been one of the founder members of Standard Liège, the son's interest in the game was predictable.

'At that time we both played football at the Fluminese. Havelange played as a half-back – central defender. Average ability. His father thought that swimming would be a better sport for João and became his swimming trainer. He trained constantly. Training without stopping. While others were swimming three hundred metres, four hundred metres, he would go to three thousand. Yes, some of this was his father's influence, but the son was already very obsessive. He would go every day of the week, even Sundays. At that time the only pool open in Rio on a Sunday was at the YMCA. He'd be there every Sunday. Now that I'm much older and reflect on these things it demonstrates to me a man that was obsessed to be number one. To be the best of all.'

In case the views of a man who, for much of the past twenty years, has been engaged in a bitter and costly legal battle with his former business partner be thought perhaps biased, those of another man who has remained a close friend for over fifty years are worth considering.

Mario Amato, President of the National Industrial Confederation – CNI – vividly recalls Havelange at the São Paulo Club Espéria.

'Havelange belongs to that class of men which no longer exists. He was an outstanding member of the water polo team. He also had the organisational skills to command all the other teams in the club. He's one of those men with so much charisma that you want to touch him to see if he's real; he's an idol. I remember once a polo team was going to play in Europe and he had the pool filled with ice. He told the team that they had to get used to the temperatures they would find there.'

At much the same time that he was impressing his Rio school friends with his determination in the water, Havelange was also beginning his lifelong interest in commerce, in turning a dollar. Though still a young student, he told me he would go to his father's Rio office and help with decoding the telegrams.

When I recounted to Havelange the tale from his lifelong friend Mario Amato of the ice-filled swimming pool he dismissed it as 'a fantasy. It never happened.' In studying the life and times of João Havelange it would seem appropriate to proceed with more than usual caution. Fantasy has been woven into the man's history in many places, often by the man himself. The early years of Havelange are important for many reasons, not least because they hold at least two important keys. One unlocks the door to his personal credibility, the other reveals the origins of his private wealth. Havelange's position is that it was acquired by hard work and honest endeavour. The extraordinary allegations that have swirled around his head for much of his presidency of FIFA suggest other explanations. That is why there is a need to examine the reality of his life during the pre-FIFA years.

What is not in doubt either during his early life or subsequently is the almost fanatical desire to succeed that is within Havelange. In and out of the water he was and indeed still is obsessed with winning. With being the best. He told me how when as a young swimmer no matter how hard he trained – 'six thousand metres in the morning and six thousand metres in the evening' – no matter how long he practised, he could not win races. That indefinable additional element continued to elude him, until …

'I don't know where it came from, but suddenly something inside of me exploded. I started to win. Four hundred, eight hundred, and one thousand metres. I won them all. I wanted to fulfil the wishes of my father and one day my condition seemed to explode and I won. For ten years I won every single race in which I competed. I was champion of Rio. Champion of São Paulo. Brazilian champion. South American champion.'

And throughout all the success his father was there. Urging him on until in 1933 his father suffered a cerebral haemorrhage. He lay close to death for many weeks. At one point he rallied and, regaining consciousness, asked his son to promise that he would continue to excel at swimming. Would make every effort to represent his country at the Berlin Olympics. Inevitably the son dutifully accepted the challenge. A few days later his father died.

The teenager continued to win every race and was selected to swim for Brazil at Berlin. His winning streak was about to come to an end.

'Today between Rio de Janeiro and Zurich you're talking about a flight of eleven, eleven and a half hours. But at the time of the Olympic Games, there were no planes, we went by boat, and so we came by boat from Rio de Janeiro to Bremerhaven and it took twenty-one days. And there was no swimming pool on board, so we arrived six days before the competition and we didn't have time to build up our condition. I did participate, but I wasn't able to come up to this condition.'

The 1936 Olympic Games in Berlin had in the minds of the organising Germans only one aim. To glorify the Nazi regime of Adolf Hitler. The Games had been awarded to Germany before Hitler attained full power. As the evil reality of the Third Reich became apparent there were growing attempts, particularly in the United States with its influential Jewish population, to organise a boycott of the Games.

Despite the fact that three years after attaining supreme power Hitler's dictatorial abuse of what had begun as a legally obtained position was obvious to all, the Games went ahead. *Heil Hitler!* had become the obligatory form of greeting; a cult of Führer worship held Germany in its thrall. Political opponents of every persuasion were purged, imprisoned or murdered. Free speech no longer existed; the supremacy of the Aryan race was an article of faith. Jews were deprived of citizenship, forbidden to marry non-Jews and barred from the liberal professions. Concentration camps contained many whose only crime was to have been born Jewish. By the time that the Games opened in mid-1936 it was equally obvious that Germany was re-arming. All of this and a great deal more was self-evident, but not to everyone.

Havelange recalled to me his impressions.

'The organisation. The attention to detail. The efficiency. The Berlin Games was one of the most excellent spectacles I have seen in my life. Everything was grandiose and perfect. You have to remember what period of history this was. Everyone admired the progress of Germany.'

Havelange applauded the extraordinary feats of the black American athlete Jesse Owens, the modest twenty-three-year-old who, through his remarkable talents, gave a definitive one-man response to Hitler's views of Aryan supremacy as he won four gold medals and out-ran and out-jumped all others. The Brazilian was unaware that Hitler stormed from the Olympic stadium rather than meet the triumphant Owens. Was equally unaware that Hitler made a point of congratulating Lutz Long, the German-born American who came second to Owens in the long jump, while ignoring the winner. Was also unaware that Minister for Propaganda Josef Goebbels had dubbed Jesse Owens and the other black Americans as 'black mercenaries'. There were other aspects that still over sixty years later came readily to mind for João Havelange:

'Once the Games were over the [German] government made it possible for any of the athletes to visit any of the cities we wanted to. And we travelled by trains which were exceptional, first class, and we had a reduction of 75 per cent on the fare.'

'And what was the impression you gained of the rest of Germany after the Olympic Games?'

'Everyone seemed happy, that was the impression I got, nothing was short, everyone was polite. Of course the young people of my time were not like youth is today. We didn't engage in politics and today young people are only interested in politics, so this is a different aspect. I must admit that the time I spent in Germany at that period was undeniably unforgettable and a wonderful time.'

In the autumn of 1936 Havelange returned to Brazil with fond memories but an uncertain future. His late father's business was long defunct. The lucrative arms deals that had put food on the table during his father's life had passed into other hands. The young man turned initially to a modern Dante's Inferno. He went to work at Siderúrgica Belgo-Mineira, an iron and steel construction company.

If his recollections of that period are as accurate as the statistics he reels out concerning his FIFA years, the four years gave him an all-round business grounding.

'I was doing all the administrative work. Dealing with the workers, receiving clients, everything to do with the organisation for about ten dollars a week. I went to the boss after four years and said, "I'm resigning. I never want to work for another boss in my life."'

By now qualified with a law degree, Havelange, according to what he told me, worked for a couple of years as a lawyer before going to São Paulo in 1940 to work in a legal capacity for a bus company. After several transport companies had merged, Havelange was appointed as a director. Since that time Havelange invariably describes himself as the owner and president of the company that is now known as Viação Cometa:

'Thirty million people a year are transported by my company, which I have now been with for fifty-eight years, fifty-four of them as President.'

Further research of the early Havelange years established a more prosaic picture. Dr Lobo is adamant that his former friend and business partner never practised as a lawyer.

'Yes, he went to university and he did graduate as a lawyer, but he never practised. Look, I graduated with an accountancy degree. I've never practised. Does that mean I'm an accountant? It's just a name.'

And president of an inter-state bus company?

'He went to São Paulo and after working for Siderúrgica Belgo-Mineira for a few years he went as a clerk to a small bus company. Some years later this company took over another, Viação Cometa. This acquisition gave the company access to inter-state routes. Havelange was indeed promoted onto the Board after some years but it was my understanding that the title of director was an honorary one. He was never president.'

Whatever the precise truth of his early years at the São Paulo-based bus company, Havelange certainly acquired a complete grounding in the nuts and bolts of running inter-state transport:

'With the war, South America had been cut off from Europe so we could no longer get spare parts. They dismantled fifty of these two hundred and fifty buses and they set up a stock of spare parts and this way we were able to continue working throughout the six years of the war with 200 buses in the city of São Paulo. When the war was over the mayor of São Paulo offered to set up a government transport company to absorb all the private companies. And I was asked to become a director of this new company. But I didn't accept because I don't work for governments. I'm too independent to submit to politicians. And so the city company, government company, was set up and the war had finished in May 1945 and at the end of '46 Viação Cometa was set up. And instead of working in the cities, we started working between the cities, say for example like between Geneva–Zurich, Zurich–Lausanne and so on.'

'And were you still on ten dollars a month at this time?'

'That's another matter. And throughout the whole network we transport thirty million passengers a year. And when Brazil was undergoing a very major financial crisis we had to cut down from sixty trips to twenty-six. With these sixty trips we had a seat occupancy rate of 80 per cent. With this crisis we had twenty-six trips, so out of sixty trips we lost thirty-four, but by selecting the best drivers and the best buses we offered a completely reliable service and increased our seat occupancy rate to 100 per cent. During this entire crisis we had fifteen thousand on the payroll and we didn't sack anyone at all. The reason for this, you get to know people during times of difficulty, not during times when everything is going well. The life of a normal bus is five years. During these five years each bus normally goes through two engines, and each engine would cover with no problem a million kilometres. So each year you renew six hundred buses and these buses are completely reconditioned, you install either a new engine or a reconditioned engine and we can issue a guarantee that this engine is going to run for a million kilometres. And we have a very large market for these reconditioned buses, because in accountancy terms, after five years, each one is devalued to the point where it's only worth a dollar. As if it didn't exist at the end of five years. So by reconditioning it and putting in an engine that was going to last another million kilometres, well, they came from Chile, Argentina, Uruguay, Paraguay to buy these buses, and they paid us in dollars and this helps us to keep the balance. So you can understand why FIFA for me is ... I didn't come here simply to watch football matches. I came here to administer this as if it was a company or an industry.'

These were invaluable lessons. Again and again throughout his life Havelange would apply that same very acute business sense. His life is riddled with such examples. Also evident throughout the years and burning just as brightly in his eighty-third year is the desire to be not just a winner but to be *the* winner. As we stood out on the second-floor patio of FIFA House in Zurich I took a moment to enjoy the stunning view. Havelange was anxious to point out to me not Lake Zurich or the

Fraumunster with its stained-glass windows by Marc Chagall or the Belvoirpark.

'Where we are standing there was when I took over in 1974 a small, two-storeyed building. There were eight staff in all. I had the building knocked down and this modern headquarters built. Over there I bought that building to house our technical staff. Over there I acquired that building. Further over where they are busy demolishing that old hotel a new building will rise for more FIFA staff. I now have over sixty full-time personnel working here. All of this has been acquired in the most desirable part of Zurich. The real estate FIFA now owns is worth at a conservative estimate over one hundred million dollars.'

In that moment I knew that when the young Havelange set out on his journey through life, whether it was bus companies, real estate, condoms or football associations, whatever he was going to get involved with he would not rest, would not pause, would not reflect until his organisation was the biggest, the best, the most valuable in the world. At a given point in his irresistible rise he chanced upon the beautiful game. In twenty-four years of supreme power he has taken it and transformed it. Revolutionised it. Whether that transformation has been for the better, whether that revolution has enhanced the game, whether the game is as innocent and as beautiful as it was when Havelange decided to make a career out of it, I leave for the reader to decide.

While demonstrating at the Viação Cometa bus company an industry and an attention to detail that at least during working hours channelled his obsessive personality, Havelange out of work still spent hours in the swimming pool, training, always training. Three times he won São Paulo's long-distance swimming race across the Tiete River. In 1952 he again represented his country, this time as a water-polo player, at the Helsinki Olympics. In 1956 he was chief of the Brazilian delegation at the Melbourne Olympics.

In the same year he was elected Vice President of the CBD, the Federation of Brazilian Sports, responsible for overseeing twenty-three different sporting disciplines. Havelange had been collecting sporting committee positions since 1937; by the time he had become number two of the most powerful sporting organisation in Brazil he had held a string of administrative positions.

His election as President of the CBD two years later in 1958 happily coincided with one spectacular sporting success for Brazil.

When Havelange had become Vice President of the CBD, one of the particular sports that he paid keen attention to was football, especially the national squad.

Today, notwithstanding what happened in World Cup 98, Brazil represent for millions around the planet all that is best about football. Style, flair, elegance, panache, accomplishment, genius. The dictionary has been ransacked for superlatives to describe successive Brazilian teams over the past forty years. Magnificent, matchless, unrivalled, supreme. The remarkable skills that the Brazilians have shown the world over four decades stay for the spectator forever frozen in the memory. It was not always so.

During the 1950s the Brazilian national team was both Dr Jekyll and Mr Hyde. Both personalities were frequently on display during the same match. Their talent was often masked and marred by a level of violence that if perpetrated off the pitch would have resulted in prison sentences. In 1954 the World Cup was held in Switzerland, for no better reason than the fact that FIFA was celebrating its fiftieth anniversary and wanted the tournament in its own backyard.

This particular World Cup saw the birth of the televised match. On 16 June, millions of new fans were converted to the sport when they saw Yugoslavia beat France 1–0. Many of the subsequent matches were also televised and the move towards the rampant commercialism of the present day had begun. If a recording exists of the quarter-final between the favourites Hungary and Brazil, and it is ever re-shown on television, it should carry a health warning for viewers of a nervous disposition. The good, the bad and the ugly were all on display during what was forever to be known as the 'Battle of Berne'. Two penalty kicks were awarded. Three players were sent off – two Brazilians, one Hungarian. When the war on the pitch reached the full-time whistle, it carried on into extra-time on the touchline and the changing rooms. The Hungarian coach Gustáv Sebes was punched in the face, the Brazilian captain Pinheiro was hit in the face by a bottle that many observers insisted had been wielded by the injured Hungarian star Ferenc Puskás, who, having watched the attrition from the sidelines, was eager to join in. The brawl involved the majority of the two teams, the police, photographers, members of both the Hungarian and Brazilian delegations. The Brazilian squad invaded the Hungarian team's dressing room. The World Cup Disciplinary Committee, who in their entirety were watching the match, declined to take any action. When English referee Arthur Ellis, the one individual to emerge from the affair with his reputation enhanced, subsequently asked Bozsik, the Hungarian captain whom he had sent off, whether he had subsequently been suspended by his national association, Bozsik replied disdainfully:

'We don't suspend deputies in Hungary.'

The moral clearly was: if you wish to behave disgracefully during a World Cup game, first get yourself elected to parliament or, in Bozsik's case, the Hungarian National Assembly.

The score – if anyone cared – was Hungary 4, Brazil 2.

Referee Arthur Ellis recently recalled the match: 'I thought it was going to be greatest game I'd ever see. I was on top of the world. It was a wholly deluded anticipation. Whether politics and religion had something to do with it, I don't know, but they behaved like animals. It was a disgrace.' Ellis was contemptuous of officialdom's response to the shambles. 'FIFA turned a blind eye. Too many committee members were afraid of losing trips to nice places.'

Perhaps beyond a certain level of desire reason goes out of the window as madness comes in the door. Four years earlier at the still unfinished Maracaná Stadium in Rio two hundred thousand spectators, virtually all cheering for the home team, had seen victory snatched from the favourites Brazil by a goal fifteen minutes from time that gave Uruguay the 1950 World Cup. By the time that the winners did their traditional lap of honour the world's largest football stadium was virtually empty. The burden of expectation had proved too heavy to bear, but still the Brazil of 1950 could take pride in their contribution to that Final. There was no pride to be taken in the débâcle in Berne.

In 1956, during Brazil's tour of Europe, the dark side of the Brazilian game was again on show. After a match in Vienna, the Brazilian team and their officials attempted to attack the referee. Brazil had become the team that all others feared playing for all the wrong reasons.

There were just two years left before the World Cup would come around again. Two years before Brazil would probably again self-destruct on a world stage. It was precisely at this time that João Havelange was elected President of CBD. Havelange, a committee man par excellence, began to demonstrate that a committee of seven works best when six are either absent or silent.

'I applied the same principles of organisation to the

problems of the national team that I had applied to Viação Cometa.'

'Running a bus company surely requires quite a different expertise to running the country's football team?'

'All that differs is the fine detail. The need for a board-based administrative concept is shared. The need for a wide range of specialists in a variety of disciplines is shared. What differs is the kind of specialist. One needs mechanics who take a bus apart, diagnose the problem and remedy it. The footballer needs not just coaches, but specialists, psychologists for instance. I appointed a new coach, Vicente Feola. He was from São Paulo, I knew him well. Another São Paulo man I appointed was the team doctor, Hilton Gosling. I appointed a team psychologist, Professor João Carvalhais. He was also from São Paulo.'

'What was the thinking behind the appointment of a psychologist?'

'I had the security of a comfortable environment to grow up in. For me to travel abroad to Berlin, Helsinki or Melbourne was not a problem. Many of these young footballers came from humble homes, from the *favelas*, from backgrounds of great deprivation. They had to make tremendous adjustments, sometimes in a very short space of time. They had to channel their natural violence, had to understand and accept discipline. Before I took control no thought had been given to these problems. We could not continue towards the 1958 World Cup in Sweden in the same manner. I was determined that what had happened at Berne and in Vienna would never happen again. One of the first things that I did was produce with the help of these professionals – doctors, psychologist and the rest of the experts – a highly detailed, very secret report on every single potential member of the national squad. Those that in our opinion could not or would not make the necessary adjustments were dropped from the squad. The psychologist played a vital role in all of this. There is no point in sending a team out that is only physically prepared. They must also be mentally fit.'

In the mid-1950s such thinking was radical in the First World. In the Third World it was unheard of. In England most First Division clubs in those pre-Premier League days had not moved very far from the 'squirt of pain relief spray, a mouthful of water and a suck on a piece of orange' school of care for their players.

The appointment of a doctor to care for the England squad did not occur until Alf Ramsey was in charge in 1963. By 1998 the number of backroom boys assisting the English manager had risen to eighteen and included Ray Clemence as special goalkeeping coach, Gary Guyan in charge of video research – particularly of opponents' previous games – and Roger Narbed as travelling chef.

The 1950s was still the era of no substitutes, not even in Cup Finals. It was a regular occurrence for men who were seriously injured to grit their teeth and move out to the wings. During the 1950s, if a player of Slaven Bilić's class had collapsed on the floor and rolled about in apparent agony after being tapped on the face, rather than the French captain Laurent Blanc being sent off, Bilic would have been laughed out of the game. What a machismo society like mid-1950s Brazil made of doctors, advisers, psychologists and the rest of Havelange's infrastructure beggars belief.

João Havelange owes a great deal to the Brazilian national squad that went to Sweden in 1958. Owes far more than he would ever admit or acknowledge. In particular he owes a debt to one player that he could never repay. Perhaps that is why Havelange, rather than acknowledge his debt to that player, has over the past decade done everything in his power to insult him and dismiss his extraordinary achievements. Inevitably his public displays of contempt have not hurt the man as much as they have diminished Havelange in the eyes of the football world. The player in question is Edson Arantes do Nascimento.

Pelé.

Yet it all began so differently.

When some of the 'experts' decided that, talented though the young Pelé undoubtedly was, he should not go to Sweden, that his time would come perhaps in Chile in 1962, Havelange was among those who argued long and hard that Pelé should be part of the squad, should indeed be part of the team that might finally win for the first time for Brazil the coveted Jules Rimet Trophy.

João Havelange has become through his long life a man who does not just like winning arguments, but a man who will go to any lengths to ensure that his point of view prevails. It was a characteristic forged through hundreds of committee meetings reaching back to 1937 when he became at twenty-one years of age Water Polo Director at Clube de Regatas Botafogo. He had not wheeled and dealed to get the top job in the world of Brazilian sports to defer to others. Since the death of his parents there is scant evidence that Havelange, until comparatively recent times, has ever deferred to anyone. Pelé went to Sweden.

In truth Brazil were lucky to qualify for the Finals. In their final qualifying match against Peru they scraped home winning 1–0. Didi executed one of his famous *foglia secca* – falling leaf – free kicks, an innovation that would in the coming years be better known as the banana shot. British sports writer Brian Glanville told me:

'Didi very nearly did not make the trip to Sweden. He was considered well past his best. He was thirty. Also he had married a white woman and furthermore questions had been raised about his level of commitment. I remember after he scored the vital winning goal in that final qualifying match he then had to wait until Havelange, his coach Vicente Feola, the doctor, the psychologist and God knows who else argued the toss about him. While this was going on, Didi remarked publicly, "It would be funny if they left me out after I paid for their ticket."'

The Havelange obsessive attention to detail was very evident at many levels. On previous World Cup expeditions the Brazilian squad had accepted whatever base was offered by the host nation. Not this time. Hilton Gosling, the squad doctor, and the psychologist João Carvalhais preceded the main party and scoured Sweden for weeks before finding a perfect location for the training camp outside Gothenburg.

Some of the travelling circus of football journalists made Brazil pre-tournament favourites on the basis that if the array of talent within the Brazilian squad performed to their full potential then the Cup was theirs for the taking. Others dismissed Brazil's chances, convinced that the dark side of the Latin American football psyche would erupt under pressure, that all it would take was a few particularly bad fouls from cynical opponents and the Battle of Berne would have a Battle of Gothenburg for company in the football hall of shame. If a national squad that contained players of such supreme talent as Didi, Garrincha – 'The Little Bird' – Nilton Santos, Vavà, Zito, Zagalo and a handful of other world-class individuals resorted to thuggery, then the game was not worth the candle and we might as well pack up and go and watch professional wrestling.

Then there was Pelé.

In the latter part of 1957, some nine months before the World Cup in Sweden, news of Pelé had begun to emerge from Brazil. In those pre-satellite and in many countries pre-television days, the news was largely by word of mouth. Could this new prodigy be as good as was claimed? Could he be half that good?

In their woodland retreat, the Brazilians went through their daily routines. Apart from the traditional training schedule, because of Havelange's various innovations, there were other more unusual sessions.

These included long conversations with the team doctor Hilton Gosling. Many of the squad used Gosling as a substitute father. They confided in him, shared their worries and preoccupations with him. Among this group was Pelé, still carrying an injury sustained back in Brazil. Concerned that his injury might not heal in time. Anxious that if it did the weight of expectation that had been placed on his shoulders should not affect his game.

There was Garrincha, the definitive free spirit, with astonishing natural gifts, remarkable speed and swaying body movements, crippled from birth, poorly educated, and against such huge odds a member of the squad. Those odds included the psychologist's evaluation that Garrincha was mentally retarded and unfit to play in the World Cup.

'The other one' was a description frequently used by the people of Brazil when referring to Garrincha. There was Pelé and 'the other one'. Born Manoel da Silva, on 18 October 1933 in Raiz da Serra, Petropolis, shortly before his family moved to a shanty town high in the hills above Rio, an environment virtually lacking every basic necessity of life. Garrincha, the 'Little Bird' – that was his other nickname – took the one escape route that was available to somebody from the shanty towns. Football.

If God had given Garrincha a twisted deformed body, the Almighty had also given him, to balance his so-called low IQ, the brain of a footballing genius. There was indeed a simple touching naiveté about Garrincha, but that was off the pitch. On the pitch few were his equal.

The masseur accompanying Brazil to Sweden was Mario Americo:

'Garrincha was the only one who did not allow his legs to

be touched, but he had great respect for me. In Sweden he had bought himself a marvellous radio for more than one hundred dollars which left me green with envy because I did not have so much money. One day when we were alone and the music stopped for the Swedish commercials, he said: "This radio won't be any good in Brazil because it only speaks Swedish. And everybody is going to laugh at it ..." And after thinking he said to me: "And what can I do?" I replied: "It's very easy. Sell it to me for forty dollars. It doesn't matter that people laugh at me. I'm not as important as you." He replied: "But I paid more than a hundred ..." "I can't do more," I said. Then he sold me the radio for forty dollars, with the promise that nobody would find out that he had paid more than a hundred "for that thing" ...'

Among the other diversions from the conventional distractions at Brazil's camp in Sweden were the sessions with the psychologist Carvalhais. His methods certainly bemused some of the press. He did not talk to the players one to one: 'This might make any problems they had become even greater,' he told the reporters. No, he did not talk to them in groups either. This, he explained, 'might bring back unpleasant memories of authority figures like teachers and produce negative results.' He liked to get the players to express themselves through drawings. He would for instance get them to draw the enemy. Those players they would soon be facing during their group matches. England, Russia and Austria.

Obviously the talents of Pelé and Garrincha at the painting easel left something to be desired. Neither was selected for the first match against Austria. Brazil won 3–0 but the normally sad-faced Vicente Feola could hardly manage a smile. He thought they should have scored many more. For the second match the coach again considered he had no need of the 'Little Bird' or Pelé. This time the opponents were England. In the first half Brazil missed a hatful of chances, in the second they were fortunate not to concede a penalty when Kevan the English centre forward was hauled to the ground by Bellini. The result was a 0–0 draw.

Before the third game the squad had a private meeting after which a deputation of players presented themselves in front of the doleful coach. Feola looked up from his deliberations. He had been busy shuffling yet another set of changes. He was destined never to play the same team twice running throughout the entire tournament.

The deputation did not profess to know much about art or who had drawn the best stick man during the training sessions, but they held very strong views about who should be playing. They demanded the inclusion of Garrincha for the match against Russia. Feola was obviously a highly unusual man. He listened to what the deputation had to say, then picked the Little Bird for the third game. For good measure he also brought in Zito and Pelé.

Russia were the first team to get a close-up view of this new team. In the first minute Garrincha hit the left-hand post. A minute later Pelé hit the right-hand post. Two minutes later Vavà went one better after a defence-splitting pass from Didi and the ball was in the back of the net. From there on it was one-way traffic with the Soviets desperately defending. There was only one more goal, again from Vavà after he had exchanged a string of passes with Pelé, but if even a small percentage of the near-misses had been converted, the Russians would have featured in the record books under the category 'Most goals conceded in a World Cup match'. The Brazilians demonstrated skills and abilities that placed them in a different league from their bemused opponents.

Garrincha in particular was unplayable and stunningly unpredictable. At one point his bemused marker Kuznetsov backed off as Garrincha yet again came swaying towards

him, then the Brazilian trapped the ball dead and ran off
into the centre leaving the dead ball for a colleague.
Kuznetsov was the picture of uncertainty torn between
following Garrincha and staring hypnotically at the dead
ball. Didi appeared and flicked it across the pitch. At
another moment Garrincha held the ball while five Russians
encircled him but none daring to lunge at the ball.

This was the team that the entire country of Brazil had
been yearning for, had fantasised about. Extraordinary
natural individual skills married into a group ability. If
Garrincha was the undisputed man of the match, Pelé
showed enough of his own range of talents to justify the
extravagant claims that had been made, not by him but by
others. Pelé himself then and now epitomised modesty.
With this performance he announced to an international
audience what had already been demonstrated for over a
year in Latin America. At the time he played against Russia
he was seventeen years of age. Brazil were now through to
the quarter-finals where they faced Wales.

Again Feola played around with his team selection. This
time he brought back Mazzola and dropped Vavà, the
scorer of the two goals against Russia. If it had been
difficult before this to know what was going on behind
Feola's tinted glasses, it now became impossible to fathom
the inner workings of the Brazilian coach's mind.

The Welsh fought a resolute rearguard action against
the rampant Brazilian forwards until the sixty-sixth minute
when the deadlock was broken. Pelé's shot took a deflection
and the ball hurtled past goalkeeper Jack Kelsey. Pelé
recalled that moment when talking to me.

'It was one of the most important goals that I ever
scored. Not one of the best, but it settled me. Calmed me.'

From now on the genius that is Pelé would be increasingly
revealed to a world audience. This young man who as a
member of a poor family living in Baura in the State of

Minas Gerais learned his football skills in what to a young boy in today's Europe would seem to be unbelievable conditions. There was no money for footballs or boots. A ball would be made out of rags and paper and played with until it disintegrated. His father was an average professional playing for the local team of Minas Gerais. Pelé wanted no more than 'to be like my Dad – a footballer'.

It was seen as a precarious living and though he was showing as a very young boy unusual control and ability, he was destined to become a shoemaker. In his early teens he was spotted by Valdemar de Brito, a former international, who was astonished at the boy's natural skills. He persuaded the fifteen-year-old's parents to forget about shoemaking and took the boy to sign on for Santos, a São Paulo club.

'My first contract was for ten dollars. Nine months later when I was sixteen and I was told I had been picked for Brazil, I got a rise. It went up to fifteen dollars a month.'

He was still playing on the same contract during the World Cup series in Sweden. Only five feet eight inches tall, weighing one hundred and forty-five pounds, the muscle tone of a perfectly proportioned athlete. He was about to show the world at large skills that are given to very, very few footballers and one of those skills has never been equalled. He was a goal-scorer supreme. Agile, resilient, he held the ball – or so it seemed – on a piece of string before releasing it again and again with a venomous right-foot shot. His ability in the air was equally devastating. And to top up the array of gifts he demonstrated a temperament that was exceptional. His coolness, his ability to keep his head when many around him were losing theirs, bordered on the unearthly. He was destined to take through his career the most brutal treatment imaginable from a succession of defenders who had concluded that even a genius like Pelé needed the use of his legs to play. The courage that he showed was as formidable as his talent. Once in a lifetime, if the onlooker is fortunate, a sportsman comes along who stands comparison with any who have ever taken part in that particular sporting discipline. Such a man is Pelé. The last hero.

Now in Sweden, 1958, only France stood between Brazil and a place in the Final. France, the tournament's high scorers with fifteen goals in four games against Brazil whose defence had yet to concede a goal.

Two minutes into the game Didi, Garrincha and Pelé combined in brilliant fashion to lay on a goal for Vavà, who had been recalled. Seven minutes later the French equivalents, Raymond Kopa and Just Fontaine showed telepathic understanding and Fontaine equalised. The Stockholm stadium exploded with excitement and the action moved from one end to the other. In the thirty-fifth minute the fate of the game was resolved. The French defender Robert Jonquet collided badly with Vavà and was carried off with a serious injury to his right knee. He returned later but was reduced to limping awkwardly along one of the wings. To play against this Brazilian team with only ten fit men was to tempt a terrible fate. Retribution was swift in coming for the unfortunate French. Didi had put Brazil ahead with Jonquet still off the pitch. In the second half Pelé shifted up several gears. He tore through the depleted French line again and again as he scored three goals and eclipsed even the fabulous Garrincha. The final score was Brazil 5, France 2.

After the game the goalkeeper Claude Abbes, speaking with great feeling, said:

'I would rather play against ten Germans than one Brazilian.'

In the Final Brazil faced the host nation, Sweden. It was precisely this fact that prompted many of the pundits, particularly the European coaches, to plump for the home team to win the World Cup. The experts were convinced that, confronted with a massive home crowd support roaring on the Swedes, the temperamental Latins would be unable to control their inner fears and would inevitably self-destruct when the moment of truth arrived. All that was needed was for Sweden to get an early goal and it would be Goodnight Rio.

In view of what had occurred in Berne and Vienna it was a valid proposition, one that was given every opportunity of success.

As the tournament had progressed, the Swedish football authorities had become increasingly concerned by the curious apathy of the home crowds. Even as Sweden began to make progress, nothing it seemed could animate the Swedish spectators to really get behind their team. For the semi-final against West Germany cheerleaders were drafted in. This then relative novelty in a football ground did the trick and to the encouragement of cheers, chants and flags, Sweden beat West Germany 3–1.

As the Final approached João Havelange, back in Rio, brooded on every aspect. He'd stayed behind 'because there were cheques that needed to be signed for the CBD'. Others in Brazil, both at the time and now, offered an alternative explanation. Fear of failure and a desire to distance himself from the team's likely defeat. On the phone at CBD headquarters in Rio, he worried about the referee and sought reassurance from the World Cup Committee that the neutral referee would stay neutral and would not bow to home crowd pressure. He worried about the cheerleaders and the general pumping up of the Swedish spectators during the semi-final. He made loud and persistent complaints to the Committee and eventually won a pre-match victory. It was announced that the Committee had forbidden in the most grave terms any manifestation that might indicate that Sweden were playing at home. The cheerleaders were banished and the Committee so put the fear of God up the already law-abiding Swedes that it was obviously seen as a breach of the peace to shout or cheer for the home team. As a result the crowd of some fifty thousand spectators were for the most part strangely quiet. The exceptions were the Brazilians who had made the trip. Presumably they did not understand the World Cup Committee's statements. In any event they ignored them and kicked up a dreadful noise.

The Swedish manager and coach George Raynor had airily declared before the start of the game:

'If the Brazilians go a goal down they'll panic all over the show.'

Thus Raynor aligned himself with what had become a very popular theory.

Four minutes into the game Sweden went a goal up. Liedholm glided past the Brazilian defenders into the penalty area and beat the Brazilian goalkeeper Gilmar with a low shot to the right-hand corner. It was the first time in the tournament that the Brazilians had trailed. The cynics waited for the storm as Didi picked the ball out of the net. Six minutes later Brazil were on equal terms, Garrincha almost inevitably being the goal-maker. Going past two defenders and leaving them floundering in his wake he crossed for Vavà to score.

Garrincha was in sublime form but the Swedes were more than making a game of it. A shot from Pelé that hit a post was answered with a Swedish attack that saw them thwarted at the last moment by Zagalo heading off his line. After thirty-two minutes Garrincha again went down the wing, crossed for Vavà to make it 2–1.

Ten minutes into the second half Pelé tore the heart out of the Swedish team. With his back to the goal he drew gasps from the crowd as he killed a high centre with his thigh. He hooked it over his head and over the Swedish centre-half, twisted around and past the startled defender, caught the ball on his instep and volleyed it past Svensson the Swedish goalkeeper.

Bravely as they stuck to their task, the tide was running irresistibly against the Swedes. No team in the world could have overcome Brazil on this day.

Zito and Didi had become like Tweedledee and Tweedledum. They changed and re-changed positions, they switched play from one side of the pitch to the other in the blink of an eye. The full-back Djalma Santos, playing in his first game of the tournament, began to behave like a forward as he indulged in foraging runs that took him deep into enemy territory. Vavà and Pelé were doing up front what Zito and Didi were doing further back. With thirteen minutes left the defender Zagalo swept into the opposing goal area and, hurtling past three defenders, scored the fourth Brazilian goal. No fists in the air, no running to the crowd to milk applause. No grabbing of the corner flag and posturing. No simulated rocking of babies. No exchanging of kisses and cuddles, either vertically or horizontally. No masturbatory gestures of any kind whatsoever. He knelt, crossed himself and shed tears of joy.

Those Brazilian fans who had not understood the World Cup Committee's strictures were by now threatening to turn the affair into an impromptu carnival. There were constant shouts of 'Samba! Samba!' Sweden scored a second goal as Simonsson took advantage of a sleeping linesman ignoring a palpable offside. But the final word was Pelé's. Leaping majestically higher than all around him to meet Zagalo's centre he headed the ball in a perfect arc over the clutching hands of Svensson.

When the final whistle went the Brazilian team ran around the pitch holding their national flag. Then they ran around again holding the Swedish flag. The Swedes had not been

disgraced. They had been outclassed. Brazil had finally, for
the first time, won the World Cup.

Over the years since that remarkable team exploded into
the public consciousness one man more than any other has
taken the credit, or rather has attempted to claim the credit
for that extraordinary achievement. Not Pelé, not
Garrincha. In fact, none of the players. Not the coach or
the doctor or the psychologist.

'I won my first World Cup in Sweden in 1958,' Dr João
Havelange said to me. It was much the same as he has been
saying to others for forty years. He also remarked:

'Pelé owes me a great deal and his debt to me began in
the 1950s when I gave him the chance of going to Sweden.'

Havelange, of course, had not bothered to go himself,
but had stayed at the office taking care of business.

'History,' it has been said, 'is but a fable agreed upon by
man.' Not if the man's name is Havelange. In his case it
gets personally rewritten.

Havelange saw the players as merely the final parts of an
elaborate master plan of his creation, a concept rather on
a par with the Allied Supreme Command who were
responsible for so much of the slaughter during the First
World War. The man in the street in Rio, on Havelange's
São Paulo omnibus, in Porto Alegre and throughout Brazil
saw the World Cup triumph quite differently. The nation
believed that the national squad in general and the men
who had played in the various games were responsible for
this famous victory. The nation exulted in their team and
in that moment of exultation the seeds were sown of the
greatest threat to the continuing irresistible rise of João
Havelange. Somehow, if Havelange was to really capitalise
personally on the World Cup triumph in Sweden, Brazil
would have to do it again.

Through this famous victory the poor, the underprivileged, the disadvantaged could for a while forget their

mean squalid lives. It was carnival time, only better and bigger and it would go on for longer. It would one way and another go on for four years. It would continue until Brazil were called upon to defend their title of World Champions in Chile in 1962.

The one non-playing member of the 1958 squad who more than any other – including Havelange – was responsible for the victory in Sweden was Paulo Machado de Carvalho. Appointed by Havelange to head the World Cup squad, it was Carvalho above all others that welded so many disparate elements into one cohesive unit and convinced the often insecure, the often unsure to believe that the dream of World Cup success could become a reality.

If Havelange had been 'too busy' to accompany the unknown Brazilian team when they set out for Sweden, he managed to have all the business taken care of by the time the acclaimed World Cup champions returned to Brazil. He accompanied them on a visit to the country's President Juscelino Kubitschek. Some time later, the President got on the phone to Havelange: 'During that World Cup in Sweden, I replaced a number of ministers and there wasn't a word about it in the newspapers. I am planning some more changes in the near future. When's the date of the next World Cup?' The President understood – as every single one of Brazil's rulers has understood since the 1930s – that with football they held in their hands a very powerful weapon.

As early as 1937, the then Brazilian dictatorship under Getúlio Vargas had created an espionage infrastructure that constantly targeted football activities. The dictatorship was obsessed with the idea that within the huge gatherings in the football stadiums communist cells were meeting to plot. This form of spying was to continue at least up to the mid-1980s. In the 1970s, when Pelé's Santos played overseas matches, regular secret reports went back to the Brazilian Secret Service. Apart from acounts of excessive partying by the Santos squad, it would appear that the team themselves did not indulge in any treasonable behaviour.

In 1974 as Havelange sought the supreme position of power in the world of football, he would boast:

'It is still Brazil who has constructed the biggest stadium in the world up to now besides a great quantity of first-class stadia through the country with an approximate total capacity of four million five hundred places.'

He did not add to those reading his sales pitch for the presidency of FIFA that the majority of those stadia were the cynical creations of successive military junta who well understood, like many dictators before and since, that football is the modern equivalent of the Roman bread and circuses. Neither did he enlighten the readers of his election manifesto that a full stadium was a Brazilian rarity long before 1974.

The domestic game in Brazil had become, after Havelange came to power in the Brazilian Sports Federation, hostage to the international game, particularly the World Cup. This trend, already evident during the latter part of the fifties and the early part of the sixties, would accelerate dramatically after April 1964 when democracy died in Brazil.

In the meantime, there was a bus company to run and soon, in addition, there would be Seguros Farroupilha, a small insurance company created in São Paulo, and in Rio Atlantica Boavista, another insurance company. These insurance companies are an early example of that mixture of business and sport which would become constantly recurring elements in Havelange's life. Atlantica Boavista had a number of connections with the Brazilian Football Federation. Most notably, it housed the Federation rent-free in return for the Federation's very lucrative insurance business. A classic example of one hand washing the other. It is also an example of the differing standards of acceptable business practice. If the President of the English Football Association indulged in such behaviour, and it was then revealed, at the very least he would be forced to resign his office immediately and might well face criminal charges.

Another business venture that Havelange part-owned was Orwec, a São Paulo company that produced chemical products that were used in the process of galvanising steel. Orwec initially had a thriving business in a totally unrelated area, one which in view of the grandiose posturing of Havelange in later years is not only ludicrous but in view of the many allegations that have been levelled at him, somewhat ironic. The company disposed of domestic garbage by burning the material. This company activity was eventually outlawed on the grounds that it caused serious pollution.

It was, however, another activity of Orwec that would lead to business activities a great deal more dubious than environmental pollution. Orwec also had a highly profitable sales market in explosives.

The ruinously expensive national championships and the poorly attended matches were not the only negative results of Havelange's reign over Brazilian football. Another was the drift of some of the country's finest players to foreign clubs, an aspect of the Brazilian football scene that has continued to the present day, leaving the domestic game poorer in every sense, a phenomenon that began as a direct result of Havelange's activities. Two of the stars of the Sweden campaign, Didi and Vavà, were transferred to Madrid. The former to Real, the latter to Atletico. Orlandoi went to a club in Argentina.

The fact that governments of every hue and colour fully understood the power and potency of football, and how it could be used for a wide variety of political ends, was underlined by the Chilean government. A series of earthquakes and droughts, particularly in 1960, had brought an already fragile economy to its knees.

There was chronic inflation, strikes, protests in the streets. The country most certainly could not afford to stage the World Cup. The money that would be needed for new stadiums, the investment that would be needed in the transport infrastructure, the whole package ran into hundreds of millions of dollars. The Chilean administration headed by Jorge Alessandri had lobbied hard and long to get the World Cup for 1962. They knew that the entire event would serve as the most marvellous distraction from grinding poverty. They also knew that they had used every argument to land the prize, including an emotional plea from the Chilean Football Federation's President, Carlos Dittborn, which included the heartfelt if illogical:

'We must have the World Cup because we have nothing.'

They knew that if they subsequently reneged, allowed reason to prevail and spent the Treasury funds on other less exciting projects, then the entire government might just as well get the next plane out of Santiago and go into exile.

Chile kept the World Cup tournament and new stadiums got built.

By the 1962 campaign Brazil's coach of the sad countenance, Vicente Feola, had been replaced by Aymore Moreira, but for the national squad there were still familiar faces. Most importantly of all, there was Paulo Machado de Carvalho attempting to anticipate every problem before it occurred. Also still there were father confessor Dr Hilton Gosling and psychologist Professor João Carvalhais. The back-up unit had grown in number, a feature of modern football where the administrative and backroom team nowadays invariably outnumbers the players.

This time Brazil were the clear favourites. The 'Brilliant Brazilians', as they had been dubbed by the press, were expected to capitalise fully on the fact that the tournament was on Latin American soil. Thinking that either shows an appalling ignorance of South American rivalries or a cynical mind that believes referees are susceptible to external pressures before, during and after the game. In the event the tournament was a triumph for those with a cynical disposition.

During the run-up, Havelange received yet another phone call from the President. Kubitschek had gone, to be replaced by João Goulart, another ruler greatly interested in football, but the new President's interest was not confined to merely exploiting World Cup success. He wanted to be involved in creating it. Havelange drove to the President's home. 'This coming World Cup in Chile. I played football once and I understand what's needed very well. I will give you my team for the World Cup in Chile.' Havelange nodded agreeably. 'OK, Jango. I fully accept you know all about football. So why don't we make a deal? You resign as President and come and be the team coach.' Both men enjoyed the joke and swapped potential team selections for over an hour while somebody else ran Brazil.

The 1962 Chilean government might well have been grossly inept at running the national economy but their reading of the national psyche was first-class. The Swedish Federation, as has been recorded, had a curious difficulty when attempting to get the nation behind their team. It was not a problem that Carlos Dittborn and his colleagues experienced. They received unexpected help in this quarter from two Italian journalists.

Shortly before the tournament and before their own squad had arrived, the reporters filed a series back to Rome and Milan. In the articles they painted a picture of life in Chile that was according to them inferior to many an under-developed Third World country in Africa or Asia. They wrote of the widespread illiteracy. The rampant problem of alcoholism with drunks all over the streets of Santiago, the capital, day and night. For good measure they created the impression that every other female resident was prepared to sell her body. They criticised the organisation of the World Cup. They asserted that there was widespread corruption with regard to the ticket arrangements.

This was read by a number of Chileans resident in Italy. Copies of the article began to arrive on the desk of the Chilean Ambassador in Rome who then sent them back to his government in Santiago. There was an instant virulently hostile campaign mounted against Italy in general and the Italian squad in particular. The players were subjected to a furious verbal assault in the Chilean press, radio and television. They were accused of being fascists, of belonging to the Mafia, of being sex maniacs. And, seizing on a recent drugs scandal involving Inter Milan, the Chileans threw in the accusation that the Italian squad were also drug addicts.

All of this was additional fuel to a fire that already burned. There had long been a deep resentment throughout Latin America because of the Mussolini-inspired theory that children born of Italian parents who were living abroad were still Italian citizens – *oriundi* – nationals of Chile, Argentina, Brazil or indeed any country, transformed courtesy of Mussolini, into Italian citizens. Thus the Brazilian Altafini, who had played for his native country during the 1958 World Cup tournament in Sweden, was now considered Italian. Humberto Maschio and Omar Sivori would have played in the same tournament for their native Argentina if Italian clubs had not jumped in during 1957 and had snapped up both players. It was policy designed to annoy the most placid of football supporters. Not a description one would normally apply to the average

Latin American fan. The final element that incensed the local population was the widely reported presence of a clutch of Italian club scouts loitering at the training grounds used by the various South American World Cup contestants.

The fact that Italy were in the same group as Chile gave a terrible inevitability to what would occur when they met.

The recently elected President of FIFA, Sir Stanley Rous, gave a public address before the opening match. The sun shone, all was sweetness and light and Switzerland obliged by rolling over and losing to Chile 3–1.

In less than a week, sweetness and light had vanished. From all four centres, Santiago, Arica, Vin del Mar and Rancagus, the same depressing story emerged. Violence on and off the pitch. Exploding tempers and serious injuries. In that first week there were more than forty casualties among the sixteen teams. The Soviet Union's full-back Dubinski, Colombia's captain Zuluagua, and the Swiss forward Eschmann were all in various hospitals with broken legs. Bulgaria had two of their key players brutally kicked out of the tournament, and four players had been sent off. The headline in the Santiago newspaper *Claron*, a paper that had done more than its fair share to stir up the atmosphere, summed up the situation with the headline, 'WORLD WAR'.

Inevitably the most serious problems occurred during the Chile v Italy game.

A number of Italian journalists would later criticise their own team for being 'too easily provoked by the Chileans'. It requires a very special self-restraint to avoid retaliating when someone is constantly spitting in your face. This was the opening gambit of the Chileans, one they pursued throughout the game. The Italians have never forgiven the English referee Ken Aston. 'Hostile', 'Provocative' and 'Incompetent' were three of the accusations they made at the time and will make again today if persuaded to recall the shambles that passed for a game of football. The Italian management had feared before the game that whatever team was selected it would be made the scapegoats for the sins and transgressions of others. They were proved to be correct. The actual team was in fact chosen more on the basis of those with exemplary self-control under provocation than for any tactical considerations.

The atmosphere in the city of Santiago hours before the game was murderous. The Italian squad, in an attempt to appease the crowd of sixty thousand, waved greetings and threw roses to the spectators before the game started. The Chilean supporters responded with screams of insults and threats.

Referee Aston seemed to justify the time-honoured fans' insult towards all referees, that of selective blindness. He saw none of the spitting, kicking and punching by the Chileans. Neither Aston nor his linesman who was standing a few feet from the incident saw the Chilean player throw a left hook and break the nose of the Italian, Maschio. It was seen worldwide on television though. What was also seen was the Italians being penalised for retaliation while the Chileans again and again walked away scot-free. First to be sent off was the Italian Ferrini. That was in the seventh minute. The next to go was his team-mate David.

Later Aston was to admit reluctantly that he had wanted to abandon the game at half-time, but fearing a riot lacked the courage to do so. The various FIFA dignitaries watching the game also demonstrated a conspicuous absence of spine. With Italy reduced to nine men, the carnage continued. Astonishingly, the Italians held out until the seventy-fifth minute when Ramirez headed in a free kick taken by Sanchez, one of the Chileans who should have been off the pitch and out of the tournament long before that moment. The Chilean Toro added a second in the last minute.

The FIFA World Cup Organising Committee, provoked by the global condemnation of what was passing for football, summoned the managers of all sixteen teams. They were warned that further violent play would result in automatic expulsion from the tournament. This would mean individually and collectively. Indeed this had already occurred once when, after breaking an opponent's leg, the Yugoslavian Mujic was sent home by his team management.

With regard to the performance by referee Ken Aston, FIFA ensured that his career did not suffer. Subsequently he was elected to membership of the exclusive FIFA's Referees' Committee and then given the responsibility for monitoring the performance of all referees during the 1966 and 1970 World Cups.

Having lost one, drawn one and won one, England had reached the quarter-finals. If that was the good news for England supporters, the bad news was that waiting for them as opponents were Brazil. They had won the first of their group matches against Mexico with Pelé, in particular, seeming to continue where he had left off in the dying minutes of the 1958 Final. His most memorable contribution occurred in the second half when he beat four Mexican defenders and then their goalkeeper with a stunning shot.

During their second game against Czechoslovakia, in the twenty-fifth minute, Pelé collected a pass from Garrincha, shot powerfully from nearly thirty yards, then fell to the floor. He had torn a thigh muscle and would take no further part in the tournament. There was still Garrincha who, like Pelé before his injury, was also showing the mesmeric ability that had confused successive defences in Sweden in 1958. From that particular tournament Garrincha had painted one image that is imperishable, when against Russia five defenders stood off hypnotised and frightened to commit themselves to a tackle on the lone Brazilian. Now against Mexico four years later Garrincha contrived to produce another exquisite miniature. Not five but eight Mexicans plus their goalkeeper, all drawn irresistibly around the Little Bird. But now Pelé, Garrincha's 'other one', was not going to be there.

It was a bitter blow for the player and his country. At twenty years of age Pelé had, since the previous World Cup, gone from strength to strength. Even now there was a belief among those who watched him that the best was yet to come. It had been thought that his peak might well happen during the World Cup, now what was already a squalid tournament had been further reduced by the loss of one of the few players capable of transforming World Cup 62 into something memorable and enduring.

To replace the injured Pelé, coach Aymore Moreira brought in the twenty-four-year-old Amarildo. He was no Pelé. There would never be an adequate substitute for Pelé, but Amarildo was a quick, inventive forward with a superb instinct for scoring goals. Simple and uncomplicated, he seemed prepared to carry the mantle of Pelé's number 10 without any undue worries.

In their final group game against Spain the Brazilians won 2–0. A victory that owed much to the unstoppable Garrincha and an ebullient Amarildo who scored both goals.

The 'Little Bird', unfortunately for England, continued in the same irresistible form during the quarter-final. The first Brazilian goal had onlookers rubbing their eyes in disbelief as the diminutive Garrincha, all five feet seven inches of him, out-jumped the English defender Maurice Norman, all six feet two inches of him, to head in a corner. England's hopes rose briefly when a Jimmy Greaves shot thundered against the crossbar and Hitchens put the rebound into the back of the net.

Five minutes into the second half Garrincha had the game won for Brazil. A free kick for Brazil was given. One of their players calmly moved the ball from the spot where the referee had placed it to ensure that Garrincha would have a clearer sight of the goal. Instead of protesting, the English players, in the words of their manager Walter Winterbottom, 'just stood around showing their naiveté'. Garrincha lashed the ball past England goalkeeper Ron Springett. The third was scored by Vavà when another Garrincha special bounced off Springett's chest and was easily converted by Vavà.

Now waiting for Brazil in the semi-final was the home team of Chile, complete with a deluded nation who believed that their team were good enough to win the World Cup.

If ever the theory that Brazil, for all their collective skills and individual talents, were a team who would implode under provocation was going to be tested to breaking point, then this was the match to do it.

Garrincha appeared to be determined to win the match single-handed. After nine minutes he cut inside, pivoted and from twenty yards sent a left foot shot into the net. In the thirty-second minute he again demonstrated his remarkable jumping ability, climbing higher than the Chilean defenders to head in another corner kick. In between kicking Garrincha and any other Brazilian within reach, Chile played some excellent football. They pulled it back to 2–1 only for Vavà to make it 3–1 as he headed in a corner from the ubiquitous Garrincha. Again the Chileans got within distance of the Brazilians. A penalty this time after a handball made the score 3–2. For a short while the Chilean fantasy stood a chance of becoming the real thing, then just when it seemed the match was liable to go either way, Zagalo moved upfield along the left wing, swerved past first one, then two, defenders, crossed to a waiting Vavà and it was 4–2.

Deprived of what they had come to believe was theirs
for the asking, the Chileans began kicking lumps of flesh
once more. Garrincha was again kicked, this time by Rojas.
After the game he insisted that he had been kicked over
fifty times by the Chileans. This time he retaliated and was
sent off. As he made his way to the dressing room he was
met by a whistling wall of hatred and derision. A bottle
struck him cutting open his head. Subsequently the Chilean
centre forward Landa was also sent off. A few minutes
later the whistle sounded for full-time. Brazil were in their
second consecutive Final but this time it would be without
Pelé and, in view of his sending off, they would also
automatically be without the one man who more than any
other was responsible for the opportunity which presented
itself to win the World Cup and make it two in a row: the
'Little Bird' – Garrincha.

Over the years the President of FIFA, Dr Havelange, has
been fond of expressing the view that politics has no place in
sport. It is of course a view that flies in the face of his actions.
Politics and sport have been linked at least as early as the
original Olympic Games, held in Greece from 776 BC.

Havelange and his colleagues on the Brazilian Federation
stood on the brink of what would be – at least in Havelange's
mind – a great personal triumph. Another World Cup
triumph. With the political situation in Brazil deteriorating
by the day, it would be a superb moment to distract the
population with another victory. That anyway was the
thinking of at least part of the Brazilian group. They got
busy. Very busy. Havelange was yet again missing from
the World Cup arena. Yet again money and business
matters detained him in Rio. Confronted with the crisis
over their most influential player, Havelange reached for
the phone.

The obstacles that had to be overcome were formidable.
After all, during the first week of the Chilean World Cup

the FIFA Organising Committee had decreed that there
would be automatic expulsion both individually and
collectively if there was any further rough play. Kicking an
opponent and getting sent off undoubtedly came into this
category. No matter that Garrincha was retaliating.
Footballers are not permitted to retaliate. The sending-off
automatically meant that at the very least he was banned
from the Final. The punishment in all likelihood would be
more severe and would possibly ban him from at least
some further games that were FIFA-controlled. Then there
was the question of whether the entire team should be
disqualified. But if they were, who would replace them in
the Final against Czechoslovakia? Surely not Chile, who
had been beaten and, furthermore, had also sustained a
sending-off during the same game.

Prompted by Havelange, the Brazilian President João
Goulart cabled the FIFA Disciplinary Committee that was
due to sit and consider the Garrincha sending-off. His
impassioned plea demanded that natural justice would be
perverted if Garrincha did not play in the Final.

Others within the Brazilian camp decided that the key
lay firstly with the Peruvian referee Arturo Yamazaqui's
report on the match and secondly with the evidence from
the Uruguayan linesman, Esteban Marino, the official who
had been closest to the incident that resulted in Garrincha
being sent off. If they could be persuaded to be the souls of
moderation, could in effect be fair-minded, even-handed
and virtually vindicate the actions of Garrincha, the
problem might well be solved.

Before the due date of the disciplinary hearing, a number
of events occurred. A large suitcase of money arrived in
Santiago from Rio. The referee's report was mild to the
point of being innocuous. On the day of the hearing the
linesman was not to be seen at the FIFA hearing in Santiago.
During the 1950s Marino had worked for the São Paulo

football championship and was well known to the chairman of that association, and also by happy coincidence to the man in charge of the Brazilian squad in Chile: Paulo Machado de Carvalho. At the time of the FIFA hearing the two Brazilians had taken the linesman into hiding in a hotel in Santiago. His crucial evidence was therefore not heard by the FIFA committee.

After due deliberation the FIFA Disciplinary Committee disappeared up its own arse as, throwing the ruling they had made in the first week of the tournament out of the window, they merely cautioned Garrincha as to his future behaviour on the pitch and told him that he was free to play in the Final, as of course were the entire Brazilian team.

In the Final, Brazil, complete with Garrincha playing yet again a key role, overcame Czechoslovakia 3–1.

The World Cup, a trophy that had been created to perpetuate the highest ideals of the sport, had been won after a tournament that had frequently debased those ideals both on and off the pitch. An ironic footnote to the World Cup tournament in Chile occurred a few years later when yet again the South American delegations to FIFA raised a matter that they were constantly complaining about. It was their collective view that FIFA gave preference to European referees and that South American referees were constantly neglected. One particular recommendation that came from a South American committee member on the Referees' Committee dealt with the inherent danger of the match referee being got at with a bribe before the game. The member suggested that in future referees for World Cup preliminary matches should be appointed at the very last minute to prevent representatives of the countries involved travelling to the home country of the referee.

As the then General Secretary of FIFA, Dr Helmut Käser, noted in a letter to the President, Sir Stanley Rous:

'According to information received, it is customary in South America to make "pilgrimages" to the referees' countries.'

With Paulo Machado de Carvalho leading them, the Brazilian pilgrims returned yet again bearing the talismanic trophy. The Jules Rimet – a holy relic capable of providing shelter for the homeless, food for the starving, work for the unemployed, of making the politically inept appear masterful in the eyes of the populace, in short capable of eliminating all that ailed a country's people. That was the theory. It still is the theory. The concept took a knock, however, when less than two years after Brazil had returned in triumph there was a coup d'état and the Brazilian military seized power.

When shortly before World Cup France 98 I interviewed Havelange during his last few remaining days as President of FIFA, I questioned him at one point about the difficulties of running the Brazilian Sports Federation at a time when democracy did not exist in Brazil.

Q: At the time when you first took over the Brazilian Sports Federation there was a democratically elected government headed if I remember correctly by President Juscelino Kubitschek?

A: Yes.

Q: Within six years the Generals were running Brazil. They took a great interest in sport generally, but they took a very deep interest in football. I'd be grateful if you would give me some illustrations of what problems you had to surmount in that situation. Dealing as you were obliged to, not with a democratically elected government, but a military junta. With a dictatorship?

A: First of all I must say to you that I have never engaged in politics, and politics do not interest me. I have never been in the employment of the government and I have never had any loans from the government of any substance, and I have never done any business with the government. Someone who is in power, I respect them and I expect also their respect, something I have always enjoyed whether they are military, politicians or anyone else. There's always this point of football being a passion. And when you have a World Cup everyone gets together to express their interest – to help – and this is how things are worked out. There was a World Cup under Mr Kubitschek and he was a personal friend of mine. There was a World Cup under Mr Goulart and he was a personal friend of mine. General Branco who was running Brazil at the time of World Cup England 1966, another friend. And World Cup 1970 in Mexico, this was the time when General Médici was in power, he was a personal friend of mine. So I had no problems and neither did football.

Q: They didn't interfere?

A: No. The Brazilian Football Federation is a private institution. It has nothing to do with the government. It's subject to civil law, of course, but it is not subject to governmental decisions.

Q: During the period that you were in charge of Brazilian football, the World Cup was won three times by your country. A phenomenal achievement. The research that I have carried out clearly shows that successive members of the various junta, including various military dictators who called themselves President, were constantly dabbling and interfering with the organisation structure, staff appointments, even team selection. There must have been on an almost daily basis an interaction with the CBD?

A: No, that's not so. The last military president for example was General Figueiredo [João Baptista de Oliveira Figueiredo]. We were more or less the same age. He attended military academy and I studied law, and we played football together and we are honorary presidents of the same club. [Fluminese.] So you see this whole idea of the military for us didn't enter into it at all. They took their part in Brazilian life. We took another part, but we continued to be friends. And especially in view of the fact that I do not engage in politics. They had their job to do. I had mine.

The facts totally refute Havelange's idealistic and totally inaccurate vision of how successive military dictatorships responded to football. Far from leaving it alone, they crawled all over it, as indeed they did with a whole range of sporting activities. In 1968, for example, the military junta expressed great concern about a wide range of sporting activities that women were participating in. They issued an edict that banned women from taking part in baseball, rugby, water-polo and football. As president of the national association that controlled all of these sports, Havelange accepted the ban without complaint. The military dictatorships that were running Brazil repeatedly saw football and international success in the game as the one way that they just might garner some popular support and some overseas credibility.

Havelange's successor as President of CBD and therefore of Brazilian football was Admiral Hélio Nunes, who was also President of the junta-created political party Arena. The dictatorship increasingly sought to strengthen its hold over the people through football and, indeed, under Admiral Nunes there was a clear policy of building a stadium and creating a team in any town or city where the Arena party were particularly despised. Between 1969 and 1975 thirteen stadiums with an average spectator capacity of 63,000 were built in Brazil. They provided distractions and they provided marvellous opportunities for corruption.

As will be recorded later in this book the military junta, not content with the above activity, began to interfere with the selection and training of the national team. All of this of course was on top of what the junta considered its real work.

'They had their job to do. I had mine.'

My last book, *To the Ends of the Earth*, recounts my hunt for the world's then most wanted man. Ilich Ramírez Sánchez – the Venezuelan Carlos the Jackal. During my hunt for the man and the truth about him I became particularly interested in another Brazilian, Antonio Pereira. In the mid-1970s he had assisted Carlos in the carrying out of a number of acts of terrorism in Europe.

I hunted for Pereira as well. During that search I discovered not only Pereira's reality but also the reality of life in Brazil between 1964 and 1974, curiously the precise period of time that I recently questioned Havelange about. The following is an extract from my last book:

ANTONIO PEREIRA'S STORY
A case history of one man's journey into terrorism
What follows is based on information acquired from a variety of sources, French and Brazilian Intelligence, Amnesty International, The International Association of Democratic Jurists, interviews, most notably with Pereira's former lawyer, Annina de Cavalho, French, Belgian and Italian legal sources.

Antonio Expedito Carvalho Pereira was born in January 1931 into a poor family in Itagui in the province of Rio Grande do Sul, Brazil.

As a result of a great deal of effort and no little talent he obtained an excellent education and graduated in law. Further study resulted in more qualifications and he obtained a University professorship; he combined this post in São Paulo with an active law practice.

Between 1961 and 1964 Brazil experienced a fertile period of political and social expression. Different sectors of society achieved remarkable progress, in organising their respective institutions, their trade unions and in their aspirations to carry out democratic reforms. Agrarian reforms began to take place, the national wealth started to be more fairly distributed, the country was beginning to move away from its almost complete reliance in so many areas on the United States. Like Carlos's native Venezuela, Brazil has had a history of dictatorships, political repression and torture; between 1960 and 1964 it was going through a period of democratic rule. Enter the Generals. In April 1964 democracy was forcibly replaced with a military dictatorship. In 1968, after four years of increasingly repressive rule, there was a 'coup within a coup' and, while still under a military regime, the country tilted even further to the right. Added to a long list of already existing curtailments to civil rights came new proclamations. The concept of Habeas Corpus was abolished, the already stringent censorship became draconian. Violence towards the individual, particularly the individual who publicly objected to this state of affairs, became institutionalised. There were Government Death Squads. Disappearances became everyday events. Guerrilla activity increased as any utterance against a government action, whether domestic or foreign, was considered by the regime to be 'an act of subversion'. All 'political offences' were tried by one of the military tribunals.

This was the reality of life for Pereira and his fellow citizens. As one of the ever-diminishing number of lawyers who took on the defence of clients accused of 'political offences', he was a marked man. He was double-marked for teaching law at São Paulo University. This placed him in the regime's category of 'dangerous intellectuals'. As a lawyer who also defended students, workers with left-wing sympathies and, on one occasion, the guerrilla leader Carlos Lamarca, it was only a matter of time before the regime came for him. They came on 3rd March 1969.

At ten in the morning fifteen officers, Army sergeants and members of the Political Police forced their way into his office in São Paulo. Another squad surrounded the building. The Brazilian standard method of arrest circa 1969 was then applied: he was handcuffed, badly beaten up, then dragged unconscious out into the street, Calle de Riachuelo, and taken to the barracks of the Army police. He was held there for seventeen days.

During each and every one of those seventeen days he was tortured. The police wanted to know his relationship and dealings with all his clients. He refused to tell them. On the first day he was suspended by his feet for seven hours, beaten continuously, kept constantly wet, subject to electric shocks in the mouth, ears, nape of the neck, genital organs and tendons. When he lost consciousness, Sergeant Roberto of the Army police pushed one electrified wire into his urethra and another into his rectum.

These tortures continued, with a number of variations. Among them was a device known as 'the Armchair of the Dragon'. The victim is sat in an armchair similar to that found in many hairdressers; it is equipped with metal arms and legs through which an electric current is passed.

Pereira continued to refuse to give his captors what they wanted. His wife, Nazareth Oliveira Pereira, was brought in, and Antonio was forced to watch while she was stripped and then tortured; she in turn was forced to watch while he was tortured. Next they brought in his three brothers, João, José and Francisco. All were tortured in his presence. Then they brought in his secretary, Celia Hatsumi Heto, and his driver, Lazaro, who were stripped and subjected to the same treatment. Finally they arrested his ten-year-old daughter, Teresa Cristina. Again Antonio Pereira was forced to watch while she was tortured under the direction of Army Captain Antonio Carlos Pivatto.

I have the full names and ranks of thirteen other creatures – I cannot call them men – who participated in these torturing sessions, as well as the names of two

Commissioner-Judges who also took part, Fernandez and Simonetti. Pivatto commanded one team of torturers, another was commanded by General Luis Felipe.

On 18th March 1969, with Pereira still refusing to oblige with either a confession or incriminating statements about his clients, he was transferred to DOPS (State Department for Political and Social Order) Central Police Station. During his two-day ordeal at this place he was subjected to the Armchair of the Dragon on at least four occasions and underwent sustained torture.

On 20th March he was brought back to the barracks and the Army police tried again for a further two weeks. He was then moved back to the central police station, where he was held in complete isolation for four months. He was subsequently transferred to the penal colony at Tiradentes. After a total of eleven months he was again interrogated before a military tribunal presided over by a judge. He was not tried but eventually returned to the Tiradentes prison. He had been held for nearly two years when a group of guerrillas seized the Swiss ambassador to Brazil, M Giovanni Enrico Bucher, on 7th December 1970 and demanded the release of seventy prisoners. Among those named was Antonio Pereira. He had never been charged, never tried, never sentenced.

In late January 1971, Pereira, along with the other sixty-nine prisoners, flew to Chile. Behind he had left his wife and daughter: the Brazilian regime had refused to allow them to leave and they had not been on the list of demands.

From Chile, via Algeria, Pereira and some of his fellow prisoners had by March 1971 reached Paris, where the French government eventually granted them the right to remain as political exiles. He began to create a new life. By 1973 he was involved with a wealthy Brazilian woman, Mohammed Boudia and Moukharbel, the Japanese Red

Army and an exclusive art gallery. The same year he met Carlos.

'They had their job to do.'

What happened to Antonio Pereira, his wife and child, his relations and his work colleagues was not unique; on the contrary, these were everyday occurrences in Brazil.

Military dictatorship continued in Brazil until the mid-1980s. The Government Death Squads, the attacks on newspapers, the tortures, the murders, the full panoply of barbarism sanctioned by a succession of men who were all close friends of Havelange, a man who during the same decade was nominated for the Nobel Peace Prize.

Havelange, who had been so impressed with the organisational ability and the splendour of Nazi Germany, was also to judge from his remarks to me entirely sanguine and content with the state of affairs in Brazil. During the time of the Generals, Havelange would be extolling the virtues of Brazil as a suitable venue for the World Cup. In 1981, for example, when the Death Squads were still murdering at the rate of over one hundred people a month just in Rio, when two hundred and fifty-eight people were murdered during the three-day carnival in Rio, when newspaper offices and news-stands were being subjected to frequent bomb attacks and when anyone raising a voice against these events was immediately silenced, permanently.

Havelange concluded this section of the interview with the observation, 'I did my work. They [the military junta] did theirs, but we continued to be friends. This was particularly because I do not engage in politics.'

'I'm stunned at that comment,' I replied. 'You don't engage in politics! Having studied your life I would say you are one of the most political people I have ever met, but let's put that to one side. The military dictators most certainly did engage in sport and that surely is inarguable.'

The long sad face looked at me, creating momentarily the impression that a huge bloodhound had been reprimanded.

It was a one of a number of moments during the two days when the ice beneath me seemed very thin. I knew from my research that Havelange has a particular style when being interviewed. He prefers to respond to a question with a speech. When the speech is finished he does not expect additional questions on the same subject. He does not give interviews. He grants an audience. I was determined that I would as far as was possible ensure that these sessions would be conversational, exchanges between two men rather than an audience with the Sun King. I was acutely aware that he has a history of reacting very violently to awkward questions. To inquiries about embezzlement, bribes, self-aggrandisement, venality, graft and simple theft, Havelange has evolved a defence of violent abuse, bombast and a very quick exit. There is nothing clever in evoking such responses from the interviewee prematurely when with time on the interviewer's side other insights, further information, may be gained merely by asking.

As World Cup 1966 grew nearer, the Brazilian military dictatorship used ever more repressive and draconian decrees to ensure that their collective point of view continued to prevail. It was readily apparent to the junta that they needed another World Cup victory to deflect mounting and increasingly organised opposition to their rule. In 1965 anti-military elements won elections in two states. The President's extraordinary powers of rule were promptly extended and all political parties were dissolved. Simultaneously monies were diverted on the junta's orders from a variety of desperately needed social programmes to ensure that Havelange and his colleagues at the Brazilian Federation had more than adequate funds as they prepared for the next World Cup tournament, this time being held in England.

Part of the Brazilian Treasury funds were spent in organising an international tournament, a form of mini World Series involving Brazil, Argentina, Portugal and England.

Havelange assisted his team in the opening match by firstly arranging the kick-off time, then ensuring that Brazil arrived over an hour late. The England team, having changed, fretted away the time in their dressing room and then lost the game 5–1. Alf Ramsey, the recently appointed England manager, learned an invaluable lesson that day. Games against Latin American teams very much involve beating the management as well as the team. When they flew out of the Brazilian capital, Ramsey was determined that come 1966 no one from Latin America was going to put one over on him or the England team. There would come a time when he would need to remember the lesson he had learned, but he failed to do so.

That England were for the first time in the history of the World Cup competition staging the event owed more than a little to the man who had been elected President of FIFA immediately before the débâcle that passed for a World Cup tournament in Chile – Sir Stanley Rous. It had been awarded to the home of the modern game before Rous became head of FIFA but his lobbying influence in the committee meetings was formidable. Rous was a man who had been using the modern techniques of 'networking' some thirty years before they were officially invented. With regard to World Cup 1966 it was nothing too subtle, simple variations on one particular theme: 'It's our turn.'

This was the last World Cup tournament to be awarded as a result of conventional lobbying. From here on it would become increasingly bitter, increasingly expensive, increasingly corrupt. Many millions of dollars were spent in 1964 by both Mexico and Argentina as they competed for the 1970 Finals. Money that Rous and other FIFA officials believed would be better spent on improving youth training, playing facilities, the whole infrastructure. The gifts from contenders to FIFA members would grow ever bigger, ever more obscene and part of the spirit of the game would be stolen. Permanently eroded. Leading inevitably to further corruption and further erosion of the ethics of the sport.

Ironically, what concerned Rous in 1964 would be a major factor in his defeat by Havelange ten years later.

The tendency to paranoia, to believe that there is a largely European-created conspiracy against them, is still very much a feature of the Latin American footballing world. Journalists, officials and players all feed off each other's fears and insecurities, and in their often intense dislike of the Old World and its ways will frequently suspect a plot. Thirty years ago this paranoia was if anything even more evident. It was to manifest itself throughout the World Cup 1966 games in England. If nothing else it is a useful guide to explaining not only the thinking but also some of the actions that were about to occur.

Paranoia Latin American-style got off to a bang before the tournament had even begun. England were drawn in Group One, which would play all of its games with one exception at Wembley. The odd game out was that between Uruguay and France that was scheduled to be played at White City. The fourth team in this group was Mexico. Progression to the quarter-finals looked a good bet for the home side.

A Football Association booklet, published before the tournament started, indicated that should England win the group they would play their quarter-final at Wembley, but the semi-final at Everton. This apparently contradicted what the World Cup Committee had decreed: namely that England were to play *all* of their matches at Wembley. To some it looked like the goalposts had been shifted to give every possible advantage to the host nation. The implication was clear, hurdles were being removed to assist England's passage. That at least was the conclusion that many of the South American journalists came to. Egged on by Havelange and other members of the Brazilian back-up group, the conspiracy theory flourished. It was taken up by the Argentinians, the Uruguayans, Mexico and Chile.

All were convinced that the hand of Stanley Rous was behind 'the plot'. In reality no decision had been made at the time that the FA booklet, which was in error, was published. Whether Rous was a good committee man or not, these kinds of decisions in the pre-Havelange days were not in the hands of one man but a World Cup Committee, who often only arrived at their collective decisions after long debate and often heated disagreements. The truth of the matter was a reverse of 'the plot'. Rous in a minority had argued for England to play their semi-final at Liverpool if the team should progress that far. He was outvoted on economic grounds: England at Wembley would ensure a ninety thousand crowd and appropriately higher receipts for FIFA.

It may all seem storm-in-a-tea-cup time, but such controversies merely fuelled the flames of South American distrust and were to have serious and far-reaching consequences.

Brazil were bidding to make it three World Cup triumphs in a row, something that had never been achieved. Not only did non-playing members of the 1958 and 1962 squads, men such as coach Vicente Feola and Dr Gosling, make the trip, but many of the 1962 World Cup team were still there and, astonishingly, even two of the senior members from the success in Sweden in 1958, the defenders Bellini and Orlando.

Also in the squad were other survivors from 1958,

Djalma Santos and Zito. Indeed, with a few notable exceptions whoever had been responsible for team selection appeared to believe that time had not just stood still, but had gone into reverse. Someone appeared to be living very dangerously in the past. The someone was João Havelange.

Havelange talks at great length about the World Cup triumphs of 1958, 1962 and 1970. He is less forthcoming with regard to 1966. The reasons for that reticence are not confined to a man wishing to restrict his recollections to his winners.

Havelange in reality had very little to do with the World Cup successes in Sweden and Chile. He was responsible for some of the innovations. The introduction of doctors and psychologists. He certainly played a leading role in doing everything possible to ensure that Garrincha, who should have been banned for the Final in Chile, was allowed to participate. As recorded earlier, those activities aside, if one non-playing member of the squad should be given the credit for ensuring that the various teams and the range of tactics were supremely successful, it is a man that Havelange never mentioned once in my interviews with him.

Just as the idea to develop and enlarge FIFA headquarters – an idea that Havelange claims as his own and seeks all the credit for – belonged to another (in that instance his predecessor, Sir Stanley Rous) so the World Cup victories of 1958 and 1962 belong very largely to someone other than Havelange. To Paulo Machado de Carvalho. This was an aspect I discussed with one of Brazil's leading sports writers, Juca Kfouri.

'Brazil won in 1958 and 1962 with Havelange as President of the Sports Federation, but at that time he was humble enough to be aware that he didn't know anything about football. At that time he knew about swimming and water polo and that was it.

'There was this other guy, Paulo Machado de Carvalho,

he was the man who organised those two delegations. Those two squads. He was the man, more than any other, who was responsible for those victories.

'When in 1966 the World Cup was to be played in England, Havelange was certain that Brazil were about to be three-times champions and that the Cup would then permanently reside in Brazil. What does he do? He gets rid of Paulo Machado. Wants to make sure that he and not Machado gets the praise and acclamation for the third victory. Havelange decided that all he needed to do was basically to just take the same team that had won twice previously and they'd do it again. Two basic problems with that. European football was far better prepared for the Brazilians, particularly the same players. To a large degree they knew what to expect. Secondly these players were eight years older. With Pelé that was not a problem. With some of the others it was. Basically the defence players that the press and the public thought should have gone to England all stayed here. Unpicked. Unselected by Havelange.'

World Cup 1966 in England appears to be the only time prior to 1974 that Havelange actually travelled with the national squad and risked being closely identified with their success or failure on the pitch.

Garrincha, the man who more than any other had won the previous World Cup for his country, was still there, but his condition was giving the team doctor cause for concern. He was still recovering from injuries sustained in a car accident but, even fully fit, Dr Gosling was of the opinion that he would have to be used sparingly. His ability to throw off the effects of a match was now much reduced, not helped by Garrincha's increasing fondness for alcohol – a problem that would ultimately lead to an early death.

But perhaps with a fit Pelé all things were possible. The teenage wonder of Stockholm was at twenty-five years of age not even at the peak of what was already a unique career.

In Eusebio, Portugal had its own equivalent of Pelé, a forward with devastating acceleration, exquisite ball control and a shot like the kick of a mule. Yet again the popular hope was that players like Pelé and Eusebio would be protected by the referees, that artistry would be allowed to flourish.

The England squad had its own contender to join such exalted ranks: Jimmy Greaves. Greaves was a goal scorer extraordinaire, a player capable of performing in an instant skills that eluded most other players throughout the game; his positional sense, his reading of the right moment to drift into the penalty box and his shooting ability were talents that placed him head and shoulders above all other rivals. Ramsey, who had never been comfortable with the precocious skills of Greaves, solved the problem of protecting the diminutive forward from the hard men who much preferred kicking the player to the ball. When the player sustained a minor injury during a first-round game against France, Ramsey dropped him from all remaining games, a decision that was greeted throughout the country initially with disbelief and then with growing anger. Greaves was destined as a direct result of this affair to follow Garrincha's example and seek solace in the bottle. Unlike the Brazilian, Greaves won his battle against alcohol and after retirement reinvented himself as a TV pundit.

While England were moving comfortably through the first round and into the quarter-finals, all was not well with the favourites, Brazil.

Having won their first match against Bulgaria 2–0, courtesy of two beautifully taken free kicks by the old firm of Pelé and Garrincha, they were to pay an unacceptably high price for that victory. Pelé had been injured and was unable to play at Everton's ground against Hungary.

Ignoring his team doctor's advice, Feola picked Garrincha for his second game within a few days. Not for the first or last time, with the Brazilian attack weakened the defence was frequently embarrassed. This time it was Hungary's turn to give the Everton audience a thrilling display of attacking football. At the end of the game, which finished with Hungary 3–1 winners, the crowd stood and acclaimed the Hungarians from the pitch.

The defeat meant that Brazil had to beat Portugal or they were out of the tournament. The pressure on Havelange and those around him that had been such a feature of the squad's preparations now reached a peak. The message coming from Rio was clear and unequivocal. 'At all costs victory must be achieved.'

'At all costs' was a particularly pertinent phrase. Within the travelling group of advisers from the Brazilian Federation, the ploy that had been used in Santiago was the subject of long and deep discussion. If a referee from Peru and a linesman from Uruguay could be persuaded to take a favourable view of events after a game to the benefit of Garrincha and Brazil, then surely a referee from Britain could be persuaded to do the same during the game?

The decision was made to bribe the English referee George McCabe before the game to ensure that Brazil won the match. One of the group, himself a referee, was designated to make the approach. Before doing so he discussed the best line to adopt with another member of the Brazilian squad who, far from offering advice on how best to nobble the ref, expressed horror at the idea.

'It's madness. I don't care who in the CBD has approved this plan. It's doomed. This isn't Chile and you're not dealing with a Peruvian. If it gets out the English won't look the other way. The President of FIFA is an Englishman, for God's sake. We'll all get arrested. You must abandon this idea otherwise none of us will be going home for a long time.'

After further discussion the plan to attempt the corruption of McCabe was, with considerable reluctance, abandoned. Brazil were going to have to win the game by conventional means.

Pelé, though still suffering from injury, returned to the side, but the panic that was running through the entire Brazilian contingent was obvious to any observer. Brazil made seven changes and after twenty-five minutes were in reality out of the tournament. They were at that stage losing 2–0. It made what subsequently occurred if anything more obscene. Pelé gathered the ball and, as he moved forward, the Portuguese defender Morais kicked him with great brutality. No attempt had been made by Morais to play the ball. Pelé staggered and, displaying extraordinary courage, moved forward again. Again Morais chopped him, this time to the ground. Again the referee McCabe stood mute, inert. Morais should have been sent off for the first tackle; that he was allowed to stay on the pitch after his second assault beggared belief. To re-watch these incidents on film is to see football at its very worst.

Pelé recalled those moments for me.

'For sure he should have been sent off. I was so intent on getting us back into the game it was only afterwards when I saw it on film that I realised just how bad those fouls really were.'

And the unrepentant Morais?

'Oh, it looked much worse than it really was. What made it look so bad was that Pelé was already injured so he was already moving with pain.'

With the Brazilian side already two down and reduced to nine fit players, the fact that Portugal eventually won 3–1 was academic.

What had occurred would have far-reaching consequences. It fuelled the already rampant hostility towards the Europeans. It was, not only to Brazil but also to other South American countries, irrefutable proof of a conspiracy, a plot, hatched by Rous and his cronies to ensure that the World Cup was won by England. The referee by his ineptitude had demostrated a rationale that for many in Rio, Santiago, Asunción and Buenos Aires would justify a rampant xenophobia. There was more to come in this World Cup that would serve as fuel for those convinced of 'the conspiracy'.

The saddest aspect of this affair was that a player of Pelé's stature had quite literally been kicked out of World Cup football. He vowed never to play in the tournament again. In his view – one shared by many who loved the game deeply – the world's greatest footballer had not been vanquished by a superior opponent but by thuggery and permissive, inept refereeing.

With the Brazilian squad departing like a group of condemned men the stage was set for two matches that would in their separate ways ensure that from 1966 onwards the South American view would be one of 'It's us against the rest of the world but particularly Europe.'

The quarter-final match between West Germany and Uruguay at Hillsborough resulted in two Uruguayans being sent off and West Germany winning 4–0. Before the quarter-finals both the Argentinian and the Uruguayan squads were to a man convinced of 'the plot, the conspiracy'. That the West Germany v Uruguay game was being refereed by another Englishman, Jim Finney, was seized on as further 'evidence'. The important aspect of this irrationality is that it was completely rational and credible to those that believed it, but then a classic sign of certain mental illnesses is to deny that one is ill.

At Hillsborough an Englishman had officiated in a game involving the Germans. At Wembley for the game between Argentina and England a German had been appointed as referee. Not the brightest of decisions by

FIFA but there is no evidence, not a shred, of 'a conspiracy' or 'the plot'.

The game at Wembley was still in its opening minutes when the pattern began to emerge. The Argentinians stifled attack after attack from England with an endless series of deliberate and cynical fouls. The excitable German referee Kreitlein, rather than acting as a calming influence, merely provoked the Argentinian defence by booking a growing number of them. Shadowing the referee through these activities was the large figure of the Argentinian captain Rattin, complaining, ever complaining. Eventually he also went into the book for a foul on Bobby Charlton.

Shortly before half-time Rattin raised strenuous objections in his native Spanish to the booking of yet another team-mate. Kreitlein neither spoke nor understood a word. He was later to say that Rattin's expression made his words entirely comprehensible. Rattin was sent off. The problem was, he refused to go. Ten minutes of arguing ensued, during which at one point the Argentinian player Albrecht attempted to persuade the entire team to leave with their captain. Ken Aston, who had refereed so lamentably the Battle of Santiago between Italy and Chile, now appeared like Banquo's ghost on the touchline. That he was now chief of the World Cup referees would have inspired little confidence in any player on the pitch with a long memory. Any England player who was foolish enough to get involved in the heaving mêlée found himself spat on by one of the Argentinians. When manager Ramsey saw England defender Nobby Stiles get a mouthful of spittle full in the face he buried his head in his hands.

After a violent tackle on a French opponent in one of the first-round games there had been great pressure brought on Ramsey to drop Stiles from his squad. The pressure had largely emanated from South American members of FIFA. Ramsey was convinced that the tackle by Stiles was without malice and that the player had genuinely mis-timed the lunge. Bowing to FIFA, members of the English Football Association had approached Ramsey with an order that Stiles must be dropped. He told them:

'If Stiles goes out of my team you can have my immediate resignation.'

Both player and manager knew that the opportunity to remove Stiles from the tournament in the event of further violent play would be seized on. Now, not for the first or last time in this crucial match, the Argentinians were deliberately provoking the gnome-like Stiles. When Ramsey raised his head expecting to find that Stiles had laid at least one Argentinian out cold on the grass, he was greeted by the sight of Stiles walking away from his assailant wiping his face with the sleeve of his shirt.

Eventually Rattin was persuaded to leave the field of play, if not the arena. I remember vividly how he performed a virtual lap of dishonour exchanging insults with the crowd and spitting at them, deliberately walking all over the red carpet to incite the spectators.

Argentina by popular consent had one of the best, if not the best, sides in the competition. If they had confined themselves merely to playing football by the rules, there is every likelihood that they would have won and it would have been they and not England who would have progressed to the semi-finals. As is so often the case, the ten men put up sterling resistance. They came close to scoring a number of times, but thirteen minutes from the end a cross from Peters to his West Ham team-mate Hurst was met with a high jump and a delightfully glanced header into the right-hand corner. England were through, but the entire continent of South America – or so it seemed at the time – was convinced beyond any doubt, reasonable or otherwise, that it had been a fix.

In time critics in South America would publicly state

that 'there was no doubt about it, the German ref was bribed. The English were determined to beat Argentina by any means.' The voice of reason was not helped by the English manager Alf Ramsey who during a post-match press conference had expressed the view that:

'We have still to produce our best football. It will come against a team who have come to play football and not act as animals.'

Ramsey had in mind not only the continuous fouling, spitting and the Argentinian response to the sending-off of Rattin, there were also the energetic attempts that members of the Argentinian team and other members of their squad had made to attack the referee at the end of the game, the wrecking of their dressing room and their attempts to smash down the door to the English dressing room to get at their rivals. The South Americans demanded an apology and threatened to withdraw from FIFA if they did not get one. They received no apology and stayed in FIFA.

The controversies that swirled around the Latin American teams during this particular tournament would become a defining moment in the transference of power from the Old World to the New and Third Worlds. A combination that has controlled world football for the past twenty-four years and is set fair to continue its domination of the world's most popular sport, short of a European revolution, for ever.

As early as 1952 at a FIFA Congress in Helsinki the writing was clearly on the wall for the Europeans. Belgian delegate José Crahay would later recall:

'One of the South American delegates had something general to say on each and every item on the agenda. We saw very clearly that each point had been carefully studied in advance and that the South American delegates had apparently been nominated to defend a certain standpoint which seldom corresponded with that of the FIFA Executive Committee.

'The FIFA General Secretary of the time, Kurt Gassman, fought back as well as he could, and all the major issues were deferred until the next Congress. But when it came to voting the European Associations each went their own way with no preconceived policy. The result was that we came close to committing a number of errors which would have done irreparable damage. May it be emphasised that our aim never was, and never shall be, to override anyone else. Europe's only aim was to defend its own interests.'

By the time of the World Cup in England in 1966, the game was well and truly afoot and not just the game played on the pitch but the one that is played far from the pitch, in smoke-filled rooms by elderly fat men. The power game.

While England prepared for their semi-final match against Portugal a number of secret, informal meetings between members of CONMEBOL, the South American Football Confederation, took place. The central theme was always the same. How to seize control of FIFA. Various strategies were explored but the central problem that was identified was to find a candidate who could attract enough votes to defeat Sir Stanley Rous. The problem remained unresolved as the various countries that had been knocked out departed for South America to confront the collective hostility that always faces losing squads arriving back home south of El Paso.

If England's match against Argentina represented for many the unacceptable face of the game, then that against Portugal reminded the spectator of many of football's positive aspects. Someone had obviously spoken to Morais and there was no repetition of his performance against Brazil in general and Pelé in particular. Possibly the prospect of missing the Final that beckoned for the winner may have had an inhibiting effect. England's own hard man, Stiles, was also a model of restraint and indeed was for many the single most decisive factor in England's victory.

Confronted with the task of marking Eusebio, the tournament's leading scorer, Stiles played magnificently and without a hint of illegal play demonstrated not only to Morais but to everyone else that it was possible to subdue one of the finest touch players in the word by outplaying him. For the English manager it was one of the sweetest aspects of a game that with its 2–1 result in favour of the home side meant that England were in their first World Cup Final, and at Wembley. Waiting for them were West Germany and yet another incident that would be seized upon by the gentlemen from South America who were justifying their various premature departures from the Finals by asserting that they never had a chance because the entire tournament had been rigged.

Certain facts were ignored. The fact that the semi-final match against Portugal had been played not only at a pulsating pace but had been brimming with skill and sportsmanship. The fact that Bobby Charlton had never played so well, that Stiles had been superb. That Bobby Moore, Jackie Charlton and the best goalkeeper in the world at that time, Gordon Banks, had defied everything that Portugal threw at them. None of this counted down south. It was a fix by those bloody English and that's all there was to it. If you needed further proof, the argument went, then just consider what happened in the Final.

The 1966 World Cup Final between England and West Germany is for the vast majority of Englishmen, who at the time were in their mid-teens or older, not unlike the assassination of President Kennedy. Everyone can tell you exactly where they were and what they were doing at the time, with one difference. The latter tragic event caught up with people doing many millions of different things. For the World Cup Final we were all in one place doing the same thing. We were all at Wembley watching England win. The stadium that at that time had a ground capacity of between ninety and one hundred thousand actually held, on Saturday, 30 July 1966, approximately seventeen million spectators. It certainly felt like it.

If the semi-final against Portugal had been vibrant, then the Final – at least for supporters of the two teams – was right off the edge of the Richter scale. The play moved ceaselessly from end to end. Germany scored first, after thirteen minutes, six minutes later England equalised. Hunt, who yet again had been preferred to Greaves, missed an open goal just before half-time. In the second half with less than thirteen minutes left to play England went in front with a goal from Martin Peters. All they had to do now was to hold out against the increasingly desperate attacks from West Germany. Four minutes from the end Hunt was clear, with Hurst and Bobby Charlton to his right and only one German defender between him and the goalkeeper. Hunt again made a hash of it, passing to Charlton a moment before the defender had been forced to commit. Charlton's hurried shot went wide. With some thirty seconds remaining Jackie Charlton and Held, the German forward, rose for the ball. Many believed that Held fouled Charlton; the Swiss referee Dienst thought otherwise and gave a free kick to West Germany, just outside the penalty box. The free kick taken by Emmerich hit one of his own players in the back, shot across to another, who sent it across the goal-mouth to be driven in by yet another, Weber. The scores were level as the whistle went. For the first time since 1934 there would be extra-time. Ten minutes into extra-time undying controversy occurred. A shot from Hurst hit the underside of the bar and bounced down. Hunt stood with his arms raised in delirious joy. For him there was no doubt that the ball had crossed the line. If he had taken the trouble to kick it back over the line all controversy would have been stillborn.

Referee Dienst was less convinced. Surrounded by petitioning German players he crossed the pitch to consult with his linesman, a Russian named Bakhramov. Two nations waited. The linesman had no doubt. It was a goal. He pointed at the centre spot and Wembley erupted. Again the West Germans refused to accept that the game was lost, their attacks came with the rhythm of waves, but the English defenders repulsed them again and again. A few moments from the end Hurst was set free by a superb long pass from Moore. The result was Hurst's third goal, the first hat-trick in a World Cup Final. It was over. The World Cup had been won in a cleanly fought contest that went some way to remove the bitter taste of much that had preceded the final game.

Television coverage in those pre-VTR days of football matches was still very much in its infancy. Fewer cameras, fewer technical facilities, the recordings of the game fail to answer the question. Was that vital third goal valid? Did Hurst's shot cross the line? Ask any German today and they are adamant it was not a goal. Ask any Englishman, they are equally dogmatic. It was most definitely a goal. The simple truth is that on the evidence that has survived on film it is impossible to tell. One piece of evidence that has, however, been largely ignored is the reaction of Hunt to the shot. If there had been the slightest doubt in Hunt's mind – and he was better placed than anyone on the pitch to judge – that the ball had not crossed the line, then it seems obvious that he would have kicked it into the net or attempted to do so. He would not have stood immobile with arms raised in celebration.

The controversy was inevitably seized upon by Havelange and others still licking their wounds. It was for them the final piece of conclusive evidence that the Europeans would stop at nothing to win. This from the head of a football association that had planned to bribe the referee officiating over the Brazil–Portugal game. This from the head of a football association that in the previous World Cup in Chile did in fact bribe at least one official and possibly two and in doing so bought their subsequent World Cup success in 1962.

Back in England the nation danced to a different tune as the celebrations engulfed the entire country. Prime Minister Harold Wilson, unlike the military junta of Brazil, had been democratically elected, but like the junta he knew very well the importance of sport in general and football in particular when it came to deflecting a nation from harsh economic realities. Less than two years into office and the Labour Government was floundering. Ten days before the Final, with much of the nation's attention focused on England's progress, Wilson imposed a pay freeze and for good measure also froze share dividends. 'The time has come to halt runaway inflation,' Wilson declared. At 5 p.m. on the 30 July the pay freeze did not seem to matter any more. Knowing a good thing when he saw it, Harold Wilson immediately invited the entire team to number 10 Downing Street. For good measure he attended the celebration banquet for the victorious squad at the Royal Garden Hotel. By now he had, in the words of Sir Stanley Rous, 'appropriated the World Cup as if it was his own or the Government's achievement ... when the crowd outside called for the players, it was Harold Wilson who swept up the cup and went out with the team to wave the golden trophy.'

Thirty-two years later it was as if time had stood still.

During the build-up to World Cup France, in the first half of 1998 it was for a moment as if we had come forward to the past. A Labour Prime Minister, one year into office and his honeymoon with the electorate showing the first inevitable signs of wearing a little thin around the edges,

played the populist football card. Not once, but twice.
First João Havelange was invited to Number Ten for tea
and biscuits. He arrived complete with World Cup footballs
and an anxious entourage from the English Football
Association. Tony Blair had created a media diversion
from political reality and footage of him spinning not
merely events but footballs duly appeared on the evening
television news. The real bonus for the Prime Minister was
when the President of FIFA emerged from Number Ten
and crossed to the waiting cameras to announce that he
believed that England should host World Cup 2006. That
news ensured a very positive front-page story on the
following day's newspapers.

Few thought to question the statement. Few it seemed
were aware that Havelange – at that time in the midst of a
very hectic campaigning schedule on behalf of his anointed
successor Sepp Blatter – had already promised the same
World Cup tournament to South Africa and Germany and
anyone else who wanted it. When the decision for World
Cup 2006 is taken, João Havelange will have been long
retired from the Presidency of FIFA. Since the moment
when he handed the World Cup to President Chirac to
present to the French captain, Didier Deschamps,
Havelange has been an ex-President. If few thought to raise
these questions then no one, it seemed, attempted to
discover precisely what had been said between the two
men before the cameras were let into Number Ten.

Prime Minister Blair's second playing of the football
card during the summer of 1998 occurred just forty-eight
hours before England's first World Cup match against
Tunisia. In a nakedly populist gesture Geoff Hurst, the
hat-trick hero of 1966, was awarded a knighthood.

According to João Havelange, the first time that the idea of
becoming President of FIFA entered his head, it was put

there by a sports journalist, the late Oduvaldo Cozzi. Havelange insists that he dismissed the idea. 'I had no ambition.' It is a statement rather on a par with his remark about not being interested or involved in politics. It flies in the face of all of the evidence of his life. Curiously for a suggestion that he claims to have dismissed, his memory of when it was made is very precise. 'On the 23rd of October 1963 in London during the centenary celebrations of the Football Association.'

Havelange insists that all he wanted was to give the World Cup to his country. Of course winning the World Cup is an excellent platform from which to launch a challenge for the supreme job in football.

Back in Brazil immediately after World Cup 66 Havelange set about winning back what he had come to regard as his own private property, the Jules Rimet trophy. The Generals shuffled political positions like an exclusive game of musical chairs, but all of them took a continuing interest in the national football team. At a time when the international perception of Brazil was largely negative and the criticism of the regime intense, one of the few positive images that the country presented to the rest of the world was the skills and talents of its footballers.

Havelange entrusted an old friend, Castor de Andrade, with the control of the Brazilian team during two South American competitions – the O'Higgins Cup in Chile in 1966 and the Rio Branco Cup in 1967 in Uruguay. Castor was a well-known figure in Rio, a patron of the Bangu Atletico Clube and a promoter of sport in general. This was by no means all that Castor promoted.

Castor de Andrade was for decades one of the leading controllers of the illegal lottery game known in Brazil as 'bicheiro'. His criminality was not confined to this one area. Illegal lotteries generate large amounts of cash. As such they present for organised crime a wonderful method of laundering cash. Castor had strong links not only with the criminal fraternities of Rio and São Paulo, but also with the Cali drug cartel in Colombia. The illegal lottery represented for the cartels just one of the assets under Andrade's control, another was his football club, Bangu Atletico. Yet again large amounts of cash were involved. Apart from the laundering, Andrade's network of lottery salesmen held for the drug cartel the prospect of an infrastructure to move marijuana, cocaine, and heroin throughout Brazil. Then there were Andrade's smuggling activities involving electronic equipment. There was also his widespread corruption of politicians, judges, police chiefs, from the most senior to the most junior. Some of the huge amounts of cash that came into his hands through his range of criminal activities was promptly given to any and all that Andrade perceived as powerful and influential friends who smiled kindly on his activities. Among this number was João Havelange.

Havelange was in the very best of company. The Governor of Rio, the mayors of both the capital and São Paulo, Presidents, police officials. Payments to the Rio police alone amounted to more than $200,000 per month. *Jogo de bichio*, which for a long time was tolerated by the authorities as a harmless contravention of the law, has since the 1970s been seen increasingly as a very dangerous potent conduit through which crime penetrates every level of Brazilian society. This is particularly self-evident when one analyses the explosion in the use and marketing of illegal narcotics that has occurred in the past twenty-five years in Brazil.

Brazil's preparation for World Cup 1970 in Mexico was, in the words of British journalist Brian Glanville, 'heavily and generously underwritten by the President of their Sports Federation, João Havelange.'

Those who were actually underwriting the preparations

were in fact the military junta. At all times paranoid and insecure, the dictatorship were determined that the 1970 World Cup experience would not be a repeat of the débâcle in England. They ensured that members of the military were in all the key positions. Chief of the delegation, of the entire squad and the personnel, was Brigadier Jeronimo Bastos. Perhaps that is what Havelange really had in mind when he talked to me about the junta having their job and he having his. Thus it was the Brigadier who organised the preparations.

That planning included a protracted and costly three-month spell when the entire national squad was kept together for intensive training and a variety of matches. The new team manager, João Saldanha, was an outspoken man with a colourful past. A former member of the Communist Party, then outlawed in Brazil, he began his tenure after Havelange appointed him in the teeth of strong opposition from members of the ruling junta.

Saldanha had always been outspoken in his criticism of the junta, a fact that was but one of the reasons he was held in such deep affection by the general public in Brazil. Admired also by the press as a man who brought a high degree of intelligence to the game, he had demonstrated while manager of Botafogo that he could produce a winning team. With his obvious talents plus a refreshing degree of vigour and enthusiasm, he appeared to be an excellent choice.

A lacklustre performance in a friendly against England at the Maracaná stadium in which Brazil scraped home to a 2–1 victory indicated there was much to be done to weld what was virtually a new squad into a fluent cohesive unit. Among those gone was the 'Little Bird', Garrincha. Never again would he be seen mesmerising defences as he came hurtling down the wing to deliver virtually on the byline a cross to be duly headed past yet another helpless goalkeeper.

Garrincha would end his days with his memories and an ever-present bottle and die at the age of fifty.

Against all the odds his team-mate Pelé was still there. He had vowed after being quite literally kicked out of the World Cup in England that never again would he expose his body either to psychopathic defenders or mindless referees. As the pain of the injuries sustained in 1966 subsided, inevitably so did the memory of how they had been inflicted, and how often they had occurred. He was finally persuaded that as he would be twenty-nine years of age by the time Mexico 70 got under way he would, barring unforeseen injury, be at his very peak. What finally decided Pelé to give it another throw of the dice was a fresh innovation from FIFA – the introduction of yellow and red cards. Provided the referees used the system correctly, Pelé and the other skilled ball players could expect some measure of protection.

Saldanha had worked the magic by the time Brazil played their qualifying games against Colombia, Paraguay and Venezuela. With Tostao in particular regularly finding the net they qualified in style for the right to play in Mexico the following year.

Saldanha, very much his own man at all times, suddenly lost the plot in November 1969. It had been four months since the squad had played an international game, yet Saldanha suddenly dropped both the goalkeeper and several other players and brought five new men into the team. The country, which to a man had been united behind the manager and his all-conquering team in August, was now outraged. The newspapers, the radio and television, were full of furious debate. It was not confined to the man on the São Paulo omnibus. The military also became involved. They had never trusted this intellectual revolutionary and it took all of Havelange's diplomatic skills to defuse the situation. Interesting that now

Havelange, as already recorded, takes the view that he did his job and the military did theirs and never the twain did meet.

In February the new team doctor, Toledo, stoked the flames of controversy when he sent two players, Toninho and Scala, home on medical grounds. In the doctor's opinion they were unfit to play. Their respective clubs had them independently examined by doctors who confirmed what the two players had already asserted. They were both fully fit. A few weeks later in early March, what was in essence Saldanha's preferred first team for the World Cup was beaten by Argentina at Porto Alegre. This by a team who had already been eliminated from the tournament by Peru. It was not seen by the nation as an ideal augury. Four days later Saldanha committed what was in the eyes of the majority an act of treason when he publicly said that he was thinking of dropping Pelé from the squad.

At this stage General Médici, the dictator currently running Brazil, got into the act and sent word that he wished to 'discuss' team selection with the manager. Before that delicate conversation could take place the Flamengo coach Iustrich added his voice to the growing criticism of the Brazilian team manager. Saldanha, who was also a master of unarmed combat, turned up at a Flamengo training ground seeking Iustrich. It was clear that he did not intend to confine himself to 'discussion' or indeed to unarmed combat. As he walked into the ground he was brandishing a revolver. It transpired that Iustrich was 'unavailable'.

The conversation with General Médici finally took place.

It is perhaps a measure of just how seriously they take their football in Brazil that this was evolving against a situation of extraordinary repression in the country. There were daily acts of terrorism both from the left and the right wings of the political spectrum. Political kidnappings, bombings, armed and bloody insurrection, citizens disappearing, torture, murder and mayhem, and in the midst of this carnage the nation's major preoccupation appears to have been the behaviour of the team manager of the national football team.

The meeting between General Médici and João Saldanha contained this memorable interchange:

Médici: 'Look, I want you to bring Dario into the team. He must play for us.'

Saldanha: 'I tell you what, Mr President. Let's make a deal. I won't tell you who to select for your government and you won't mess with my team.'

Médici was apparently unimpressed with this suggestion. He ordered João ('I did my job, they did theirs') Havelange to fire the team manager. Instantly. Havelange obeyed the order and Zagalo, a World Cup winner in 1958 and 1962, replaced Saldanha. Zagalo would still be there, still managing Brazil in World Cup France 98, but after what occurred both before the 98 Final and during the match in the Stade de France-Saint-Denis, Zagalo was destined to become an ex-Brazilian manager shortly after the squad's dismal return home to Brazil on two airliners named by the occupants Zidane One and Zidane Two. Even in 1970 Zagalo's promotion had not been a universally acclaimed appointment. In the years since 1970 there have been many who believed Zagalo has only retained his position because of Havelange's patronage. The team manager has also been subjected to fierce criticism because of the frequency that the national team play in meaningless competitions for apparently the sole benefit of their sponsor, Nike. Again over the years his critics have formed the view that Zagalo often selects particular players not on merit but to boost their transfer value on the international market. That was all in the future in March 1970 as Zagalo attempted to pick up the pieces of a demoralised squad while the nation continued to debate on a daily basis the rights and wrongs of 'L'affaire Saldanha'.

Zagalo has always had the reputation for being a man endowed with more than his fair share of luck. He was certainly fortunate in the squad he inherited from Saldanha. During their qualifying matches Brazil had scored twenty-three goals in six games, nine of them by Tostao and six by Pelé.

Before the 1970 World Cup tournament began all thirty referees were given very strict instructions that they were to take a severe line with dirty and violent play.

As is so frequently the case, the opening game was a dreary, unutterably boring game between the host nation Mexico and the USSR. They drew 0–0. The most passionate moment occurred before kick-off when during the parade of the competing nations England's Union Jack was greeted with long and sustained whistling. The holders of the World Cup were thus given a rapid reminder that hostilities with Latin America had been resumed.

The most distinguished performance during the actual game was from the referee, German Kurt Tschenscher. He had taken the injunction from the FIFA Referees' Committee very much to heart at least as far the Soviet team was concerned – a succession of very largely mild tackles was followed by a succession of names going into the black book. Curiously, when it came to viewing what was for many independent observers the far more violent tackling by the Mexican players, Tschenscher saw no wrong. His is a name to remember. It is certainly one that João Havelange has never forgotten.

Brazil were in the same group as England and their arrival at Guadalajara would have provided some excellent lessons for the England manager Alf Ramsey if he had been watching. Not lessons in football, but public relations, and if any team manager ever needed those, it was the brusque, taciturn Ramsey. In his dealings with the press he was invariably abrasive and frequently humourless. He lacked tact and he lacked patience when dealing with the media, and that was just when confronted with a very largely supportive English press.

When Brazil came to Mexico for the 1970 World Cup, instead of promptly disappearing to their training outside the city, on Havelange's instructions the squad went on a charm offensive. The players distributed flags and pennants to the populace, made visits, pressed the flesh and constantly proclaimed their undying love, affection and respect for all things Mexican. It has often been said that a team playing at home with good strong vocal support has an instant advantage of a goal. No one taking part in this tournament could afford to give this particular Brazilian squad a goal start.

In the previous year Ramsey had brought the England squad to Mexico. The intention, according to the England manager, was to 'make friends and create a warm friendly climate'. It was good thinking. Such an atmosphere would enhance the team's possibility of retaining the World Cup the following year. After England and Mexico played out a goalless match Ramsey held a short press conference outside the dressing rooms. The dressing rooms were always in Ramsey's time as team manager a no-go area for the press. He was asked if he had anything to say to the Mexican press. His response in part was:

'There was a band playing outside our hotel until five o'clock in the morning. We were promised a motorcycle escort to the stadium. It never arrived. When our players went out onto the pitch they were abused and jeered by the crowd. I would have thought the Mexican public would have been delighted to welcome England. Then when the game began they could cheer for their own team as much as they liked.'

He was about to return to the dressing room when something else occurred to him.

'We are delighted to be in Mexico and the Mexican people are wonderful people.'

The afterthought did not get reported by the Mexican media.

A few days later, after England had beaten Mexico 4–0, the Governor of the State of Jalisco wished to make a presentation to Ramsey. He was escorted into the team dressing room. The Mexican press promptly followed. With equal promptness they were thrown out by the England manager.

The following year, immediately before the World Cup tournament, Ramsey took the full England squad on a four-match tour of Colombia and Ecuador. Again the thinking was excellent, exposing the squad as it did not only to the heat and humidity but also the high altitude, all of which were problems that lay waiting for them in Mexico. Wretched circumstances decided to put a few more problems in the team's way, particularly the captain Bobby Moore.

With Bobby Charlton, Moore visited a jewellery store in the Bogotá hotel where the team was staying. Leaving without making any purchase, the two players were shortly afterwards confronted with a Colombian version of the badger game. It probably has its origins in the Stone Age. One timeless version is to confront a man in a hotel bedroom with a woman other than his wife. The other woman will usually be someone he has picked up in the hotel bar. Among the group confronting will be an irate 'husband' and possibly a 'hotel manager'. Threats are made. Money is paid. The accomplices leave in search of their next victim.

What Charlton and Moore were exposed to was an accusation that a valuable bracelet had gone missing. Moore was identified as the 'thief'; he was arrested and detained at a downtown police station. Allowed out on bail, Moore rejoined his England team-mates for their match against Colombia, which they won. They then travelled to Quito, the capital of Ecuador, and beat the national team. Returning to Bogotá, Bobby Moore was re-arrested as the team was in the process of catching a plane to the World Cup tournament.

He was eventually placed under house arrest in the care of the president of a local football club. In view of the number of people who swore on oath to a certainty that they had seen Moore pocket the bracelet, which had apparently vanished from the face of the earth, it is remarkable that either Moore or Charlton was allowed to leave the jewellery store and sit down in the hotel corridor. Following diplomatic intervention by the British Consul, bail was granted and Moore was allowed to go to Mexico to play in the World Cup.

The England captain's composure throughout the ordeal had been quite remarkable. Through all the hysterical denunciations he had calmly declared his innocence. The whole affair was at least an attempt to extort money from both Moore and the England management in return for agreeing to drop the charges. Those behind the scam were eventually arrested two years later and charged with conspiracy. It may well have had from the outset another agenda. Quite a number of those gathering in Mexico for the World Cup would have been delighted to learn that the England captain, who had had an outstanding World Cup four years earlier in England, would not be getting the opportunity to repeat that performance. At least these individuals could be relatively certain that even if he played in any of the games, Moore's focus and concentration would be very seriously affected with such grave charges hanging over him. In the event, Bobby Moore played brilliantly during World Cup 70.

When the team arrived from Colombia the forward Jeff

Astle, a man with a pathological fear of flying, was visibly the worse for wear and thus contributed to the Mexican newspaper headlines which proclaimed that England were 'a team of drunks and thieves'.

The various incidents may well seem with the passage of time and distance to be minor affairs that were quickly forgotten. In Brazil in February 1998 while researching this book I had each and every one of them seriously recounted to me, not once but several times, as important elements in the creation of an atmosphere where senior figures in South American football finally decided once and for all to wrest the power away from Europe in general and England in particular.

To many in South America the fact that Bobby Moore was completely exonerated was 'all part of the plot'. The fact that the England manager continually displayed what they saw as not merely arrogance from an inadequate individual but racist attitudes that, in the minds of those South Americans, were also secretly held by Sir Stanley Rous and his mainly European colleagues in FIFA was further 'evidence' – if it be needed after the South American débâcle of World Cup 1966 – that the game was being run by and for an exclusive club which, if its rules did not exactly state was for 'Europeans only', suffered the rest of the world badly.

England, having beaten Romania 1–0 in their opening match of the 1970 World Cup, prepared to face a Brazilian team that was very largely the creation of the gun-toting unarmed-combat expert Saldanha with some fine tuning by Zagalo. Brazil began with the 4–0 demolition of Czechoslovakia. It was apparent that Zagalo's legendary luck was holding. He had inherited a squad with an embarrassment of riches, including as it did Rivelino, Gerson, Tostao, Carlos Alberto, Jairzinho and Pelé.

On the eve of England's match against Brazil, the holders against the previous holders, Ramsey's decision to stay in the heart of the city at the Guadalajara Hilton was put to the test. The trinkets and the charm offensive that the Brazilian squad had previously demonstrated paid a powerful dividend.

The invasion began during dinner. A sprinkling of Brazilians with hundreds upon hundreds of Mexicans descended on the Hilton. They came on foot, by car and by motorcycle. By eight in the evening they had begun to circle around and around the hotel honking and tooting continuously, chanting without pause, *'Brasil! Brasil!'* As it grew later the crowd grew bigger and noisier. There was no let-up. It went on all night. Most of the English had no sleep at all. Mention this to those South Americans who talk of plots and conspiracies and they will invariably laugh and give you the Spanish or Portuguese equivalent of 'boys will be boys'.

To many observers this was the real Final, no matter that it was only a Group One qualifying game. England were given news shortly before the game that more than compensated for a sleepless night. Gerson had a thigh injury and would miss the match.

Against the Czechs early in the second half Gerson from deep midfield had hit a ball all of fifty yards to Pelé, who while being challenged trapped the ball on his chest, turned and struck the ball all in one exquisite flowing movement. It was a goal so beautifully created and taken that team-mate Clodoaldo dropped to his knees and cried. But this time Gerson, a forty-cigarettes-a-day man, would not be there to link up with the man who some were saying before the tournament was well past his best. Pelé had simultaneously silenced the critics and reduced a team-mate to tears of thanksgiving that he should be on the same pitch.

Now the fire and passion of Brazil confronted the ice and control of England in a collision of two diametrically opposed football philosophies. In the tenth minute Jairzinho accelerated past Cooper, the England left-back, raced to the byline and centred. Pelé's head moved and headed the ball down inside the left-hand post.

Recalling the moment, Pelé said to me: 'I was already shouting goal when Banks appeared from nowhere. One moment he was by the right-hand post as I headed down. The next moment. No, the same moment, he was by the left-hand post and he'd scooped the ball up and over the bar.'

The save that Gordon Banks had made was televised around the world and was acclaimed by, among others, Pelé as the greatest ever. Journalist John Moynihan was behind Banks's net as:

'Pelé hurtled in leaping over Mullery, and all for one were shouting "Goal!" and rising to acclaim the "King". Then an outrageous flash of movement, a combination of sprawling arms and legs. Banks was suddenly over to the right of goal lying sideways with his left leg thrust straight out, his other bent at right angles and his groping right hand scooping the ball up and over the crossbar. Banks, in this attitude of a praying mantis after spinning to a new twig, had played the ball up and away into oblivion. It tumbled over the bar and rolled slowly onto the other side of the net with the sudden abatement of an ocean wave breaking on a rock. And one wondered, amid all the shouting and screaming and commotion, whether England's goalkeeper had broken his arm and suffered grievous damage; he lay on his back with his shoulders on the grass, his colleagues standing around too nonplussed to yell their praise. Already the moment had become a legend, a piece of unique folklore, a gymnastic impossibility. "Did you see that?" roared Harry, turning round to me. His nicotined fingers were trembling with tension. "Christ! Did you see that!"'

The temperature reached ninety-eight degrees during this game. No English player lost less than ten pounds in weight. The English team doctor pointed out after the game that an American Army manual forbade even training when the temperature exceeded eighty-five degrees. To quote Brian Glanville again:

'The World Cup Committee had prostituted their tournament and sacrificed its players to the demands of European television.'

Fourteen minutes into the second half, Tostao beat three English defenders, including a foul on Moore that went unpunished, before passing to Pelé, who flicked the ball across to his right for Jairzinho to close in and score. It was the only goal in what was a definitive example of exactly what Pelé had in mind when a few years later he referred to 'the beautiful game'.

England had had their moments. Indeed, late in the game Jeff Astle, who had come on to replace an exhausted Hurst, missed an easy chance of an open goal from a few yards out, one of a number that were squandered by the cup-holders.

Brazil, very much relieved, departed convinced that they had just met the team that they would have to play in the Final. If the England v Brazil game had shown a global audience all that was good about the game, other matches gave those who saw them a glimpse of the other side of the coin, the referee's coin.

Hosts Mexico's first goal against El Salvador ranks as one of the all-time top ten in the category of worst referee decisions. Referee Hussain Kandil of Egypt awarded El Salvador a free kick. It was immediately taken not by an El Salvadorian player but by Perez of Mexico, who pushed it to a colleague who centred the ball to Valdivia of Mexico, who stood in a deserted goal mouth, the El Salvador team very largely being congregated upfield where they had gathered to take their free kick. Valdivia scored. Despite protests from the El Salvador players the goal inexplicably was allowed to stand, to the intense delight of the Mexico crowd.

The home fans were even more delighted in Mexico's game against Belgium when Mexico's centre-forward Valdivia, hurrying back out of the Belgium goal-mouth after an attack had failed, fell over his own legs and was promptly awarded a penalty by Coerezza the referee. Señor Coerezza was Argentinian. The goal that resulted from this decision took Mexico into the quarter-finals. Much more refereeing like this and they would have won the World Cup without even turning up. Fortunately they faced Italy in the next round and their luck ran out, Italy winning 4–1.

If folklore had been created by Banks against Brazil then both he and his substitute Bonetti conspired unwittingly to contribute to an imperishable myth concerning the quarter-final against West Germany. The myth goes that when the 'world's best goalkeeper', as his team-mates called Banks, developed a severe dose of Montezuma's revenge from a dubious bottle of beer and went sick the day before the match, his place went to Peter Bonetti and the game went to West Germany. Facts have never been allowed to stand in the way of a good myth.

Forty minutes from the end England were winning 2–0. After extra-time they were beaten 3–2. Thus West Germany gained revenge for England's victory over them at Wembley in 1966. Ramsey, who of course dictated the tactics from first to last, had decreed that the match would be played without wingers, something he was very prone to do. Indeed, his teams were often called 'the wingless wonders'. A number of the England squad were unhappy and concerned about this tactic. It had been employed against the Brazilians and they had lost.

The German substitutions during the game brought two pairs of fresh legs that lifted their entire team. Ramsey replaced Bobby Charlton and Martin Peters with Bell and Hunter, two substitutions that were dismal failures. The first German goal unarguably was Bonetti's fault: going down too late to a Beckenbauer shot, the ball ran under him. The second came from Seeler, totally unmarked in the England penalty box. Likewise Müller, also totally unmarked in extra-time when he scored the third goal.

Bonetti served as a convenient scapegoat for a manager who began with the wrong tactics, then compounded that error with the wrong substitutions. Peter Bonetti never again played for England.

In the semi-finals Brazil were confronted with Uruguay, who complained – quite rightly – that the match should not have been played at Guadalajara, which was to all intents and purposes Brazil's home ground, but at Mexico City. Their protests were over-ruled. They responded by deliberately arriving late for the game and refusing to attend the Governor's reception. When eventually they took to the pitch and the game commenced their behaviour went further downhill. Confronted with one of the most skilful teams, not just of this particular tournament but ever, Uruguay concluded that the only way they could win was to kick the opposition and continue to kick them until the final whistle. If they had concentrated on playing to their full potential they would perhaps still have been defeated but they just might have stolen the game. If this Brazilian side had a forward line and a midfield that was peerless, their defence all the way back to goalkeeper Felix was vulnerable. As if to underline this fact, Uruguay scored first. A basic goalkeeping error of positioning and the ball languidly bounced past Felix from the foot of Cubilla into the back of the net.

Gerson held his head as if cutting out the jubilant shouts of the Uruguayan players would make the moment an awful dream. Carlos Alberto looked momentarily drained of all energy. Then there was the stirring image of Pelé running through his own demoralised ranks. Running to collect the ball from the back of the net and carry it to the centre spot to get on with the game. To get back into the game. No longer the innocent seventeen-year-old of Sweden, he was now seen by many in the squad as the father figure, a man for all football seasons. He turned and spoke to his team-mates:

'Right. Let's see who is going to be first to score against these bastards.'

The Brazilians probed at the Uruguayan defence as they attempted to find an answer to the frequently brutal man-to-man marking that was being employed against them. Gerson was suffering from continuously having his marker Cortes climb all over, following him everywhere. Pelé was being crowded and suffocated by Castillo. Gerson, one of the most intelligent of players, began to consider the problem like a chess grand master.

'First I went to the left, then I went to the right. Then I moved up to their penalty area and still Cortes stayed with me. So I decided there was one place to take him. They were only interested in defending, so I took him back to our penalty area. That meant one body out of the way of our attackers. I told Clodoaldo to go forward and do my job, that I would stay behind with their number 20. Clodoaldo scored our equaliser from my position. Then the whole game changed and we could not lose.'

At half-time the only adjustment that Zagalo made was to tell Rivelino to play a little further to his right in the midfield, thus allowing Pelé and Tostao the space to make their runs on the left, a piece of fine tuning that was to prove crucial.

During the second half Tostao, making devastating use of the extra space, found Jairzinho who, leaving his marker floundering, slashed the ball past the Uruguayan goalkeeper.

In the final minute with Uruguay driven desperately to counter-attack, Pelé dragged the defence with him before stroking the ball into the path of the approaching Rivelino. 3–1.

Brazil were in the Final and the attention to detail that João Havelange so prides himself on was about to pay a very rich dividend. With Mexico out of the competition the Mexican nation turned its support to Brazil. They became in effect the 'home' team and the home team has won the World Cup five times. Ramsey and the English management were not the only organisation who could have learned much from studying the Brazilian squad *off* the pitch as well as on it. Maintaining a fortress mentality and keeping contact with the host nation to a minimum wins few friends.

West Germany met Italy in the other semi-final and Italy, a team obsessed with defence, for once threw off that obsession and narrowly prevailed 4–3 after extra-time. The West German captain Beckenbauer had been crippled by a series of brutal and cynical fouls, all perpetrated outside the penalty box. That a team playing such negative, sterile football as Italy had played throughout the entire tournament, with the exception of this one match, should get to the Final pleased no one but the Italian supporters. This particular Final was seen by a great many as the Forces of Light against the Forces of Darkness.

Both nations had previously won the Jules Rimet trophy twice, therefore the winner would take permanent possession and a new cup would be created. It was a match with a wide range of possibilities. The Italians had all the goal-scoring potential in the world. Riva, Boninsegna, Mazzola and Rivera each had the skill and ability to turn the game single-handedly, but first the Italians had to break free of their own self-made straitjacket, the *catenaccio* defence, a philosophy that dominated their game. It was sterile. It was negative. It did not create, it destroyed. *Catenaccio* – a great big chain – employs a chain of defenders designed to negate all attack from the other team. Three full-backs are given strict man-to-man marking duties. Behind them is the *libero* or free man with no specific opponent; his task is to patrol the entire central defence area ready and alert to plug any gap created by an error from any of the defenders in front of him. It was not and never has been a philosophy designed to win games. Its purpose is to avoid losing heavily. It has for decades, for fifty years to be precise, eaten away at the very heart of football, particularly Italian football. In the summer of 1970 it was to be given the definitive test. Could it smother and subdue the flair and imagination of Brazil? Could it snuff out Pelé's genius? The vision of Gerson? The subtleties of Tostao? Could this Italian team which in fact contained such an abundance of talent throw off its totally defensive posture and create rather than destroy? One thing was for sure: if the Italians sat back and let the Brazilians come at them they were asking for trouble.

It soon became very clear that Italy had come to play negatively, hoping for a chance to break on a counter-attack. They sat back. They let the Brazilians come at them. They got trouble.

Gerson dominated the midfield. Jairzinho, taking a leaf from Gerson's book on how to overcome man-to-man marking, took Facchetti continuously into the midfield, which allowed Carlos Alberto, a defender who was never happier than when going forward, to spend the entire afternoon doing precisely that as time and again he advanced down an empty right wing. The Italians, courtesy of *catenaccio*, were not playing with a left winger. Less than twenty minutes into the game Brazil went ahead. A throw-in by Tostao to Rivelino, who lofted a harmless looking cross in the general direction of the Italian goal. Pelé climbed higher than the defenders around him. He twisted in the air as he appeared to hang there like a high diver caught and frozen in mid-air by a photographer, his head connected and the ball was in the back of the net.

Mazzola and Boninsegna were playing like men possessed, but around them too many of their team were content to patrol the last third of the Italian end of the pitch. It would take something very spectacular to get Italy back into the game.

When it came, it was from a Brazilian, a spectacular mistake. Clodoaldo had a sudden rush of blood to the head and inexplicably back-heeled the ball towards the Brazilian goal. It became a superb pass to Boninsegna, who, given the opportunity to capitalise on the confusion, took the ball past Felix in the Brazilian goal. At that moment, as Pelé recently confirmed to me, the Italians had the game in the palm of their hands. Brazil were demoralised, their heads down. If Italy had surged forward, had attacked the Brazilian defence consistently, the game was theirs for the taking.

The home crowd was not the only advantage the Brazilians had that day in Mexico City. They also had *catenaccio* going for them. The Italians could not break free of the all-pervasive defensiveness that was so integral to their game.

Brazil were thus given the space to re-group. To draw encouragement from small success. To rediscover their belief in their collective talent.

Sixty four minutes, and well into the second half, Gerson, still being allowed to dominate the midfield, received a pass some forty yards from the Italian goal. Two touches with that left foot took him past a defender, he swivelled and from twenty-five yards or more the ball rocketed into the net.

Sixty-nine minutes and Gerson took a free kick which found Pelé. Pelé did not appear to look up. It seemed that he knew that Jairzinho would be there. The forty-yard kick from Gerson came flying towards Pelé, who delicately flicked it down into the path of Jairzinho, who, without pausing, ran the ball into the Italian goal.

Three minutes from the end came something sublime.

Tostão tackled and won the ball some ten yards from his own penalty area. He played the first of what were to be nine passes between Brazilian team-mates, passes that were interspersed with an exquisite variation on the team samba by an adlib from Clodoaldo swaying and swerving and sidestepping as he beat four men in the space of a few yards and then touched the ball to Rivelino. From Rivelino to Jairzinho. Jairzinho cut inside, a change of direction that confused two of Italy's defenders and allowed Jairzinho to lay the ball across to Pelé. Pelé paused, taking four touches. He had sensed that roaring up the right wing Carlos Alberto was approaching. 'The weight,' recalls Carlos Alberto with a smile. 'I never had a powerful shot, you know, but Pelé made me take this one in my stride and that's why the goalkeeper had no chance. I was lucky.' So were we all.

So Brazil won 4–1. The score was only a small part of the story. Light had indeed defeated darkness. The jubilation from the Brazilian players and the rest of their squad, from their back-up team, from their fans, stirred the heart. They had won the cup as now they were celebrating that victory, with panache. With joy. They had reminded all who were very privileged to see this match, either as spectators in the stadium at Mexico City or as part of the global audience watching on television, that above everything else football was a glorious game, one to be savoured and enjoyed.

This match was football's masterpiece. The Citizen Kane of the game.

Brazil went home with the trophy and, courtesy of João Havelange, a twenty-thousand-dollar bonus per man. It was huge money in 1970. Today there are players earning more than that in one hour of their working week.

The Italians went home to what had become a traditional greeting when they return empty-handed – insults and rotten fruit.

Pelé had vowed after being so viciously attacked during

the 1966 World Cup in England that he would never again play in the World Cup. Many had gone to work to persuade him to change his mind. In particular João Havelange had gone to great lengths to reassure Pelé. There still existed at this time a very close bond between Pelé and Havelange. Still father and son. There is much to take Havelange to task for with regard to his involvement in the game. Much to condemn. There is also inarguably the credit side to his involvement in football, and this included persuading Pelé to play in the 1970 World Cup. By convincing the man who is for so many millions the world's greatest footballer, ever, to reach beyond the darkness of the game, Havelange places all who love football in his debt. That handful of games alone. Those six performances from Pelé, this gentle, soft-spoken, modest man, ensured that his abilities will remain forever imperishable. *This* was the game.

And therein is the supreme irony. The most bitter paradox. From having significantly contributed to all that is beautiful about the game, by persuading Pelé to play yet again in the World Cup, João Havelange embarked on a campaign to initially seize control of, then to subsequently steal the game.

And at the very heart of this campaign was that same player.

Havelange had told me of how he had 'won my first World Cup in Sweden in 1958'. He had also said:

'Pelé owes me a great deal and his debt to me began in the 1950s when I gave him the chance to go to Sweden.'

Any debt real or imagined by Havelange has surely been repaid many times over with what Pelé has contributed to the game. What Havelange in his turn has never repaid is his own very real debt to Pelé. Quite simply, if any one single person is responsible for Havelange capturing supreme power in football, that person is Edson Arantes do Nascimento. Pelé.

Part Two

'I still had no ambition to become President of FIFA.' 'But Dr Havelange, within twelve months of Brazil winning the World Cup in Mexico you were actively campaigning for the post.'

'All I wanted was to win the World Cup for my country, and I was very successful. We played five and won three.'

Again I checked myself from stating the obvious about who had actually won these trophies and allowed Havelange to tell me how he without ambition had gone campaigning for the top job in world football. That famous total recall of his yet again appeared to have hit a black hole. An abortive attempt had been made to get Havelange's presidential aspirations off the launch pad in 1968 at a CONMEBOL (South American Football Confederation) meeting that took place in October that year at Guadalajara. Impassioned declarations extolling the virtues that Havelange would bring to the FIFA presidency were made by a number of delegates. Less than three years later there was another attempt and this time Havelange remembered it:

'The presidents of the federations of Argentina and Uruguay came to Rio in 1971 to ask permission to put forward my name as candidate for the Presidency.'

'They wanted to nominate you as the official candidate of the South American Football Confederation?'

'That's right. The Presidency had always been occupied by Europeans. They thought it was time for a South American to have the job.'

'Did you share this view?'

'Of course. Initially I was unsure about running myself, then I talked the matter over with two other CBD directors, Silvio Paceco and Abilio de Almeida. Then I decided to run.'

Three months later in a scene that would not have been out of place in a *Godfather* movie, the other eight presidents of the South American federations met with Havelange and his Brazilian supporters for a banquet in Tijuca, Rio. Amid much kissing and embracing all present made public commitment to Havelange.

It was an impressive beginning, but the constitution of FIFA is no respecter of a country's size. All votes are of equal weight. One vote per country. South America with its ten federations, one per country, was just ten votes. Havelange needed over sixty to win. To snatch the crown from Sir Stanley Rous. He was largely unknown outside Latin America. He held no position in FIFA and was not even one of his country's delegates to the organisation. Sir Stanley had been President since 1961 and whatever faults either real or imagined Havelange and his supporters saw in the President, he was internationally known and respected. With South America in his pocket, Havelange began to develop a strategy.

'At that time the British links with their former Empire were weakening. An employee, when he leaves a company and goes out to make his own way, run his own company, is normally against his ex-boss.'

He began visiting former British colonies in Africa and Asia. He is disinclined to mention it today, but on a great many of these trips he was accompanied. Havelange was most definitely completely unknown outside a minority of countries. The man he took with him was known throughout the world. Was along with four or five other individuals one of the best-known people on the planet. Pelé.

It was a shrewd ploy. In 1967 during the civil war between Nigeria and the breakaway state of Biafra, the slaughter was halted for twenty-four hours on both sides so that people could watch Pelé take part in an exhibition game. Santos were touring through Africa. Like a travelling rock'n'roll star they were playing a series of one-night stands. Kinshasa, Brazzaville, Libreville, Abidjan, Cotonou, Lagos and many more. Everywhere the team went Pelé was treated as a god. As he himself acknowledged, 'I represented to the blacks in those countries what a black man could accomplish in a country where there was little racial prejudice, as well as providing physical evidence that a black man could become rich, even in a white man's country.' Every match was played in front of a packed stadium. Every airport was choked with thousands and thousands of people hoping to catch a glimpse of this black athlete who somehow represented for all of them a ray of hope, a possible escape hatch.

Now in 1971–72 Havelange moved through the African countries with Pelé. Lobbying for votes. Promising much in return for those votes.

Some of the promises – a commitment to enlarge the World Cup with a promise of more places for African states; a promise to ensure that South Africa was isolated permanently until apartheid was abolished – mixed the idealistic with the politically astute very neatly. Other promises catered to more basic desires in those who were the recipients.

Many of the Associations in the Third World rarely if ever attended FIFA Congress; they simply did not have the money for such trips or finance to cover hotel expenses.

The 1974 Congress was, as is the custom, going to take place in the host country staging that year's World Cup, in this instance Germany. Frankfurt, the location for the Congress, might just as well have been on the moon for men eking out a living in Malta, let alone Ethiopia or the other thirty African associations. It is perhaps difficult to grasp the fact that in the 1970s FIFA saw the world at least in some respects as a place where sportsmen and their various associations still clung to amateur traditions. Paying out large amounts of money for officials to fly to foreign places for sustained junketing was not in the mind of Sir Stanley Rous part of those traditions.

Havelange had a different view of the world. He was a founder member of that branch of philosophy that has debunked the concept of a free lunch. To Havelange, in this life you invariably get what you pay for. His offer to pay from his own pocket all expenses, plus handsome spending allowances, presented for many delegates an attractive package to men who had never been out of their own countries. No one could cavil at Havelange's generosity when it came to expenses. Tessima of Ethiopia, for example, received more than three hundred thousand in Swiss Francs plus free return flights to Europe.

From Africa thirty-seven FIFA delegates came to Frankfurt, virtually all of them courtesy of Havelange's benevolence.

As a campaign it never lacked for versatility. In 1972 Havelange organised an all-expenses-paid alternative World Cup tournament in Brazil. The Mini Copa. Twenty teams played in the tournament which significantly was boycotted by the most important European footballing countries including England, Italy and Germany. Everyone got a free trip and a free holiday and at the end of the day a lot more delegates had heard what Havelange was promising if elected. To persuade Venezuela to take part,

Havelange paid their football association $25,000, which guaranteed him their vote at the next FIFA Congress. The tournament had a financial loss for CBD of more than $10 million. It had cost over US$21 million to stage. Not everyone in the military junta saw it as a good investment, but then not everyone in the military junta or the government thought it would be a good idea if Havelange became President of FIFA. In June 1973 there were calls in the Brazilian parliament for a commission to be set up to investigate the financial losses of CBD, which were generally acknowledged to be totally related to Havelange's campaign for the FIFA presidency. The other cloud over that particular event was Pelé's flat refusal to take part in the tournament. By now, he told me, he had been made fully aware of just how corrupt the junta were, of how they were using his footballing abilities to present an acceptable image to the rest of the world. He would have no more of it.

Pelé would continue to play, but never again for the national team. The military had now fully taken over the running of the national squad.

The training camp for the Brazilian team resembled in some respects a concentration camp. None of the squad could leave without specific permission. All of the infrastructure was either run by people actually in the military or people closely connected to it. As Juca Kfouri, the Brazilian sports journalist and unremitting critic of Havelange, explained:

'They were very competent. Very efficient. They took the view that football was too important to be left in the hands of footballers. They decided to militarise it. There was a huge disappointment in the country when Brazil did not win the World Cup in England in 1966. Although there was of course a dictatorship in place at the time. It got much tougher after 1968. The people looked back and thought, well, the good times were when we were winning

World Cups. Good times were the other governments. Previous governments. This was very dangerous for the military. That's why the victory in Mexico in 1970 was so important for the junta. That's why Havelange's organising an independent tournament in 1972 was important for the junta, just as it was important for Havelange's ambitions to become FIFA's President.'

Havelange showed the same kind of planning that he had brought to Viação Cometa. The same attention to detail that he had brought to the Brazilian Sports Federation was now brought to bear on defeating Sir Stanley.

Whenever he met the president of an association or delegates of any federation he would always insist on being photographed with them. He told me:

'Then I memorised these photographs because if a man is in Fumincino airport, or Orly, or Heathrow, and if I bump into them and I don't greet them, then this would be a vote I would lose, because people are very sensitive and so I paid particular attention. And, I have a very good memory.'

So simple. So effective.

Havelange also brought to this campaign that obsessiveness that has always been a feature of his life. Intensive research, detailed analysis, inexhaustible energy. He worked tirelessly. If a FIFA delegate wanted to meet Pelé, no problem, Pelé was whisked to the delegate's country. If the delegate wanted to meet the entire Brazilian team or have them play in his home town, no problem, it was done. FIFA was going to get for the first time in its history the best election that money could buy.

To the non-European delegates Havelange attacked European domination of FIFA. It was, he argued, time for a change and he was the change that was on offer.

To the African delegates he promised to enlarge the World Cup competition from its current sixteen finalists. As a first step he promised to enlarge that to twenty-four.

To all the developing nations he promised money, buckets of it, for new stadiums, courses for referees, for doctors, for trainers, for anyone. There would be more lucrative competitions in the Third World.

To those many countries who wished to see China readmitted as a member of FIFA he promised it would happen.

To those who wished to attend a lavish cocktail party given by an ambassador, Havelange arranged a series of such events around the world at Brazilian embassies. At one such party, for example, in Cairo in 1974, Havelange promised the assembled delegates who represented every FIFA-affiliated country on the continent of Africa with the exception of white South Africa that, if elected, the South Africans would remain permanently suspended from FIFA until apartheid no longer existed in that country.

In this Havelange was quite deliberately exposing the Achilles heel of his rival, the incumbent Sir Stanley.

For over three years Havelange planned and schemed by every conceivable means to increase those original ten votes to a plus-sixty total.

'In one period of two and a half months, some ten weeks, I visited eighty-six countries. My air ticket weighed several kilos. Near the end of my campaign in five days I was in six countries in Central America and Mexico. From there I went directly to London, where I chartered a Mystère-Falcon jet, and then I flew to Strasbourg, where the Brazilian team was playing that night in a game prior to the World Cup of 1974. When the match was over I returned to the airport, where the Mystère-Falcon was waiting for me. Back to London, where I had a coffee. Took a bath, locked my hotel door, disconnected the phone and slept for twenty-four hours in a row. The following day I flew to Frankfurt for the election.'

His campaign literature is very typical of the man. No

one having to vote in this election could complain that having read the material they remained ignorant of where Havelange was coming from and what his life to date had been about. It was selective. Highly selective. Campaign literature always is. It left many questions unanswered and many gaps in Havelange's life unfilled.

There were a dozen photographs charting various stages of Havelange's career. In the majority of the shots Havelange has been photographically highlighted. Five shots of the would-be President in his swimming trunks and water-polo kit may well have bemused some of the less well-informed FIFA delegates when they first received their mail shot. Quite what they were to make of a photograph of the front door of the CBD offices in Rio still remains a mystery. Havelange's list of the various titles he had received – fifty – and the decorations he had been awarded – sixteen – gave very clear indications that Havelange was not alone in thinking he was a very fine fellow. Quite what FIFA delegates made of the information that the man who wished to become their President, while not a member of the South American Football Federation, was nevertheless an honorary citizen of Teresopolis City who held the Santos Dumont Order (aeronautics) has remained a mystery.

In his election address to the delegates there is much reference to the fact that South America had only hosted three out of the nine World Cup competitions held up to that time. There are also several paragraphs extolling the virtues of João Havelange, one of the final vanities being to compare himself very favourably with the father figure of FIFA, Jules Rimet. Perhaps at the end of the day it was just the envelopes of dollars that so many of the delegates received from Havelange rather than his awards and honours that swayed the electorate. It certainly was not the idealistic picture of everyday Brazilian life that the document contained. To judge from the election address of Dr Havelange, Brazil as of 1974 resounded not to the screams of the tortured, the bullets and bombs of the left and right and the lament from victims' families. All that could be heard in Havelange's Brazil was the sound of football in packed stadiums 'with a total capacity throughout the country of four million, five hundred places'.

Throughout this entire campaign Havelange not only conducted a continuous global canvass of the some one hundred and thirty delegates, he was also very active within his own country. One minute ensuring that the transport company of Viação Cometa was running smoothly, the next casting an anxious eye over the activities of Atlantica Boavista or looking in at the offices of Orwec.

Then there was the Brazilian Sports Federation to run. Twenty-three sporting disciplines to keep an eye on. Yet another World Cup to prepare for. This time of course the tournament in Germany would be immediately preceded by the election.

One question more than any other comes to mind. Who paid for it all? Who paid to finance an election campaign that even by the most conservative estimate must have cost between two and three million dollars? Havelange's ten-week, eighty-six-country tour, for example, where did the money come from for that?

In 1986 *Playboy* magazine interviewed Havelange.

'Visiting eighty-six countries costs a lot. Who paid for the trip?'

'I myself paid for it. After working for nearly fifty years I can allow myself a few luxuries. This was at the time that I decided to be the President of FIFA.'

'And how much did you spend?'

'I haven't the faintest idea.'

This response from a man who reels off facts and figures,

amounts of money, distances travelled, stops made, meetings held, as if his very existence depended on imparting such information. He can tell you to the cent what he was earning before the Second World War, tell you the current real estate value of FIFA's property portfolio to four decimal places. Tell you what he claims was in the FIFA cash till when he outflanked and outbid Sir Stanley Rous. Tell you how much he is leaving as his bequest to FIFA over the next ten years, yet he has not the faintest idea what he spent to get the job.

The same interview contains another example of Havelange's reticence when it comes to his personal finances. He was asked about the salaries of the staff based at FIFA House in Zurich.

'Do they earn a lot of money?'

'A great deal. My Secretary General receives around ten thousand dollars a month. My secretary earns six thousand dollars a month. The lowest salary is three thousand dollars a month.'

'And you?'

'Oh, please don't ask me something like that. I have income from Cometa, of which I am the main shareholder. I provide FIFA with my services for free. I receive my bare expenses for tickets, accommodation, entertainment and travelling, plus a daily subsistence allowance.'

At the time of this interview Havelange owned a superb flat in Rio in a very salubrious part of town and a magnificent house in Angro dos Reis on the Fluminese coast.

Havelange has invariably trotted out the transport company Viação Cometa when asked about his money. He is frequently described as being 'fabulously wealthy'. He is undoubtedly capable of acts of generosity, but it is often the kind of generosity that has strings attached to it. A vote bought. An income tax investigation soft-pedalled. A favour sought or granted. Havelange has for most of his life inhabited a world in which one hand washes the other.

As for the bus company, of which he claims to be the main shareholder, being the source of his wealth, the documentary evidence contradicts this. In 1993, for example, the published accounts of Viação Cometa indicate that Havelange is not the main shareholder, that he occupies what is in effect an honorary position on the board without any real influence and that he was paid for his troubles precisely the same amount that a few years earlier he was telling a journalist was the sum his FIFA secretary in Zurich earns. Six thousand dollars per month. Set against the sums Havelange was giving to FIFA delegates in 1974, six thousand dollars would not even represent a 10 per cent deposit on what Havelange allegedly paid for the Ethiopian vote.

If the funding for the FIFA campaign did not come from Cometa, where then did the money come from? It was a question I put to Dr Lobo, Havelange's former business partner. At exactly the time of Havelange's campaign – 1971 onwards – Lobo was a fellow director and part owner of Orwec. By this time the refuse-burning had been decreed a health hazard by local authorities and brought to an end. That left two elements to the company – the chemical and metallurgical activities, its most profitable activity being a chemical process to galvanise steel; the other being the selling of explosives and mines.

'Dr Lobo, do you know how João Havelange financed his candidacy for the FIFA presidency?'

'Part of the money came from embezzled funds from the Brazilian Sports Federation. The other part came from Orwec.'

'And was that legal?'

'Ah, he was a partner, he would take it from the company account and put it into his own private account.'

'Was that legal?'

'If his partners allowed it, yes.'

'Did you as a partner sanction this?'

'No, but as a minority partner and at that time a friend ...' Haddock Lobo shrugged. 'It was a debt that he owed Orwec, a running debt. He owed the company more than 1.2 million cruzeros. [In 1972 values, approximately $200,000. Current equivalent $850,000.] This, plus money stolen from the CBD, was what financed his campaign.'

The Havelange that Dr Lobo described to me is in sharp, stunning contrast to the image that the man himself projects. A self-made rich man indulging a whim to seek the most influential position in the world of football who uses his own financial resources to conduct a three-year electoral campaign or a venal man who appropriates company funds without reference to a fellow director and augments that money with funds stolen from the country's sports federation?

Then there is the other line of business that Orwec did. Explosives and bombs. It began innocently enough as Lobo explained.

'Orwec also was in the explosives business. During those years there was much development throughout Brazil. A great deal of expansion. New football stadiums. New roads. New towns. There was a need to dynamite a way through previously impenetrable terrain.'

Enter the Portuguese.

In the early 1970s many members of the late Antonio Salazar's regime, confronted with a situation that had been progressively deteriorating since the dictator's death, had, like others before them, seen Brazil as a safe haven. These particular men had among their number the former Portuguese Minister for Finance, Luis Maria Teixeira Pinto. Again like others before them, they knew that to re-establish themselves in a foreign country was a costly affair. Brazil offered them the same native tongue. It also had a thriving arms business.

It could be fairly said of the Portuguese Finance Minister that nothing in his government life became him like the leaving of it. He stole a sum variously estimated at being between five hundred million and one billion dollars.

In the first instance this money was diverted to New York and sprayed into a wide range of bank accounts. Much of it is still there today. Other tranches were used to buy ongoing businesses. One particular enterprise, called very grandly Emprecendimentos Portuguese do Brasil Participacoes with a capital of over $300 million, had as its central ambition to buy up the majority of explosives and arms companies within Brazil.

Havelange's company Orwec was seen as the perfect laundry. Once they controlled this company, large amounts from the New York accounts could be channelled into Brazil for further acquisitions thus circumventing Brazil's then stringent controls of foreign currency movements into the country.

At the time the Portuguese appeared Orwec was, financially speaking, on its knees. It had twice been pulled back from bankruptcy by injections of large amounts borrowed from a relation of Dr Lobo – company debts that were still on the books when the Portuguese came. The Portuguese made a 'loan' to the three Orwec directors to ensure that when they bought the company it was solvent and was not carrying forward significant debt. The amount that was handed over by Pinto and his colleagues was five million cruzeros (1972 – $1 million; 1998 – $8 million). With the company now able to show a clean bill of financial health the Portuguese bought 51 per cent. Having got their foot in the door they then bought further companies, including one that specialised in bomb and rocket manufacture. With Havelange on the parent board still retaining 49 per cent, history had now repeated itself and João Havelange, like his father before him, was in the arms trade.

When the Portuguese had advanced the five million cruzeros to the three partners, Havelange attempted to defraud Lobo of most of his rightful share. The exchange of letters between the two men and the subsequent settlement by Havelange overwhelmingly confirms this.

'At the time this argument broke out, Havelange's election campaign was becoming increasingly active. I was attempting to get Havelange to settle. All I wanted was what was legally mine. He was prevaricating. Then his lawyer called me. "He's going to Europe ... Going to be too busy to deal with this matter now ..." I told Havelange's lawyer, "Either he pays me now or I'm going to court."'

'Of course by making that threat at that time, if you had taken him to court, if this whole affair came out, become public knowledge, that would have been the end of his chances of becoming President of FIFA?'

'Naturally. His lawyer paid me the full amount within the week.'

It was not the end of Lobo's problems with Havelange. Both men are still to this day partners in Orwec. Lobo has been attempting for over twenty years through the courts of Brazil to get Orwec legally dissolved, his main complaint being allegations of consistent and serious fraud. In view of its activities immediately after he broke with Havelange in 1973, dissolution would seem to be an excellent idea.

There was, for example, the deal that the Portuguese and Havelange concocted with the Bolivian dictator Hugo Banzer and the other members of his military junta. João Havelange has remained remarkably consistent throughout his life concerning the kind of people he prefers. Hitler and the Third Reich. The Brazilian Generals. Salazar's colleagues. Banzer and the other members of the Bolivian junta.

The deal between Havelange and the Portuguese and the Bolivians has criminal fraud, fraudulent accounting, theft and conspiracy to defraud written all over it. Those aspects apart it is a model business transaction.

Like their spiritual brothers in Sicily, the individuals controlling Orwec knew how to move bits of paper around. They also knew how to run a second set of books, an illegal account whose sole intention was to defraud the tax authorities. Throughout at least the first six years of Havelange's FIFA presidency, his company Orwec also operated a slush fund. Despite consistent losses since its inception, Orwec has been able to persuade a variety of Brazilian banks to lend it many millions of dollars – loans that appear to have been repaid by the use of some very dubious transactions which have involved many millions of dollars being moved from Nassau in the Bahamas into Orwec. This represents prima facie evidence of a money-laundering exercise that went on over many years. The object of the exercise, as organised crime all over the world has demonstrated on countless occasions, is to distance yourself from the crime while simultaneously benefiting from it.

Orwec, namely Havelange and his Portuguese partners, bought Industria Quimica Mantiqueira, an arms company that controlled yet another company, Valparaiba. The deal with the Bolivian regime involved selling them eighty thousand hand grenades. The order was placed in writing with an unusual condition. The deal was dependent on Havelange's company borrowing the money from the Banco do Brasil to pay for the grenades they were selling. The maximum cost of eighty thousand grenades at that time would have been $1.2 million. The written order called for payment to be made of $5.3 million, at today's values over $21 million. The 'loan' that Havelange and his colleagues so kindly arranged for the Bolivians, so that they could pay five times what everyone involved knew was the value, was paid directly from Banco do Brasil to the Havelange company. If the reader remains a trifle confused, it should be remembered that the intention of all parties was to create two things: maximum confusion and maximum profit.

Having concluded this business, João Havelange got back to the task of convincing the FIFA delegates scattered around the world that he was the ideal man to run football and manage its finances. His vote-collecting gathered pace and always showed enterprise. Yugoslavia had a number of international players on yellow cards who were obliged to sit out an international match before they could yet again play for their country. Havelange had the answer. He arranged for the Atletico club from the Brazilian state of Minas Gerais to travel to Europe as a Brazilian international eleven and play against Yugoslavia, thus freeing the Yugoslavs for their next proper international game. On 6 June 1973 Brazil played Tunisia and Havelange very kindly reduced the amount that Brazil would normally take from the gross receipts from $50,000 to $30,000. He now had the votes of the Yugoslavian and Tunisian delegates in his back pocket for the coming election.

The man he would be hoping to unseat – his opponent Sir Stanley Rous – came from a rather different background.

Stanley Rous, son of a grocer, born in the late Victorian age, was a quintessential man of his times. Born in a Suffolk village, he could in later life vividly recall seeing some of the men who were the footballing greats of the early twentieth century.

'I used to cycle some fifteen miles from Nutford to watch Norwich. Harold Fleming was a great favourite. C. B. Fry was another. Strong, very fast, a good tackler, used his shoulder a lot I remember, and J. U. Smith the famous Corinthian.'

Rous remained throughout his life true to the early values of football and became in his own way a very famous Corinthian himself. By the time of the Presidential election of 1974 in Frankfurt there was very little of the Corinthian spirit left in the game and certainly precious few of those early Corinthian ideals.

Rous was not of course a wealthy amateur playing the game for the sheer love of it and paying for the pleasure of playing. He was born to the wrong class to be able to indulge in such elegant activities. Not that the famous Corinthian football team declined money. By the 1880s they were asking for the very princely sum for the time of £150 per match. Rous was – or so it seemed to this observer – always the enthusiastic amateur. He resumed his degree studies after the First World War and in 1921 became a master at Watford Grammar School. By this time he had already taken a very keen interest in refereeing and in 1927 – the year, if his election manifesto is to be believed, that the ten-year-old Havelange was organising swimming committees in Brazil – Stanley Rous became a league referee.

In 1934 he won what was then the supreme honour for an English referee. He was put in charge of the Cup Final. Manchester City v Portsmouth.

'I remember the Graf Zeppelin from Germany flew over the ground .... There was a young wing-half playing. Got to know him rather well in later years. Busby. Matt Busby. Brooks was playing at outside-left up against an Irishman playing at right-back. At one stage I heard him threaten Brooks who was very clever. He'd dribbled past the Irishman several times, finally the Irishman told him what he was going to do. "I'll break your legs if you try that again." I said to him, "If you do that I'll send you off." "Oh, you'd never do that. You'd never send me off in a Cup Final." "Well, you try it and you'll find yourself in the dressing room." The rest of the game was smooth and easy.'

It was another world, light years away from instant replays, mind-numbing commentaries, banal punditry and the relentless pursuit of money, always more money. In those pre-Second World War days product placement meant a tin board with Oxo written on it. It was a time when very largely football was not considered too important to be run and controlled by footballers or individuals with a knowledge of the actual game.

The 1934 Cup Final saw the introduction by Rous of a daring innovation. The diagonal system of refereeing. The method is still in use today. Still waiting is an even more daring innovation. That referees should be full-time professionals with a top age limit of forty years.

In August 1934, Stanley Rous was interviewed for the vacant post of Secretary to the Football Association. It was, as he later recalled while being interviewed by that doyen amongst sports journalists, Bryon Butler, late on a hot afternoon. He was the last of six to be interviewed. The Chairman was Sir Charles Clegg; another member of the board was a Mr Pickford. As Rous entered the room, Pickford said to him, 'Don't address your remarks to the Chairman, he's deaf and can't hear you, and don't shout at me because I've just had a heart attack.' Not the most promising of starts. Some ten minutes later the Chairman suddenly spoke to Stanley Rous in a high-pitched voice.

'Have you any questions to ask?'

Rous recalls: 'Well, now. When I was teaching at Watford, I also undertook voluntarily to attend a deaf and dumb school, a very select deaf and dumb school, and I had to learn to lip-read. So I looked at Sir Charles, looked him straight in the face and said, "Yes, sir. Is the post pensionable?" And he understood me perfectly, to everybody's surprise. They looked up and paid greater attention. And he said to me, "You don't have to worry, young man, your predecessor was well treated by us." I said, "My predecessor, sir? Am I appointed?" "No," he said, "that was a slip of the tongue." But I did get the job.

'Two years later a lady came up to me when I was flying out of Northolt. She introduced herself as Sir Charles Clegg's sister and told me, "I well remember him coming home to dinner in London one night and saying, We've appointed a nice young man to be Secretary to follow Sir Frederick Wall. He's the only one I had a conversation with!"'

Stanley Rous remained as Secretary to the Football Association for twenty-seven years. As a guide to the continuing rise in the popularity of football, when he began there would be a maximum of fifty letters a day for Rous and his staff of five to deal with. In 1961 when he left to become President of FIFA, the thirty staff were dealing with three sacks a day.

During the intervening years, apart from running the game at the highest level in the country, Stanley Rous was clocking up a considerable list of achievements.

He helped form the Central Council of Physical Recreation, becoming its chairman. He played a major role in organising the 1948 Olympic Games in London for which he received his knighthood. He was instrumental in ensuring the Duke of Edinburgh's Award Scheme became a lasting success story; raised over three million pounds for the Red Cross; led the British Football Association back into the FIFA fold after a long-standing disagreement over broken-time payments to amateurs; was one of the initiators of the European football competitions. His most significant contribution to football during this period was to re-write the laws of the game and with Walter Winterbottom he introduced a coaching manual and coaching courses. The first of their kind.

Sir Stanley may have had his roots in Victorian England, but his vision of the future directions that football would take in the second half of the twentieth century was extraordinarily prophetic.

Football legend Stanley Matthews recalled Rous sharing some of that vision.

'He could see the future, and remember this was just after the Second World War, about 1946. He said the future of football is going to be in Europe and there'll be a European League and English clubs will be playing across Europe. Fast air flights will make that possible.'

Rous also foresaw all-seater stadiums at a time when the vast majority of spectators still stood, and most intriguingly predicted that an African country would win the World Cup by the year 2000. That final prediction will not happen, but several African nations are on course to make it a reality early in the twenty-first century.

In 1961, after two ballots and at the age of sixty-six, he was elected President of FIFA. He was older than FIFA itself at the time he assumed office.

Like the man who was destined to challenge him, Sir Stanley Rous knew how to handle committees. Harry Cavan, Vice President of FIFA, recalled receiving some sage advice.

'No, old boy, you or I can never think or speak like a Frenchman or a Spaniard, what you've got to do is to do your homework. And when you go to the meeting or the conference, you've got to be sure that you know more about the subject matter than most of the other people in the room and they'll have to listen to you.'

Or on manipulating a committee:

'When I saw a proposition on the agenda, I would always

select the right man to either oppose it or enlist a man who would talk too much or too long, annoy the rest of the committee and provoke them into ruling the proposition out of order. On the other hand if I wanted a proposition passed, I used to select a man who could talk very concisely but pointedly and get it through. One had to be a leader, that's what I would call myself, not a dictator, but a leader.'

By his own admittance he was a man who 'used to live for FIFA and football'.

He was a curious and interesting mix of a man. A visionary who could predict with extraordinary clarity the future, yet a man who in many respects continued to live with views more consistent with the Colonial age and the era of British Empire that was at its apotheosis when he was a young boy.

He was a firm advocate that the frontiers of football should be pushed back. That the game should expand and flourish in all countries, but that it should basically remain under the auspices of the Europeans. An Englishman had been in control of FIFA since Arthur Drewry's appointment as Sir Stanley's predecessor in 1956 and Rous saw no reason why that happy state of affairs should not continue into the foreseeable future.

He was deeply suspicious of the cabals that were emerging, particularly from Africa and South America. He retained the original ideals of FIFA's founders, that football should be one large family, but every family in Rous's view requires a head, preferably male, ideally English. After all, the English had invented the modern version of the game.

CONMEBOL, the South American Football Confederation, was viewed by many at FIFA in the decades that preceded the 1974 election as inefficient at best and corrupt at worst. Thus there was at the time a paternalistic attitude implicit in much of Rous's thinking, the issue of South Africa being a good example of this attitude.

Rous did not believe that sport should be used as a weapon to force the white minority government of South Africa to change its internal sports policy, particularly as it applied to apartheid. In his view, by the late 1960s in South Africa there was indeed opportunity for all to participate. He also believed in holding the line with official British government policy, whatever it happened to be.

Asked in the run-up to the 1974 election by Mawad Wade, then secretary of the Senegal Football Association: 'If you are elected, can you keep South Africa out of FIFA until apartheid goes down?' Sir Stanley Rous replied:

'I can't promise you that because I follow my country, the United Kingdom.'

That interchange ensured that all Havelange had to do was to come up with the right amount of money and the African vote was his for the asking. Havelange, a man who protested to me that he never got involved in politics, in truth was never uninvolved in them. Emerging as he had from a multi-racial society, his environment, even one where only French was spoken in the Havelange home, would have left him well disposed on the apartheid issue.

One of Havelange's first actions in 1971 after he had decided to run was, according to him, to fly to England and have lunch with Sir Stanley Rous. During the meal, Dr Havelange told Rous of his intention to stand against him. He expressed the view that the better man should win. Rous, now dead, makes no mention of this meeting either in his memoirs or during his long BBC Radio interview in the 1980s with Bryon Butler, from which Sir Stanley's various remarks quoted in this book largely come. Indeed, Rous went on record subsequently to say that Havelange had previously 'promised not to stand against me'.

What is curious about the incident is Havelange's view of what it meant.

'I said I wanted to inform him personally. As a former

swimmer I said, "There is only one medal. Either you will get it or I will." We finished our lunch and parted. This is what I call loyalty. And this is the behaviour I myself would have expected.'

Even with the African vote added to the delegates from South America, he was still approximately twenty votes short of victory. Europe or most of it – 33 votes – would stay loyal to Rous. CONCACAF, the confederation covering Central America, Canada, the Caribbean and the United States, would also vote for Rous. The United States delegate, former Celtic player Jimmy McGuire, a FIFA senior Vice President, controlled the voting inclinations of these various countries at that time and would duly deliver them to Sir Stanley.

As World Cup 74 drew ever nearer Havelange's activities grew ever more frenetic. He was nibbling around the edges of the Rous constituency. India. Indonesia. He was also extremely busy getting a variety of individuals from a variety of African countries to register at their embassies that they had become, some of them overnight, duly elected FIFA delegates.

Havelange had another card up his sleeve, one that he told me about with obvious relish.

'I conducted my campaign entirely on my own, and I never bothered anyone.'

He proceeded to tell me in great detail of 'the only niceness or politeness that he had received', a phrase which in Havelange's world means someone putting money or help his way. This 'niceness' had come from a long-term friend whom he had first met at the Berlin Olympics. The friend had subsequently become a director at Lufthansa. Working in Brazil he was offered a promotion to Australia which did not appeal to him. He planned to leave the airline, but Havelange persuaded him to take the promotion and extolled the virtues of Australia. Years later after the

Olympic Games in Japan in 1972, Havelange went to Sydney to visit his long-time friend who was living very happily in his newly adopted country.

'I'd like to thank you for the advice you gave me. This election in Frankfurt. I think I'll come and I can offer you six free flights to Frankfurt. I'll bring six delegates for you who have promised to vote for you.'

Havelange told me of other help he was offered that in this instance was declined.

'In 1973 Horst Dassler of Adidas sent one of his directors to Brazil to have CBD sign a contract concerning the supply of equipment by adidas. Apparently some of my fellow directors had been secretly negotiating with Adidas. It was to be an exclusive tie-in. The national football team, our swimmers, runners, basketball players, every conceivable sporting discipline. We would be paid a large amount of money and all our sportsmen and women would wear only Adidas clothing – shoes, tracksuits, the whole range. This equipment would of course be part of the deal and supplied free of any charge. The contract was brought to me, which was the first I had heard of it. I refused to sign. Now what I haven't told you was that a further part of the deal was that Dassler would use all of his very considerable influence to get me elected.'

'What were your reasons for declining to sign this deal?'

'I had Brazilian companies who were serving CBD, there was no reason for me to sign to Adidas.'

'What was Dassler's reaction?'

'He switched very quickly to the campaign for Sir Stanley Rous.'

'Really?'

'Oh yes.'

Horst Dassler was destined to play a major part after the Frankfurt election in the world of football and indeed in the world of sport. Dassler was a man who knew the price of everything and the value of nothing. Dassler is a leading member of that select group of individuals who stole the game. He was, as Havelange said to me, 'a man with very considerable influence'. He was also a man with access to money. Mountains of it. As long as you were someone in the sports world during the 1970s and 1980s that Dassler perceived as worth buying, then he bought you.

Havelange rarely missed a trick during his campaign. One of the FIFA Vice Presidents during the Rous presidency was Harry Cavan, a senior figure in Northern Ireland football. Sensing like Dassler the wind of change blowing through FIFA House in Zurich, Cavan shrewdly began to reposition his allegiances. The versatility of some of the game's great players of this century is as nothing compared with the ability of many FIFA delegates to reinvent themselves, adopt new positions and remain on the winning side.

Cavan cleverly arranged for a certain initiative to come not from himself, after all Rous might yet win, but from his friends south of the border in Dublin.

João Havelange: 'Before the World Cup in 1974, Dublin asked me as President of the CBD if I would arrange a match. A selected Brazilian team against the Republic of Ireland. I said, yes, no problem. One condition. Six of their team should come from the south of Ireland and five from the north of Ireland. Otherwise we would not come. They agreed. It was a huge success.'

Indeed it was, with the profits from the match going to a good cause. This enterprise had nothing whatsoever to do with Dr Havelange, something that it would have been difficult to learn from his election address in which Havelange rhetorically asked, 'Who has put Brazilian football at the services of mankind's greatest causes without any profit or advantage for himself, as it was recently done when the Brazilian team visited Dublin, playing for the benefit of the underprivileged children of the world [UNICEF]?' The answer, Havelange told his potential voters, was João Havelange.

A FIFA Congress is a curious affair to attend. A large gathering, virtually all middle-aged or very elderly fat men, most of them smoking at the slightest opportunity and many of them eating and drinking throughout the proceedings sitting in judgment on the whys and wherefores of the world's most popular sport. A sport in which the current exponents at international level are frequently young enough to be the grandchildren of the undead who administer the game.

The one significant difference in the 1974 conference was the number of people that neither Sir Stanley Rous nor any other member of the FIFA Executive Committee had ever clapped eyes on before. Whether all of those who voted were actually entitled to vote is very dubious. But before the vote Havelange had yet another card he intended to play.

Havelange had frankly admitted to me:

'I didn't have the means to pay everyone.'

But now in the conference hall he had the opportunity shortly before the vote to influence the entire assembly, including those who had actually got to Germany without any assistance from either Dr Havelange or his executive friend in Lufthansa.

'The day of the Congress, one of the items on the agenda was the question of China. Should they be re-admitted to the FIFA family? The Brazilian government had sent me a telegram through the Ministry of Foreign Affairs not to address this issue. At that time Brazil did not have diplomatic relations with mainland China. I ignored the telegram and when the item came up I intervened. I spoke strongly in favour of China being re-admitted. When I returned to my seat, another delegate who was a Brazilian minister said to me, "Listen to the amount of applause you're getting. You're going to win the election."'

Many others believed that too. Some of them had publicly predicted that if indeed Havelange did snatch the crown from Rous then there would be a schism in football. They saw the contest very much as Europe versus the rest and believed that if the South American prevailed at the ballot box then one day there may come a 'parting of the ways, with the two hemispheres running their separate world competitions'. This was the view of the British newspaper, *The Times*, who saw Havelange as 'a challenging activist who has spread largesse liberally in many quarters in an effort to win support in bringing down the establishment'.

To win on the first ballot either candidate required a two-thirds majority, seventy-nine votes. The first ballot was Havelange sixty-two votes, Rous fifty-six votes. Thirty minutes later the Russian senior Vice President of FIFA announced that an era had ended, Havelange requiring merely a simple majority on the second ballot had polled sixty-eight votes, Sir Stanley Rous had fifty-two votes. Havelange was the new President of FIFA, the overlord of the world's most popular game. A position he would continue to hold until June 1998.

Virtually his first words after the second ballot were:

'It is a great day for South American football. This has been a great victory for South America.'

It was a triumphantly held belief that has continued to dominate the administration of football ever since it was uttered. FIFA committees are increasingly stacked with South Americans. Some good, some bad. Some law-abiding, some venal criminals.

Havelange proudly climbed onto the rostrum to take his seat. Unfortunately, the organisers had not anticipated the result. There was no seat available for the new President. It was a bitter echo of an event that had taken place on the previous evening. When João Havelange recalled it to me just a few days before the 1998 Paris election that would decide his successor, the bitterness, the hurt and the pain were very evident. This was twenty-four years after the incident. It might have been something that had occurred just an hour or so before we spoke.

'In the evening before the FIFA Congress, before the election, Adidas offered a huge banquet in a castle in honour of Sir Stanley Rous. I had received an invitation and when I arrived at the door I handed over my invitation. The person read it and said, "You have no business here." I said, "Well, I've come because I have this invitation and I wish to honour it." This is how they treated me. It's rather different from what has been reported. It's because I come from a country "over there". The only thing that was missing was my Indian skin.'

Over the ensuing years Dr João Havelange was to exact a long and lasting revenge for such insults – and slights, either real or imagined, are all real to this man.

'They had always pushed us aside. But today they have to recognise us and for that I really worked like a madman. At least I've been able to show the world that my country may have a lot of faults but we also have people who can be very useful and I think I was very useful.'

The delegates, having in many instances merely voted which way the dollar was pointing, stood and gave Rous a standing ovation as he and three other long-serving members of FIFA were presented with bouquets. Rous was having considerable difficulty in hiding his bitterness. He considered the vote to be an act of betrayal by a number of the men now on their feet lustily cheering him. God protect any man from a vote of thanks. Accepting the flowers, Rous smiled and said:

'My colleagues are receiving bouquets. I am receiving a wreath.'

Horst Dassler of Adidas quietly observed the proceedings and before the Congress had finished had invited Havelange to dinner. Yet again Dassler had 'switched quickly'.

Sir Stanley Rous would no longer be 'very useful'. After voting him out of office, the delegates voted to make him 'Honorary President'. This meant that he could attend but take no active part in any meetings.

Subsequently Havelange attempted to persuade Rous to accept a FIFA pension. One of SF (Swiss francs) 6,000 per month. This is the first recorded example during the presidency of João Havelange of his legendary generosity – with other people's money. The Sterling equivalent as at 1974 of Havelange's offer is just over £2,500 per month – at 1998 values this is now £5,100 per month or £1,250 per week. Rous declined the offer, arguing that it was wrong when leaving the unpaid job of President to then accept payment for work you were no longer doing. Havelange tried again. Through the Brazilian Federation the suggestion was made to name the new World Cup the Stanley Rous Cup. Again Rous declined to accept the gesture. It simply wasn't his style.

The first ballot that had been so crucial in showing which way the Congress was leaning had been won by the contender by just six votes. João Havelange wanted to make quite certain that I understood the significance of that figure. Whoever won the first ballot was almost certain to build a momentum and win outright on the second ballot.

'My friend in Lufthansa Airlines kept his promise. He brought six delegates over from various countries. Six who had promised to vote for me. I won by six votes.'

Also in Frankfurt on the day of the vote was Pelé. No longer preparing to wear that number 10 shirt. Despite being offered £200,000 by Adidas as part of a sponsorship deal to ensure that World Cup 74 attracted maximum media and public interest, Pelé had determined to go out of international football while at his peak. He did not need the money. During the previous season with Santos, he had donated his salary of £6,000 a month to charity and retained his match fee for overseas friendlies – some £3,500 per match. There was also another reason for his refusal to play for Brazil:

'By 1971 I was beginning to really learn some of the truth about what was going on in my country. The torture, the killings, the disappeared. I didn't want to pull on a Brazilian shirt while the military were running the country.'

His last international had been at the Maracaná stadium in Rio. Brazil v Yugoslavia. At the end of the game Pelé ran around the ground waving to the crowd of over one hundred and eighty thousand spectators. They chanted as they had chanted continuously throughout the game: '*Fica! Fica!* – Stay! Stay!'

Apart from the reality of everyday life in Brazil there had been for Pelé other factors that had influenced his decision.

'I wanted to leave the national team while I was fit and in good enough condition to continue if I had wanted to. If I had stayed on I would have only been thirty-three years of age in 1974, the next World Cup. Both Nilton and Djalma Santos played World Cup football at the age of thirty-eight. But I didn't want to wait until the fans were booing me off of the pitch like they had done other players. Apart from that, by vacating my place in 1971, it gave a young player plenty of time to get the experience he would need to be ready for 1974.'

Pelé continued to play for his club Santos and to plan for a future when he would no longer be playing professionally. He had given hugely to the game. More than he will ever realise. The same year, 1971, he had an opportunity to give even more and in an unusual manner. Pelé was approached by Pepsi-Cola. They wanted him to teach football around the world to children. A series of football seminars fitted around the almost continuous football tours that Santos did. Part of the disease that has attacked Brazilian football for decades is the endless pursuit of the next dollar by so many involved in the game.

'Santos was a club that had to pay a lot for its players, so they played many games on top of their Brazilian League commitments. January and February in Latin America. June and July in Europe. Every year they would go on tours. At this time of course there was no concept of selling TV rights for large amounts of money.'

'How many games would you have played in a year at that time?'

'Around one hundred games. Yes, it got to a hundred games. Let me tell you something funny, David. All these tours. Every European country we visited we would buy up everything. The jeans, the shirts, every conceivable thing for the family. That was really something in those days. You'd come back loaded up like Santa Claus. Today you have everything here, in São Paulo. You don't have to move out of the city for anything. Such a different time. What makes me feel sad as a human being is that today it's a much more commercial world than it used to be. People sell themselves much easier than they used to do.'

Pelé the supreme football artiste was one thing, although even in that role he had had his critics, his detractors. Appearing at the World Cup 1974 as a commentator for a Brazilian network and doing PR for Pepsi-Cola, it was inevitable that there would be adverse comment. Some could not cope with the world's most famous footballer attempting to take the first tentative steps towards a new career. They would have preferred that when the day came and he took off his boots for the last time he should perhaps attempt to melt away into the night. It would have been a clever trick. An impossible one.

Two decades after Pelé last scored a goal in a professional game, MasterCard International conducted an exhaustive research programme in one hundred and fifty countries. The subject: sports icons. In February 1998 the senior Vice President of the company revealed, 'Pelé surfaced not only as the most popular among football stars, but among all sports stars.'

So, courtesy of Pepsi-Cola and Banderantes Television, Pelé cast a critical eye over the World Cup 1974 in general and Brazil in particular.

It was highly appropriate, if depressing, that the romanticism of Brazil's football of 1970 had given way to the negative approach of 1974. Appropriate because the Stanley Rous era for all its manifest faults both in the President of FIFA and the world of football in general had retained much of the refreshing innocence that was such a feature of post-war football during the years 1945 to 1970. The decades of Matthews, Mannion, Carter, Lawton and Finney. Of the brilliant Torino team that contained eight of Italy's current national team, all killed when their plane crashed. Of the Hungarians Puskas, Kocsis, Hidegkuti, Bozsik who on one extraordinary grey winter's afternoon at Wembley inflicted on England their first defeat ever by a foreign team on English soil. No, it was not just a defeat: it was a burying of a country's delusions about their football team. The score was England 3, Hungary 6.

These were the decades that gave us Busby's Babes. A Manchester United team of the highest quality that, like the Torino team, had died in a plane crash. Roger Byrne, Duncan Edwards and Tommy Taylor would have been in the England team at World Cup Sweden in 1958 but for that plane crash four months earlier. Mark Jones, Geoff Bent, Eddie Colman, David Pegg, Bill Whelan. All gone too soon. Far too soon. Among the reporters that died that day, former England goalkeeper Frank Swift.

There is a golden thread of quite magical artistry running through the game between 1945 and 1970. Much of it jinking and feinting to a samba beat, but by no means all. No one knew it at the time, but that performance by Brazil in the World Cup Final of 1970 against Italy would come to be seen as *the* high point of that and every subsequent World Cup tournament.

Now with a new President at the helm at FIFA, a man almost totally motivated in terms of his involvement with the game of football by money, the percentage, and particularly the bottom line, it was appropriate that the team from Brazil should, courtesy of its manager Zagalo, reflect that same narrow view of the game on the pitch. They had come to Germany in 1974 to play *defensively*. To play percentage football. Take minimal risk. Defend in depth.

As for the preoccupation with money, Paulo Cesar, one of only three remaining members of that 1970 team accurately reflects that obsession.

Pelé went on that first night in Frankfurt to visit the Brazilian team, to wish them luck and to see how their morale was before they faced Yugoslavia in the opening game on the following day.

'When I went to say hello to Paulo Cesar, I thought that maybe he would want to talk about possible tactics for the match. Or how the training had been going for their opponents. He asked me for my opinion about something that was obviously more important to him. "Pelé. I've been offered a fantastic transfer to a French club once the World Cup is over. I'll be paid far more than I'm getting now. I'm going to accept, but I don't know if I should ask for more. It's a real problem. What do you think?"'

Pelé was stunned. 'I couldn't believe my ears. This was

just a few hours before a World Cup game. I reminded him of that. "And all you're thinking about is this job offer. Forget the offer. Concentrate on the games you have to play, starting with the one against Yugoslavia tomorrow. When you've won the Cup, then think about the offer, but if that's all that's on your mind I don't think you'll be seeing the Final.'"

The result of that first game in which Zagalo ordered Brazil to play defensively was a 0–0 draw. Their second game against Scotland again ended in a 0–0 draw. Again Zagalo had decreed that Brazil would play without a recognised centre forward. And this was the tournament that many of the pundits were describing as The World Cup of Total Football. A wonderfully pretentious phrase to describe letting the sweeper roam where he felt like roaming. Total football assumed that all players had all abilities. That all were interchangeable. Defenders dramatically becoming attackers. Attackers with equal suddenness becoming defenders. It seemed to some to be rather what Brazil had been doing so brilliantly for years.

But not any longer.

Brazil's squad were not the only footballers at Germany in 1974 with a largely mercenary outlook. Holland spent far more energy arguing about terms, conditions, bonuses, than they ever spent discussing football tactics. They were constantly demanding more money in the run-up to the Finals. Finally, after cavilling at a vastly inflated improvement, their manager Rinus Michels told the squad:

'Any who are still not satisfied with the money that is currently being offered can drop out of the team now.'

Undeterred, the Dutch players marched to what was becoming the universal language of football. Money. Money. Money. The undoubted talent in the team was more than matched by their greed, and when one recalls that this squad included Cruyff, Van Hanegem, Neeskens,

Suurbjer and Krol it will give an indication of just how greedy the Dutch class of 1974 was. A number of the Ajax players declined for a long time to speak directly to Feyenoord players; presumably they communicated through their investment consultants.

The Scots were yet another squad to catch this new virus, which left the sufferers' hands forever outstretched in the search for more cash. The Scots squad appointed Billy Bremner to negotiate all commercial aspects for the team. The result was a series of arguments and squabbles. None of the footballers, it seemed, could or would focus on the matter in hand, playing football.

The team from Haiti were rocked by a positive drug test on their centre-half. The Argentinians were distracted by one of their number being accused of assaulting a chambermaid. When East Germany and West Germany met for the first time on a football pitch, there seemed to be as many guns in attendance as spectators. Helicopters constantly circled the stadium. There had been threats of a guided missile rocket attack. It was not made clear if the intended victims were East or West Germany. In the event there were no attacks and East Germany against all popular expectation ran out 1–0 winners. Their West German opponents, like so many of these World Cup finalists, were yet another team that had spent much time and energy arguing about money, contracts, bonuses and fees before the tournament.

To add to the squalid atmosphere there were the inevitable outbreaks of violent play on the pitch. Forgotten along with the scintillating play of World Cup 1970 was the promise to protect the touch players. The saddest sight of the entire tournament was undoubtedly the Brazil v Holland match. On paper it should have been a glittering occasion, a showcase for the game.

That the Brazilian team should have initiated the violence

was to turn the clock back to the Brazil of the early 1950s, to a time before they discovered the joy of winning through wonderful free-flowing football. The notorious Battle of Berne flickered again in the memory, as did Vienna 1956.

At Dortmund against the Dutch, the Brazilians chopped, hacked and kicked at their opponents. The Dutch retaliated with interest. Thus one team, Brazil, whose Generals had spent over five million dollars preparing for this tournament, did their best to maim the other team, the Dutch, who were each on a guaranteed payment of $24,000 plus 70 per cent of the profits that the Dutch FA made from this tournament. Players vied with each other to inflict permanent injury on the opposition. The poverty of the football on offer was, courtesy of spectators watching on television, obvious to the entire planet. It was hardly the most auspicious of occasions for the newly elected President. His sensibilities had taken a knock even before the game had started:

'Kissinger arrived at the Dortmund stadium with thirty-eight security men. Virtually every guest in the box had to be moved out. Not just for Kissinger, but so that these oafs could sit with him.'

During the first half Neeskens was knocked unconscious by Mario Marinho. In the second he was hacked to the ground by Luis Pereira, and the Brazilian was sent off by the referee who had been so busy with his notebook and pen during the opening game of the Mexico World Cup tournament four years earlier, Kurt Tschenscher. After that, victory for Holland was inevitable. They scored twice. When Cruyff superbly volleyed home Krol's left-wing centre for the second goal, Kissinger rose from his seat to acclaim the Dutchman's footballing genius. Havelange, sitting next to him, grabbed him by the shoulder and hauled him back into his seat. The Dutch were in the Final and the Brazilians were no longer the best team in the world.

I talked to Pelé about this match.

'The press in your country, and indeed throughout Europe, blamed Brazil for the violence. What I did not see in the papers was that the Dutch were just as bad. They were just more cunning about it. They knew how to foul and how to hurt without getting caught. After that game I went into the Brazilian dressing room. It was like a hospital. There was not a single member of that team who was injury-free. They had cuts, they had bruises, Marinho had a gash on one leg from his knee to his ankle.'

With regard to this particular defeat, the response of the newly elected President of FIFA when he was asked for an explanation is most illuminating. If this view came from a fan on the terraces it would be no more than one would expect in view of the terminal myopia that so many fans of all nations suffer from. To come from a man holding the highest office in football, a position that is seen as putting the individual above the fray, above all partisanship, it offers a revealing insight not only into Havelange's thinking but of the man's values.

'Because I had been elected President of FIFA and had beaten Sir Stanley Rous they wanted to get revenge. They designated a referee, the German Kurt Tschenscher, to make sure that Brazil would not be world champions for the fourth time. The sending-off of Luis Pereira was totally unjust. There was no way that we could win after that.'

Havelange continued with other more rational explanations for the defeat. Jairzinho past his best, Paulo Cesar injured, but the idea that Rous and his colleagues should conspire with a referee to ensure that Brazil were cheated of victory says much about Havelange.

The defeat was greeted in Brazil with widespread disbelief. The nation was so used to winning the World Cup. To the military junta's dismay a mood of deep bitterness began to manifest itself. The junta had not invested over five million dollars in the team's preparations for this. The Generals began to take a long hard look at the manner in which Havelange had been running the CBD. They did not consider they were getting value for money. With Havelange still in Europe, preoccupied with the aftermath of his election, President Geisel discussed the problem at length with General Adalberto Nunes. For Havelange, still savouring his newly acquired power as he watched the closing stages of the World Cup in Germany, this was a potentially dangerous development. He and General Nunes were bitter enemies. There would be no favours from that quarter.

In Munich Havelange watched Brazil, reduced now to the sideshow, a play-off for third place against Poland. The match was so boring that the crowd continually booed both teams. Poland won 1–0 and no one gave a damn.

The Final was between West Germany and Holland, or media-reduced to a contest between the two best players in the tournament, Beckenbauer v Cruyff.

Holland had, at least temporarily, taken on the mantle of Brazil – brilliant attack, suspect defence. Conventional wisdom concluded that to win, Holland would have to score three because their defence was sure to let in two. For once good old conventional wisdom got it right.

The Dutch got off to a blinding start playing possession football as if the game was an exhibition match. When Cruyff set off on a beautiful run, went around his marker Vogts and racing into the penalty area was tripped by Hoeness for a penalty, this was less than two minutes into the game. Neeskens scored from the spot and the Dutch supporters in the crowd knew very precisely at that moment how their English counterparts had felt at Wembley in 1966. Holland had put sixteen passes together without a German player touching the ball and now it was nestling in the back of the German net behind goalkeeper Maier.

Up in the VIP section of the Munich stadium all was far from well. The new President of FIFA was furious. The kick-off had been somewhat delayed for a variety of reasons. There had been the vocal entertainment provided by a choir approaching two thousand people who acknowledged Holland by singing 'Tulips from Amsterdam' and West Germany with Beethoven's 'Ode to Joy' – hardly an even contest. The start was further delayed by the late arrival of Secretary of State Henry Kissinger and it was this that had really upset João Havelange. What occurred was a re-run of what had happened during the Brazil v Holland match.

As previously recorded, when it comes to those who have insulted or offended him, Dr Havelange has total recall. There would come a moment in the future when he would exact revenge.

With Kissinger and his security entourage finally seated, the match was about to commence when it was noticed there were no corner flags. In the light of what had occurred inside the first two minutes of the game, the West Germans might well have been wishing that the flags had stayed permanently hidden. For the next twenty-five minutes Holland did much as they pleased with the ball, with one exception. They conspicuously failed to get it into the net.

Thirty minutes later and the scores were level as the result of another penalty, then just before half-time Müller got the second for West Germany. Despite repeated Dutch attacks during the second half, the score remained 2–1. West Germany had won the 1974 World Cup. There was a great deal of truth in Cruyff's bitter after-match observation. 'Germany did not win the World Cup. We lost it.'

There had been much speculation before Havelange had been elected President that if he did indeed ascend to the FIFA throne it would provoke a split in the ranks with

Europe going its own way and forming a rival organisation. That had been before the vote. After the vote all talk of civil war was removed from the European agenda. Some delegates felt that Havelange would rapidly be floundering as he struggled to deal with a long list of interminable issues. Others felt he would come to grief as he attempted to keep his pre-election commitments. These electoral promises would involve huge amounts of money and if the statements Havelange made to me are to be believed, the FIFA coffers were empty when he took over in 1974.

'FIFA had no money. Not a cent' has varied with 'There was barely thirty dollars in the cash box.'

Dr João Havelange is not to be believed. As in so much connected with this man, close analysis of the actual facts surrounding his version of events reveals again and again the image of a man who has over the years continuously reinvented the truth. The Gospel according to Havelange states that he has transformed an organisation that stood on the edge of bankruptcy when he took over. That he has, almost single-handed, made FIFA and football a multi-million dollar success.

The World Cup tournament of 1974 was in financial terms the most successful event in the competition's history. To quote from FIFA's financial report for 1974:

'... The financial results of all previous Tournaments have been greatly exceeded in all spheres: the DM36.3 millions gross income from the sale of entrance tickets set a new record. The income from other financing sources (television, film, stadium advertising, etc) had never reached or even nearly reached what was achieved at the time of the World Cup in 1974.'

The report, the last one overseen by Sir Stanley Rous, is a model of clarity and explanation. What it clearly shows is that football in commercial terms was growing ever more successful. That the money to be generated and made from the game was constantly growing higher and was reaching hitherto undreamed of levels.

The 1974 report, for example, records the fact that at the time of the Mexico World Cup in 1970 the income from sources other than the sale of tickets had reached what was then a staggering 20 per cent of the total income. Now in 1974 that had become 46 per cent of the total revenue. The total profit for the World Cup 1974 was in excess of DM50 million – approximately $19 million – which in today's 1998 value is over $60 million.

It is an indisputable fact that the current 1998 World Cup will show a profit hugely in excess of that figure. That is not the issue. What is at issue is the veracity of Dr Havelange. It would appear that in his overwhelming desire to take almost sole credit for every sunbeam that shines on the world's most popular sport, the man from Rio is in considerable danger of permanently departing from reality. By implying that there was a 'hole' in FIFA accounts when he took over, Havelange may of course be guilty of no more than a confusion of mind. Perhaps he had mixed up the accounts of FIFA in Zurich with the accounts of the Brazilian Sports Federation in Rio.

If there was no shortage of funds at FIFA there was most certainly a very serious hole at CBD headquarters.

General Nunes had been engaged upon a treasure hunt through the front door of CBD, the door that had featured so prominently in Havelange's campaign literature. The General had not found a great deal of money; on the contrary he had found a great lack of it.

During the Havelange reign of sixteen years, the Brazilian Sports Federation had been regularly and systematically robbed. Money amounting to many millions of dollars had gone missing. Between the years 1958 and 1974, $6.6 million had vanished without trace. In today's values that represented over $20 million. That was officially. That was the hole revealed by the official accounts of the Sports Federation. The reality was undoubtedly far worse. The official figures were false. The real loss certainly was much higher. In 1974, the year that João Havelange was considered not merely a fit and proper person to become President of FIFA but presumably the very best possible candidate for the job, he was directly responsible for rendering a false account to the Brazilian Treasury and also for hiding the fact that far from having a surplus for 1974 there was a deficit of $1.7 million, in today's values over five million dollars.

The investigation of the CBD went on into the following year. It was early 1975 before the 'secret and confidential' report landed on President Geisel's desk.

Many in the junta, particularly General Adalberto Nunes, wanted to press charges and put Havelange on trial for corruption. Geisel was equally outraged at the clear evidence of sustained and systematic embezzlement, but the President did not fail to see the irony in the affair. Havelange, like the rest of them, had ridden to the crest of popularity in Brazil on the backs of the victorious Brazilian football teams. Those sporting triumphs had given not only the junta but also Havelange the aura of respectability. From 1958 onwards successive Brazilian teams had again and again shown the world the positive side of their country. They had become its greatest ambassadors. Then Havelange had wanted to ride the waves even higher, even further. He had wanted like General Ernesto Geisel to become President, not of his country, but of world football, a potentially far more powerful position. The money that he had taken from his own company, Orwec, taken without reference to his partner Dr Lobo, was certainly not enough to finance what Havelange had in mind. Buying a FIFA majority does not come cheaply. Nor did the continual air trips, the hotels, the Mystère jet, hired and kept running like a personal taxi. Using Pelé, the most famous sports icon in the world, as his personal talisman, Havelange had begun to stack up votes. The alternative World Cup tournament also cost a great deal of money, but it brought in more votes. Then – and this would have given President Geisel pause for thought – there were all those Brazilian Embassy functions, paid for by the country for the greater glory of Havelange. Now he had been duly elected. The junta had been instrumental in creating a South American Frankenstein's Monster. It was now out of control. It was also, as far as President Geisel was concerned, untouchable.

To pursue Havelange through the Brazilian courts, to indict him, to have him found guilty and sentenced, would be to demonstrate to the world that a Brazilian crook was sitting on the FIFA throne in Zurich. It would not merely destroy João Havelange. It would bring great and lasting international shame upon Brazil.

In a government report dated 7 March 1975, the instruction was given to offer 'technical support' to the CBD. The technical support took the form of a state-owned bank putting the amount missing for the year 1974 into CBD's bank accounts. Thus over $5 million at today's values was paid over. The bank, Caixa Economica Federal, later debited this transfer to the Social Assistance Fund. What had been done in 1974 was no different from what had been done in previous years. Filling financial holes created by Havelange and his colleagues at CBD had become regular practice.

João Havelange, displaying extraordinary chutzpah, initially resisted all attempts to remove him from the Presidency of the Brazilian Sports Federation. He thought he could continue. General Geisel thought otherwise. Havelange was replaced by the brother of his adversary General Adalberto Nunes, Admiral Heleno Nunes.

Havelange, thus relieved of his responsibilities to

Brazilian sport in general and football in particular, was free to concentrate on the fact that he had promises to keep. Costly promises.

Havelange had promised to increase the number of countries that could compete in the World Cup Finals. He was committed to increasing the number of finalists from sixteen to twenty-four. To do so imposes a financial strain not only on the competing teams as they play their eliminating matches, but also the host country. It would require a great deal of money. To deliver on the first stage of that promise, an undertaking to increase the number of World Cup finalists from sixteen to twenty for World Cup 1978 in Argentina, was already looking unlikely. He had promised to create a FIFA World Youth Championship for players under twenty years of age. Again it would cost a great deal of money. He had promised a development programme to take top-quality players from Europe and Latin America to the Third World, to the emerging countries in Africa and Asia. Yet again a great deal of money would have to be found. Havelange has said, 'I am a businessman and I have far too much money to make even more from soccer.' It was an observation made some time after the discovery of the multi-million-dollar hole in CBD's accounts. Certainly as he wandered around the old FIFA headquarters with his General Secretary Dr Helmut Käser, the new President was in acute need of some wealthy benefactor. Enter Horst Dassler and his business colleague Patrick Nally. Although Havelange had not been made to feel particularly welcome at the Adidas dinner on the eve of his election, Dassler certainly compensated for that omission after the vote.

Dassler wanted to get the various national football federations throughout the world to commit exclusively to the Adidas brand. Boots, socks, shirts, everything. He had a dream. A world clad totally in Adidas products. He did not, however, have the kind of money that Havelange needed, but it was just possible that Nally might have the key to that door.

Patrick Nally lays claim to being a founder member of modern sports sponsorship. The next time you cannot get a seat to see a World Cup match because a huge percentage of the tickets have been allocated to Coca-Cola or Gillette or any one of nearly two hundred sponsors, you will know who to blame.

Nally is a public relations and marketing man who in the late 1960s teamed up with sports commentator Peter West. By the time they met West's career as the doyen of cricket commentators was drawing to a close, but because of the constant exposure he enjoyed on television, he had become that most amorphous of things, a TV celebrity.

Shrewdly seeing a potential, they formed a company with the principal aim of exploiting sport commercially. Put in marketing speak, forming a partnership between a company and those controlling a sporting event which would give the company product availability, advertising, promotion tie-ins and trademark presence. Put in everyday language, Nally and West set about convincing companies to hand over money to sponsor events.

One of their first ventures was to persuade Green Shield Stamps to sponsor a tennis training scheme to break down the class prejudice that still bedevilled the growth of lawn tennis in this country.

From such modest beginnings in the late 1960s sports sponsorship and event marketing has in less than forty years exploded to create an industry today with a $16 billion turnover.

In this country it would take a long memory to recall that there was initially bitter opposition from a wide range of vested interests. Newspapers and commercial television saw potential advertising revenue being diverted away from them and initially censored all references to the sponsor. Others such as the BBC were petrified that they were in breach of their broadcasting charter; they were also terrified of what the Football Association reaction would be if, for example, they showed a Ford Fives competition – a five-a-side tournament sponsored by Ford Motor Company that featured old football stars.

The then Secretary of the Football Association, Alan Hardaker, was from the 'live football on television will only happen over my dead body' school of administration. Today in contrast, the Football Association, using every media trick in the book, leads a campaign to win the right to stage the World Cup in 2006, the campaign alone will cost at least £10 million. All matches will of course be seen live on television. This revolution has occurred during the tenure of João Havelange's presidency of FIFA, something of which he is at constant pains to remind his listeners. He is less forthcoming about Dassler. Of Patrick Nally there is no mention at all.

Horst Dassler and Patrick Nally were very much made for each other. They shared a vision of the future. One in which ever-larger amounts of money poured into every conceivable sport. Money from the coffers of an ever-growing list of sponsors. TV rights for sporting events which in 1970 were sold for minimal amounts. When Canon were first persuaded by the events marketing consultancy CSS to sponsor Football Association League matches the annual fee was as small as £100,000, a figure that today has been surpassed five times over to sign a thirteen-year-old schoolboy to a Premier League club.

Dassler believed that the more money that was pumped into sport – athletics, football, rugby, the whole spectrum – the more desirable it would be to control the various federations who ran these various sporting disciplines. Long before Nally joined forces with him, Dassler was buying up individual sports stars to ensure that it was a pair of Adidas rugby boots that the audience saw on their TV screens when the penalty kick was taken. It was a pair of Adidas running shoes that the Olympic winner ran in. When the Men's Singles Champion stepped forward on the Centre Court to accept the trophy it was the Adidas motif of three wavy lines the viewer at home saw.

Now with the potential of boatloads of money arriving at the dock, Dassler made the quantum leap. Sports sponsorship by major companies would make it much more important to control the federation the sportsman belonged to than the sportsman.

Dassler brought an almost scientific approach to the task of the attempted corruption of all sports federations.

He created what he grandiosely called his 'political team' – a group that was responsible for global monitoring and infiltration. Federations, sports politicians, journalists. If you had influence in the world of sport in the 1970s and 1980s, there was an excellent chance that sooner or later Dassler or one of his people would appear in your life making you an offer that hopefully you would find irresistible.

Dassler personally looked after Central and South America. The word according to Adidas began to spread far and wide. It really was extraordinary what favours would be granted by officials in return for some free Adidas equipment.

Havelange, if Dassler and Nally could land him, would be the biggest catch imaginable. As President of FIFA he held the key to a potential gold mine. As a member of the International Olympic Committee he offered for Dassler access to a second potential fortune. The two had so much to talk about over dinner in 1974.

At the end of the meal Dassler had one hand almost on the gold mine. If he was going to secure the huge benefits of exclusive deals with FIFA and through the international organisation exclusive deals with the national federations worldwide, then all he had to do was find the price to make Havelange's extravagant promises to his electorate a reality.

Very typically, when Dassler with the crucial help of Patrick Nally made a reality of the fantasies that João Havelange had so impressed the various football federations with, it was the President of FIFA who ensured that he got all the credit. On his eightieth birthday, when a host of footballing dignitaries vied with each other to heap praise on the President, there was a full account of the stirring years under the man from Rio including his concerns immediately after being elected.

They included, as he had promised they would, a comprehensive, worldwide, development programme. The account continues:

'As FIFA did not have the necessary financial means, the FIFA President implemented his vast experience and fantasy as a businessman in order to materialise these ambitious plans.'

This does not mean that he went back to the creative accounting techniques that had been such a feature of his years running the Brazilian Sports Federation. It means that Nally struck solid twenty-two carat gold. More accurately, he conducted a tireless mining exercise for eighteen months before laying in front of Dassler the biggest blue chip on the block. Coca-Cola.

Coca-Cola, after what Nally was to recall as 'an incredibly stormy board meeting in Atlanta', agreed to commit to a worldwide sponsorship programme.

It meant that Dassler would get his exclusivity deal with FIFA. It meant that Havelange had the financial muscle to make what had been mere pipe dreams into a reality. During my conversations with Havelange we talked of that moment.

'There is a point that I have to say in favour of Mr Dassler. When I wanted to set up development programmes, he came to FIFA and he said, "I have the possibility to put you into contact with the people from Coca-Cola." Before signing the contract with Coca-Cola I went in 1975 to New York to Warner Brothers; they were in control of Pepsi-Cola. I submitted to them the various FIFA projects that needed to be funded. I asked them about sponsoring these projects. They said, "We'll reply shortly." I've been waiting twenty-four years. In the meantime I signed with Coca-Cola.'

I asked João Havelange to elaborate on the Coca-Cola deal. I had heard there had been some unusual clauses added to the contract. The question obviously struck several very specific memory chords.

'The day I signed with Coca-Cola. The contract was signed in London with the President of Coca-Cola, Mr Al Killeen. After the signing there was a press conference. A British journalist asked, "What is your interest in this contract?" Namely, how did I personally benefit? I let about a minute go by before I answered the man. "Oh, about once a year I drink a glass of Coca-Cola." Everyone started laughing and the man got up and walked out.'

Throughout the two days I spent with him, Havelange drank a great deal and it was always Coca-Cola. I had no way of knowing that his relationship with the soft drinks giant is a particularly sensitive element in a man with so many areas of sensitivity. I was soon to find out, but before that Havelange responded to my question about contract details.

'When we signed the contract there were two particular requirements imposed by Coca-Cola that I objected to. It had to be signed in dollars and that was for me unacceptable. My Swiss bankers had recommended that the deal should be done in either Swiss francs or German marks. These two currencies are economic factors and are reasonably stable, whereas the dollar is a political currency so one day you might profit by fifty million dollars on your investment, the next you might lose a hundred million. They signed for the deal to be done in Swiss francs.'

'And the second requirement?'

'If there were any legal problems subsequent to the signing at any time with the contract – its interpretation, breach, anything – they wanted the place of jurisdiction to be Atlanta, the city where their headquarters are. I said no, it must be Zurich. They were not happy about that. "Why don't you accept our headquarters?" they asked. I said, "Look, I'm not Swiss. This is an international body and the respect of an international body, its integrity, should be maintained."'

A short while later I drew the conversation back to Coca-Cola. I had been trying for many months to establish precisely how much these various sponsorship deals were worth. Not just the one with Coca-Cola, but the whole range of what FIFA calls Category One sponsors. I had experienced the greatest difficulty. By comparison it made establishing the voting figures in a Conclave of Cardinals electing a new Pope a relatively simple task, and in theory they are a permanent, carefully guarded secret.

Coca-Cola, like every other corporation that enters into a deal with Horst Dassler's ISL and therefore with FIFA, is contractually restrained from making the amount of money involved public knowledge. In view of the fact that the majority of these organisations are publicly owned with quoted shares on the world's exchanges, this stipulation would appear to contravene a very basic right of the shareholder: to know how the company he or she has invested in, which the shareholder in part owns, is spending that investment.

The analogy drawn above of a corporate secrecy comparable to a Vatican Conclave may sound overly dramatic to some. If so, they should perhaps approach Coca-Cola, Canon and the other conglomerates as I have done. Some ignore a polite request for information. Others plead pressure of work, particularly in a World Cup year. Others such as Coca-Cola and McDonald's give what information they can under the restraints of their contracts.

The experience was very reminiscent of my efforts some years ago when I attempted, ultimately with success, to establish just how much money the Vatican controlled. It transpired that the reluctance to reveal just how many billions they were worth was in no small part due to the fact that criminal activity of the most appalling nature was involved in the Vatican's financial administration.

I began to wonder if the same reason masked a similar reluctance to reveal the truth on this occasion. Not just a reluctance from the corporations, but from ISL, the Horst Dassler-created company that since 1982 has had a stranglehold on the marketing and media rights not only for successive World Cups but for a whole rack of other sporting events. Dassler and Nally's grip on the World Cup goes back beyond the time when ISL was created, goes back to the magical day that Coca-Cola said 'yes'.

'Would you put a global figure on what the Coca-Cola contract has been worth? I don't mean per year. I mean historically. From when you signed that first contract in 1975 up to the present day. A gross amount?'

'Firstly you will never have heard of a contract being signed for twenty-five years like the one we have signed with Coca-Cola. It is a perfect marriage. Secondly, the Coca-Cola money does not come to FIFA. Coca-Cola pays all the development courses which FIFA organises throughout the world, so you have so many courses per year and so many people involved in these courses, there are the instructors, the whole infrastructure pays for that. So they don't need to give me any money. There's the world championship for the Under-20s that's held every two years. There were sixteen teams, now there are twenty-four. Coca-Cola pays for everything.'

Havelange had not of course mentioned any figures. There were other omissions.

'Yes, but aside from those amounts that Coca-Cola invests. They also pay to ISL marketing fees. For example, the right to be one of your Category One top ten sponsors. The right to be the exclusive soft drink at all World Cup venues. For this and other privileges FIFA, through your virtual in-house associate ISL, receives many millions of dollars. I don't want you necessarily to break it down. A global figure will suffice. One that includes everything including the training schemes.'

Havelange erupted. Physically as well as verbally. He stood up from behind his desk. In the light of his eighty-two years he appears to be in an extraordinarily fit and healthy condition. Apart from a little extra weight around the stomach he would seem to represent a superb advertisement for exercise, particularly daily swimming. He is by any criteria an impressive figure. He is also a bully. Research had demonstrated again and again that he does not merely rely on the force of his argument. Nor does he assume that his charisma will carry the day, though these are two powerful tools that the man uses to the full. Guido Tognoni, FIFA's Director of Communications until Blatter and Havelange needed a scapegoat in 1994, had talked to me in Zurich only a few weeks before my meeting with the President of FIFA about Havelange's persuasive abilities.

'You can go in to see him knowing that the sky is blue. He will convince you, I mean convince you, that the sky is in fact red, or black. When you leave his office you will look up and see a blue sky and you will say, God's got it wrong again.'

If that was an example of his power of argument, I had also been given several other examples of Havelange's behaviour that shed light on the man's personality. His sense of his own importance is quite unusual, but then if an individual considers he is the most powerful man on the planet it would presumably affect his outlook on life and other people.

Keith Cooper, FIFA's current Director of Communications, talked to me of the President's obsession with punctuality. Other people's punctuality.

'I remember once in Madrid at a time when both France and Morocco were competing for the privilege of hosting World Cup 98. King Hassan II of Morocco kept President Havelange waiting for two hours because he was held up in a meeting with King Juan Carlos of Spain. Havelange was furious. In a few weeks' time World Cup 98 kicks off in France, not Morocco.'

The King of Morocco is indeed one of the most unpunctual people on this planet. On one occasion he kept Her Majesty the Queen waiting even longer than Havelange waited. Havelange would certainly be able to give Her Majesty a few tips on dealing with large egos. Mark McCormack expressed a desire to meet Havelange either in Rio or Zurich. In view of the fact that the all-powerful marketing man was in the midst of a round-the-world trip and part of his itinerary took him to Buenos Aires, he suggested a Rio meeting; it would for him be very convenient. The mistake McCormack made was to tell this to Havelange, who promptly refused to see him in Rio. 'I'm not going to be just a convenient stop on your journey. You want to talk business, then come to Zurich. I'm not going to see you in Rio because you happen to be passing through.'

This had been told to me by Havelange himself. He also recounted, almost with a touch of personal hurt, how the newspaper tycoon Rupert Murdoch had shown him less than the proper respect.

'I was at the Final of the CONCACAF Gold Cup in Los Angeles. It was between Brazil and Mexico. A man came into the VIP area and was introduced to me. He told me that Mr Murdoch would like to talk with me. I was about to agree when this man added that Murdoch would only be able to spare me fifteen minutes. I said that I was there to watch a football match, not talk business. If Mr Murdoch wanted to talk with me he should make an appointment with my Zurich office. I'd be happy to talk to him there. Any time. Apparently Murdoch was given the message, left for the airport, then flew back to New York. That was the last I heard from him. I consider myself important, and I am important, but FIFA is important also and people should respect FIFA. I as its President in my own way made Mr Murdoch respect FIFA.'

Now this same individual was exploding in front of me.

'You always want to see money, it's always the same thing. No, I'm not getting a penny out of this.'

It was such an extraordinary response as the questions recorded verbatim from tape transcripts make clear. My preoccupation at this stage was to discover FIFA's wealth, not Havelange's. There was no doubt that my interpreter, a man I have worked with for over fifteen years, had correctly translated.

Indeed, Andreas Herren, FIFA's Information Officer, who was present throughout the two-day interview, attempted at my suggestion to reassure Havelange, to calm the raging bull that had suddenly taken over the President of FIFA's office. In vain did the two men try for some minutes. Eventually it began to percolate through to Havelange that he had indeed very much snatched at the wrong end of the stick. He offered me the nearest to an apology that I suspect he has ever offered anyone interviewing him.

'It's not personal. It's just the impression people always have, that I'm getting money.'

He was calm again now. He sat as I again doggedly asked for some factual details on the contracts. He obliged.

'Look at the Adidas contract for ten years. A hundred million dollars. For that we give them the two most important elements of football. For one hundred million dollars they get the ball and the badge on the referee's jersey. When you go to a football match, stop for a moment and consider what you are doing. Stop for a moment and consider what you are looking at. You're looking at the ball and you watch the referee. This is what we are giving to Adidas in return for one hundred million dollars.'

If there is a life hereafter then Dassler must be chuckling. Nothing has changed since he paid Scotland's penalty-taker more than the rest of the team put together simply because of the TV close-ups of the player's boot the moment before he took the place kicks.

In fact my research indicates that Coca-Cola pay considerably more than $100 million over ten years. They have paid out that amount for the privilege of being the only soft drink sponsoring World Cup 2002 and World Cup 2006. Their commitment for the training programmes, for the wide range of other tournaments they part-sponsor, would more than double that figure. The average paid by Category One sponsors for World Cup brand exclusivity is at least $40 million per sponsor. These closely guarded figures have not only been denied to the public, they have also been denied to FIFA itself. Dassler was obviously not a man to play poker with.

Since the beginning of Dassler's involvement with Havelange at FIFA, right up to the present time, all contracts between ISL and FIFA have contained some very unusual clauses. Havelange and many others at FIFA do not regard football as a sport. It is a product, something to be marketed. Something that the controlling body should squeeze the last ounce of profit from. This being so it makes their collective attitude towards their marketing partner ISL inexplicable. Contract after contract has been 'negotiated' – and that word is used here with considerable hesitation because what has been going on here defies definition – without escalators, without profit sharing, without ancillary rights profits. It has been a simple straight buy-out of football for an agreed figure. If ISL and their partners then sell the rights on for twice as much, three times as much, a hundred times as much, then not a cent of that additional money finds its way back into FIFA's coffers.

For the good of the game?

From its inception ISL had as a major partner Dentsu, the Japanese advertising conglomerate. Dentsu owned 49 per cent of ISL with Dassler or his nominees owning the other 51 per cent. There have been repeated attempts for years to discover precisely how much commission ISL was paid. From time to time an ISL spokesman will airily talk of his company getting 'the normal rates of commission'. It all depends on what you mean by 'normal'. Dentsu have confirmed to me in writing that the commission rate they receive from all ISL deals is 50 per cent.

Consequently when nine multi-national companies – Visa, Brother, Federal Express, 3M, Time-Life, National Panasonic, Kodak, Philips and, of course, Coca-Cola – signed up for the 1988 Olympics and handed over in excess of $100 million, based on what Dentsu have confirmed, $50 million hit ISL's bank accounts in Switzerland.

As far as the game of football is concerned, Horst Dassler and Patrick Nally redefined its historical context. Now there was BC and AC. Before Coke and After Coke.

Having got what was in marketing terms a world-class act in place in the shape of the soft drinks giant, to persuade other big corporations to join became progressively easier.

Haddock Lobo had remarked to me during my conversations with him in his Rio home that 'João Havelange would say hello with another man's hat. His generosity always came from another's pocket, never his own, or his own hat. After he went to FIFA it was much easier. As for this coming election [this interview was conducted in February 1998] Havelange will either offer himself yet again as a compromise candidate or he will work night and day to get Sepp Blatter elected. Blatter is his spiritual heir. A creation of Havelange's.'

The comments about the election that would occur in Paris on Monday, 8 June 1998, were to prove very prophetic. His remark about Havelange always saying hello with another man's hat is, based upon my own research, equally accurate.

The FIFA development programmes in which the best talents in Europe and South America took their collective skills to Africa and Asia were transformed from vague election promises to reality by Dassler and Nally and the late Klaus Willing. The coaching concepts, administration, even medical care, the nuts and bolts of these innovative plans came from Dassler and company. The Coca-Cola-sponsored youth tournament, the football skills programme, these too were created not by FIFA's new President but by the man from Adidas.

Dassler was content to let João Havelange take the credit; after all, in terms of increased turnover and the exploding profits at Adidas, Dassler was taking the money.

The first World Cup that Coca-Cola was 'proud to be partners with FIFA' in was a tournament that remains one of the most shameful chapters in the history of FIFA. World Cup 78 in Argentina. João Havelange cannot be blamed for the decision to let the country host the event.

They had been awarded the honour by his predecessor Sir Stanley Rous. But that had been in 1966 at the time that the Argentine national team were fouling, kicking and spitting their way to defeat against England. Since that time what had been going on in Argentina had given anarchy a bad name.

Perón was dead; his wife Maria Estela (Isabel) who had replaced him as President was thrown out of power in March 1976 after a military coup led by army commander General Jorge Videla. The Generals were in control. In view of the fact that Havelange already numbered among some of his closest friends the successive dictators running his own country, and sold arms to the Bolivian dictatorship, perhaps it should not come as a surprise that he dismissed a growing worldwide protest about staging the 1978 World Cup Finals in Argentina.

Civil war was raging. All political activity and trade union rights were suspended. Press censorship banning the reporting of 'political violence' was imposed. Right-wing paramilitary groups had embarked on their own version of ethnic cleansing, which included murdering priests, left-wing refugees from Chile and Uruguay and Jews. At that time Argentina had the world's fourth largest Jewish community, with some sixty thousand members.

Bombing of what were designated as 'strategic targets' was another regular feature of everyday life as were kidnappings, particularly of senior employees of foreign companies. Some were lucky and survived to be released after huge ransoms had been paid. Others, including executives from Fiat, Monofort Cement and Sudamericana Petrochemical Company were murdered. Power cuts continued for many days after repeated bombing of generators. And in the midst of this carnage the military junta began to prepare for the World Cup tournament.

The Generals, like their Brazilian colleagues to the north,

like their spiritual brothers in many another Latin American country, knew full well the power, the potency, of football. They knew that at a time when their international image was hideous, a World Cup competition could be their salvation, and if by some miracle Argentina should win the World Cup, then the military would be forgiven much by their people.

Thus Videla and his colleagues set up alongside the various military committees, whose work was of a more base nature, an organising committee for World Cup 78, the Ente Autarquico Mundial (EAM). At its head as its chairman, General Carlos Omar Actis, a highly respected engineer. Videla had chosen shrewdly. Actis carried no history of the night with him, no involvement with the junta's excesses. He was honest and incorruptible. At a time when state funds were already overly stretched, it was vital that such a man should be in supreme control of this enterprise. The Vice-Chairman of the organising committee was a different proposition. As a mere naval captain, Lacoste was comprehensively outranked by Actis, but he was a man of unbridled ambition.

Having been appointed in July 1976 at the head of the committee, virtually the first action that Actis took was to ensure that Lacoste would have no input as to how the budget for the World Cup was to be spent. Lacoste had agitated for new stadiums, for the installation of a domestic colour TV transmission system. Actis over-ruled him. The country could not afford such luxuries. This became a major issue. He scheduled an international press conference for 19 August so that he could explain to the world's media what he was planning. In fact he intended to ensure that overseas transmissions for foreign television would be in colour; it was just the home audience that would be restricted to viewing in black and white. He may have been unaware that the pressure for colour transmission did not originate from one ambitious naval captain.

The impetus for what would be for the host country a very costly innovation came from FIFA, from Havelange and from Dassler. The man from Adidas was horrified that a sporting event they had just sold to Coca-Cola as the event of the decade might end up being seen on the television screens of the world in black and white. Hardly state of the art circa late 1970s.

On his way to that 19 August press conference General Actis, head of the World Cup organising committee, was assassinated. The attack was blamed on the left-wing guerrillas – the Montoneros. The following day the mutilated bodies of thirty people were found in a field near Buenos Aires. The killings were 'a reprisal' by the right-wing death squads for the murder of Actis. Many had their doubts that the Montoneros were responsible; among that number was the Argentinian writer Eugenio Benjamin Mendez. He began to investigate.

Lacoste was promoted and placed in charge of the organising committee. In Zurich, Havelange continued to ignore, with what seemed to FIFA's General Secretary Dr Helmut Käser to be glacial indifference, the demands to relocate the tournament. In the Plaza de Mayo in the heart of Buenos Aires a growing number of extremely brave and courageous women had begun to make regular protests. They became known as the mothers of Plaza de Mayo. They had also been the mothers of many of the *desaparecidos*, the disappeared. Between 1976 and 1983 more than thirty thousand men, women and children would be made to disappear. Most of them permanently.

The Montoneros issued a statement. They denied they had had any part in the killing of Actis. They declared that it was not and never had been any part of their campaign to disrupt the World Cup. '*Estamos hombres y mujeres del pueblo* – We are men and women of the people.'

Mendez continued very delicately to probe. Self-evidently

this was an investigation that would take a very long time. One indiscreet word, perhaps to a police informer, and Mendez would join the ranks of the vanished.

Lacoste was beginning to expand, to fill the role he had inherited. He took to issuing grandiose statements. Inevitably they all contained stirring messages of support for General Videla; after all it was cousin Videla who had given him the job.

Launching a bitter complaint on those who had gone before him and their failure over successive years to organise for the coming World Cup, Lacoste castigated the Peronists:

'Between 1973 and 1976 they talked a great deal but did nothing to prepare for this great tournament. We are replacing their talk, their bits of paper, with reality. With buildings, with stadiums. Under the Peronists you had three days of work and three hundred and sixty-two days of strikes. Today there are no strikes. We've banned them.'

Even in a dictatorship where not only strikes were banned but also, for a great many, the right to live, a junta can only do so much with strained resources. Patrick Nally and Horst Dassler persuaded Coca-Cola to underwrite the World Cup to the amount of $8 million, but it was too little, too late for Havelange to have any chance of the military junta bearing the additional burden of an enlarged World Cup. Plans to increase the number of teams from sixteen to twenty were quietly postponed. This would open up the potential insanity of World Cup 82 leaping in the number of finalists by a third to twenty-four.

The junta claimed that it was spending over $200 million improving the roads, railways, airports and communications systems.

Three new stadiums were built and three others renovated. By the time the first match kicked off in the summer of 1978, few it seemed remembered General Carlos Omar Actis.

Colour television was introduced for the World Cup within Argentina, but it was confined to the press centres for the delectation of the nearly five thousand journalists and reporters covering the event.

The press photographers worked in conditions that a mere twenty years later sound Victorian. They developed their film and made prints in small cramped darkrooms inside each stadium. These black-and-white prints were then scanned line for line by a very slowly spinning drum connected to an expensive and highly erratic international telephone line. The photographs were wired over the phone lines to the waiting newspapers often many thousands of miles away to be stared at by the reader over the following day's coffee. It seemed at the time quite wonderful.

During World Cup 98 the photographers loaded images captured on digital cameras directly onto their laptops and sent them by mobile phone to be placed on the worldwide web within minutes of the game ending.

In the weeks before the opening game the pressure to find an alternative venue reached a crescendo. Amnesty International were particularly active in leading the campaign. Far from giving the military junta what it had hoped for, they had a PR disaster on their hands. An event that was predicted to leave the country with a loss of $750 million had been the direct cause of much of the world learning for the first time just how bestial life in Argentina had become for much of the population.

Johann Cruyff had already withdrawn, not for political reasons, but personal ones, or, as the German tabloid *Bild* delicately put it: 'Cruyff, champagne and naked women.' Rumours flew that the entire Dutch squad would pull out. The next hot rumour was that the tournament would be relocated in Holland or Belgium. Notwithstanding what the left-wing guerrillas had stated, other elements would have seized any opportunity during the tournament to create havoc. If West Germany in 1974 had been considered a security problem because of its potential vulnerability to terrorist attack, then Argentina four years later was a disaster waiting to happen. Then there was the problem of the Argentinian fans and their players. An international reputation for violence on and off the pitch had not been acquired just because of the events at Wembley in 1966. It was true that the new Argentinian manager had eschewed the violent approach. The chain-smoking César Luis Menotti, a man who could have hired out his body as an extra for morgue scenes on television, morosely shared his inner thoughts on the subject.

'If a team could still kick its way to a World Cup then I would pick just such a side, but it is no longer possible. Such methods are obsolete. The emphasis must be on skill.'

Just one year before the World Cup, England and Scotland both played against Argentina and were therefore well placed to observe this newfound Argentinian reliance on skill.

The England player Trevor Cherry was punched in the mouth by Argentinian Daniel Bertoni. The Uruguayan referee sent them both off. The following week Scotland's Willie Johnston was laid out with a vicious punch to the kidneys by Pernia of Argentina. Again the referee sent off both players.

Apart from the implicit violence that seemed to permeate the very air, the preoccupation with materialism, with money, always more money, that had been such a feature of the 1974 World Cup had not abated during the intervening years. England suffered from a truly appalling manager by the name of Don Revie who before he could be rightfully dismissed decamped to a lucrative contract in the Middle East. He had previously been so incompetent that England's failure to qualify had become entirely predictable.

Scotland's manager Ally MacLeod talked a great game of football, for a fee. The precise amount that he made in the twelve-month run-up to the Finals is unclear. He was not alone. Indeed, the constant theme among the Scots squad of players was much what it had been four years earlier. Money.

Just over a year before the Finals, with his nation confidently expecting him to lead them to glory again, West Germany's Franz Beckenbauer exemplified the new breed of footballer and went the way the dollar pointed – in his case $2.5 million – by joining Cosmos in New York

Silly money was not confined to deals involving entrepreneurial Americans and Germans with deep pockets.

In Italy just two months before the World Cup the President of the Italian League resigned in protest when Lanerossi Vicenzi put a £3 million valuation on Paolo Rossi. At 1998 prices, Rossi was a snip.

Lacoste boasted that this particular World Cup would be a smoothly run affair from first to last. In view of the fact that if it had indeed been without its attendant problems it would have been for the first time in the history of the event, he was undoubtedly tempting providence. Providence duly obliged.

Shortly before the opening game a bomb was found, despite blanket security, in the Press Centre in Buenos Aires. It exploded as it was being moved, killing a policeman.

The junta, or rather the building contractors that Lacoste had chosen, had rebuilt the River Plate Stadium. They may well have been first-class builders, but whoever was in charge of the pitch knew little about maintenance. It was watered regularly with seawater. The salt killed the grass. Just before the first game a new pitch was hastily relaid. It looked good. The bounce was something else. At a second stadium at Mar del Plata constant heavy rain failed to drain adequately, cutting up the surface, which rapidly resembled a ploughed field. Through all of these problems the Generals in Rio kept repeating their offer to take over the World Cup. The Generals in Buenos Aires would have none of it and thanked their brother officers at regular intervals through gritted teeth.

Whatever the military might do, Havelange would not have moved the event anyway. With a rival in the form of Admiral Nunes, the possibility of Brazil staging the tournament was simply not a subject for discussion with the President of FIFA.

After yet another dreadful opening game, once more a 0–0 draw, this time between Cup-holders West Germany and Poland, the tournament creaked to a start.

Shortly before Hungary played the hosts, their manager while in England had expressed his fears for what lay ahead, not just for his team but for all of them: 'Everything, even the air, will favour Argentina. All will favour them. I'm sure that the referee will donate a couple of penalties to them.'

His final utterance in the light of what was to occur resonates grimly down the years: 'The success of the Argentinian team is finally so important to the tournament.'

The Hungary v Argentina match had a wide range of elements. Unfortunately they included some appalling refereeing that resulted in first one, then a second Hungarian being sent off. Score: Hungary 1, Argentina 2, Referee 2.

The hosts' next game was against France. They had lost their first match against Italy, in no small part due to a squad preoccupation before the game with money. The French team were focused all right, but not on football, just football boots. They were engaged in a bitter argument with Dassler and Adidas. Training had been abandoned on a number of occasions to facilitate negotiations with

Adidas. Michel Platini and his fellow team members, having failed to agree terms to their satisfaction, had taken the field against Italy with the three Adidas stripes on their boots painted out.

The fact that France also lost their second game had nothing to do with their financial preoccupations. They outplayed Argentina for most of the game. Outplaying the referee they found much more difficult.

During injury time at the end of the first half, when French defender Tresor fell while challenging the Argentinian Luque, Tresor fell on the ball with his hand. The referee, M Jean Dubach from Switzerland, was well behind the play. To the astonishment of observers, he ran over to his Canadian linesman who was even further back from the incident.

After consultation he pointed to the penalty spot. The Argentinian captain accepted the gift with grace and converted the penalty. It was so clearly not a penalty that even at the time there were some members of the press from neutral countries who were convinced that the referee had been got at. It is a view that perhaps should at least be given serious consideration in the light of the linesman's subsequent revelation:

'The referee spoke to me in German. "Inside or outside?" was what Dubach wanted to know.' An indication not only of the distance he was from the incident but also of failing eyesight.

In the second half France fought back bravely, equalising through Platini. Completely against the run of play Argentina went ahead again, then eleven minutes from the end the Frenchman Didier Six was pulled down in the Argentine penalty area. The referee on this occasion was very close to the incident. He continued to stare at Six as he lay on the ground, then turned his back and moved away. Score: France 1, Argentina 2, Referee 2.

In their final Group One match Argentina played Italy. Both teams were already through to the next stage. The referee was Abraham Klein, an Israeli official well known for a temperament that was not susceptible to bribes, bullying or intimidation. Italy 1, Argentina 0.

The Brazilian junta, ever ánxious for the positive image that invariably flows from winning the World Cup, had ordered the man who had deposed Havelange at the CBD to accompany the squad. Thus among the many members of the military at the Brazil base was Admiral Nunes and the manager of the team, Captain Claudio Coutinho. Coutinho, who had come to management of Brazil's national team via physical training, may well have been one of the world's leading authorities on exercise. Subsequent events indicated that his knowledge of football and the tactics of the game left something to be desired. His philosophy brought a new word to the game. He wanted his team to embrace the concept of 'polyvalence'. There is no evidence to indicate if any of the then crop of Brazil's football stars also had a degree in chemistry. It may be therefore that Rivelino, Oscar, Roberto and the rest of the squad experienced some initial difficulties in following orders. It transpired that what Coutinho was talking about when he referred to atoms that can combine with one element, then partly with another, was Total Football. Full backs were encouraged to become forwards, those up front were encouraged to face back and defend. Above everything the opposition had to be stopped one way or another. It seems such a pity that Coutinho did not attend any of Menotti's master classes on skill. With Admiral Nunes undermining the manager at every turn; with the manager and Zico, one of his most gifted players, hardly talking to each other; with Reinaldo under a cloud for publicly talking about the thousands of political prisoners, it is surprising that Brazil made any progress at all in the competition. Somehow they too scraped through their first-round group matches. The Brazilian supporters who had travelled to watch the matches were by this time so incensed that they burned an effigy of Coutinho in the streets of Mar del Plata. Admiral Nunes publicly humiliated the manager by announcing that he had been relieved of all his duties, then allowed him to stay on after Brazil progressed to the second round.

Argentina again benefited in a second-round match from the contribution of their twelfth player. With the host nation beating Poland 1–0, Kempes saved a certain equalising goal by punching the ball off the line. The referee saw nothing untoward and the game continued. Result: Argentina 2, Poland 0, Referee 1.

In their next game the host nation played Brazil. The concept of 'polyvalence' was to be demonstrated to the host nation. The Brazilians for their part were about to get a close-up of Argentinian manager César Menotti's 'emphasis on skill'. Within the first ten seconds the Brazilian half-back Batista was hacked to the ground by Luque. Palotai, the Hungarian referee, took no action. In the second half Batista was yet again kicked viciously to the ground, this time by Argentina's Villa. Again the referee took no action. Result: Argentina 0, Brazil 0, Referee 2.

For their next trick the Argentinians did not rely on the referee. They put their faith in EAM – their own World Cup Organising Committee headed by Captain Lacoste. Brazil with goal advantage over Argentina were to play Poland. Argentina were to play Peru. Only one team could progress. Lacoste's committee promptly scheduled Brazil to play in the afternoon and Argentina to play in the evening. This ensured that when they began their match against Peru the Argentinians would know exactly what was needed to ensure they and not Brazil went into the Final.

Admiral Nunes and Coutinho, for once united, protested to the committee. The protest was overruled. Nunes had already heaped further humiliation on his wretched manager in another long public denunciation. He described Coutinho as a man 'with scarce technical abilities. That Brazil have progressed so far has nothing to do with Coutinho. It is due to the players and the wise officials.'

For once Brazil were the equal not only of their opponents but also the abysmal refereeing. This time perpetrated by a Chilean, Juan Silvagno. They beat Poland 3–1. This meant that in the evening Argentina had to beat Peru by at least four clear goals. In their first-round group matches Peru had finished top of their section, beating Scotland 3–1, Iran 4–1 and drawing 0–0 with Holland. The fact that Scotland had gone on to beat Holland 3–2 and that Holland would eventually be one of the finalists would indicate a form book that gave Peru every chance of beating Argentina.

Now in the second-round group they had no chance of proceeding to the Final. All they had to play for was their own self-respect and for their country. In the event they forfeited the former by obliging the latter.

It would take eight years for the truth to become public, but immediately after the match there were allegations that the result had been fixed. The Brazilian manager Coutinho was but one of those who were convinced that the Argentina v Peru match had nothing to do with football. Coutinho declared that Peru's players would feel no pride when they heard their national anthem being played at the next World Cup. Others were more direct. They wanted to know how much the Peruvians had been paid to throw the match.

The Argentinians were quick with the counter-punch. Their newspapers were full of stories of representatives from Brazil, including men from the CBD, arriving at the hotel where the Peruvian team were staying. This was allegedly before the game. The men from Rio were carrying suitcases full of money for the Peruvian players. There were also promises of large tracts of land for the team. All they had to do was to win or draw or avoid defeat by four clear goals. It must be the only attempt in the history of the game where allegedly an attempt has been made to *bribe* a team to win.

The Brazilians came back again. It was an indisputable fact that Peru's goalkeeper Ramon Quiroga had been born in Argentina. Would he want to be remembered in his home country as the man who prevented Argentina from getting to the Final?

At the time Peru's goalkeeper issued a vehement denial that he had been part of any conspiracy to fix the match. Four years later he was allegedly quoted as saying: 'The truth is that I feel cheated. If so many dollars were paid out, I was not included. I think that I have the right to participate in it.'

None of this scratched the surface of what had really gone on before the Argentina v Peru match.

In June 1986 journalist Maria-Laura Avignolo, an Argentinian, was the first writer to reveal exactly what had occurred. In early 1998 while in South America I was able to obtain independent corroboration of many of the essential facts. In addition, I interviewed at length two additional key witnesses to the affair.

The order to fix the result came directly from the man then heading the military junta, General Jorge Videla. The man he gave the orders to was Captain Lacoste. Then if you wanted to fix a football match, who better to turn to than the chairman of the organising committee for the World Cup?

Lacoste carried out a series of detailed negotiations with three senior officials travelling with the Peru squad. The bribes took a variety of forms. Thirty-five thousand tons of grain to be shipped from Argentina to Peru. The unfreezing of a $50 million credit line to Peru. Substantial bribes were also paid directly to Peruvian officials from accounts held by the Argentinian Navy. Lacoste's contacts were particularly useful in that area, work that would be acknowledged soon after the World Cup by a series of rapid promotions to the position of Vice Admiral. A substantial piece of the $50 million credit that became available was subsequently sprayed around among members of Peru's military junta. None of this would be effective without taking care of the last vital link in the chain of bribery and corruption. Selected team members were approached in the days leading up to the match. I have spoken at length to three of the squad who each independently confirmed that they had been offered money to ensure the correct result. They were approached by a senior member of the ruling junta separately. They could not confirm if any of the other team members had been bribed. In view of what was at stake, the amounts that these three players took were pitifully small – $20,000 dollars per man. All had spoken, as did everyone else connected with this affair, on the strict understanding that their anonymity would be preserved. As one of them pointed out to me:

'If my identity became known there would certainly be reprisals, not only against me, but also my family.'

Carlos Ares, an Argentinian journalist who at the time of the World Cup worked for a pro-junta newspaper, had been given unrivalled access to the Argentinian squad and their base. He was writing an official biography of the team. He was certain from what he saw and heard that the game against Peru was fixed. After the game he voiced his suspicions to Lacoste.

'He threatened to have me killed. I had to leave the country and go into exile in Spain.'

And what Ares saw going on within the Argentinian

squad shortly before the match was odd to the point of bizarre. The goalkeeper was banned from the pre-match tactical talk by manager César Luis Menotti. Also banned were all non-playing members of the squad. This was the only occasion during Menotti's long reign as manager that such steps were taken.

The fact that there is also strong evidence that many of the Argentinian team were on drugs, not merely during this match but through the World Cup tournament, seems to be almost an irrelevant postscript. According to an Argentinian official the drug-takers avoided detection via their urine samples by a simple device. The urine samples were all supplied to the all-Argentinian team of inspecting doctors by the team water boy, Ocampo.

As for the match, Peru opened proceedings as if they really intended to make a game of it. For the first fifteen minutes they were all over the Argentinians, but somehow they just failed to score, not once but several times. Sir Walter Winterbottom, the former England manager, was watching the match. He later recalled in an interview* how a Peruvian player missed 'the best chance of goal-scoring I had ever seen in my life. The bloke mis-kicked it and he was only about four yards out of goal and he had an open goal.'

Chances were sent begging by a number of the Peruvians. Then it was all over. Argentina scored, again, and again, and again. They eventually ran up not the four goals required, but for good measure an additional two. Just to make doubly sure that the game would eventually end with the result that all – except for the waiting Brazilian team – desired, the Peruvian manager used four inexperienced substitutes. For good measure he also moved one of his defenders into the forward line. Before the game the Peruvian manager had asked his team to refrain from playing in their

---

* *FIFA and the Contest for World Football* by John Sugden and Alan Tomlinson

official national colours but instead to go through this charade wearing white shirts. How appropriate.

Argentina, having bought their way into the Final of the World Cup, now had to play Holland. Brazil won the consolation prize of third place after beating Italy 2–1. Coutinho's last word on the squalid affair was, 'We are the moral champions.' He then returned to Rio and was instantly dismissed by Admiral Nunes.

By now the mood throughout the host country was continuous high tension. As Argentina had progressed nearer and nearer to the Holy Grail, cynical dismissal of the team's chances had inexorably given way to fevered, nationalistic fervour. The junta finally had, domestically at least, what they had dreamed of. The country's mood as the Final approached was one of continuous frenzy. There could only be one result. There had to be only one result.

Shades of Brazil when playing England in Rio in 1964. The visiting Dutch took the field ten minutes before kick-off and waited. The Argentinians eventually strolled out five minutes late. Gamesmanship designed to wind up the opposition. Then to compound it they complained about a lightweight plaster cast being worn by the Dutch winger Rene Van de Kerkhof. He had worn the dressing in Holland's previous games and there had been no complaints.

The tactics were not only targeted at the Dutch. The Argentinians were rapidly establishing what kind of referee they were dealing with. Sergio Gonella from Italy made no complaint when the Argentinians strolled out late, then he upheld their protests about the medical dressing. The hosts were satisfied they had a compliant, weak referee, something to be worked on during the course of the game.

After the game the Argentinian captain Passarella attempted to justify the frenzied hysterical complaints that he and his teammates had made about the dressing: 'We could not allow ourselves to concede any advantage. Luque [another Argentinian player] saw the danger the bandage could be and I as captain had the obligation to protest.'

Twenty years later almost to the day, on 30 June 1998, those same tactics, that same meanness of spirit, were still alive and well in the Argentinian approach to football. England v Argentina, playing for a quarter-final place in World Cup France 98. In a game that contained so much excellent football and the stunning emergence on a world stage of eighteen-year-old Michael Owen, there was also on show the street Arab side of Argentinian football. Not the handball they got away with; not the Campbell goal that was disallowed; not even the Argentinian captain Simeone disgracefully playacting in front of the referee – acting that undoubtedly influenced a decision to bring out a yellow card for Beckham and persuaded a change of mind to red. None of these incensed quite as much as two moments that passed without comment.

Owen the boy wonder was fouled late in the game. To compound the foul the Argentinian player kicked Owen on the face and then the head. Owen quite clearly was only half-conscious as he lay on the ground. The Danish referee Neilsen beckoned for trainers, for medical attention. As English medics hurried out to Owen and attempted to assess his injuries, Balbo of Argentina appeared. He gesticulated to the referee that he wanted Owen removed immediately from the pitch on a stretcher. He wanted to capitalise on the foul by thus reducing England to nine men. The referee quite clearly spoke sharply to Balbo, who, one moment all bluster, hunched his shoulders in that oh so typical Latin gesture of hurt innocence.

When the period of extra-time had reached halfway and the two teams moved to change ends, back-up men from both squads ran onto the pitch to give water, advice, encouragement. Passarella, the then Argentinian manager

– a man who if he had been obliged to play his football under today's FIFA rules on foul play would not last ten minutes on a pitch – had learnt nothing about football's morality since 1978. He complained bitterly to the referee that the England manager Hoddle and his colleagues were actually talking to players, actually giving them a drink of water. Passarella ignored the fact that his own squad were doing precisely the same thing. It was all part of the same tactics. Attack the ref, undermine his self-confidence, intimidate him. On 30 June 1998, the Danish referee had the presence of mind to wave Passarella away like an irritating wasp. His Italian counterpart of twenty years ago unfortunately lacked that same ability.

Gonella proceeded to let the game slip away from him. Gallego the Argentinian midfield player twice deliberately handled the ball without being booked. At all times if there was a fifty–fifty situation that required a decision from the referee, it was given to the home team. Predictably the Dutch, already fuming about the pre-match gamesmanship, began to lose the plot. At the end of a largely forgettable match – unless you happened to be Argentinian – the host nation had won 3–1 and the country erupted with joy as their victorious team went up to collect the trophy on which so much time, effort and money had been expended by the military junta.

Lacoste had promised a trouble-free period during the World Cup. The Montoneros, breaking their word to the ordinary people of Argentina, carried out fifteen attacks during the period of the World Cup; four members of the Argentinian Communist Party were 'disappeared'; bombs exploded at a wide variety of locations throughout the country and the police tear-gassed the Roman Catholic faithful who were leaving Church after celebrating Mass on the fourth anniversary of Perón's death.

Lacoste would go from strength to strength in the coming

years. President of Argentina during an eleven-day handover period between leading junta members. A distinguished career in FIFA as Vice President, second in power only to Havelange. They were the very best of friends. Lacoste would be a key figure in the planning of the next World Cup to be held in Spain in 1982.

The evening after the 1978 World Cup Final there was a lavish celebratory banquet in Buenos Aires. It was attended by all senior members of the ruling military junta. General Videla and his colleagues welcomed Havelange and his fellow FIFA executives with a great deal of hugging and kissing. In proposing a vote of thanks to the junta and particular Carlos Alberto Lacoste, Havelange eulogised the tournament and observed, 'Now the world has seen the true face of Argentina.'

A few days earlier his colleague, FIFA Vice President Herman Neuberger, had refused to accept from Amnesty International a fully documented report that detailed the torture, kidnapping and murders committed at the orders of the military junta.

In 1984 Eugenio Mendez published the conclusions of his investigation in a book entitled, *Admiral Lacoste. Who killed General Actis?* The delay and then the timing of the publication were significant. The delay was for self-preservation. If Mendez had attempted to publish during the time of the Generals no publisher in Argentina would have dared to put the book into print and the author would undoubtedly have been murdered. In December 1983, democracy was finally restored to the country and Raul Alfonsin, the first civilian president for eight years, took office. Finally the truth that Mendez had so courageously established could be shared with the nation.

In view of the allegations contained in the book Alfonsin ordered an immediate investigation to establish the answer to the question that the title of the book had posed.

At the end of that investigation Admiral Lacoste was charged with a wide variety of crimes. Some were fiscal and alleged that he had stolen funds from the World Cup Organising Committee's accounts. One of the other charges was that he was responsible for the murder of General Actis.

President Havelange, confronted with this situation, responded in a manner not dissimilar to his reaction when a large hole was found in the Brazilian Sports Federation Funds. Then Havelange had wanted to keep his job as President of CBD. Now he considered that his dear friend Lacoste should be allowed to stay as Vice President of FIFA. His efforts on behalf of Lacoste were so strenuous that observers both inside and outside FIFA felt that there had to be a secret agenda between the two men. The newly elected President of Argentina insisted that Lacoste be removed from his FIFA position and in 1984 the Admiral very reluctantly resigned.

Subsequently Lacoste was asked by the State Prosecutor to justify his sworn deposition that a large piece of land he had bought in Punta del Este in Uruguay had been acquired with a bank loan. There was no evidence of any such bank loan. That, explained Lacoste, was because the loan had actually come from his close friend João Havelange, who confirmed the transaction. The sum involved was half a million dollars.

The legal process against Lacoste was suspended on a number of occasions and finally the former Admiral escaped jail after a general pardon and amnesty was declared in 1989. No evidence has ever surfaced that indicates Lacoste repaid the half-a-million-dollar loan from his good friend João Havelange.

Lacoste certainly benefited in a variety of ways from World Cup 78, as did Havelange. The official FIFA financial analysis of the tournament reveals that for all the financial input of Coca-Cola and other organisations, the net profit was slightly down on the Stanley Rous-organised event of 1974. One of the reasons was the increased amount spent on insurance. In the light of the instability in Argentina at the time, increased premiums are hardly surprising. What is surprising is that an insurance company called Atlantica Boavista received some 25 per cent of the insurance business. The senior director of the company is João Havelange. When challenged on this issue by a British reporter, Havelange initially used his familiar tactic of walking out of the interview. Subsequently he blamed the FIFA General Secretary, Dr Helmut Käser. Quite why the General Secretary of FIFA should channel lucrative business to a Havelange-controlled company without discussing the matter with Havelange was never explained. The insurance business for the tournament was worth SF2.3 million.

Among those who also benefited greatly from World Cup 78 were Patrick Nally and Horst Dassler. Understandably they were eager for more of the same.

Returning from a Rio meeting with Havelange, the man from Adidas talked to his marketing partner. He told Nally of the progress he had made in his attempts to persuade Havelange to give them the marketing rights for World Cup 82 in Spain. The game was getting faster. The stakes were getting higher. For Argentina, Nally had contracted six main sponsors. For Spain he would need more. Many more.

Before the Rio trip Nally and Dassler had concluded that the amount they would need to raise from the corporations to keep the Spanish government and its World Cup committee sweet was $4 million. They had not allowed for the pressures that João Havelange was now under. He had failed to deliver an enlarged tournament in 1978 to Argentina, when the number of finalists that he had promised should have been increased from sixteen to twenty. He had bought himself a little time with his electorate, but 1982 in Spain had to be pay-back time or it might mean the Havelange reign was over.

As Dassler recounted his conversations with Havelange to his business partner, Nally was stunned. The ante had not merely been raised: it had gone right through the ceiling. Havelange wanted to persuade Spain to take twenty-four finalists. The financial burden would be massive. The 'bribe' or 'financial inducement' that had to be dangled in front of the organising committee had to be equally big. Not $4 million, but SF36 million – at 1998 values, $42 million. Then there was an additional one million dollars to be found. That was for Havelange. Everyone, it seems, was to get a sweetener.

Author Andrew Jennings* recounted to me that when Nally and Dassler had this conversation they were in the gentlemen's toilets in the Placo de Congresso in Madrid. In view of the shock to Nally's system it would appear to have been a very wise precaution.

Having taken a very deep breath, Nally zipped up his trousers, went back out into the corporate marketplace and began to pitch to Category One companies. Dassler also jacked up the price that Coca-Cola, Canon and the other organisations that were already on board for World Cup 82 had agreed to pay. The official figures show that Nally and Dassler achieved their target and the demand for SF36 million was met. Adidas got exclusive control of all marketing rights plus North American TV rights, but Nally and Dassler did not live happily ever afterwards. They parted company in 1982 when a rather confused Nally had become uncertain whether his primary role was helping his clients, or Dassler and Adidas. Dassler suffered no such

---

* *The Lords of the Rings* by Andrew Jennings and Vyv Simson

conflicts. He knew that all of his actions, all of his strategies, had but one aim: to enrich Adidas and thus enrich Dassler.

The riches that went to Spain in connection with World Cup 82 were not confined to the SF36 million. The Spanish negotiated something worth immeasurably more from Havelange. In a meeting between King Juan Carlos of Spain and the Spanish organising committee for the 1982 World Cup and President Havelange, it was also agreed that if Spain accepted the expansion from sixteen to twenty-four teams, the Third World countries who were clearly going to benefit from the larger tournament would also vote for Juan Antonio Samaranch as the next President of the International Olympic Committee and that Havelange would use his excellent contacts with a variety of other countries to ensure that Samaranch of Spain was in the Olympic driving seat. Samaranch was duly elected President of the IOC on the first ballot on 16 July 1980. One of the many benefits flowing to Spain from this election was of course the award to Barcelona of the 1992 Olympic Games.

In the run-up to World Cup 82, having promised Coca-Cola product exclusivity, as indeed all Category One sponsors require, Dassler found that at the Bernabeu football stadium in Madrid the rival Pepsi-Cola already had the franchise. They had to go. They did. All stadiums had to be 'clean' – meaning free of all advertising other than that purchased via the sponsorship deals from Nally and Dassler.

By early 1980 Havelange, who throughout his entire presidency has made an eternal virtue again and again in interviews of the fact that he was not paid a cent, had 'expenses' running at a quarter of a million dollars a year. This would move inexorably up and up over the years until the personal amount of expenses Havelange was being paid exceeded $1 million per year.

The President was not alone in enjoying the fruits of the

reservoir of marketing and television money that was beginning to flood in. The bill for bringing the FIFA officials to Spain for World Cup 82 was over $3 million – more than it cost to transport and accommodate the twenty-four teams. In the two years 1982 to 1984 FIFA spent a further $1.5 million on travel expenses and gifts, excluding the President's expenses.

The spending spree that Havelange embarked on soon after his election in 1974 was yet another example of the President saying hello with another man's hat. The forty or so special guests who were flown into Buenos Aires for their all-expenses-paid World Cup 78 experience would be forever indebted to their generous host, João Havelange. It is quite extraordinary just how much value powerful and influential men will put on a few tickets for some World Cup matches. And if the tickets and the air fares and the hotel bills can all be given to the FIFA General Secretary for payment, so much the better. Problems are only likely to occur if the General Secretary begins to query such largesse. Problems began to occur.

The General Secretary that Havelange had inherited from Sir Stanley Rous had been functioning very effectively in that position for a great many years. Indeed Rous himself had inherited Dr Helmut Käser from the previous President of FIFA, Arthur Drewry.

Käser held very strong views on fiscal propriety. Before Rous had been elected President in 1961, Käser had circulated a memo to all delegates that Rous was in all probability ruled out of consideration because as a paid official he would not be eligible. This was a reference to Rous's work as Secretary of the English Football Association. In fact Sir Stanley had resigned from that post in order to avoid precisely that controversy. After a relatively short period Rous and Käser were able to form an excellent working relationship.

Confronted with Havelange with or without another man's hat, it was only a matter of time before the General Secretary and the President had their problems.

In truth their problems began before they had even started trying to work together. Like many others, General Secretary Helmut Käser had read Havelange's election manifesto and his curriculum vitae with great interest. As Havelange had never been a member of the South American Football Association and had not therefore ever been a FIFA delegate, Käser made a number of inquiries to learn more about this man from Rio who wanted to take over FIFA. What he learned puzzled him. Havelange claimed to own Viação Cometa. The inquiries confirmed he had worked for them, but that he had never owned or even part-owned the company. Then information came back to Käser about Atlantica Boavista, the insurance company that – unlike the bus company – was at least part-owned by Havelange. From what Käser learned, the relationship between the insurance company and the Brazilian Sports Federation was an unusually close one with Atlantica Boavista picking up virtually all of the Federation's insurance business. Then there were the rumours about how the accounts were operated inside CBD.

At the time of the Frankfurt election in 1974, Dr Käser no longer had to rely on information from third parties. Many of the African delegates, the Maltese delegate, others from the Far East, all told Käser, 'If Dr Havelange had not been kind enough to pay for my air tickets, my hotel bills and my out-of-pocket expenses I would never have been able to come to vote for him.'

Helmut Käser watched quietly as Havelange continued lobbying right up to the vote. He was struck by a curious phenomenon. After engaging Havelange for a while in deep conversation, a large number of delegates moved away and each appeared to be clutching a white envelope.

After the election the General Secretary's misgivings rapidly increased when Dassler and Nally became frequent visitors to FIFA House. Dassler was well known to Käser, known as a man determined to enlarge the Adidas corporation by any means possible. Dassler had frequently attempted to persuade Käser to use his influence on Rous with a view to putting potential business Dassler's way. Rous too had direct experience of Dassler's lobbying techniques and had not been above using them during the election.

As Havelange did deal after deal with Dassler and Nally and the President's expenses began to rocket, Käser queried a great many of the expense claims that were made. Rous had never felt it necessary to have extraordinarily expensive meetings at the Savoy Hotel in Zurich, nor had Sir Stanley felt it necessary to invite forty guests to an all-expenses-paid World Cup holiday. Then there were the additional bills: twelve thousand Swiss francs for additional tickets supplied by Havelange; Longines Swiss watches costing more than one hundred thousand Swiss francs for over one hundred guests at a Zurich dinner party; hotel bills for one hundred guests – these last two items connected with Havelange's need to celebrate the 75th anniversary of FIFA in what he deemed to be an appropriate manner. This was the period when the Sun King metamorphosed out of the man from Rio who had businesses that in the recent past had teetered on the edge of bankruptcy and a Sports Federation with a multi-million-dollar hole in its accounts. Now João Havelange had become President Havelange, a man who 'if there is not a first-class seat on the plane or first-class hotel accommodation, then I don't get on the plane and I don't go to the hotel.'

Dr Käser and Stanley Rous had run FIFA with a staff of half a dozen. Rous had been planning to move FIFA to more spacious accommodation and enlarge the number of staff. The success of the 1974 World Cup confirmed for

Rous a trend he had already identified. Football was an ever-growing success story. With television beginning to play an ever more important role, Rous saw that in the very near future the game would be generating many more millions. He lamented the fact that in football the talk, the subject, the preoccupation was always now concerning money, and realised that his own personal lack of concern with the material side of the game might seem to others outdated and amateurish. Despite his misgivings, he was prepared to build for the future. Havelange, with the assistance of Nally and Dassler – three individuals who, far from lamenting the increased preoccupation with money, positively relished the changing situation – merely picked up the same baton and ran with it. This included building the current edifice to that market success, the new FIFA House. It needs to be a big building to contain the huge oil painting and the equally large photographs of Havelange that seem to be on virtually every wall, very reminiscent of visiting Assad of Syria or Saddam Hussein.

General Secretary Käser saw and heard much that gave him cause for concern. He was of the old school: he liked to stick by the rules, if there was an official procedure then it must be followed. It became clear to Käser that Nally and Dassler were at the time of the 1978 World Cup in Argentina operating a tax-evasion scheme involving letterbox companies. French tax investigators who were probing Dassler's affairs came knocking at FIFA's door looking for answers. It had all been so different when Rous was running the show.

Käser was outraged when Havelange attempted to blame him for the fact that the British media had obtained irrefutable evidence of corrupt dealing with regard to the lucrative insurance business.

Havelange had instructed a Munich-based insurance company Albignia, controlled by insurance broker Erwin

Himmelseher: 'If you want the insurance business for World Cup 82 in Spain then 20 per cent of it must be funnelled to Atlantica Boavista.' That might pass for good business practice in Rio. Under Swiss law it was a serious offence.

It seemed that every way Helmut Käser turned there was evidence of Havelange's very dubious approach to business. A simple matter like negotiating a contract to produce commemorative coins for World Cup 82 became, after Havelange got involved, a hornets' nest. He personally negotiated a deal with a Spanish businessman, Ricardo Cistare. When Käser finally got his hands on the contract that had been signed in Rome on 1 December 1980, he was horrified. Havelange had not merely neglected to include Käser in the negotiations, he had also kept out all members of the FIFA Executive Committee. The contract breached an existing exclusivity agreement for commemorative coins with a company called Sport-Billy.

The million-dollar bribe that Dassler had discussed with Nally – money that would open the door to the lucrative Spain 82 contracts – had become by early 1980 an open secret in FIFA and also the corridors of the European Football Association. Artemo Franchi, the President of UEFA, discussed the problem with Käser and made it clear that the evidence was overwhelming.

Käser's reaction was to go at the first opportunity to Havelange and tell him that, according to rumour, the President had taken a million-dollar bribe from Horst Dassler. It was at the very least an unwise move after the various events recorded above that had occurred during the previous six years. Käser is now dead and beyond explaining his motives. Clearly, despite all that had gone on before the General Secretary could not believe that he was working with a man who could be bought.

Havelange's reaction was, according to Helmut Käser,

'venomous' – very reminiscent of his responses over the years to any such allegations. This time the anger contained a threat: 'I'll take these people to court. I'll get a lawyer and I'll sue. I haven't been given a million dollars by Dassler.'

Havelange never instructed a lawyer and never went near a courtroom. For a man in his position his inaction is mystifying. Perhaps the fact that the financial records at Adidas show that a million-dollar payment was made to João Havelange had something to do with his failure to instigate legal proceedings. In the light of those financial records a court action would not have been desired by Horst Dassler and what Mr Dassler wanted he usually got.

A number of FIFA officials who, during the first ten years or so of the Havelange reign, were close observers of proceedings inside FIFA House have spoken to me of the Havelange–Dassler relationship. Quite independently of each other, one particular word came up in each of these interviews. *Drahtzieher*: wirepuller; puppetmaster – and for each of these people the man pulling the strings was Dassler. Each was quite sure that he controlled Havelange. The idea of anyone controlling the Sun King in his full pomp is difficult to accept, but then the idea that one small piddling little company owned by Dassler should seize control not only of football but also the Olympics is even more preposterous; yet it happened.

The idea that Dassler could, for example, acquire the marketing rights for Mexico World Cup 86 from Havelange for SF45 million and then sell them on for more than SF200 million to twelve multi-nationals is of course unbelievable, yet it happened. Opel and Coca-Cola and the others became 'official sponsors'. Horst Dassler became even richer.

Dassler's bank accounts were far from being the only ones showing increased activity. Even the ordinary staff at

FIFA began to feel certain benefits. Increased salaries, a delightful tax-avoidance scam – one that is still in operation today – ensured that 40 per cent of salary came out of a World Cup account and was tax-free. At the upper end of the scale the non-salaried President was moving into a high all-expenses-paid decade. Havelange operated a bewildering number of bank accounts during his reign at FIFA. There was an account at Pictat, a private bank in Geneva; another at a second private bank, Bank für Handel & Effekten in Zurich; another at Chase Manhattan in New York. This last one was particularly active as a device to circumvent prying eyes in Brazil. It was a dollar account into which hundreds of thousands of dollars covering 'rent for Rio office and office costs' would find their way. Havelange also moved money the other way from Rio to Zurich; never through the banks, but physically in suitcases – an operation that was totally illegal. On one occasion he asked his General Secretary to take thirty thousand dollars cash out of Rio back to Switzerland. Käser declined to act as a currency smuggler.

The relationship between the two men had by late 1980 deteriorated so much that Havelange was excluding Käser again and again from official FIFA business and conducting meetings and negotiations quite improperly without any involvement from his General Secretary. One of their running battles concerned the profligacy of Havelange. Again and again Käser would remonstrate with him. 'The Coca-Cola money is running out. You must stop treating it as your own.'

To avoid the lectures Havelange took evasive action and, contrary to official procedure, began slipping his ever-larger expense claims to Armen Rauber, the accounts clerk.

During November 1980 it became open warfare. Havelange got off the first blast. In his letter to Käser dated 'Rome, November 30th 1980' he defined his own role.

'The President represents the Federation. He also represents it at law, both as plaintiff and as respondent.' Having quoted extracts of Articles 19 and 20 of the FIFA Statutes at Käser to demonstrate that as the Sun King he had absolute power and authority, Havelange then went on over three pages to define the role of the General Secretary.

It would not be unreasonable to assume that Käser, who had worked with three FIFA presidents over a twenty-year period might, by late 1980, have got the hang of the job. As an exercise in humiliation it was first-class. Käser realised as he studied the letter that it would have been translated by a member of his staff and that those working under him would have been fully aware of the letter's contents before he was. It includes such directives as:

1 All departments of the General Secretariat must work in close collaboration for the success of FIFA's obligations;

2 Each time the President is working at FIFA headquarters, the General Secretary must prepare a meeting with the Heads of Departments;

3 Each time the President of FIFA arrives in Zurich for business purposes, the Head of Protocol [Käser] must be present when he arrives;

6 An inventory of all PR material (pennants, ties, cufflinks, scarves, watches, pencils, etc) must be submitted to the President of the Finance Commission by 15th January 1981 with a copy to the President.

What makes this such an extraordinary document is that it very graphically demonstrates the state of affairs at the heart of FIFA as football went into a new and crucial decade. That the supreme head of football should be preoccupied with the number of cufflinks FIFA was holding is demonstrably absurd. Havelange was not of course concerned about such trivia. For a man who had only shortly before spent over SF100,000 of FIFA's money on expensive Swiss watches for his friends, plus picking up the bill for their hotel expenses, a few mass-produced cufflinks were neither here nor there.

The object of the exercise, masterminded by Dassler, was to make life impossible for the General Secretary, to hound him out of FIFA House. Dassler had already groomed his successor, a man who had previously been working for Longines – the same company where Havelange so enjoyed bulk-buying his watches: Sepp Blatter.

Blatter had in fact been originally employed at FIFA by Käser in 1975. Looking to the future, Käser thought that eventually Blatter might well take over from him. 'Eventually' had come much quicker than Käser had planned for. (It often does in this life.)

When it became apparent to both Dassler and Havelange that Käser was not going to roll over and allow them to run FIFA and football as they saw fit, Horst Dassler concluded that Blatter should be groomed at Adidas. He absorbed the Dassler philosophy with such enthusiasm that by 1977 he had been promoted to Technical Director at FIFA. Now all that was required before he took over the chair of the General Secretary was to push the present incumbent out of the window.

So close was the Blatter–Dassler relationship that Blatter's salary was paid by Adidas even though he was working for FIFA – an exercise that was as questionable as Havelange channelling insurance business to his own company, but then if Dassler was indeed the puppetmaster then the more puppets he could pull the strings on inside FIFA House, the better.

Having considered the implications of what Havelange had written, Helmut Käser retaliated in January 1981. He too went public, in his case sharing not only his thoughts but also a selection of the correspondence that had passed between the two men with the entire FIFA Executive Committee.

The unevenly matched contest was always going to have only one result. In July 1981 Havelange announced that Dr Helmut Käser no longer sat in the General Secretary's chair. His contract had been terminated. Announcing his 'retirement', Havelange said it was an 'amicable arrangement'. In fact the negotiations had been long and bitter and included a SF1.5 million pay-off plus a generous pension.

The coup de grâce had been delivered by Havelange at a FIFA meeting on 7 May. Käser has been forced to sit outside the room while Havelange launched into a character assassination. He complained to the Executive Committee that Käser was refusing to carry out his instructions and that this attitude showed a lack of both discipline and respect. Ironically the first item on that day's agenda unwittingly underlined the real issue between the two men. There was a running FIFA deficit. More money going out than was coming in.

Sepp Blatter became General Secretary a few months later in November. Two years later he married Barbara, Helmut Käser's daughter. Dr Käser was not invited to the wedding. When he heard of the event he broke down and cried.

With Dassler's anointed choice now working alongside Havelange there would no longer be any tiresome arguments about the President's expenses, nor would there be any disagreements about his per diem – his daily spending money. Over the years this would be subject to regular increases until it reached SF2000 per day. At current rates of exchange, nearly £800 or over $1,300 per day. Some time ago, referring to his per diem but without revealing just how large it was, João Havelange said, 'It hardly covers my daily living.' Clearly his extravagant tastes have not deserted him in his old age.

After Dr Helmut Käser died on 11 May 1994, FIFA paid

tribute to his work as General Secretary which 'had been a model of competence and integrity'.

In 1981, with the problem of the General Secretary finally resolved to the satisfaction of Dassler and Havelange, it was time to look to the future, to World Cup Spain 1982 and beyond. Dassler, never a man to rest on current achievements, was already planning well into the future. He had talked to a number of people about cutting adrift from Patrick Nally. For a man as Machiavellian and paranoid as he undoubtedly was, Dassler could be spectacularly indiscreet, but it was a selective indiscretion. He never talked outside closed rooms about which sportsmen and -women had taken illegal payments over the years. To have done so would of course have been to cut his own throat and Dassler was far too busy cutting everyone else's.

When they parted company in 1982 Nally discovered just how Machiavellian his former business partner was. Dassler took with him the marketing rights to international football and that is where they have remained ever since, and are contracted to remain at least until the year 2010. The fact that Havelange and Blatter have disposed of their most precious asset for such a long period of time does not appear to have disturbed the tranquillity of the majority of the FIFA membership. It would be a curious way to run a sweetshop, let alone a billion-dollar enterprise, which is what football has now become.

Dassler needed a company. He promptly founded ISL. To Nally's astonishment, he discovered that Dassler had already formed a new partnership before he had ended their relationship. He had exchanged Nally for one of the very biggest, if not the biggest, advertising agencies in the world, the Japanese giant Dentsu, which owns a part of much of the country's commercial business, press, publishing and TV.

Nally had unwittingly brought about his own replacement. During the years when he was bringing the world's
top corporations to Dassler, one of the Category One
sponsors he had snared for the World Cup had been the
Japanese electronics manufacturer, JVC. For good measure
Nally had also obtained a long-term commitment from Fuji
Film. When negotiating with the two companies, Nally had
worked through a Japanese advertising agency, Hukuhodo,
the number two agency and Dentsu's biggest rival.

Dassler had kept back from his dear friend Nally, the
man who had brought him Coca-Cola and all of the other
blue-chip sponsors, the fact that Dentsu were desperate to
replace Hukuhodo. They wanted to buy into Dassler's
company. Thus ISL was set up and they duly bought in for
several large boatloads of dollars.

From now on the money that the corporate sponsors
would pay, not only for football but also for the Olympic
Games, was going to get bigger and bigger between the
beginning of the 1980s and the end of the decade. The
money that ISL would extract from the corporate sponsors
went from millions to hundreds of millions to billions. And
all of it controlled by a secretive private company that
declined to tell FIFA just how much it was selling football
for. It was indeed a steal.

Before that, courtesy of Nally, Dassler and Havelange,
there was 'Spain 1982 – the biggest and the best World
Cup ever'. Well, it was the biggest. Havelange, eight years
after his promises and his money had got him elected to
football's most important job, finally delivered on the
promise of an increased Final tournament.

With an eye to future presidential elections, Africa now
got two slots instead of one, as did Asia/Oceania and
CONCACAF – the North and Central and Caribbean
region. South America now had four teams instead of
three. The biggest winner was Europe. UEFA had been

bitterly opposed to what many considered a grotesque bloating of the tournament. Opposition vanished overnight when Havelange decreed that Europe would have four additional places at the Final.

It was a cynicism that England and other European countries would show again in 1998 when they voted for a candidate to replace Havelange, not out of conviction but out of a desire to influence the location of the World Cup in 2006.

Havelange praised Spain for having accepted the challenge of a greatly enlarged competition in the spirit of Don Quixote. He neglected to observe that the Spanish organising committee had shown a great deal more realism than the Knight of the Sad Countenance had. They had insisted on a guaranteed advertising revenue of thirty-six million Swiss francs. Due very much to the efforts of Patrick Nally they had got their money.

If an award were ever created for the worst-organised World Cup in the history of the tournament, Mexico would be one of the favourites, as would France after a succession of débâcles during the summer of 1998. A student of form might, however, be seen making discreet inquiries concerning the odds on Spain 82. In terms of cock-ups it has so much going for it.

Confronted for the first time with twenty-four teams, the organisers of this, the supreme event in the world's most popular sport, worked long and hard to ensure the maximum amount of aggravation would be given to the greatest number of people.

The tournament was spread throughout the length and breadth of Spain. Fifty-two games were to be played in fourteen different cities. At the draw made in January in Madrid there was a hint of what the summer would hold for any who ventured either to participate in or watch the football.

One of the revolving drums from which the balls were being picked stopped revolving. A ball broke into pieces. Neuberger, the FIFA Vice President who considered the entire Argentinian junta to be above reproach, did not feel the same way about the proceedings in Madrid. The balls were being selected by a group of orphans. One of their number was subjected to a verbal attack by Neuberger, a moment that was observed by a huge international audience on television. The balls representing Scotland and Belgium were drawn too early, thus defeating the object of this entire charade, which was to keep the South American teams well apart in the opening games.

In June the full insanity of this Havelange-created scenario became apparent to the general public. There would be six groups of teams, comprising four teams per group. The first two in each group would qualify for the second round. This was to be played exclusively in Madrid and Barcelona between four groups each consisting of three teams. Points would decide; if points were level, then goal difference. If that could not resolve who should progress, then Havelange and his World Cup Committee had decreed that goal average from the previous round would be brought into the equation. The one manager who might just have been able to follow these rules was Coutinho of Brazil – he had after all displayed in the past a profound working knowledge of polyvalence – but he had been fired long ago and had subsequently drowned. His place at the Brazilian helm had been taken by Tele Santano.

Having got, via the second-round matches, four semi-finalists, the World Cup Committee had then produced one of its best tricks. It would be logical to assume that, having got the four teams in either Madrid or Barcelona, then the two semi-finals would take place in these cities. Logic had nothing to do with this World Cup. Barcelona would have one of the matches, the other would be played in Seville. This naturally gave a great advantage to the two teams in Barcelona. Whoever won that game would go into the Final without tasting the delights of a trip to Seville and then a trip to Madrid.

Just in case anyone involved in all of this still felt cocky about their expertise at organising their World Cup itinerary, the Spanish Football Federation played their master-stroke. They had handed over, lock stock and tickets, the organisation of the hotels and the ticketing to the Mundiespana organisation. This group were destined to make an art form out of incompetence.

Sometimes life is well written; an incident occurs that one has either devoutly wished to happen or delighted in when it has happened.

During World Cup Spain 1982 Havelange received from the organiser of the tournament the four hundred tickets that he had asked for. This by Havelange's demands was an average quota of tickets for a game. In this instance the tickets were for Brazil's opening game of the competition against Russia. When he checked the seating location Havelange was enraged to discover that his friends, cronies and delegates who had been promised special treatment were not to be seated in the VIP boxes but behind one of the goals. Surrounded by ordinary people. The Brazilian politicos, the judges, the senior lawyers, the newspaper proprietors, the owners of various big football teams, friends that worked in the tax offices, all of these, like the President who had organised the outing, do not consider themselves to be ordinary people.

The following morning at half-past eight Havelange appeared at the office of the ticket organiser Raimundo Saporta. The office was empty. The President of FIFA sat down and waited. Thirty minutes later the unsuspecting Saporta entered. Havelange put the four hundred tickets on the table saying, 'You can keep these tickets, they are not for FIFA. I've come for the four hundred tickets that were promised.'

On the office wall was a plan showing the seating arrangements for the stadium. Havelange stood, his figure towering over the diminutive Spaniard. He pointed to the VIP section on the plan. 'That's where I want my four hundred friends seated.'

Saporta looked up at him. 'I haven't got them.'

Havelange nodded. It was an answer he had expected. Crossing to the door, he locked it, removed the key and came back to the centre of the room. He studied the office then moving around, closed all of the windows. Satisfied, he returned to the middle of the room and addressed an apprehensive Saporta.

'I can stay here for seventy-two hours without having a piss, a shit, food or sleep. You on the other hand might well die, because I am not going to let you leave until I've got the tickets in my hands.'

Saporta began to hyperventilate at the very prospect. He struggled to speak. Like the majority of people involved in running international football at the highest level, Saporta was heavily overweight and badly out of condition. The sixty-six-year-old Havelange, looking at the time a very fit fifty-year-old, fixed his baleful eyes on Saporta. 'Now, it's your problem not mine.' Then Havelange very calmly sat down. Señor Saporta had a brainwave. 'Why don't you call ...' 'No, I don't work for you,' Havelange said. 'You call.'

The heat of the day was beginning to pick up. Perspiration was running down Saporta's face while Havelange sat looking as cool as an autumn breeze. This was a man totally at ease in a heavy suit in a heatwave. An ability he has demonstrated at football matches on countless occasions.

Raimundo Saporta began to dial. He made one phone

call, then another, then another, each more urgent than the last. Twenty minutes later the President of FIFA left Saporta's office. He had in his hands four hundred tickets for the Brazil v Russia game. The allocation was for seats in the VIP section of the stadium.

The commitment that FIFA had made before the 1970 World Cup in Mexico – that artistry would be protected, that ball-playing skills would not be penalised by defenders who had but one solution to all problems: to kick and maim their way of difficulty – that commitment had long been forgotten in the intervening years.

The promise had come largely because of the treatment that Pelé had suffered in England during the World Cup of 1966. In Spain 82 the touch players were considered fair game.

The first to suffer was Diego Maradona. Twenty-one years of age. Powerful thighs that triggered an extraordinary acceleration. A footballing mind as quick as his body. Tactically astute and a lethal finisher. After a dove of peace had been released before the opening game between the cup-holders Argentina and Belgium, Maradona was hacked and kicked to the ground repeatedly. He was subjected to violent tackling from behind, he was pushed off the ball, pulled off the ball. Referee Vojtech Christov saw nothing to disturb his tranquillity. He appeared to wander through the game on his own private cloud. For the first time in twenty years the opening match produced a goal; sadly it went not to the side trying to play football, but to the side that packed its defence and rarely strayed upfield. Belgium won the match 1–0. They won no friends among the neutrals watching.

If the refereeing of that first match was bad, what was destined to follow during the tournament on a number of occasions was quite abysmal. Still FIFA persists with the myth that middle-aged amateurs can effectively control young top-class professional athletes. At Spain 82 there were forty-one referees from the four corners of the earth. Men from Australia in theory reading the game exactly the same way as their colleagues from Libya, from Hong Kong, from Bolivia.

In Italy's second game of the tournament against Peru, Claudio Gentile, Italy's current version of the creature from the black lagoon, perpetrated a dreadful foul on the Peruvian winger Oblitas. This was inside the penalty box. The referee Eschweiler ignored the foul and concentrated on his own personal problem. He had been hit in the stomach by the ball shortly before the foul. Any competent referee would have immediately whistled up and stopped play until he had recovered. He would also have consulted his linesman about the foul on Oblitas. Eschweiler lifted a hand from his stomach and waved play on. The Italians had enough problems without Gentile adding to them. The squad yet again were refusing to talk to the press, yet again they objected to the justifiable criticism about the size of the bonuses they were receiving.

The match that President Havelange had been so determined to see, but only from a VIP seat, produced further evidence that there was something very rotten in FIFA and that the something had a name. Referees Committee.

Brazil beat the USSR 2–1. Brazil came with rich talent in their midfield: Zico, Socrates, Cerezo and Falcao, but the forward line yet again proved, if further proof was needed, that Pelé, Garrincha and the other gems of times past were irreplaceable. Every independent observer believed that the Soviets should have been awarded two penalties. Some also felt that the Brazilians should have been awarded a penalty as well. The Spanish referee Lamo Castillo declined to award any.

In Spain's first match they were trailing 1–0 to Honduras

– the under-dogs of the tournament who had scored in the seventh minute. From then on it seemed that the Spanish tactical plan was to try to get the ball into the Honduras penalty box and then promptly fall over while screaming for a penalty. It failed to impress the referee until well into the second half, when he succumbed and awarded the home team one of the traditional World Cup perks that is usually given to the hosts: a free shot at goal. Having equalised, Spain were in no mood for further adventure and gratefully accepted the draw.

In their second game their opponents, Yugoslavia, also found that they were obliged to play against twelve men. Like Honduras before them, they were leading by an early goal, always a dangerous thing to be doing against a Spanish team playing at home. Spain were awarded a penalty after what was obviously a foul. The problem was – and this was confirmed by constant television replays – it was also obviously a foul that had occurred outside the penalty box.

The Spanish player Ufarte shot wide. The Danish referee, Lund, was more than a match for that. He ordered the kick to be retaken. It was, this time by Juanito, who scored. Later in the game Spain got a second for what was to be their only win of the tournament.

Everywhere one looked the spectator saw not only glimpses of great football but with depressing frequency bizarre and unacceptable refereeing.

France v Kuwait. A beautiful ball from Platini had his team-mate Giresse dance through the Kuwaiti defence while some of the defenders appeared to have been turned to stone. Giresse scored. The Russian referee Miroslav Stupar pointed to the centre. It was France's fourth goal. The Kuwaitis protested violently. The reason they had watched immobile while Giresse went on his merry way was because the referee had blown up for offside. The referee was adamant. He had not blown up and it was a goal. The Kuwaitis grew more excited. Grew more vehement in their protests. If the referee had not blown then someone in the terraces had.

Up in the stands in his VIP peasant-free zone sat the President of the Kuwaiti Soccer Federation, Prince Fahed. He started beckoning to his team, motioning that they should leave the pitch. The Kuwaitis began to make their way off the field, then the Prince appeared by the touchline. Now it seemed he was telling them to stay on. At this stage the Russian referee decided to add further to the excitement. He now announced that he had disallowed the goal. Now the French started to protest. Eventually, what passed for order in this match was restored and with the goal staying disallowed they got on with the football. In the event before the farce finished France scored another goal.

The game between Germany and Austria was no laughing matter. In its own way it was as disgraceful an affair as the Argentina v Peru game had been in 1978. It was the final game of their group. It exemplified all that was rotten not merely with the refereeing committee at FIFA House in Zurich, but with the whole Executive Committee from Havelange down.

Both Germany and Austria were aware before the kick-off that a 1–0 win for Germany would ensure that both Germany and Austria would progress to the next round at the expense of Algeria. If Germany won by more than the odd goal or the match was drawn, or Austria won, then Algeria not Germany would progress. After ten minutes Germany scored. The following eighty minutes had to be seen to be believed. Neither team made any attempt to score or to play football. A neighbourly arrangement.

Algeria protested and demanded that both Germany and Austria should be thrown out of the competition for violating the very spirit of the game. Havelange remained silent. His close friend, the German Neuberger, FIFA's senior Vice President, remained silent. FIFA rejected the Algerian protest and it was the Algerians who departed. Yet again football had been reduced by the corrupt and venal to the level of professional wrestling.

Hidalgo the French manager, whose team were due to face Austria in the next round, had gone to watch France's next opponents and to take notes. In the event he made no notes and publicly suggested that the Nobel Peace Prize should be awarded to both teams.

The second round saw a standard of refereeing that beggared belief. If collectively the referees in the Group One matches had hit rock bottom, then in some of the second-round matches they began drilling. Diego Maradona must have felt after the opening match against Belgium that things could only get better. He was wrong.

Gentile should never have been playing in this second round match. His behaviour during the Group One matches should have ensured at least a two-match ban but here he was alive and kicking – in this case Maradona, from start to finish. It was dreadful to behold. The clock had run backwards. It was Portugal v Brazil 1966 all over again with a wonderful precocious talent being kicked, whacked, punched, kneed out of the game. The Romanian referee Nicolae Rainea saw no evil in Gentile and allowed him free rein to indulge in a range of violence that merited criminal charges. Finally, after Maradona was yet again hacked to the ground by Gentile, the referee was moved to produce a yellow card. It was for Maradona. In the referee's mind the Argentinian was protesting unduly. Six minutes from the end the referee got out a red card. This one went to the Argentinian, Americo Gallego. The Italians won 2–1.

Argentina now had to beat Brazil, the third member of their mini-league, to have any chance of progressing further. After their experience at the hands of Italy, their manager Menotti addressed the press:

'I believe there is a rule that a player who fouls repeatedly must be rejected, no?'

In the case of Gentile, it had indeed been 'no'.

Now against Brazil, Menotti was finally to see a red card after an incident involving Maradona, but it was Maradona who was expelled, five minutes from the end of a game that Brazil deservedly won 3–1.

All of the frustrations and injuries had finally got to the young Argentinian. His foul on Batista was inexcusable and with so much promise unfulfilled he walked off and out of World Cup 82.

The final game of this group between Italy and Brazil would decide who progressed further. Brazil needed but to draw, Italy had to win.

If one could ignore Gentile's contribution to the game, it was a match fit to be the Final. However, neither the spectator nor Zico, who had the misfortune to have Gentile marking him in every sense of that word, could ignore the Italian psychopath. This time he did actually get a yellow card, but undeterred carried on kicking, hacking and pulling at Zico, to such an extent that Zico's shirt was shredded. The Brazilian drew the referee's attention to his bare chest, but Klein of Israel was having, by his previous standards, an off-day. He waved Zico away. This was the dark side of Italian football that was on display during the match. There was also the delicious talent of Paolo Rossi to relish. He had been well below par in Italy's previous games, but dramatically in this crucial game the pieces of his delicate game finally all fell into place. Rossi scored a memorable and brilliant hat-trick against a Brazilian defence that, like so many before and indeed so many later, was there to be taken. Goals by Socrates and Falcao were nearly enough to see Brazil through, but at the end Rossi's dramatic return to top form was too much for them.

If the refereeing of this match by Klein had been bad, Charles Corver, the Dutch referee in charge of the France v Germany semi-final, easily surpassed Klein's ineptitude. The match was finely balanced at 1–1 ten minutes into the second half when the Frenchman Patrick Battiston, who had only been on the pitch for a few minutes, moved through the German defence chasing a long ball. He beat the German goalkeeper Schumacher to it. The goalkeeper, making no attempt to play the ball, smashed Battiston in the face with a forearm chop.

Battiston fell like a stone. His body did not move. Schumacher compounded his appalling attack by callously ignoring the unconscious player. It was as brutal a foul as any seen in this entire tournament.

The Seville police, in keeping with the general level of squalid incompetence that bedevilled this World Cup, had banned the Red Cross from the side of the pitch. It was more than three minutes before medical aid got to Battiston, who many feared was dead. Thankfully his injuries were restricted to severe concussion and the loss of two teeth. Schumacher should clearly have been sent off and a penalty awarded to the French. Neither happened. The referee considered nothing untoward had happened. He had not seen the incident. His linesman made no attempt to tell him what had happened.

Referee Corver had yet another telling contribution to make to this game. With the score 3–1 to France, Rummenigge of Germany scored a second for his country. The fact that there had been two blatant fouls on French players by Rummenigge before he scored was also ignored by the referee. After extra-time the score was 3–3, so for the first time a World Cup game was to be decided by the ultimate farce that has reduced the beautiful game to a lottery: a penalty shoot-out. West Germany won the lottery because their goalkeeper Schumacher, who should have been sent off in the fifty-seventh minute of the second half, saved two penalties.

Italy had beaten Poland 2–0 in the other semi-final, and the Final therefore would be between Italy complete with Signor Gentile and West Germany with Herr Schumacher between the goalposts. It was time for the Spanish organiser to throw another joker onto the table. The French team attempted to catch a plane from Seville back to Barcelona. Amid the chaos, totally exhausted players sat on their suitcases as plane after plane arrived and departed. It was yet another unforgettable performance by Mundiespana, who inevitably had been responsible for booking the flights. They had also ensured that an equally exhausted German team would, after a traumatic game, extra-time and a penalty shoot-out, spend half the night at Seville before flying to Madrid to face a fresh Italian side in the Final of the World Cup.

The first half of the Final very largely consisted of two teams determined to prevent each other from playing football. Watching paint dry would have been an appealing alternative. The Italians missed a penalty in the twenty-fifth minute but the most welcoming sight during the first forty-five minutes was the Brazilian referee, Coelho, putting the whistle to his lips to blow for half-time with the score 0–0. Stielike, the German defender, should have been sent off for a foul on Oriali four minutes before the interval, but presumably referee Coelho was determined that the refereeing standards that had been set during the previous games of the tournament should be maintained until the bitter end.

His foul and the fact that he had got away with it obviously set Stielike up for the interval. The West German dressing room was the scene of far greater activity than anything that had preceded half-time. Stielike ranted uncontrollably that Rummenigge, who was carrying a muscle injury, should not have played. Eventually tiring of the hysteria, Rummenigge asked a team-mate to hit Stielike for him.

If football is a game for those who enjoy irony, then some ten minutes into the second half must have been particularly sweet for them. The man that Stielike had so badly fouled in the first half had been the Italian Oriali. Now the same Italian player was fouled again. This time by the injured Rummenigge. A quick free kick found Gentile of all people on the right wing. His cross went flying across the German goal, to be met by Rossi, who headed past Schumacher.

Tardelli got a second and Altobelli a third. Near the end Breitner pulled one back for West Germany, but the match and the Cup was Italy's, 3–1. They had joined Brazil, the only other nation to win the Cup three times. The tournament had been a powerful demonstration that the old maxim of 'if you throw enough money at a problem, the problem will vanish' was, like many an old maxim, a load of balls, of the non-Adidas variety.

FIFA, amply aided by its World Cup Committee and Mundiespana, had given the public the worst tournament in the history of the competition. It was entirely appropriate that the closing images of the Final should include a delightful vignette. Havelange standing importantly next to King Juan Carlos while Zoff the Italian captain proudly waved the trophy, and below the gantry the Madrid police clubbing photographers with their truncheons. In 1982 the Spanish police force still clung to many of its fascist traditions. The idea that the press should be allowed to photograph the King while he handed over the Cup was obviously absurd.

Before the World Cup 82 in Spain had commenced, FIFA had asked all the participating countries to sign a commitment, a public promise. For the good of the game.

'Violence distorts and disgraces sport ... We are aware of our responsibilities and undertaken to play with respect for the rules, the referees, and our opponents.'

If FIFA had also made this legally binding, had stated that if it was contravened then automatic disqualification from the tournament would follow, then the declaration might well have had some effect and influence on what passed for a football tournament during the summer of 1982. They did not and the statement remained mere hyperbole. The loathsome Gentile was allowed to take the field for the Final and to subsequently receive a winner's medal. The equally obnoxious Schumacher also played in the same match. A class act in the shape of Diego Maradona had, like Pelé before him, been brutally kicked out of the tournament. Austria and Germany had successfully conspired to cheat the Algerians. The quality of the refereeing had frequently reached levels that would have disgraced Sunday soccer on an English village green. The hosts, fully aware that their mediocre side was virtually devoid of flair, originality and basic ability, had settled for the acting award with players dropping like Spanish flies in the penalty box.

One man, however, was thrilled and delighted with all that he had seen. The man who had dreamed up the declaration of fair play.

Havelange, the man who was very largely responsible for the mess, who had forced on Spain and the wider international audience the unutterable tedium of a fifty-two-game competition that went on and on and on, pronounced World Cup 82, 'A truly splendid success. A glittering occasion.'

He told reporters that he was 'looking forward with great eagerness to World Cup 86 in Colombia'. Bidding his farewells, Havelange departed for Madrid International airport. There, accompanied by Guillermo Cañedo, former

President of the Mexican Football Federation, he boarded the private jet of Emilio Azcarraga, head of Televisa Mexicana. The plane headed for Mexico City and the secret plan to replace Colombia with Mexico as the next venue for the World Cup took another step towards fulfilment.

By the time Havelange had become President of FIFA in June 1974 the allocation to Colombia of the World Cup for 1986 was established fact. The newly elected President had other ideas, but even a man as arrogant as Havelange shrank from attempting to overturn a decision so recently made, particularly when he planned to give the tournament to the nation that had just staged the last one. It was a question of waiting and planning. Much of the planning took place between Havelange and Dassler and excluded Nally. The meetings pre-dated Nally's departure, but even then, in early 1980, the man from Adidas was preparing to dump the man to whom he owed so much.

Mexico, in the minds of Havelange and Dassler, had so much to commend it. Much of the 1970 infrastructure was still in place. Only one new stadium at the most would be needed. Colombia might well have been able to accommodate a sixteen-team tournament, but Havelange had taken care of that. It was twenty-four teams and if that figure was ever to move, it would be upwards.

Then there was the endemic violence, corruption and drugs problem that beset Colombia. Not very good PR for inducing thousands of foreign visitors for the tournament. Of course, exactly the same problems beset Mexico, but at least there was not a full-scale incessant civil war raging there.

The United States and Brazil would undoubtedly wish to be considered as alternatives in line with FIFA tradition that the tournament had always alternated between Europe and Latin America. They were both logical candidates, but

Havelange has never been a man to be overly impressed with logic. Apart from any other factor, Mexico had one hell of a plus going for it. It had Emilio Azcarraga. Among other assets he had his own private television network, Televisa Mexicana; he also owned the Spanish International Network in the United States; then there were the radio stations, the newspapers, the cable channels, movie companies, music companies; his Televisa Mexicana company broadcast over 18,000 hours of programmes a year – more than ABC, CBS and NBC combined. He was Mexico's Rupert Murdoch before anyone had ever heard of Rupert Murdoch.

Havelange secretly struck a deal with Azcarraga, who because of his immense wealth was able personally to guarantee and underwrite the entire tournament. Initially the deal was only in principle. Both men knew that much remained to be done before World Cup Mexico 86 became a reality. Dassler, ever the modern Machiavelli, could not resist planting in October 1980 in the periodical *Sport Intern* the following:

'The 1986 Football World Championship will probably be given to Mexico if Colombia returns its mandate, a possibility which, in the meantime, is almost being counted on by the International Football Federation (FIFA). Even Brazil is considered in leading circles of the FIFA only as "second choice", even if FIFA President Dr João Havelange uses all the prestige of his position to add weight to his homeland's candidacy. These circles view as "completely absurd and almost ridiculous" the suggestions ... to stage the championship in the USA. This even more so since the interest in soccer in the USA is noticeably declining. Some observers even see the existence of the North American Soccer League as being put into question.'

The quote dismissing a potential pitch from the United States came directly from Havelange. The reader may recall the incident during the World Cup in Germany in 1974 when Kissinger and his hordes descended on the VIP box. Certainly Havelange recalled it. As has been made clear, Havelange feels very strongly about who should and should not be occupying VIP boxes at football stadiums. He knew that Kissinger would be fronting any pitch made by the United States. It made his proposed plan all the sweeter.

As for the reference to Havelange loyally pushing Brazil's candidacy, this is an example of Dassler at his most Machiavellian. Never a man to admit defeat when it came to a lucrative market, he lusted after Brazil and the huge market it represented for Adidas.

Havelange had recounted during my interviews with him how Dassler came calling, offering to sell Sir Stanley Rous down the river and help Havelange into the President's chair in exchange for a deal that tied Brazilian sports in general, but most important of all, Brazilian football in particular, to his company. Havelange claimed to have spurned the offer and given the business to a rival. After he and Dassler began to work closely together Dassler worked on the President at every opportunity to bring his influence to bear back in Rio to get the clothing and equipment contract for Adidas. He was clearly successful. By the time Giulite Soutinho became President of the Brazilian Football Federation in 1980. Adidas had the contract; football was no longer under the broad umbrella of all Brazilian sports, but was controlled separately and known as CBF. During my interview in Rio in February 1998 with Giulite Soutinho he told me what then happened.

'When I took the post as President of CBF, there were contracts, the last contracts were with Adidas. What I did was to invite a tender for a new contract. Four companies bid for the contract. We opened the envelopes and Topper had made the best offer. They won.'

Soutinho's six years as President of CBF are a shining example of how to run such an organisation. He published annual accounts. He published attendance records, he rationalised at least part of the insanity of Brazilian football that he had inherited from Admiral Nunes and from Havelange. His business dealings on behalf of CBF were always conducted with the maximum of transparency. He was in fact everything to Brazilian football administration that Havelange was not. The two men could not be said to enjoy a warm friendship.

Dassler was distressed at the loss of the lucrative business that would have continued to pour into Adidas if they had remained the exclusive suppliers to the most famous football country in the world. But his pique was nothing compared to President Havelange's anger. Soutinho had to go, and Havelange had just the man to replace him. Ricardo Teixeira.

Teixeira was a law graduate with an undistinguished career, but he had one huge asset in his favour. He was married to Havelange's daughter. This meant that despite his total ignorance of football administration and finance, he was ideal material for the most important position in Brazilian football. All of this was beginning to ferment long before Havelange got on a plane to Mexico City.

Havelange would have made a formidable general and indeed his life is not dissimilar to that of a sixteenth-century conquistador. If he can prevail with guile and cunning he will; if it becomes necessary to coerce he will. After a brilliant campaign he had seized the throne and become a first-class warrior king. First-class at least when it came to expenses.

At the time of the World Cup in Spain, Colombia's newly elected President Belisario Betancur advised FIFA that he was fully prepared to reaffirm all the guarantees that had been made by his predecessor Dr Borrero. He was not to know that his cause was lost before he had even begun to fight for it. Havelange despatched a FIFA commission to Colombia. Their brief was to check out 'the entire infrastructure that would be necessary for a World Cup tournament, roads, rail, airlines, stadiums, hotels, the whole multi-million dollar package that FIFA considers absolutely essential to stage the competition.' The fact that Spain had just staggered through a World Cup without many of those absolute bottom-line essentials was not a subject for discussion, certainly not among the FIFA delegates who set off for Colombia. Havelange had fully briefed them before departure, and insiders were convinced that their colleagues were going an awfully long way to say something that they had already concluded on before they left Zurich. There was no intention of giving Colombia a clean bill of health.

In January 1983 the Colombian government admitted defeat. Suddenly, to the great surprise of no one on the executive floor of FIFA House, World Cup 86 was looking for a new home.

Four contenders declared themselves. Canada, the United States, Brazil and Mexico.

Giulite Soutinho gave it his best shot.

'In fact, I fought a long hard battle to bring the World Cup to Brazil when Colombia gave up. In truth it was war. I had the support of all the Brazilian press, of the people, of Congress, but in the end the decision went against Brazil.'

It went against Brazil because the Brazilian President of FIFA had been very busy working on his good friend the President of Brazil, João Baptista de Figueiredo – 'my João' as Havelange calls him – and, for good measure, the President's son. 'Brazil has such a heavy balance of payments debt. It would be imprudent to add to it with such a huge outlay. The stadiums you know, my João, they would need to be renovated. My committee tells me that the total cost to Brazil would be $400 million. My major concern, however, is the local administration. The CBF. They just are not up to it. When there's a change of leadership, a new man at the top, then that will be a different story ....'

Havelange made it abundantly clear not only to 'my João', his friend for decades, but also to a great many other leading figures in Brazil. 'While Soutinho is President of CBF the World Cup will not be coming to Brazil.'

Such economy is impressive. Killing two birds with one stone is always a clever trick. Havelange had simultaneously fired the opening shots in a campaign to get Ricardo Teixeira his son-in-law elected as President of CBF and also eliminated one of the main contenders for World Cup 86. That left the United States, Canada and Mexico. Which meant that it left Mexico.

On 20 May 1983 the FIFA Executive Committee met at a Stockholm hotel. Their purpose was to give due consideration to the three applications for World Cup 86. First in to bat was Canada, then came Mexico. They made a vague desultory statement lasting seven minutes. Departing, they went down to the lobby and ordered champagne. Lots of it.

Next up to bat was the former Secretary of State Dr Henry Kissinger.

Apart from Havelange, among the others sitting there as Kissinger and his team warmed to their task was the man soon to be charged with a wide variety of crimes including murder, the Argentinian Carlos Alberto Lacoste, and the gentleman who had shared the plane trip from Madrid to Mexico with Havelange, Guillermo Cañedo, who apart from being a FIFA Vice President, was also a senior executive of Televisa Mexicana, the media conglomerate owned by Azcarraga. Even that was not an end to Cañedo's busy professional life. He had also after a bitter fight managed to get himself elected as the chairman of Mexico's World Cup Organising Committee.

Kissinger is in a number of respects a man very similar to Havelange. Both appear to be totally without modesty, false or any other kind; both have gone through this life very largely getting their own way. What Kissinger wanted that morning was the prize of World Cup 86.

His presentation lasted well over an hour. He extolled the growing interest in football within the United States, reminded the Committee that the giant conglomerate Warner Communication had poured money into the North American Soccer League (NASL), paid tribute to the talents that had come to the States to help the growth of the game. Men like Pelé, Beckenbauer and Carlos Alberto had shared the Indian summer of their careers at New York Cosmos.

Kissinger had just moved up a gear and into his second hour when an aide came and whispered in his ear. The Mexicans down below were apparently very busy organising a victory celebration.

No one had ever treated Kissinger like this. He stormed out humiliated. There was talk of Kissinger and the others of the US delegation suing FIFA, particularly when they learned that the decision had been made before breakfast by the Executive Committee and that the entire morning had been merely empty ritual.

More devastating than the loss of face that Kissinger suffered was the effect this decision had on football in the United States.

Soccer's popularity in the USA had been building steadily. It was always going to be a long hard haul before it could hope to compete for public attention at anywhere near the level of support that American Football, basketball and baseball commanded. The big hope among those involved in the NASL was that the United States would get selected as the venue for World Cup 86. When it did not happen Warner Communication pulled the plug. They could not accept that Mexico had more to offer than the United States. Without corporate support the North American Soccer League collapsed.

Havelange's need to put Kissinger in his place was satisfied at an enormous cost to the game, certainly within the United States. The Havelange decision put the growth back many years. When they finally got to stage a World Cup in 1994, it was too late to capitalise on the initial momentum that football had created in the 1970s and early 1980s. The momentum had lost interest and gone looking for other diversions.

In such a manner then did Havelange sell the 86 World Cup to Mexico. The country that had been preferred to the world's super-power was by any economic criteria a basket case.

At the time of that meeting in Stockholm, Mexico had a deficit of more than $80 billion. Inflation was nudging 100 per cent. The peso had been devalued by two-thirds during the previous twelve months.

Colombia had been rejected for a number of reasons, including a foreign debt then standing at $7.2 billion. Now it had been replaced by a country that was being asked to present itself in full formal evening dress when it did not even own a shirt.

So Mexico began its preparation for World Cup 86. It began to build a plush International Press Centre and to interview attractive women to work as hostesses for the visiting journalists. All those chosen to work in the Press Centre were white – this in a country where 90 per cent of the population is of mixed blood and most of the rest are Indians.

They began to build walls which would be painted white and rise to over seven feet high to hide the rat-infested squalid shanties that were behind them.

The order went out that before the World Cup all street vendors, beggars and children washing car windows were to be removed and kept off the streets for the duration of the tournament. The drug trade would be harder to hide. One-third of the heroin and marijuana consumed in the United States passes through Mexico, a trade that already by the mid-1980s was worth billions of dollars. It would take more than a seven-foot-high wall to hide that.

Just after seven on the morning of 19 September 1985, one of the most powerful earthquakes ever recorded hit downtown Mexico City. The quake had registered 8.1 on the Richter scale. The death toll was over seven thousand people. Thirty thousand people were made homeless.

In a stunning demonstration of insensitivity, Havelange announced that he was flying immediately to Mexico to check out the stadiums. Of the death and carnage he made no mention.

It transpired that none of the stadiums had sustained any damage, but did the people care a damn about staging a football tournament at such a time? The answer was that they wanted it more than ever, at least that was the word on Azcarraga's television channels, in his papers, magazines and radio.

On 30 December, rather like the Pope, the President of the United States and Her Majesty the Queen, João Havelange gave an end-of-year message to the world's football community.

He talked initially of the Heysel stadium disaster which had occurred in the previous May in which thirty-nine people had died, and said that such events 'must never be allowed to happen again'. Then he talked of the year ending on 'a more positive note'. Because 'Mexico's preparations were full of promise ... If we take the new media installations as an example of the standard of efficiency of the Mexican organisers, we can indeed look forward to a brilliant World Cup ... Mexico was the best possible choice. The Mexico Finals will be more than ever a media event. I therefore urgently appeal to all media representatives to support us in our fights for the ideals of fair play ... The fact that a large part of the sport has in the recent past turned from pure recreation into a professionally managed entertainment industry with big financial consequences must in no way be taken as a reason for disregarding sportsmanship and fairness.'

It had disturbing echoes to that pledge that the competing teams had signed prior to Spain 82. During the 1980s decade with its market-forces mentality and compassion virtually a swear word, to talk of sportsmanship and fairness to the average professional footballer participating at the World Cup Finals in Mexico was to risk a trip, a shirt tug, one elbow in the ribs and the other in the face.

This was the decade when cheating whether in commerce, politics or sport was legitimised; when the only crime was getting caught. Football is not something separate from society, it is a part, an integral part, of our lives. What happens on the field of play has merely become far too often the cheats taking physical exercise. Mexico 86 was to give many examples of this, including one that must have sent any who still clung to fragments of the Corinthian ideals in search of the sick bag.

Whatever else Mexico 86 offered, it gave Havelange's insurance company yet another healthy injection of funds. Insurance costs for the tournament were over six and a half million Swiss francs.

One player for good and for bad would dominate this tournament and in one particular game he would within the space of five minutes first cheat and then charm his way into headlines that went around the world.

FIFA, having concluded after the previous tournament in Spain that there was still potential to ruin the game even

more than they had done, on that occasion decided once
more to mess around with the match structure.

Realising that the entire event was as Havelange had
noted from his Zurich balcony at the end of the previous
year 'a professionally managed entertainment industry',
FIFA got busy with some show-business concepts.

The name of the game was to turn up the drama button.
This time, sixteen teams would advance from the first
round, the first and second in each first-round group plus
the four best third-place finishers.

One day, but not in this century, the concept of 'the
opening game' will be scrapped in favour of a whole raft of
games being played on the first day of the tournament.

This one was Italy v Bulgaria, FIFA's answer to insomnia.
There was a lively festival of Mexican dances and mariachi
music, a speech from President Miguel de la Madrid which
was whistled and booed by the Mexican spectators who to
a man, woman and child knew that much of the money
that had poured into Mexico after the earthquake for relief
work and charity had been stolen by the government. After
the singing and dancing and the booing and whistling,
everything went downhill.

The referee blew his whistle to start the game. It ended
as a 1–1 draw. It was a match to remind one of a particular
occasion at Wembley when the Queen was obliged to
watch a particularly dull Cup Final. After the game as Sir
Stanley Rous escorted Her Majesty to the waiting car, he
inquired, 'Did you think anyone played well today,
Ma'am?' The Queen considered for a moment and then
replied, 'Yes, the band.'

At the end of the first round the press were advised at the
all-white sumptuous International Media Centre that
Bulgaria would be going forward into the next round.
Bulgaria had finished bottom of their group. They had
drawn two matches and lost one. Their goal average was

2–4. Also excitingly through, entirely on the merit of their play, were Uruguay. They had drawn two, lost one and had an even worse goal average – 2–7.

Uruguay had clearly embarked on a fully committed attempt to enter the record books as the most undisciplined team in the history of the World Cup. In view of some of the games already recorded within this book they had a formidable task in front of them, but they were obviously going to give it their best shot.

The bookings in their first game against West Germany were accompanied by extraordinary behaviour from their bench with their manager Borras leading frequent charges onto the pitch. After the game there was complete havoc during the drug-control tests with the randomly selected Uruguayans screaming, shouting and threatening the examining doctors with physical violence. FIFA issued the Uruguayans with a stern warning concerning future behaviour. They were unimpressed. When they played Denmark two yellow cards and a red were interspersed with a 6–1 drubbing. When they played their third crucial game with a second-round place at stake the Uruguayans, fearing that this might well be their last opportunity to add to their blemished record, went for broke. José Batista's name is today remembered by few, yet he is in World Cup record books. Fastest sending off in the history of the World Cup – fifty-three seconds. The same match also contained a number of Uruguayan goal kicks that each took over a minute to occur.

After the game, a 0–0 draw which enabled them to scrape into the next round, their coach Omar Borras commented, 'We have survived the so-called Group of Death. That's what it was today, there was a murderer on the field. The referee.'

FIFA summoned a disciplinary hearing which resulted in the Uruguayan Federation being cautioned, fined twenty-five thousand Swiss francs, threatened with expulsion if their riotous behaviour continued and their manager Omar Borras being banned from the bench during their next game for calling the referee a murderer.

At the end of this first round of matches more than a quarter of the players who had taken part had been booked (eighty-two) or sent off (six). Havelange assured the press:

'This proves that the referees are doing their job. I have no concern about the players, they are not getting out of hand.'

Some of the press went after Havelange. They had so much ammunition and for once some of their number decided to forget the first law of newspaper reporting, which is that accreditation comes before information, namely, if you wish to keep getting access to the event do not offend those controlling it.

'What about the Portuguese ...?' was one question, a reference to the fact that the squad from Portugal, like the majority of the other squads, were very much focused on money, particularly the size of their bonuses. The squad's relationship with its own federation had deteriorated so badly that Portuguese officials asked FIFA for permission to fly in an alternative squad of twenty-two, an interesting idea. FIFA declined the request presumably fearing it could start a very dangerous precedent. Portugal were eliminated at the end of the first round.

'What about the refereeing?' was another question that rebounded around the Media Centre. 'What about ... the mounting violence; the rampant time-wasting; four defeated teams being able to qualify for the second round; incompetent match supervisors; an invitation to a political criminal; and, Dr Havelange, what about your financial involvement and the allegations about you concerning a one-million-dollar bribe from Dassler of Adidas?'

This last item had surfaced in the current edition of *Der*

Spiegel. In a long and very detailed examination of the Adidas empire, the German magazine gave details of the Nally–Dassler conversation concerning their attempts to gain control of the marketing rights for World Cup 78 in Argentina and the comment of Dassler's, 'If the Brazilian were to be bribed with a million dollars the rights would be ours.'

Havelange replied, 'I will only smile. People can write what they like.' For a man with such a highly developed sense of his own importance and the respect that he insists upon always being shown, it was an extraordinary response. Equally curious was his reaction to the allegation that he was financially linked to Emilio Azcarraga and Televisa Mexicana. He denied any link, but said, 'If I decided to be financially linked it would be quite legitimate.' Many of the reporters present were convinced that the link that bound Havelange to Azcarraga had been forged long before and that it was indeed financial. Other questions exploring their relationship were ignored. João Havelange is an expert at answering a question that has not been asked.

The fact that sitting next to him was his fellow plane traveller Guillermo Cañedo smiling enigmatically throughout the proceedings added a certain irony to the situation. An irony that deepened when his master's television conglomerate came in for some scathing criticism.

Here was a World Cup tournament that was being completely run by a television company, Televisa, who were making the biggest cock-up imaginable, and making it in front of billions of viewers. In Holland they got a reasonable picture but no sound. In Brazil they got the Italian commentary. In Colombia they got the Portuguese commentary. In France they got neither pictures nor sound. The majority of countries were forced to resort to commentary via the ordinary telephone network.

The European Broadcasting Union, who had paid a

fortune for the rights, were beside themselves with fury. Uniquely, they went public, calling what was coming – or rather not coming – out of Mexico 'the biggest disaster in the history of broadcasting'. It accused the Mexicans of incompetence. Then it went further. 'It is hard not to believe that what has happened is not as the direct result of deliberate sabotage. The members of the EBU have paid over \$30 million for the broadcasting rights to World Cup 86. Get it fixed. Now. Or we will sue for the return of our \$30 million.'

By the time of this press conference the communications fiasco had been resolved. Havelange was questioned about what had occurred. He waved it away, describing it as 'a minor television problem'.

The question about an invitation to a political criminal was a reference to what had occurred in the Press Centre two days earlier. Chatting happily and walking arm-in-arm came Guillermo Cañedo and Vice Admiral Carlos Alberto Lacoste. The normally noisy Press Centre suddenly went very quiet in one particular section. The Argentinian section. Reporters who had been in the middle of filing stories on their team, and particularly on Maradona, froze. Lines to Buenos Aires were suddenly terminated as the entire Argentinian group who were present at the time, some ten to a dozen, stood up and left the room.

Cañedo, nonplussed, dismissed the departing reporters as 'merely rats'.

Now, faced by hostile questions from those same reporters, the other FIFA members left the ball to Cañedo.

'Carlos Lacoste is a good friend. An old friend of mine. I personally invited him here. His visit gives me real satisfaction. Whatever he may have done politically is of no interest to me. I am an apolitical FIFA official.'

Herman Neuberger and Havelange and Blatter nodded in agreement.

One of the many shared activities that the good friends Havelange and Lacoste had in common was an interest in transportation. It is to be hoped that Viação Cometa confines itself to carrying passengers. Lacoste's car-hire business in Cali carried a far more lucrative commodity. Cocaine. Castor de Andrade. Admiral Lacoste. Two of President Havelange's closest friends, who had so many shared interests. Money laundering. Football and illegal narcotics.

Apart from Uruguay and Bulgaria there were, thankfully, a number of teams that could actually play football who had advanced through into the second round.

West Germany. A World Cup tournament without West Germany in the Finals was by now inconceivable. Since their re-admittance to the tournament in World Cup 54 in Switzerland, they had appeared in every final stage of the competition and won the trophy twice. Now in Mexico they had as their team manager a veritable talisman: Franz Beckenbauer. His squad was a mixture of old and new – a combination that fails as often as it succeeds. Schumacher, who had been guilty of the appalling atack on the Frenchman Patrick Battiston, was still there. The experience in Spain had not been character-building. When he heard that his rival, the younger goalkeeper Stein, had replaced him in one of the earlier matches of the tournament, he promptly injured another German player during training. With Battiston still playing for France, it was to be sincerely hoped that the two teams were not destined to meet on the pitch.

Brazil were the bookmakers' favourites, though with so many of their mid-field players – Zico, Falcao, Cerezo, Socrates – all carrying injuries, the quantity of matches to be played at altitude argued against their going all the way. Among the others still there as the second round began were England, their indecision on the pitch very accurately reflecting the usual state of mind of their manager Bobby Robson. There was still room for improvement after they had completed their round-one matches. A solitary win against Poland, a fortunate draw against Morocco and a defeat at the hands of Portugal was not the stuff of world champions.

Also into the second round were the Jekyll and Hyde of the tournament: Argentina, now under the management of studious Dr Carlos Bilardo. There had been moments when Bilardo had in the past been somewhat less academic. He had played for the notorious Estudiantes de la Plata team in the late 1960s – a squad who made the Wild Bunch look like Girl Guides. Nobby Stiles, whose aggressiveness had so worried not only opponents but also FIFA in 1966, will bear the marks of his encounter with Bilardo to the end of his days: a head-butt over the eye. Bilardo's assistant was another charmer: Carlos Pachame. He had split open Bobby Charlton's shin in the same match.

Manager Bilardo also used tactics that left much to be desired – a sweeper, two markers, five men across the midfield and just one striker. Reminiscent of many English clubs playing an away league match. But the one forward happened to be Diego Maradona. If any one player could impose himself on this tournament, it was Maradona.

Maradona's response in Argentina's first game, against South Korea, to the kicking, tugging and mauling he received was the best of all possible forms of retaliation. He created all three goals that Argentina scored. The word went out that the little man was back and buzzing.

France had also made it through the first round, their elegant midfielder Platini bent on a last hurrah as he still searched for that elusive winner's medal.

One of the most positive aspects of the second-round matches was the elimination of both Uruguay – at the hands of Argentina 1–0 – and Bulgaria – beaten by the host country Mexico. The presence of Bulgaria and Uruguay at these finals was a powerful argument for reducing the number of finalists.

France, with a half-fit Platini, also went through, beating Italy 2–0. Brazil gave Poland a comprehensive lesson in controlling the midfield in their 4–0 victory and England, despite a Paraguayan defence that resorted to karate chopping Gary Lineker at one point, showed encouraging improvement in accomplishing a 3–0 win.

West Germany, meanwhile, though not exactly setting the tournament on fire, were making steady progress. They defeated Morocco 1–0 to move into the quarter-finals.

Three of the quarter-finals could only be resolved after resorting to the artificial penalty shoot-out. Thus France, Germany and Belgium went through into the semi-finals courtesy of the lottery.

One particular quarter-final match stays indelibly in the memory. It was the first time that the two countries had met since their nations had been engaged in war. The Falklands War. England v Argentina.

The press build-up in both countries bordered from some sections of the fourth estate on the hysterical. On match day there was a massive army presence in and around the Azteca stadium where the game was to be played. There were tanks in the streets and the number of Mexican military in attendance easily outnumbered the supporters of both teams.

The second half had opened with the game goalless. Some five minutes in, Maradona lost the ball in the England area. It went out to English defender Hodge who hooked it over his head, always a dangerous gambit, but this was intended for the best goalkeeper in the tournament, Peter Shilton. As the English goalkeeper rose to punch the ball clear another figure challenged him. Maradona. It was no contest. Shilton stood over six feet tall in his stocking feet,

Maradona barely five feet eight. In the air there was no way Maradona could outjump the outstretched arm of Shilton. No way, except one. He punched the ball over Shilton and into the net with a clenched fist. The linesman had a perfect view and as England defender Terry Fenwick recently recalled, 'he bottled it'. The referee, a Tunisian, Ali Ben Naceur, pointed to the centre spot. It must be remembered that this was the 1980s. Cheating was perfectly all right if you did not get caught. The linesman and the referee had elected not to catch Maradona. Despite protests from the English players, the goal was allowed to stand.

In the baking oven that the Azteca stadium had become, some English heads drooped. Others were moving on the pitch like dazed survivors of some appalling accident. This had been no accident. They needed to hang on, re-group, draw strength from each other. Maradona, having shown those watching the dark malignant part of his personality, took this moment to show the pure, untainted creativity that simultaneously lived within him.

The Argentinian defence were playing possession football in their own half. Maradona called for the ball. When the ball was played to him, he was facing his own goal. Three England players – Reid, Hodge and Beardsley – were around him. He had nowhere to go. Spinning like a top as Beardsley moved in to tackle him, Maradona twisted himself around. He flicked the ball forward and accelerated out of his own half and towards England's goal. Reid came after him as Terry Butcher attempted to tackle. Maradona moved inside, leaving them both floundering in his wake. He moved past the English defender Fenwick as if he was not there, while Butcher chased back attempting desperately to get in a late tackle. Maradona pushed the ball past the diving Shilton and into the net. In the space of a few minutes the little man had played both Beauty and the Beast.

Drawing deeply on their own innate belief in themselves, the England players battled gamely to get back into the match. After sixty-five minutes manager Bobby Robson began ringing the changes. Trevor Steven and Steve Hodge were achieving little down the wings. Peter Reid was struggling with an ankle injury; he was pulled off and replaced by Chris Waddle: fast, two-footed and erratic – if he fooled goalkeepers with his direction he sometimes fooled himself. His initial impact on the game was minimal. After seventy-four minutes John Barnes came on for Trevor Steven and things finally began to happen. Barnes, who through his career often produced frustrating lacklustre displays – frustrating because one had also seen on other occasions world-class ability – on this day in the Azteca stadium showed the full range of his talents. He began to run at the Argentinian defence. No defence likes to have a world-class winger running at them. This one was no exception. His marker Giusti was left bothered and bewildered continuously. Five minutes after Barnes had come on he again went past Giusti and centred for Lineker to head in. Two–one. Three minutes from the end, Barnes did it again. Gary Lineker rose. It seemed he must score, then suddenly Lineker was in the net but the ball was not. He'd just failed to connect.

Argentina had won. They would now go forward to the semi-finals and England would go home.

After the game Maradona brushed away repeated questions about what had happened with a blasphemous response:

'If there was a handball, it was the Hand of God.'

They loved that in Buenos Aires. They were less amused when they learned that the same day one of their countrywomen had revealed in the *Sunday Times* the truth concerning how not just one Argentinian but the entire government had colluded with Peru and ensured that

Argentina cheated its way to the World Cup Final of 1978 and eventually to the World Cup itself.

Recently during World Cup 98 Maradona publicly apologised for what he had done against England in the game in the Azteca stadium. Apparently he would like to come to England and manage one of our Premier League clubs.

English defender Terry Fenwick was one of the players that Maradona dribbled past on the way to his 'other goal'. His great goal.

'I'm glad that a marvellous goal stood between the two teams at the end. It would be rotten to think that that little bastard cheated us out of it.'

But he had. As an Italian journalist observed at the time to his British colleague Brian Glanville when they discussed that 'other goal':

'England were still in a state of shock, like a man who's just had his wallet stolen.'

It was, as Glanville observed, an apt description 'for Maradona's first goal was an act of theft'.

After the game the England squad replayed the match as all losing teams do. Shilton pointed out to the others that England had had an excellent chance denied when a free kick was chipped to John Barnes who struck what looked a goal-bound shot when it hit the referee who had stationed himself at the end of the Argentinian wall. The Tunisian referee ran around to the England players saying, 'Sorry. Sorry.' One can only wonder how he felt in the summer of 1998 when they told him that Maradona had finally apologised for cheating against England in World Cup 86.

In the semi-finals Argentina faced the dark horses of the tournament, Belgium, who had only squeezed into the second round as one of the beneficiaries of the dubious best third-team rule. Grasping this lifeline, they had dramatically hit a rich seam against Russia, running out eventual winners 4–3. In the quarter-finals they had won their particular penalty shoot-out lottery against Spain and now stood waiting for Maradona and his men.

The other semi-final produced a match that many had feared from the outset: France v West Germany, or Shumacher v Battiston. Would Platini of France or Rummenigge of West Germany, both in the closing stages of their illustrious international careers, move to within touching distance of the trophy?

Schumacher, at the instigation of Beckenbauer, shook hands with Battiston before the kick-off. Ten minutes in it was the French goalkeeper who made a name for himself, and back in France it would not have been a particularly good one. Seeing a Brehme free kick late, he dived for the ball, which slid from his chest, under his body and into the net. The rest of the game was a story of France missing excellent opportunities to level the score. In the last minute and against the run of much of the play, West Germany got a second and yet again were through to a World Cup Final.

If the Falklands War had motivated Argentina against England, then the memory of how Belgium had kicked Maradona all over the pitch in Spain during World Cup 82 fulfilled that role in the semi-final.

In the first half Argentina finally got the ball into the net. Despite the massed Belgian defence Valdona, following Maradona's example, had punched the ball in. Different referee, different result. The 'goal' was disallowed.

In the second half, with the game crying out for a flash of brilliance to enliven a drab affair, the little man answered the call. Gliding into the penalty area six minutes into the second half, Maradona cut through two defenders and with the outside of his left foot hit the ball past Pfaff in the Belgian goal. Twelve minutes later – penned in just as in the past Pelé, Garrincha, Matthews, di Stefano and other players of genius had been penned in – Maradona did what only such players can. Just on the edge of the Belgian penalty box he swerved one way, surged another, dummied, swayed, and left four defenders for dead as he put the ball for the second time past Pfaff. Argentina 2, Belgium 0. Without the use of his hands Maradona, ably assisted by his colleagues, had put his country into their third World Cup Final.

Asked on the eve of the Final if he would be going to watch it, Michel Platini had responded:

'No, I won't be going. There will be nothing to learn from this match.'

West Germany had throughout the tournament sadly failed to excite the neutrals. Dogged resilience and stubborn rearguard actions are admirable, but defending in depth does need to be relieved with the occasional attack. To judge from his line-up, it would have been reasonable to conclude that the German manager Franz Beckenbauer was playing for the penalty shoot-out. His most versatile mid-field playmaker, Matthäus, had been delegated to mark Maradona. A triumph of negativity over creativity. It got its just response when twenty-two minutes into the first half Matthäus hacked Maradona to the ground. The resulting free kick by Burruchaga found José Luis Brown lurking by the far post and Argentina were one up. From a goalkeeping error made by Schumacher.

Ten minutes into the second half Schumacher hesitated as Valdano ran at him. Perhaps that dreadful clash with Battiston four years earlier had left its mark on the perpetrator as well. Valdano beat him with ease and Argentina were two up. Twenty-eight minutes into the second half and Rummenigge pulled one back. With eight minutes to go they were level. A header from Voeller. It underlined what has become a fact of life about the World Cup. Germany are not beaten until the final whistle is blown.

Maradona had been subdued throughout much of the game. Now with just five minutes left, he roused himself. A run, a shuffle, an exquisite delightful pass to Jorge Burruchaga and the game and the World Cup were Argentina's.

Over the Azteca stadium throughout the Final between Argentina and West Germany floated a huge yellow balloon advertising Camel cigarettes. Many criticised the image as setting a very bad example to our young.

Questioned about the implicit contradiction of football being used to sell cigarettes, President João Havelange appeared to be bemused. He had never smoked, what was the problem, and apart from that, 'I've got a twenty-four-team tournament to run. I need all the money I can get from every sponsor.'

Dassler must have enjoyed that, knowing as he did that he had scooped the pool.

Gross income for Mexico 86 was just over SF144 million – $96 million. Virtually one-third of that, $32 million, had come from the marketing and advertising. This was the figure that Dassler had paid for the privilege of controlling those rights. He had then sold them on to the Category One sponsors, primarily, Coca-Cola, Fuji Film, Gillette, Canon, Opel and the rest of the top twelve. His profit on the deal was SF200 million – $128 million dollars. Dassler's net profit was therefore greater by approximately one-third than the entire gross take for the tournament. It was money lost to football forever: $128 million.

It was a situation that would be repeated at regular intervals. Horst Dassler died of cancer on 10 April 1987, but ISL, the private company he created, is alive and well. It continues to benefit hugely from its intimate relationship with both Havelange and Sepp Blatter. Competitive tenders do not threaten this relationship. Competitive tenders are not seriously considered. Who gains from such a situation? Certainly not football.

When FIFA was founded in Paris in 1904 it had been about football and little else. It remained largely unchanged in its ethos under successive Presidents, two Frenchmen, a Belgian and three Englishmen, until a Brazilian occupied the throne in 1974. Within a few years its ethos began to change. Within a decade it had been totally transformed. It was no longer about football. It was about product, it was about sponsoring, advertising and marketing that product. It was about money. The game? That had been stolen. Like professional art thieves stealing a masterpiece, the original had been replaced by a clever copy. The fake fooled a great many people. It is to be devoutly hoped that Abraham Lincoln was right when he expressed his views on 'fooling the people'.

Part Three

They were still counting the takings in Mexico when in November 1986 the first press conference for Italia 90 took place. The Sun King was present, which ensured that the theme was not football, but marketing the product. There was interminable talk about the marketing contracts, the Category One sponsors, who was going to supply what. The President of Italy, Francesco Cossiga, like all politicians, knew well the value of hosting the World Cup. Never mind if the streets of Rome, Florence, Milan and every other major city were awash with narcotics. Ignore the Mafia. Forget P2. Dismiss inflation along with poverty and unemployment. Roberto Baggio and Gianlucca Vialli will win the World Cup for us.

Cossiga demonstrated that Havelange was not the only President who could talk telephone numbers. He announced that the twelve cities where the games would be played would have the sum of $5 billion spent on them. This was to upgrade stadiums, and the entire communication infrastructure. It was a fantasy figure that existed only in the minds of the Italian government but it made a great many people happy, at least until Italy got knocked out of the tournament.

Money would certainly have to be allocated to deal with a recurring problem: those who would come to Italy seeking off-pitch violence. The hooligans.

With a European-based tournament the problem of violent criminals causing havoc throughout the World Cup was that much greater than Mexico 86 and there a limited threat had caused the government to bring out the tanks when England played Argentina. This time FIFA and the Italians decided that the answer to the English criminals was to quarantine them during the opening round. Sardinia would play host to England. That just left the Dutch, the Germans, the Italians and the lunatics from the other countries to sort out.

Further evidence was forthcoming during the qualifying rounds that illegal behaviour was not confined to off-the-pitch activities. Nothing had changed it seemed in some countries since Rous and his FIFA officials had concerned themselves about dubious activities in Latin America.

Brazil v Chile, their first qualifying match, became two matches, one involving two teams of eleven players, the other involving two managers. Played in Santiago, the match was drawn 1–1, the contest between the two managers ended with the Chilean manager Orlando Aravena being removed by the police and the Brazilian manager Sebastio Lazaroni apparently going violently insane.

Before the second leg in Brazil's Maracaná stadium Rojas, the Chilean captain and goalkeeper, warned, 'At the first sign of trouble, we're coming off the field.'

With twenty minutes left Brazil were leading 1–0. Among the watching one hundred and fifty thousand spectators a flare suddenly went into orbit and dropped in front of the Chilean goal. A moment later and Rojas could be seen laid out on the ground. He was holding his head. He was carried off the pitch soaked in blood. The rest of his team came with him and refused to return. The game was abandoned.

A place in the World Cup Finals hung in the balance. FIFA launched an urgent investigation. Its conclusion was that Chile had attempted to cheat their way into the Finals. The injury to Rojas was self-inflicted. FIFA banned the Chilean captain for life. Concluding that what had occurred was not isolated to the single player, FIFA also handed out a life ban to the President of the Chilean Football Federation, Sergio Stoppel. The team doctor, the manager, the centre half, the kit man, the physiotherapist, all received bans of varying lengths. The Chilean Federation was also fined $60,000 and thrown out of the World Cup 94 tournament. FIFA described the entire affair as 'the most ignoble incident of attempted fraud in the history of FIFA'. That conclusion should be weighed against the various other 'ignoble incidents' recorded earlier.

The Mexicans also found themselves banned from Italia 90 when their youth team were caught using false passports during a qualifying round of the 1989 World Youth Championship. A number of the team, it transpired, were not youthful enough.

The dreaded opening game of World Cup 90 produced a sensational result. Nearly thirty years earlier Sir Stanley Rous had prophesied that an African nation would win the World Cup by the year 2000. At the end of the first match of the tournament that prediction began to look just possible. Cameroon had beaten the world champions Argentina complete with Maradona 1–0.

They had considerable skill, sadly it was outweighed by their capacity for violence. Three yellow cards and then two red. Astonishingly the nine men held out after scoring halfway through the second half, the extraordinary Roger Milla only getting on for Cameroon six minutes from the end. Their performance left many wondering just how far they could progress if their defence could curb its collective tendency to mug an opponent who even vaguely looked like taking an interest in the ball. In Omam Biyik, the scorer of the sole goal, they had a very useful striker, but their class act was undoubtedly Milla. At the time he was at least thirty-eight years of age, but informed opinion put him nearer his mid-forties. He would become the definitive super-sub of the competition.

Maradona had taken a terrible pounding from the Cameroon defence and another one from the crowd. Playing for Naples, he had twice been largely instrumental in his team winning the Italian championship, to the intense dismay of much of Italy, particularly the north. His sex life, his drug taking, his lack of discipline, all of which were accepted in Naples without comment, confirmed to the Milanese in particular what they had always 'known' about the Neapolitans. When shortly before the World Cup he had asked the people of Naples to cheer not for Italy but for Argentina, he lit a fire of resentment and hatred that, including a significant amount of racism, was to burn right to the end of the tournament.

This particular controversy threatened at times to dominate World Cup 90. Antonio Mataresse, President of the Italian Football Federation, went on television to make a public appeal to the citizens of Naples to prove that their team was the *azzuri*: the national team. Polls were conducted by a number of radio stations and newspapers to establish just how patriotic the people of Naples were.

Responding directly to Mataresse's remarks, Maradona was defiant. He addressed the following remarks directly to the people of Naples:

'For three hundred and sixty-four days of the year you are considered by the rest of this country to be foreigners, in your own country; today you must do what they want by supporting the Italian team. I, on the other hand, am a Neapolitan for three hundred and sixty-five days of the year.'

Trouble looked like it was going to follow the diminutive Argentinian wherever he went. In his country's next game against the USSR the Argentinian goalkeeper Pumpido was stretchered off after only ten minutes. The Soviets eagerly poured forward to put his replacement Sergio Goycochea under pressure. Winning a corner the ball was swung over and Oleg Kuznetsov rose majestically and headed the ball. It was speeding into the net when Maradona appeared and with his right hand punched the ball down to his feet. The referee Erik Fredricksson was standing just a few yards away, perfectly placed. He continued to stand and stare as Maradona cleared the ball. Argentina went on to win 2–0.

After the game the Brazil manager Lazaroni who had been watching the game said:

'What a versatile player Maradona is. He can score goals with his left hand and save them with his right'.

Drawing their final first-round game against Romania 1–1 the world champions scraped into the second round.

The fact that Lazaroni could still see the funny side of life was remarkable in view of the mood that prevailed inside the Brazilian training camp at Asti.

The money bug had caught the Brazilians, who were disgruntled with everyone, including each other. Dunga, the small, rock-hard defender, thought he should be running the show. Careca, a forward, thought he was the obvious person to be captain of the ship. The hotel manager was disenchanted with the entire squad and talked to the media of unpaid bar bills. The squad's sponsor Asti 90 was equally peeved with the entire team, who had been paid handsomely for services that were not being rendered. Lazaroni had gone into the qualifying matches playing a sweeper, Mauro Calvao, who was to be Brazil's Franz Beckenbauer, circa 1990. It was a European concept that many both in and out of the team objected to. The manager had persevered with the concept and his critics had persevered with their objections.

Nine of Brazil's automatic first team earned their living

playing in Europe. This was a cause of deep conflict between the nine and the Brazilian media who regarded the nine as virtual foreigners. The press took a chauvinistic position with regard to the exiles. 'How can these men understand Brazil? They've forgotten what it's like to be Brazilian. They don't understand either us or our game. We play the game to the rhythm of the samba, not some Teutonic march.'

When the Brazilians won their first game against Sweden 2–1, the critics were not over-impressed. When Brazil could only beat tiny Costa Rica 1–0, it was open season again for the Brazilian reporters. To judge from their comments one would think that their team had lost to Costa Rica. They wanted to see *jogo bonito* – the beautiful game. Dunga was defiant. 'There will be no more *jogo bonito*. This is the Brazil of sweat and sacrifice.'

Pelé's riposte was a succinct one-liner.

'As soon as we play a good team we'll lose.'

Scotland, Brazil's next opponents, failed to come into that category and were dispatched 1–0, yet again making a sad early first-round departure from the World Cup, their one victory against Sweden having been nullified by a defeat at the hands of Costa Rica.

England, the latterday Napoleons, having been exiled to Sardinia, showed less than impressive form during the first-round matches. Managing only one win and that by a bare goal against rank outsiders Egypt, after drawing with Holland and again with Ireland they, and Ireland, went into the second round. Neither team had made many friends among the neutrals. One Italian review of the England–Ireland 1–1 draw was headlined: 'NO FOOTBALL, PLEASE, WE'RE BRITISH'.

Indeed the long-ball game that Ireland's manager Jack Charlton had decreed showed a total contempt for paying spectators. Charlton was heard to observe, 'We could win the World Cup without scoring a goal in open play.'

Cameroon was the name on most lips when the first-round matches were complete. In their second match, against Romania, Roger Milla made what was to become his customary late appearance. This time fifty-eight minutes into the game. Twenty minutes later he became the oldest player ever to score in a World Cup game. Three minutes from the end Milla got a second. Though Romania pulled one back, it was too little, too late. A famous victory to Cameroon 2–1.

This was the cue for pundits to tell the rest of us the secret of Milla's success. It was his diet. It was his lifestyle. It was the fact that he came from an *inland* part of West Africa. It was because he had the powerful muscles associated with living on the West *Coast* of Africa. Obviously if he moved about at that kind of speed as a baby it was hardly surprising that he had developed powerful muscles.

The hooligans had not been inactive during the first-round matches. The German thugs had opened proceedings, but the main action was very predictably between the English and the Dutch. The Italians put four thousand police into the stadium and a further two thousand in the streets of Cagliari. Heads were cracked by the police, and vitriol splashed by those sections of the press who never miss an opportunity to condemn all English supporters. Hands were wrung by Conservative ministers who neither knew nor cared about the game. It is a curious paradox that so many of the mindless were Thatcher's children. They adored a prime minister who had nothing but contempt for the game of football.

The Italians after their final round-one game against Czechoslovakia finally had something to really get excited about. An injury to Gianlucca Vialli had forced the Italian manager to pair Roberto Baggio and Schillaci for the first time. The result was an effervescent display, both men scored and the country was alight.

In the second round the Italians turned over Uruguay 2–0, Schillaci again on the score sheet, this time accompanied by Serena. That intolerable pressure that is such a constant factor for an Italian World Cup team was beginning to reassert itself. They were the host nation. This was to be their year. It all had an ominously familiar ring about it.

Ireland went through to the quarter-finals, still without scoring a goal in open play. They won the penalty shoot-out against Romania 5–4. Pelé once famously remarked that to score from a penalty was a cowardly way to score a goal and that was said before the obscenity of penalty shoot-outs was introduced.

Cameroon had no need of such dubious means to resolve their second-round match against Colombia. Yet again it was that man Milla coming on early in the second half of a free-flowing end-to-end game. There were a host of near-misses, but no goals after ninety minutes. In extra-time the oldest man on the pitch yet again demonstrated an extraordinary turn of speed. Taking a cleverly angled pass from fellow striker Biyik, he went past Perea as if he wasn't there, hurdled over Escobar and struck the ball with his left foot well wide of goalkeeper Higuita.

The Colombian goalkeeper was well known for his forays up the pitch. Seeking an equaliser, he set off from his goal and some forty yards out had the misfortune to meet Milla. He attempted to dribble around him and lost the ball. Milla set off and moments later the ball was in the back of the net. Valderrama, blond dreadlocks flying, set up Redin for a goal, but it was too late to find another. The under-dogs were through to the quarter-finals.

Higuita, the Colombian goalkeeper, appeared at the post-match press conference.

'I have asked my team-mates to forgive me. It has never happened to me before, but it was a mistake that a lot of people were waiting for. Well, you all saw it, it was as big as a house.'

'As soon as we play a good team we'll lose,' Pelé had predicted. Argentina were a good team. Good enough to put a Brazil team who had been trained to play in an alien European way out of the World Cup.

It was the first time in four matches that their neighbours to the south had triumphed. Defeat came after a flash of brilliance from – who else? – Maradona.

Maradona fought on two fronts throughout this World Cup. The first battle against Italy continued to take place off the pitch. The second against a variety of players whose one intent was to maim him. It was remarkable after the treatment that had been dished out, particularly by Cameroon, that Maradona was still standing. By the time Argentina played Brazil Maradona's legs and thighs were covered in bruises and his left ankle had been kicked so frequently that it was permanently swollen, yet still his manager Carlos Bilardo persisted in playing Maradona in a central striking role. Eight years earlier Menotti had exposed his star to that gambit during the World Cup in Spain. The result was Gentile kicking the little Argentinian again and again, until he kicked him right out of the World Cup. Whatever he lacked with regard to ethics and to honesty, Maradona never lacked for courage; he accepted the high-risk role that left him terribly exposed. Why common-sense did not prevail and dictate that Maradona play deeper with some protection around him, play from a position where he could use his devastating acceleration to suddenly run at defences, is a mystery.

Against Brazil he was reduced by his injuries to playing much of the game at little more than walking pace. Eight minutes from the end with extra time and a penalty shoot-out looming, Maradona went for broke. His adrenalin rush masking the pain, he accelerated into the heart of the

Brazilian defence. Ran at them. Almost hypnotised by his mazy run, four defenders converged on him, inevitably leaving men unmarked. With the sweetest timing, Maradona threaded the ball through the defence to the unmarked Caniggia who, drifting across the face of the goal, swivelled to put the ball past Taffarel, the Brazilian goalkeeper.

Brazil were not content to have been beaten by a piece of exquisite play. To excuse his own part in the goal, the Brazilian left-back Branco accused the Argentinian bench of handing him a bottle of drugged water. A pathetic excuse from a pathetic Brazil. One banner in the crowd had very adequately summed up what was wrong and who was responsible.

'IF LAZARONI IS A COACH, I'M THE POPE.'

It was a view widely shared both in and out of Brazil. When the squad returned home Lazaroni was dismissed.

Shortly before World Cup 90, I happened to be doing some last-minute shopping at Heathrow before catching a flight. Into the shop came the England manager Bobby Robson. He began to examine a wide selection of ties, then selecting one, moved towards the counter. Halfway there he changed his mind and went back to the tie rack. I watched with increasing fascination as the man, who more than any other held England's chances in World Cup 90 in his hands, agonised. Back and forth he went, twice, three times. He caught me looking at him and grinned sheepishly. 'I have such a problem making my mind up about ties,' he self-evidently said. He had equal difficulty when it came to choosing a team.

He'd had problems selecting Glenn Hoddle for the 1986 World Cup; he'd had a problem letting go of a palpably unfit Bryan Robson and had lied to the press about the extent of his namesake's shoulder injury; he'd had problems with a team revolt in the middle of Mexico 86. Gary

Lineker had ended the tournament as top scorer with six goals, but there was precious little else to celebrate, apart from a string of outstanding performances by Peter Shilton in goal. For far too many seasons, Shilton's wonderful ability masked fatal flaws from some of those in front of him. Peter Beardsley, who, when Robson eventually picked him, shone like a beacon in the night, was another who suffered from his manager's indecision; John Barnes was yet another. If Barnes had started the game against Argentina in Mexico 86 many believed England would have won, hand of God notwithstanding.

Getting to Italy 90 was for England, yet again, largely due to the fact that we had the world's best goalkeeper. The final qualifying match had virtually been Poland v Shilton. England were not a happy squad in Italy. Bobby Robson's private life had been splashed across the tabloids. An enlightened attitude about extra-marital affairs had yet to percolate into the offices of the Football Association. Robson had been told that it would not matter if he came back clutching the World Cup, his contract would not be renewed. In view of the fact that he was the manager of England's football team, the connection between his private life and his public duties was not readily apparent, but then the Football Association – like much of England – are preoccupied rather than occupied with sex.

So England's squad with a disgruntled manager at the helm had settled into their exile in Cagliari with a certain attitude problem. Taking their cue from Robson they treated the press reporters as 'the enemy'. In their midst was yet another player who like so many before him had inspired in his manager chronic indecision: Paul Gascoigne – Gazza. Like all flair players that have emerged in England since the Second World War, Gazza worried his manager. He worried Robson just as Greaves had worried Ramsey; just as Matthews had worried Winterbottom; just as

Michael Owen worried Hoddle and, ironically, Hoddle had worried Bobby Robson.

Gazza had forced his way into Robson's squad after a breathtaking performance against Czechoslovakia when he made three goals and scored the fourth. A bit difficult to ignore after that.

England's second-round opponents were Belgium, usually dour, always difficult to beat. Inevitably the Belgian defence proved obdurate. Barnes had what seemed a good goal disallowed, Lineker went close. In extra-time a wonderfully flighted free kick from Gascoigne's right foot was met by a flying David Platt, who volleyed the ball into the net for the only goal. England were into the quarter-finals: waiting for them the shock success story of the tournament – Cameroon.

Italy won their quarter-final match against Ireland with a goal yet again from the irrepressible Schillaci, a simple tap-in after goalkeeper Bonner had failed to hold the ball.

With West Germany scraping through their quarter-final against Czechoslovakia with a goal scored from the penalty spot and Argentina doing the same – in their case winning the penalty shoot-out – there was a chronic shortage of goals in the quarter-finals. The England v Cameroon game was about to remedy that problem.

Cameroon were forced to rearrange their defence drastically. They had four players suspended from earlier matches. Inevitably they yet again began without Roger Milla. Platt opened the scoring with a header from a left-wing cross by Stuart Pearce. In the second half with Milla now on England should have had a second when Platt was blatantly brought down in the penalty box. The Mexican referee thought otherwise and waved play on. When Gascoigne brought Milla down in England's penalty area two minutes later the referee had no hesitation in awarding a penalty. Kunde narrowly beat Shilton from the spot.

Three minutes later Cameroon went ahead when Milla put his countryman Ekeke through. A famous victory, or conversely, a notorious defeat, looked on the cards.

Manager Robson pulled Terry Butcher off and put Trevor Steven on. With eight minutes remaining England snatched an equaliser. This time appeals for a penalty when Lineker was brought down in the box were heeded and taking the kick himself, Lineker scored. Defender Mark Wright emerged from a clash with Milla with blood pouring down his face from a gash above his right eye. England went into extra-time with ten fit men. Fifteen minutes into extra-time and a defence-splitting pass from Gascoigne found Lineker; turning to shoot, he was brought down again in the penalty box. Again he converted from the spot. The notorious defeat had been avoided. England went into the semi-finals. There they met West Germany.

The further they went in this tournament the better England had played, but only fitfully. It seemed that manager Robson's dithering about team selection affected the entire team. On a practical level, the best eleven so rarely played together. Psychologically it was clearly unsettling the players. For the second World Cup running the manager faced an English-style dressing room rebellion as senior players quietly but firmly questioned tactics.

The day after defeating Cameroon manager Robson observed, 'A flat back four saved us.' It had indeed, which of course almost certainly would mean another change of tactics for the semi-final. Looking towards the next match, the England manager said:

'We've got here, but I don't know how.'

The other semi-final match promised extraordinary drama. Italy the hosts v Argentina the cup-holders. Add Maradona and do not wait for it to boil.

The venue? Naples.

Again there were pleas from Maradona for the city to

support Argentina. Again he was denounced. The only one who did not get in on the act was a former goalkeeper now residing inside the Vatican.

Vicini, the Italian manager, demonstrated that uncertainty was not confined to the English manager. He dropped Baggio and brought back Vialli. After seventeen minutes a thundering shot from Vialli was too hot for the Argentinian goalkeeper Goycochea to hold. Schillaci, like all great goal poachers, was on hand again. Italy 1, Argentina 0.

The Italians had already earned $120,000 per man for reaching the semi-finals. Another $40,000 was theirs if they won this one. Midway through the second half Maradona switched play to the left flank and sent Olarticoechea roaring down the wing. The cross was met by Caniggia and the score was level. No more goals in the game, not even after extra-time, meant that a football game was finished and a lottery commenced. The penalty shoot-out was won by Argentina and a nation mourned before turning their sorrow into anger. Whoever won the other semi-final was going to have the entire Italian nation cheering for them against Argentina.

England dominated the first half of their game against West Germany with Paul Gascoigne outstanding. He totally outplayed his opposite number Lothar Matthäus. After sixty minutes and against the run of play, West Germany went in front from a freak goal – a German free kick hitting English defender Paul Parker's foot, the ball rose over Shilton's head and into the net. With ten minutes left Lineker took advantage of confusion in the German ranks and stole in to equalise. In extra-time Gascoigne and Thomas Berthold chased a ball that was going out of play. They tangled and the referee gave Gascoigne a yellow card. The realisation that he would miss the Final if England won hit Gascoigne forcibly. He had received a yellow card in an earlier game. Two yellow cards and the player automatically missed the next match. *The* match. Tears welled up in the distraught player's eyes and rolled down his cheeks. Lineker saw what was happening and mimed to the bench Gascoigne's distress. These moments, captured on television, went around the world. They exemplified the passion that so many players and spectators alike feel for this game. His tears touched millions, just as his talent before and since the incident has touched millions.

Extra-time finished without further score. Again the circus was back in town. Again FIFA Incorporated's edict that 'the product' must have a showbusiness end prevailed. Stuart Pearce and Chris Waddle failed to convert and West Germany were through to face Argentina in the Final.

The Final was a dreadful, negative affair having as much to do with football as penalty shoot-outs. Argentina had four players unable to take part because of suspensions. A further two were sent off during the game. Maradona was booed continuously by the majority of the spectators. The only goal came from a highly dubious penalty given to West Germany. At the end of the game Maradona's tear-stained face appeared on the large screens around the ground and the spectators screamed with delight. As for Maradona, he refused to shake the hand of Havelange when he took his loser's medal.

'This is a plot by FIFA. We have been punished for beating Italy, which was the team FIFA desired to win this World Cup. There is a Mafia in the soccer world. That penalty did not exist. It was awarded to let the Germans win.'

Sometimes, Diego, what goes around, comes around.

It was generally considered to have been the worst Final match in the history of the tournament, but then it had climaxed a truly dreadful tournament. The quality of the play had been at an all-time low. The number of goals was at an all-time low, an average of just two per game. The footballing public were paying in every sense of the word a high price for Havelange's election promises. The grossly inflated tournament simply did not work. Too many games produced not an excess of goals, but injuries. The corporate sponsors were naturally delighted. More games, more commercial slots. More inertia and boredom. What the hell? The gross take was at an all-time high, SF226,250,000. Havelange and ISL and Blatter must be doing something right, surely? Surely?

Former Secretary of State Henry Kissinger has never been a man to be easily dissuaded from an objective. If a week in politics is, as we are constantly being told, a long time, then an imperious rejection of an application from the United States in May 1983 was a world away long before Mexico 86. Off-the-record meetings took place between USA Federation officials and members of FIFA's Executive Committee. Everyone agreed that the United States should not be subjected to the embarrassment of another public refusal. That was stage one. Stage two – again off the record – was confirmation to the American Football Association that if they applied for World Cup 94 they would get it.

On 15 April 1987 the United States Federation confirmed its candidacy to FIFA, that it wished to host World Cup 94. Other candidates who declared their desire to host that tournament were Brazil, Chile and Morocco. Chile dropped by the wayside. Morocco had a King who was unpunctual. Brazil did not yet have Havelange's choice in place as President of CBF. On 4 July 1988 FIFA announced the United States as host country for World Cup 1994.

The FIFA custom, that every four years immediately before the current World Cup tournament João Havelange was re-elected unopposed, was seriously questioned for the first time after an event that occurred in December 1993. Pelé was banned from the podium during the draw for World Cup 94. Banned by João Havelange.

This action and the background leading up to it convinced many FIFA delegates that the time had come to remove a man who was being increasingly described by fellow FIFA members as 'the dictator'.

During an interview earlier in 1993 Pelé had stated that a member of CBF had asked for a $1 million bribe to ensure that Pelé's application for the broadcasting rights for the 1994 Brazilian championship went to his company. He refused to pay and the contract went to a competitor.

Ricardo Teixeira, Havelange's son-in-law, decided that as he was the President of the CBF, the allegation referred to him. In itself a curious piece of reasoning as Pelé had not identified the individual, Teixeira brought an action against Pelé alleging slander. This was the background to the President of FIFA banning not only the most famous footballer in the world but the one footballer that millions of Americans knew.

When Pelé's career at Santos finished in 1974, he had joined Cosmos in New York. He was well paid for playing for them, but the key to his move had been the fact that the Americans had persuaded him that if he and other players of international stature came to the United States, then football might finally conquer the one major nation in the world that had yet to truly take the game to its heart.

Between 1974 and his second and final retirement in October 1977, Pelé by his talents, his humility, his charm, did more positive good for the game within the United States than anyone before or since. An indication of the very deep affection in which he was held in America can be gauged from the various events surrounding that final game for New York Cosmos in 1977.

Seventy-eight thousand, seven hundred fans, many of

whom had bought tickets at least six months earlier, watched his final game. This man had only two clubs throughout his entire career. Santos and Cosmos. For his final match they played each other, Pelé playing the first half for Cosmos and the second for Santos.

Former Brazilian team manager João Saldanha was not a man whom Pelé would number among his closest friends. On this night Saldanha said:

'Pelé is to Brazilian football what Shakespeare is to English literature.'

In the dressing room after the game Muhammad Ali, at thirty-five just one year younger than Pelé and still fighting, stood crying with emotion. He hugged Pelé and said, 'My friend. My friend. Now there are two of the greatest.'

Sports columns that week were full of praise for Pelé, describing him as a 'football missionary and gentle courtier of the sport'. They wrote, 'This one man has given the game of football credence in our country.'

The language that Havelange used when he defended his action served merely to compound his dictatorial arrogance.

'I have given every attention and kindness to this lad. But playing soccer is one thing, being a businessman is another. This lad shouldn't have done what he did. Ricardo is married to my only daughter. He's the father of my grandchildren. Whatever he needs, I will do for him.

'When I was a boy my father used to slap me if I was disrespectful. That is what I have done metaphorically to Pelé. He must learn to show respect. I launched Pelé in the national team when he was only seventeen.'

Asked for his reaction, Pelé said:

'Havelange has been my idol since the 1958 World Cup, and because he's the boss of FIFA, he can say who comes in and who stays out. But his son-in-law is President of the Brazilian Federation and I will not serve corruption.'

At seventy-eight years of age, it seemed to close observers

that the President's mind was going. A few months after causing universal offence and outrage by his exclusion of Pelé, Havelange attended a FIFA reception in New York and repeatedly called the female governor of New Jersey 'sir'. It was noticeable that aides moved him around at receptions as if he was a tailor's dummy on wheels.

The European element of FIFA were particularly exercised. They had long ago concluded that Havelange was a liability. The problem was finding a candidate strong enough to mount a serious challenge. The name of the Italian Federation President emerged from the pack in early March 1994. For a while Antonio Matarresse seemed to have the support of the Europeans, then his name melted away as rapidly as it had surfaced. Lennart Johansson of Sweden was talked of, then the name of Sepp Blatter was mentioned with increasing frequency.

Blatter, though he would subsequently deny it, was more than up for the challenge. Better than any he knew just how much damage Havelange was doing to the image of international football. Blatter was also very well positioned to have an informed view of how valid were the allegations of corruption concerning the Brazilian Federation. Issa Hayatou, President of the African Confederation, was another who had excellent credentials and was tipped as a likely runner.

A number of problems faced any potential candidate. Havelange had beaten Stanley Rous after a long, expensive campaign and that was before the matter of delegates' air fares, hotel bills and white envelopes was addressed. Courtesy of Nally and Dassler, Havelange had delivered on his election promises. Even mainland China was now in the FIFA fold. The World Cup had been enlarged to the delight of a number of very mediocre footballing nations but, more importantly, to the intense joy of the corporate sponsors who equalled more teams with more markets. A string of youth tournaments, indoor football competitions, women's football tournaments, had been initiated. The game was awash with money. Who could want for more than all this?

Apart from these practical considerations there was another that profoundly inhibited many of the delegates as they considered their options. Fear. Many were genuinely frightened of Havelange. Frightened of his power. Frightened of his wrath. Frightened of what reprisals he would indulge in if the attempt failed and the Sun King emerged from the Chicago vote still safely ensconced on his throne.

Havelange has over the years been called The Godfather on a number of occasions and indeed there has been about his reign over football a brooding malevolence. Like a Mafia leader he has demanded total loyalty and absolute obedience. Consultation with colleagues. Consideration of another's point of view. Mature reflection leading to the admittance that perhaps he has been in error. None of these has featured significantly during the Sun King's reign from his Zurich and Rio palaces.

In the early months of 1994 the view from the smoke-filled delegates' rooms, at UEFA and at AFC and CAF, the Asian and African confederations, were confused. Blatter talked to the UEFA delegates. He attempted to persuade them to back his candidacy. Lennart Johansson, the President of the European Confederation, and his fellow committee members have never liked Blatter, more to the point they have never trusted him. He is seen by them, and indeed by most FIFA members, as Havelange's creation. Time would ultimately prove that this was not a liability. In early 1994 it most certainly was a handicap to Blatter's presidential ambitions.

During a UEFA Executive Committee meeting in Holland Sepp Blatter stunned Lennart Johansson and his colleagues with one particular proposal. He was attending the meeting in his capacity as General Secretary of FIFA.

'I believe the time has come to get rid of Havelange. If you are prepared to nominate me I believe that with UEFA's support I can beat him this June.'

The European position was summed up by Ellert Schram, at that time Icelandic member of UEFA's Executive Committee, subsequently President of the Icelandic Sports League:

'We shouldn't be discussing the deposing of Havelange, but rather the deposing of his disloyal General Secretary.'

Without UEFA's fifty-one votes Blatter would struggle to acquire an absolute majority. One of the gambits he attempted to play to create a favourable climate was to try to persuade FIFA's Press Officer, Guido Tognoni, to plant a series of stories in the news media that would show the President's failings. Tognoni declined on the grounds that such actions would be disloyal to Havelange.

One aspect in particular inhibited pretenders to the throne. Havelange was not going to go quietly. Aware that he was threatened, he pulled every trick in the book. Some, like calling in a wide variety of favours owed by voting delegates, were done quietly, privately. Then there were the 'financial inducements' to delegates to ensure that the status quo would continue after June. Then there were the public pronouncements. A pyrotechnic display from the Sun King. Defiance, threats, boasts and reminders that with him sitting on the throne FIFA had not only the Sun King but Superman.

'I get up at six in Rio. I work all day at my various companies. I get home. I have a bath. I pick up a suitcase, go to the airport. I do not sleep on the plane – that is the time for working and reading – and when I arrive in Zurich at ten the following morning I go straight to the FIFA offices. There I work until seven. Usually there is a dinner party afterwards. And then eventually I get to bed. I am never tired or irritated. I am never arrogant.'

Having in his own humble way described his average forty-five-hour day, the Sun King turned his basilisk look in the direction of his main rival.

'Mr Blatter came to FIFA in 1975. I gave him responsibility, and promoted him to his current post. And he did an outstanding job.'

It was beginning to sound like an obituary.

'But in the last few months there have been certain manoeuvrings aimed at having Mr Blatter become President of FIFA. I should have been informed. Things should not have been done behind my back.'

It was a wonderfully veiled reminder to Sepp Blatter of the fate of his predecessor Dr Helmut Käser.

As the Chicago election in June grew ever close, Havelange upped the ante.

'As everyone knows, it has been our custom at the end of each World Cup to have a match between the winners and a team from the rest of the world, with the receipts in dollars, usually of about one million, going to UNICEF. I feel we should build on this concept by asking the great companies of America, Japan and Europe to join us in starting a foundation so the problems of youth can be addressed. If each company would contribute a quarter of a million dollars, I believe we could raise for a start twenty million dollars. It could then be deposited in the three main Swiss banks in Zurich, and the interest be sent to the children in Asia, in Africa to make them grow in the world of football.'

He also called for Saudi Arabia to join this scheme and then concluded with information to gladden the hearts of his opponents.

'This then is my mission – and in 1998 I shall say farewell and go back to my country.'

What many both inside and outside FIFA wanted to know was who Havelange had in mind for his successor if he did indeed bow out in 1998. The over-riding fear, even among many of his friends, was that he was grooming his son-in-law Ricardo Teixeira to take over from him. Deprived of a son of his own, was football's Godfather preparing the ground for Teixeira? There is no doubt in my mind that this was very much what the Sun King desired, and if it became a reality based on his son-in-law's performance as President of Brazilian football, unmitigated disaster would hit FIFA and the organisation would collapse.

Havelange had remained defiant with regard to his banishment of Pelé from the World Cup 94 draw, though the issue did enormous damage not to Pelé's standing, but to Havelange's. In the eyes of the press and the general public it was apparent long before the election that no one was prepared to take him on except Blatter. Without at least one Confederation supporting him, Blatter's cause was lost before the fight had even begun.

Sepp Blatter tiptoed from the field of battle with his powder still dry, devoutly hoping that he would be able to convince 'The Old Man' that it was all just media talk.

By the first week of April it was all over bar the general acclamation of joy that Havelange was going to give FIFA 'four more years'. UEFA had stated that as long as Havelange stood he would not be opposed by a UEFA candidate. The European Federation had just over fifty votes, more than a third of the then electorate. All further talk of rebellion evaporated. It was exactly at this time that Havelange received some alarming news from Rio.

The President's network of contacts in Brazil reaches from the highest to the lowest. It is my understanding that the information Havelange received came from the Brazilian Secret Service. Castor de Andrade's home had been raided at the instigation of Judge Denis Frossard. The problem of precisely who was going to carry out the raid must have severely vexed the judge. All of Rio's senior police officers were on the payroll of de Andrade, described as 'top organiser of Rio's Mafia', as were a great many of Brazil's great and good including President João Havelange.

The web of corruption that surrounded de Andrade touched every single element of power in the country.

The illegal gambling that de Andrade and the other syndicate heads control has, by official estimates, an annual turnover of $1.3 billion and employs over fifty thousand people in Rio alone.

What also came to light, simultaneously, was an extraordinary letter written by Havelange on 2 October 1987. It was in essence a character reference for his good devoted friend de Andrade. Since its writing, de Andrade had used it continuously every time criminal proceedings had been brought against him. In view of the fact that indisputably de Andrade had close links with organised crime, including the Cali Cartel, and that these links were over many decades, some of Havelange's comments have an almost surreal ring about them.

'... I know that he is a pious Catholic and has shown his faith in acts of devotion to Our Lady of Aparecida ... Castor de Andrade is a sportsman. I am President of the International Federation of Football Associations (FIFA) and Castor is an outstanding promoter of this sport in Rio de Janeiro where he is patron of Bangu Atletico Clube. For his distinguished contributions, Castor has received decorations from Football Federations of the States of Rio de Janeiro and Minas Gerais.

'Due to his dedication and skills, Castor de Andrade was in charge of Brazilian national teams which succeeded in foreign fields, such as in the O'Higgins Cup in 1966, in Chile, and the Rio Branco Cup in 1967 in Uruguay.

'I'd like to leave record here that Castor de Andrade is respected and admired by his friends for his fine education. I also know that he provides relevant and abnegate services to many charities that protect abandoned children and assists the handicapped in Bangu.

'Castor de Andrade, a controversial man with a strong personality, is an amiable and pleasant creature, who can make friends due to a predominant feature in his character: loyalty ... Castor de Andrade is a good family man, a devoted friend and is admired as sports administrator and director of an escola de samba, in addition to being an abnegate protector of the elderly and children in need.

'Those who attack him perhaps ignore these positive traits of his personality. I authorise Castor de Andrade to use this statement as he deems appropriate.'

A copy of this was also found among the lists of those that de Andrade had bribed and corrupted. Against Havelange's name was written '$17,640. Box at the Sambodromo.' A reference to Havelange's VIP seating arrangements to view that Rio Carnival.

When Havelange received news that this scandal was about to break he was in Madrid. He immediately issued a press statement. Not about his relationship of thirty years' standing with a senior member of Brazil's organised crime, but about an astonishing change to the composition of the World Cup. It had been the view of an increasing number of observers that increasing the number of finalists from sixteen to twenty-four simply was not working. Excessive injuries, public boredom with an elongated tournament. An inevitable reduction in the quality of football. These had been just some of the objections raised. Now Havelange announced that he proposed that from France 98 the number of finalists should be increased yet again. From twenty-four to thirty-two. If re-elected that June, Havelange's proposal was that there would be eight groups of four teams per group in the Finals with two qualifiers from each group going forward to the knock-out stage. Eight cities would be used and the competition would still be contained in one month.

The proposals, with just one slight adjustment – ten cities instead of eight – were accepted. The timing of the announcement would quite coincidentally ensure that the media focused not on a scandal in Brazil but on a World Cup in France 98. Those who have enjoyed the surfeit of football – sixty-four games in one month – during the summer of 1998 might well wish to offer a thank-you to one of Brazil's leading criminals for over thirty years. The late Castor de Andrade.

At the forty-ninth FIFA Congress in Chicago on 16 June 1994, João Havelange was re-elected unopposed for a further four years as President of FIFA.

One of the individuals watching Havelange's re-election was the Chairman, President and Chief Executive Officer of the American World Cup Organizing Committee, Alan I. Rothenburg. He was working without taking any salary. He had rejected taking a regular wage on the understanding that he would 'eventually be compensated as deemed fair'. It strikes a chord with President Havelange's 'I take no salary, just enough expenses to get by on' philosophy. The end product was quite similar too.

When World Cup 94 in the United States was all over and the profits were all counted up, it was announced in October 1994 that Rothenberg was being rewarded with a $3 million bonus. The press release that informed the media of this fact neglected to say that Rothenberg would also be getting a salary of $4 million. This the World Cup Committee said came from a five-year contract at $800,000 a year. In view of the fact that Rothenberg's contract had begun in November 1991 this meant that he would continue to draw $800,000 a year until 1996, two years after the World Cup had finished. Ten thousand unpaid volunteers who had worked night and day to make the event a success were not asked either individually or collectively for an opinion on Alan I. Rothenberg.

The path to World Cup 94 in the USA, as has already been noted, was not a smooth one. Little more than a year after the Havelange-dominated Executive Committee had said yes to the bid, they were bitterly regretting their decision. FIFA, the most market-forces-led sports organisation in the world, was confronted with the country who during the twentieth century had perfected the concept of market forces.

First major cause of dissension was the marketing rights. The President of the United States Federation, Werner Fricker, believed his organisation controlled them. Havelange read him the law according to ISL. Fricker huffed and puffed and stood firm. Havelange threatened to take World Cup 94 away from the United States and Fricker stopped huffing and puffing.

Second cause of dissension was the TV rights in the United States. Fricker worked out what he considered to be an excellent deal with NBC to televise the event. The problem was that the other networks who had been excluded did not consider it an excellent deal. Neither did FIFA.

Havelange knew how to deal with a recurring problem. Get rid of the problem. FIFA were legally bound to deal with USSF, the United States Federation, but that did not mean you could not change their President. Elections for the USSF presidency were due to be held. Just two weeks before the elections FIFA executives persuaded Los Angeles lawyer Rothenberg to run against Fricker. Rothenberg was reluctant. With just two weeks to canvass support how on earth could he possibly beat the man who had put together the successful United States application for the World

Cup? The answer had only one word to it. Havelange. Ensuring that his men won elections in the world of football politics was what the President did. That more than anything else is what he had been doing for decades.

FIFA began to promote Rothenberg. It championed his cause so blatantly that the voting delegates were all fully aware that if they had the temerity to vote their President back in, then FIFA would take the World Cup away from the United States. It did not matter that Havelange was not empowered to make such a threat. It had never mattered in the past when he failed to consult his Executive Committee, why should it matter on this occasion?

On the morning of the election Guido Tognoni, FIFA's Press Officer, telephoned from Zurich to the USSF Treasurer, Paul Stiehl, who was also running against the incumbent Fricker. Havelange was concerned that the vote against Fricker might be fatally split. Tognoni asked him to withdraw. Stiehl expressed astonishment at the FIFA interference and refused to oblige the Sun King. Rothenberg won.

That World Cup 94 would be a resounding financial success was an easy prediction to make. When it comes to marketing a sporting event, particularly one that has major United States corporate backing, commercial success is relatively assured. As FIFA's primary aim under João Havelange has been to make the maximum amount of money regardless of virtually any other consideration, then World Cup 94 must be judged a stunning success.

If, however, the object of the exercise is to lay before the public, both in the stadium and the wider public watching around the world on television, a tournament that constantly thrills and excites and builds to a Final that lives on in the memory, then World Cup 94 was a stunning failure.

If the World Cup Organizing Committee had devoted

the same amount of energy to actually promoting the game that they gave to marketing 'the product' then there would have been long-term benefits to the growth of football in the United States. Instead golden opportunities to convince cynical news media were wasted.

With Rothenberg safely installed courtesy of Havelange's threat, a major news conference was called in New York during December 1990. In theory it was to mark the official launch of World Cup USA 94. In practice it became a news conference without a focal point. No football personalities. No content that related to the game. Instead there was a wealth of information about money, sponsors and historic marketing agreements. Just another day on Wall Street.

On the eve of the tournament, *USA Today* published the results of a Harris opinion poll on the event. According to Harris only 25 per cent of all American adults knew the World Cup was about to be held in their country. When the others were told what was about to begin, only 15 per cent said they were likely to watch any of the games. The poll bore no relation to the attendances at the games, nor to the viewing figures that would be attained.

On 17 June at Soldier's Field, Chicago, the opening game between holders Germany and Bolivia was watched in stifling heat by a capacity crowd that included President Clinton and a fully suited President Havelange.

Shortly before the tournament had begun FIFA announced that a new rule ratified in the previous March by the International Board would apply for the World Cup. Any tackle from behind would be a red-card offence.

João Havelange announced, 'Any referee who doesn't show a red card for a tackle from behind will be going home on the first plane the following day.'

The referee for the opening game was the Mexican Arturo Brizio Carter, who shortly before the competition had been described by FIFA as 'the world's best referee'.

Such a description would be a heavy cross to bear for any man. The weight was to prove too much for Carter.

After six minutes Germany's Jurgen Kohler brought down Bolivia's Baldiviesco, not from behind but still a stiff challenge. The yellow card was produced and those among the watching audience who favoured the total abolition of the rear tackle were gratified. Less than ten minutes later another Bolivian was on the deck: this time Thomas Hässler went in hard from behind on Luis Critaldo. Referee Carter was very close to the incident. He gave a free kick and devotees of the ban waited. They are still waiting: no red, no yellow, but the referee did remonstrate with the Bolivian laid out on the grass recovering: apparently he was taking too long to get to his feet.

The FIFA-nominated world's best referee also missed a blatant hand ball early in the second half when Hässler palmed the ball to Klinsmann who then scored the only goal of the game.

On the following day, for non-Italians there was a delightful surprise. The *azzuri* were beaten by Ireland. In the Giants Stadium, New York, seventy-five thousand predominantly Irish supporters had a day to remember as Jack Charlton's under-dogs beat one of the hot favourites to lift the Cup. The only goal came from Ray Houghton, a delightful chip over a dreaming Pagliuca in the Italian goal.

Confounding Harris poll-takers and the cynics, the crowds continued to come to World Cup 94. Nearly eighty-two thousand people watched in the blazing sun as Russia went down 2–0 to Brazil. Romario, ringing alarm bells to all the rival teams, was in devastating form. Making one and scoring another, Romario was yet another example of managerial inability to work with rather than against a flair player. It seemed that even a Brazilian manager of all people could display short-sightedness when it came to creative genius. The current team manager Carlos Alberto

Parreira, like Brazilian managers before him, was much taken with 'Europeanising' his squad. He wanted fewer surging runs down the wing from backs and more stringent marking from his defenders. Parreira had dropped Romario from his squad before Brazil had embarked on their qualifying matches for World Cup 94. What happened is such a familiar story. Brazil struggled to qualify. Public unrest. Sporting journalists critical. Manager ignores demands to bring Romario into the team. Further defeats for Brazil. Demands now at a crescendo. Manager relents at the eleventh hour and picks Romario for crucial game. If Brazil lose this one then they will not be at World Cup 94. It's against the old enemy, Uruguay. Twenty minutes to go the score is still 0–0. Brazil have to win to qualify. Then in the next ten minutes it's all over. Romario has scored not one, but two, stunning goals. Brazil are through to the World Cup Finals and manager Parreira can stand down the bodyguards.

For a man who was destined to get a multi-million-dollar bonus for his brilliant management of this World Cup, Alan I. Rothenberg left rather too much to be desired. If in the classic American tradition the buck should stop on the top man's desk, then Rothenberg should have been made to answer for the farce of the indoor Silverdome at Pontiac, near Detroit. The host team were due to play their first match at this vast airless place. No one had thought about laying the grass pitch until the decision to play there had been taken. After countless scientific brainstorming sessions, the Americans grew the grass in California and then spent a fortune moving it to Detroit. What no one ever thought of was air-conditioning. The Silverdome did not have any. The nearly seventy-four-thousand-strong crowd endured a Turkish bath. The players were exhausted and dehydrated twenty minutes into the first half. The US ground out a stultifying 1–1 draw with Switzerland.

Their next game was against Colombia, a team that many had felt would be the ultimate champions. Putting far too much reliance on the talented Carlos Valderrama, the Colombians had gone down to a shock 3–1 defeat at the hands of Romania in their first game. Next up was their match against the hosts, USA.

The drug cartels had already made their presence felt outside the stadiums. Huge additional quantities of cocaine had been shipped into the country from Cali and Medellín. Aware that there would be hundreds of thousands of overseas visitors to the tournaments, the Cartels saw the possibility of an increase in sales and, like any professional organisation, moved to meet potential demand.

Their presence was felt inside the stadiums too. Certainly inside the arenas where their home team was playing. The Cartels and football had long been bound together. Drug lords like Pablo Escobar owned professional clubs. Money was laundered at many grounds and not only in Colombia. Cali in particular were highly proficient at having foreign assets laundered through football revenue. Brazil. Paraguay and Uruguay. Mexico, Spain, Italy and France and Germany, a cocaine trail goes right through the turnstiles at grounds in all of these countries. Now in the middle of the people's game the Cartels reached out from Colombia. Threats were made by Cartel members to individual Colombian players. Large bets on the results had been made. In view of the fact that some Cartel members had bet on Colombia to win and others had bet on them to lose, the match against the USA was going to end in deep trouble for someone. A fax arrived before the game at the hotel where the Colombian squad were staying. It was addressed to Gabriel Gomez, a midfield player. It stated that if he played against the USA his home would be blown up. Gomez did not play. The smart money in Medellín placed at very good odds was on Colombia to lose to the unfancied host team.

Thirty-five minutes into the game the Colombian back Andres Escobar – no relation to the drug lord in Medellín – stuck out a leg to intercept a cross and scored an own goal. In the second half Stewart of the United States made it 2–0 and over ninety-three thousand spectators in the Rose Bowl went wild.

Colombia through Valencia scored in the final minute to make it 2–1, but Colombia were out of the World Cup. They went on to win an irrelevant match against Switzerland, then, demoralised, departed for Colombia. Their manager Francisco Maturana went into hiding, with good reason. Before the game against the USA he had received death threats.

A few days after the squad had returned home, Andres Escobar was leaving a restaurant in Las Palmas, a suburb in Medellín. He was a regular there, popular and well liked. At least there he and his girlfriend could be sure that there would be no taunts about the own goal he had unwittingly given away. Returning to his car he was recognised by a group of men as he sat with his fiancée next to him. An argument developed. A gun was produced and both Escobar and his girlfriend were shot repeatedly. As each bullet hit their bodies there was a shout of 'Goal!' from the killers. No one has ever been charged for his murder.

The Italian goalkeeper Gianlucca Pagliuca, having been caught napping in their first match against Ireland, was obviously fired up for the second game. Too fired up. Against Norway a through ball found its way through the Italian defence. Rushing out of his area with a Norwegian forward descending on him, Pagliuca handled the ball outside the box and was sent off. Time to put on the substitute goalkeeper Marchegiani. To make way for the goalkeeper the Italian manager Sacchi joined the ranks of those who cannot live with flair and originality. He pulled off his best player Roberto Baggio. The Italian supporters in the crowd whistled and booed and Baggio was clearly not too pleased either.

Arrigo Sacchi was already struggling against an increasing wave of hostile criticism. Dismissed by many of the pundits because he had never played football at the highest level, he had responded with: 'You don't have to be a horse to be a jockey.' After the untimely removal of Baggio, notwithstanding that the Italians went on to scrape a 1–0 victory, many doubted whether the manager had the brains to be a horse, never mind a jockey.

Narcotics were never far away during this World Cup. Argentina had qualified narrowly for the tournament. In their hour of need they had once again turned to Diego Maradona, but this was a Maradona who had been to hell and back. While playing for Naples he had tested positive for cocaine and had been suspended for one year. He was at this time heavily addicted to the drug and significant evidence linked him with the Camorra as a drug supplier for the Neapolitan version of the Mafia. In the next twelve months under judicial supervision he was re-born. The extra weight had been shed and magically the little man had not merely made time stand still, but had turned the clock back. They thrashed Greece 4–0, Batistuta scoring a hat-trick and Maradona the fourth. A disturbing image hit the television screens around the world: after his goal Maradona had run to a ground-level television camera. Eyes popping, he screamed defiance at the world.

Against Nigeria, Maradona had never demonstrated greater commitment or energy: he covered every inch of the pitch and with striker Claudio Caniggia – another reformed cocaine addict – posed questions that the Nigerians had no answers to. Caniggia scored twice and the Argentinian quest for another World Cup was looking increasingly like becoming a reality.

Random drug testing had been introduced by FIFA at the time of the World Cup in England in 1966. The first player to test positive had been the Haitian Ernst Jean-Joseph during the 1974 World Cup in Germany. Willy Johnston of Scotland had been sent home from Argentina during World Cup 78 after being caught using the pep pill fencamfamin. Now on 30 June 1994 came the next one. An Argentinian. *The* Argentinian. Maradona's urine sample after the Nigerian game had revealed a range of ephedrine-related drugs. They are frequently used to help weight reduction and Maradona had lost nearly two stone in a frighteningly short space of time shortly before the World Cup had started. FIFA's head of the medical committee, Dr Michel D'Hooghe, said, 'Maradona must have taken a cocktail of drugs, these substances are not available in one medicine.' The drug, apart from acting as an appetite suppressant, is also a stimulant. For some, they now had the explanation of Maradona's astonishing level of energy during the Nigerian game. Julio Grondona, President of the Argentinian Football Association and a FIFA Vice President, salvaged what he could. He announced that Maradona had been withdrawn from the tournament. By acting quickly on what had been Havelange's confidential advice, Grondona pre-empted any move from the World Cup Committee to throw Argentina out of the tournament. Protesting his innocence, Maradona was then banned from football worldwide for fifteen months. In essence his international career was over, but many were uneasy. Within his own country many believed that this was yet another part of the much publicised feud between Maradona and Havelange. Support came for Maradona from a variety of sources. Most surprisingly of all, from the operatic tenor Luciano Pavarotti.

'I am upset at FIFA's stupidity. I consider ephedrine a medicine, and I take it every day to be at my best for my public.'

Without their focal point a lack-lustre Argentina were beaten in their next match by Bulgaria 2–0. Though they made the next round, that was as far as they could go without the little man. They lost to Romania 3–2.

It was an ironic variation on 'the plot' and 'the conspiracy'. In early pre-Havelange years, the Argentinians, the Brazilians and the rest of Latin America were sure to a certainty that 'they' had plotted against them. 'They' being the Europeans in general and Sir Stanley Rous in particular. Now with the initially unfancied Argentinians threatening to get hold of World Cup 94 by the scruff of the neck, with their star rejuvenated and in the full pomp and majesty of his remarkable talents leading the Argentinian charge, they had been thwarted. Wickedly prevented from winning what was rightfully theirs by ... By whom? Surely not FIFA's Executive Committee or its standing committees? With Brazil holding thirteen seats? With England holding only two? Surely not by Havelange's son-in-law Ricardo Teixeira of Brazil or Cañedo of Mexico or Grondona of Argentina, all honest serving members of the Executive Committee? Wherever one looked on FIFA's many committees it was wall-to-wall with Latin Americans. And if not Latin Americans, then puppets like Harry Cavan, an Ulsterman whose total obedience to the President's every whim resulted in Havelange promoting him to chairman of five major committees. Havelange by such measures had made very sure that over the years no one could get past men like Cavan to launch an attack on the Sun King. Who then was behind this injustice to Diego Maradona?

The thrust of the various theories that have been published since World Cup 94 is this:

FIFA were so concerned that the coming tournament in the United States lacked star quality, lacked box office appeal, that they promised Maradona immunity from any drug testing. FIFA then forged documentation that he was

clean of drugs and threw down the red carpet for the little
man. He duly responded, lost far too much weight too
quickly for his own good, but astonishingly began to
deliver the goods in large quantities. FIFA then panicked.
Maradona was not supposed to be this good. He might
well take them all the way. Brazil and particularly the
President of the CBF must be protected against that. 'The
path of Brazil to their rightful place as winners must be
smoothed.' Thus QED the man behind 'the plot' must be
the Brazilian at the top, João Havelange.

Well, I suppose if you believe Sir Stanley Rous was
capable of fixing a match you might just believe anything.
Maradona was caught cheating and was banned. End of
story. A far more interesting question might be, why wasn't
Maradona caught cheating when he punched the ball past
Peter Shilton?

The Argentinian was not the only individual in trouble
with officialdom during this World Cup. Jack Charlton,
Ireland's English manager, was involved with a number of
officious FIFA officials. If a game of football brings out the
worst in some of the supporters watching, it is equally true
that a World Cup brings out something equally unappetising
in a variety of FIFA personnel. All Charlton was concerned
about was the fact that in the arid enervating conditions in
Orlando his players were demonstrably dehydrating before
his and everyone else's eyes. His attempts to get substitute
John Aldridge onto the pitch were extraordinary to behold.
An interminable time elapsed before any of the officials
would let Aldridge on. It was outrageous to watch. God
only knows what it was like to be either Charlton or
Aldridge. FIFA knew what to do and it wasn't to reprimand
their officials. They banned Charlton from the bench for
the next game and fined him $15,000. For good measure
they also fined Aldridge nearly $2,000. A great many
people who had seen what had happened decided to make

their feelings known. Money began to pour in to pay the fines. Jack Charlton ended up with $100,000. He gave the money to the family of the murdered Colombian player Andres Escobar.

Through this tournament the refereeing fluctuated wildly. During Germany's second-round 3–2 defeat of Belgium, German defender Thomas Helmer brought Weber down in the penalty area. Swiss referee Kurt Rothlisberger must have been looking the other way. No penalty. Havelange was watching though. The next day Herr Rothlisberger was flying back home.

Kurt Rothlisberger was no stranger to controversy. A year before the World Cup tournament in the USA he had been in charge of the Galatasary–Manchester United game. When the game finished Eric Cantona, exasperated at the dubious standard of refereeing, went on television and accused Rothlisberger of taking a bribe. Cantona received a four-match ban for making the accusation.

Two years after being sent home by FIFA for what was at the very least grossly inept control of the Germany v Belgium game, Rothlisberger approached Erich Vogel, the general manager of Grasshopper Zurich. Grasshopper had recently played the first leg of a Champions League tie against Auxerre and had lost 1–0. Rothlisberger wanted to know if Grasshopper Zurich would be interested in the appointed referee for the second leg, Vadim Zhuk of Belarus, 'giving favourable decisions for the Swiss club in return for financial compensation, something in the region say of £45,000?'

Vogel reported the referee to UEFA who banned him for life for attempted bribery.

Refereeing the Italy v Nigeria game was 'the best referee in the world', Arturo Brizio Carter. The pre-match build-up indicated that Carter would need to be at his very best. The President of the Nigerian Federation, Samson Emeka

Omeruah, declared to a group of Italian journalist who had come to the Nigerian training camp:

'I'm not scared of Italy. We're the champions of Africa. Who are you? Italy is world famous for the Mafia and Fiat, not for football.'

Just to make sure that the Italian media understood how the Nigerians felt about them, an Italian TV crew were beaten up for having the temerity to try to film a Nigerian training session.

During the course of the game Carter gave out nine yellow cards, sent off Gianfranco Zola, denied the Italians two obvious penalties, ignored a terrible foul by Maldini that merited a red card, and near the end awarded Italy a penalty which won them the game 2–1 after extra-time. FIFA announced after the game that the world's best referee would not be getting any more games to control.

News of the fact that Carter had achieved a bizarre World Cup record – nine yellows and a red in one match – travelled rapidly. The news clearly reached the Syrian referee Jamal Al Sharif very quickly. The same day he was in charge of the Bulgaria v Mexico game. He handed out nine yellow cards as well, then topped that with two red cards. He was yet another referee who would be permanently rested after the game ended, appropriately in a penalty shoot-out that was won by Bulgaria.

At the quarter-final stage a number of potentially exciting Finals were on the cards. The form four to go through to the semi-finals were Italy, Brazil, Germany and Sweden. In the event the bookies got three out of four right. The shock result of the round occurred in the Bulgaria v Germany match.

Germany had appeared in every Final since 1978. For many, a new World Cup meant trying to guess who would meet Germany in the Final. That unfancied Bulgaria should defeat them hardly seemed credible.

Germany had gone in front early in the second half after Letchkov had tripped Jürgen Klinsmann and Matthäus had converted the penalty kick. Fifteen minutes from the end Stoichkov, challenged by Möller, went down. After the game Möller was adamant that there had not been a foul, that the Bulgarian had dived and conned the referee. Stoichkov took the free kick himself and the ball had hit the back of the net without goalkeeper Ilgner moving. Three minutes later, a high cross came in from the Bulgarian right wing. Normally one of the tall German defenders would have headed the ball upfield. The problem was a shortage of tall German defenders to meet the cross. The only German around was the smallest member of the team, the diminutive Thomas Hässler, no match for Yordan Letchkov, who headed the winning goal.

The United States team had gone out to Brazil in the second round. Their performances had been largely negative, like a team playing for the penalty shoot-outs. In truth they had done extremely well to progress out of a very tough Group A. After their dismissal most of their support seemed to fasten onto Brazil.

The Holland v Brazil quarter-final was a curious affair: a first half as dreary as the second was enthralling. During the first forty-five minutes the Dutch, most unusually for them, had played a tight defensive game that lacked any spirit of adventure. Wave after wave of Brazilian attacks broke down against the massed lines of Holland.

Ten minutes into the second half the Brazilians finally picked the lock: Romario got the first, Bebeto got the second. Holland rallied. Receiving the ball from a throw-in, Dennis Bergkamp ran at the Brazilian defence. There are few sights more exhilarating than seeing a class forward directly take on a defence. Inevitably there is panic, often a fatal mistake through a challenge delayed too long. Taffarel was beaten comprehensively by a shot that made it 2–1.

Twelve minutes later an Overmars corner, the leaping form of Holland's defender Aron Winter, and Taffarel was beaten again. 2–2.

With nine minutes left Brazilian left back Branco let go with a thirty-foot drive that gave De Goey in the Dutch goal absolutely no chance. Three–two and Brazil were in the semi-finals.

The luckiest team to join Brazil and Bulgaria in the semi-finals was undoubtedly Italy. They led at half-time from a goal by Baggio – not Roberto, but his namesake Dino, the hardworking midfield player who was beginning to make a habit of scoring vital goals. This time a rasping twenty-five-yard drive sailed past the Spanish goalkeeper, Zurbizarreta.

Earlier the Spanish defender Abelardo had escaped with a yellow card when his foul on Roberto Baggio deserved a red in the eyes of all except referee Sandor Puhl. The second half was largely dominated by Spain with their midfield player José Caminero continuously running at the Italian defence. Thirteen minutes into the second half he equalled for Spain, who then surged forward, eagerly sensing victory. Italy are at their most lethal when they counter-attack. This time the Italian scorer was Roberto Baggio; a lob deep from the Italian defence found him and the score was 2–1. Still Spain went forward in numbers. A cross from the right wing had the Spanish forward Luis Enrique racing into the Italian penalty area, the Italian defender Tassotti closed on him and Enrique was sent crashing to the ground having been elbowed in the face. When the referee failed to react, Enrique, with blood streaming down his face, stood screaming for justice. Neither the referee nor the linesman had seen anything wrong and the game continued for one more minute before the final whistle sent Italy one match away from the Final.

The match officials may have been blind, but the

television camerawork had clearly shown a dreadful foul on Enrique. FIFA had no alternative but to officially view the evidence. The Disciplinary Committee handed down an eight-match ban on Tassotti. No consolation to Enrique or Spain, who should have been awarded a penalty. Tassotti, of course, should have been shown the red card and dismissed. Italy were in the semi-finals and Spain were on their way home.

The other quarter-final between Sweden and Romania was a drab, negative match. The American spectators proved to be bright students of what was good and what was bad about this game of football. They booed both teams for much of the match. Sweden eventually prevailed after the penalty shoot-out.

That period of extra-time was to take its toll. When the Swedes faced Brazil in the first semi-final they looked right from the start like a team that had just played ninety minutes. During the opening stages of the game, there was considerably more activity in the VIP section of the stadium than on the pitch. Lennart Johansson, President of UEFA, recalled for me:

'What happened on the day of the semi-final? Well, the captain of the Swedish team, midfield player Jonas Thern, was sent off after eighteen minutes by a referee who came from South America. Now, the Minister of Finance and the Minister of Sport and four other members of the Swedish Government came in and I could not offer them a place. Could not offer them a seat. I felt embarrassed to tell these gentlemen, who I personally knew and who were from my own country, that despite the fact that Sweden were playing in the semi-final, there was no place for them to watch the game. The reason was because all around the seats were occupied by friends of Havelange. I was subsequently told that he had between two and three hundred guests, many having arrived in private planes.'

I asked him: 'The sending-off of Thern was of course crucial to the final result, Brazil winning by a solitary goal. I've been told that the referee for that match had been selected because Havelange insisted upon him controlling that semi-final.'

'That is what I have been told and that happens obviously very frequently that Havelange has an impact on the choice of referees.'

'I understand something similar happened prior to the Final and that this time the Referees Committee dug in and objected and had a fight with Havelange about this issue.'

'Yes, you're correct. That is my understanding of what occurred.'

Romario had got the only goal in the eightieth minute. Would Italy or Bulgaria join Brazil in the Final?

The Bulgarians had obviously peaked in their game against Germany. That was one explanation. The other was that they simply had no answer to Roberto Baggio – 'The Divine Ponytail' as his countrymen called him. Baggio scored two scintillating goals and Bulgaria converted the gift of a penalty to make the final score 2–1. Italy were in the Final against Brazil, but the match had left its mark on their star, Roberto Baggio. He had limped off with a strained hamstring; his presence in the Final thrown into uncertainty.

Brazil's manager Parreira paid tribute to the opponents his team would soon face.

'Italy has grown with the days. It's not just Baggio. We've earned the right to play in the Final through our consistency. Italy have earned the right with their last brilliant performance.'

Yet again Brazilian critics took a less generous view of their team's progress to the Final. Chico Mai, a radio reporter from Belo Horizonte, summed up what many of his colleagues felt:

'We journalists consider it an error to Europeanise the play of our national team. We have a tradition, a credibility, and we're not disposed to sell it off or bargain it away.'

Four years later, to the day, that same sad lament and a great deal more would be heard in the land. In the hours and days following World Cup 98 in France.

Twenty-four years before the World Cup 94 Final these two teams, Italy and Brazil, had met in what is still – and these words are written after the Final in France – the best World Cup Final in the history of the tournament.

The 1970 Final had produced a match that was a celebration of the game. It had been the perfect example of what attacking football could produce. It had been theatre of the highest order. In Pelé's performance everything that is wonderful about the game of football was distilled into one man. Any who came away from watching that game unmoved were to be pitied. It was the last pre-Havelange World Cup Final.

In 1994 in what was the penultimate Havelange Final, the audience was somewhat larger. Apart from the ninety-four thousand people packed into the Rose Bowl Stadium in Los Angeles, there was the wider global television audience. FIFA estimated that the size of the television audience for the entire World Cup 94 was cumulatively 31.2 billion people – more than five times the entire number of people on the planet. What those who were watching the Brazil v Italy Final in 1994 saw was a sterile, dull, defensive game which, having ended without a single goal being scored, was reduced to the ultimate banality of a penalty shoot-out which Brazil 'won'. That a World Cup Final should be reduced to a showbiz ending speaks more eloquently than any words of how the game has been prostituted since those ninety minutes of absolute magic in Mexico in 1970.

The total receipts for World Cup 94 were an all-time

record. A triumphant accolade to brilliant marketing skills. The gross was a staggering SF 292,843,000 – $235 million. If just a small percentage of these profits had been donated to research, to study, an attempt to find ways to improve the 'product' that was being sold, who knows? FIFA Incorporated might have begun to gain a little credibility to their self-description – 'For the Good of the Game' – a slogan that invites legal action under the Trade Descriptions Act.

With the commercial success of the World Cup tournament in the United States now a reality, the Sun King was able to focus on the next item on the agenda. Revenge.

On 27 October with the final figures for World Cup 94 having been freshly announced a mere nine days earlier, Havelange struck. In his view certain members of his court had shown disloyalty earlier in the year during the run-up to the Chicago Congress. Attempts to unseat him had been very rapidly destroyed, but Havelange desired to send out a clear warning of what happened to those who plotted against him.

There are of course set procedures, rules and a wide variety of statutes to ensure that a form of democratic process is applied within FIFA. These apply to every member of FIFA save one. The Sun King.

Presumably Havelange has a very special set of FIFA's statutes. An edited version that excludes for example:

'The President shall have an ordinary vote, and when the votes are equal, the casting vote.'

At the FIFA Executive meeting in New York, Havelange allowed the various items on the official agenda to progress until he introduced as the final item some changes he had made to various committees. He handed out copies of the lists to the Executive members. To ensure that no one had been able to get advance warning of what he was up to, he had personally photocopied his own list of appointees to the committees. Before the Committee could respond or study the list Havelange, standing on the dais, said:

'I now declare those lists approved and the meeting closed.'

With that the Sun King exited, leaving an initially bewildered and stunned court behind him. As they began to read, their bemusement changed to anger.

Purged from their posts were some of the very best of FIFA. Peter Velappan of Asia, Gerd Aigner of Europe, Chuck Blazer of the United States Federation, Mustapha Famy of Africa. From the Referees Committee, the Italian Paolo Casarin. Head of the Italian Referees Federation, Casarin had been widely praised for his attempts to upgrade the standard of refereeing and for his meticulous research on the subject. Casarin had committed an unforgivable sin: he had appointed to referee the World Cup Final in the United States the Hungarian Sandor Puhl. Ignoring the fact that this decision was not within his ambit, the President had sought to influence the choice. He had failed, so Casarin had to go. Also removed from this important committee were two other very respected referees, Karoly Palotai and Alexis Ponnet. Havelange had also replaced the deputy chairman, the Brazilian Abilio D'Almeida. In this instance with another Brazilian. His own son-in-law, Ricardo Teixeira.

Havelange also got rid of FIFA's Press Officer, Guido Tognoni – a man who had given eleven years of unstinting loyalty to Havelange and to FIFA. There was one extraordinary omission from the list. One name that should have been at the top of the list was not on it at all. Sepp Blatter, the General Secretary of FIFA. Havelange had demonstrated in 1981 that removing even someone at that level was not for the President an insurmountable problem. Dr Helmut Käser had been summarily dismissed.

Blatter, when I interviewed him, flatly denied the initiative to run against Havelange was his. He insisted that it came from the senior members of FIFA. From their Executive Committee. He also said that the President of UEFA, Lennart Johansson, had confirmed this. Johansson and his fellow UEFA members were adamant. They told me the suggestion came from Blatter. These accusations and counter-accusations were made to me only weeks before Johansson and Blatter were due to win or lose the fight to take over from Havelange. What shines through clearly is that there is no doubt that Blatter was, for a while, in the run-up to Chicago 94, a very serious contender for the crown. Why then did he survive the purge? The answer that came back to me when I asked that question was always the same. 'Because of what he had on Havelange.' What would vary was exactly what it was that the General Secretary 'had' on his President. The range of possibilities was extensive, but invariably involved money. Large amounts of it. If nothing else, this issue serves powerfully to underline the need for total transparency in all of FIFA's financial dealings. This money is not Havelange's or Blatter's. It is ours, held on trust by FIFA's officials.

I had been told that after the night of the long knives in New York, Blatter was subjected to over a year of ice from the Sun King. Their previous close relationship full of '*Du*' was reduced to '*Sie*' and that well into 1996 Havelange would totally ignore his General Secretary. It is behaviour that is very consistent with the João Havelange I have come to know. Blatter recalls it differently. There was '… for a month, for August, when we came back from the World Cup, a frostiness. I had been told he was very unhappy. I asked him, João, do you really want to get rid of me? Do you want to do a buy-out?'

It's clear that that is exactly what Havelange wanted.

Somehow Blatter 'persuaded' the President to forget his grievances. The only recorded occasion in his entire life when a man who still spoke bitterly to me of a 1974 insult twenty-four years later has been prepared to bury the hatchet other than in his opponent's head.

There were five defining moments that led ultimately to the close of Havelange's reign over football.

The first had been his treatment of Pelé at the World Cup draw in Los Angeles. Havelange has over the years been feared. He has also been respected. He has never, outside his family circle, been loved. To treat an icon with such contempt and one who is indeed much loved, ensured that many viewed Havelange with derision. His action rebounded and led many FIFA delegates to condemn him publicly for the first time.

The second incident that hastened his departure from FIFA was the night-of-the-long-knives meeting, which resulted in Havelange alienating so many.

Just over a year after the New York committee, the third key event in the inevitable demise occurred. João Havelange has always been a sucker for an award. The list that he has accumulated over the years, rather than adding lustre to his reputation, collapses his image like an over-cooked soufflé. His lust for such baubles took him in November 1995 to Nigeria to a treble-kissing of General Abacha, yet another dictator to add to the number that Havelange counted – at least until Abacha's recent death – as a 'good friend'.

In the days leading up to Havelange's visit there had been mounting worldwide pressure on Abacha to commute the sentence of death that had been passed on nine dissidents, including the playwright and human rights campaigner Ken Saro-Wiwa.

Nigeria, because of the military junta running the country, was considered by world opinion to have no place

in civilised society. Enter Havelange. He was anxious to
reassure General Abacha that Nigeria might after all get to
host the 1997 World Youth football tournament. It was
the best piece of public relations that Abacha had had for
a long time. The delighted General awarded an equally
thrilled Havelange an honorary chieftainship. Simultaneously he ordered that the nine human rights
campaigners should be executed, an order that was carried
out within twenty-four hours. Havelange could see no
wrong in either his or Abacha's actions. Defending his
meeting with the dictator, he said:

'If in a certain country I am taken to see the Head of
State, out of education and respect I do it; it's my function
and my obligation. If FIFA start to get involved in political
questions, it would disappear. Recently, a journalist asked
me about the French nuclear tests and I told him it was a
matter for the United Nations because they do politics,
while we do sport. And my answer now regarding Nigeria
is the same.'

Presumably keeping South Africa out of FIFA until
apartheid was abolished; bringing mainland China back
into FIFA; recognising Croatia, Lithuania and Estonia very
rapidly after the collapse of Communism and at a time
when the Kremlin was still taking a very hard line,
particularly on the Baltic States; suspending Yugoslavia in
line with a United Nations sanction from World Cup
qualifying matches, none of this is 'doing' politics?

The President of FIFA had ensured by his own actions
that the organisation he headed was, not unlike the
disgusting regime who had just honoured him, held
internationally in contempt.

When the controversy over his visit was at its height,
Lennart Johansson, UEFA's President, finally decided that
enough was more than enough. He announced his
candidacy for the next Presidency. The elections would be

held in Paris immediately before the kick-off of World Cup 98.

The French Football Association was also now viewing Havelange with exasperation. When France had put in its bid to run World Cup 98 it was based on the fact that there would be twenty-four teams competing in the Finals. Despite the fact that Havelange had repeatedly declared after that bid had been accepted that it was 'impossible to conceive of a time when the number of finalists could be increased ... the idea that there could be thirty-two finalists is absurd', the French learned through the newspapers that absurdity had now become reality. There would now be sixty-four games instead of fifty-two. A logistical and security nightmare beckoned. With an initial commitment to spend $235 million renovating nine stadiums and a further minimum $541 million on building the new Grande Stade in the suburbs of Paris, the French Committee went hurrying to Zurich seeking a firm underwriting of the additional cost that would be incurred with an enlarged tournament. Havelange obliged, courtesy of Coca-Cola and the other Category One sponsors. Nothing had changed since the days of Dassler and Nally. The same corporate giants bailing out the same President of FIFA.

One result of these blunders by Havelange was an attempted reining-in of his powers to ensure that further abuses were limited. Reforms proposed by Johansson included redefining the power balance between FIFA and the confederations to ensure a greater degree of democracy after more than twenty years of autocratic rule by Havelange.

The other proposal was a direct attack on the citadels of ISL and the European Broadcasting Union (EBU). UEFA urged competitive marketing of the World Cup Finals and an insistence that the profits made be shared out more evenly. Havelange's critics were particularly exercised by the fact that the amounts being generated in successive World Cup Finals were massively below what the market would pay. In 1986 Havelange, a man who at all times projects an image of a super-sharp businessman, compounded the naiveté he had shown in earlier dealings with Dassler by signing a twelve-year marketing agreement with ISL and an agreement for the same length for television rights with the EBU. Havelange had excluded his Executive Committee from these negotiations, which were conducted by himself, Blatter and Guillermo Cañedo. What this autocracy has cost football over the past twelve years is incalculable. The loss can be conservatively estimated at between $500 million and $1 billion.

Havelange, who also boasts of the millions he has made as an astute operator in Brazil – millions that most certainly have not come from any of his known business interests – did not think to put a cap on the profits that first Dassler and then his heirs would make at ISL. Neither did he think to demand a profit participation scheme or an escalator clause in the FIFA contracts for television rights that were continuously awarded to the EBU, but then these basic concepts also appeared to have passed by Blatter and Cañedo.

The effect of these four incidents on the thinking of the majority of delegates within the confederations was to make them stop and re-evaluate João Havelange. Many for the first time since his election in 1974 began to seriously question whether the President had become a liability to football. Some had always held that view, but for decades they had been the silent minority, often afraid to publicly say what they had frequently said in off-the-record briefings. They saw what had happened to various secretaries of the Confederations, full-time employees in the world of football who had been removed from influential committees by Havelange. That removal had meant they no longer got on planes to a variety of foreign locations and met other like-minded anti-Havelange members of FIFA. They had been subbed by the manager. Difficult to influence the game from the sidelines. Now Johansson had declared he was going to run for election in June 1998 the dissidents had a focal point.

The focal point became even more clearly defined when the fifth and final crucial moment occurred in early 1996. The issue of World Cup 2002. Which country should host the tournament? Who should have the TV and marketing rights?

It was an open secret that Havelange, while officially declaring himself to be neutral in the Japan v South Korea bidding war that had been going on virtually since the last ball had been kicked in the 1994 tournament, intended to give the prize to the Japanese.

It was also an open secret by April 1996 that, despite agreeing four months earlier that there would be far greater consultation concerning the negotiations for the TV and marketing rights, Havelange had once again acted as if these rights were his personal property. Never mind rival bids from Mark McCormack's organisation. Never mind a lack of consultation with his Executive Committee. The double act of Havelange and Blatter had yet again done the business.

The issue of the venue for World Cup 2002 had the world and his wife getting in on the act. There were inspired leaks to favoured reporters. Secret meetings between the former Prime Ministers of Japan and South Korea. Candle-lit dinners between Havelange and his old comrade-in-arms, the President of the International Olympic Committee, Juan Antonio Samaranch, who dangled in front of Havelange the prospect of awarding the Olympic Games for 2004 to Rio as a reward for climbing down and putting to one side his implacable opposition to South

Korea hosting World Cup 2002. Everyone, it seemed, was primarily concerned with only one objective. Not to lose face.

For two years Japan and Korea had been continuously raising the ante. Gifts poured in to any FIFA official that either country thought capable of influencing the outcome. What began with a trickle of cameras, watches and electronic equipment of every conceivable kind moved on to motor cars, extensive all-expenses-paid overseas trips, women, men, and when their minds had run the gamut of corruption, the two by now hysterically warring camps resorted to that old standby: money.

Every single member of the FIFA Executive Committee was targeted by the Japanese and South Korean Federations. The majority of the FIFA Committee accepted gifts while simultaneously ordering the Japanese and south Koreans to desist. This Committee included, after President Havelange, the most senior members of FIFA, yet even members such as Vice-President David Will apparently saw nothing wrong in accepting gifts worth thousands of pounds. Will was subsequently to say that he had helped to curb the gift-giving bonanza by campaigning with other FIFA officials to introduce a new code of conduct, banning gifts totalling more than £60. As Will has confirmed, 'I, together with other Europeans, immediately contacted the two bidding bodies and said, "Now, look, we do not wish to receive gifts in this way." I was not a person who just merrily received these gifts and did nothing about it.'

The level of sleaze appalled even those realists who know that 'the sweetener', 'the financial adjustment', 'the commission' are facts of everyday life. Sultan Ahmad Shah, the Malaysian President of the Asian Confederation, wrote a confidential letter to the heads of the other FIFA confederations.

'AFC [Asian Football Confederation] is embarrassed

with the intensive campaigns in every continent. The campaigns have gone beyond the limit of normalcy. It is unhealthy for FIFA and the AFC and for the future of the World Cup. Therefore as responsible leaders of world football, it is our duty to take control of the situation so that sanity and morality of football are maintained at all times.'

Havelange's response indicated what he considered a desirable level of sanity and morality should be within football. He orchestrated a collective vote among his five South American colleagues on the Executive Committee in favour of giving World Cup 2002 to Japan.

Coincidentally the issue of the marketing and TV rights for the same event was bubbling to the surface as another contentious issue. South Korea's Chung Mong Joon, the Vice Chairman of the FIFA Media Committee, pointed out to the President what was an established fact. The rights had been seriously undervalued for many years. He drew attention to the Olympic Committee, who earned approximately seven times more from TV and marketing. Havelange told Chung:

'I think you should concentrate on more mundane matters, like the catering arrangements for the press.'

Chung was subjected to a Blatter-inspired whispering campaign in an attempt to discredit him. Sticking doggedly to his belief that Havelange and Blatter were selling football very seriously short, Chung drew attention to the bid from Mark McCormack's International Management Group. He believed that the presence of these rival bidders to ISL could push the price up for the marketing and TV rights for World Cup 2002 to two billion dollars. That would leave scope for over three hundred million dollars to be distributed to football at grassroots level through the Federations.

Chung Mong Joon also played a very important ethical

card with regard to the bitter fight still raging about who would be awarded the World Cup venue for 2002.

'I wish to state unequivocally that if South Korea hosts this tournament then all profits will be given back to football. One-tenth to FIFA and nine-tenths to the football confederations.'

This would ensure that the huge profits generated at World Cup tournaments would go not to the powerful – the top thirty-two for example that contested the Finals in France 98 – but also to the small developing football nations, the grass roots of the game.

Havelange was under siege and he hated it. When Lennart Johansson's carefully considered, cautiously worded document, 'Vision One', was given to him during an Executive Committee meeting, he exploded in rage and threw it across the room. He wanted no part of any attempt to bring about either 'greater democracy' or 'more openness in FIFA'. He was satisfied with the way that he was running it.

Havelange attempted to bounce his colleagues into a premature decision on the issue of World Cup 2002 some six months before the due date. He announced a 'unanimous decision' of the Executive Committee to bring the vote forward to January 1996 because 'Korea's aggressive lobbying was causing bad feelings all round'. The presidents of the six confederations discreetly vetoed this decision that had been taken by a minority. A South American minority.

Havelange had now taken to the trenches. By April 1996 he had let it be known that Korea would be awarded the World Cup 'over my dead body' – a dangerous gambit.

To confirm that the politics of this issue were not confined to FIFA members but also involved two governments, the then Japanese Prime Minister Hashimoto dismissed the suggestion that had come from Lennart Johansson's UEFA. Co-hosting. The Prime Minister wanted the event exclusively for Japan. Quite why Havelange had so deeply committed himself to Japan's bid appears to puzzle many observers. The fact that Dentsu, the huge Japanese advertising conglomerate, still owned at this time 49 per cent of ISL was presumably not widely known among certain sections of the press. What was totally unknown was exactly how much Dentsu had benefited in the past from this holding. From their involvement in the early 1980s Dentsu had been earning an extraordinary 50 per cent commission on all profits. Thus Dassler's coup in selling on the marketing rights of World Cup 82 in Spain for a gross profit of $96 million immediately put $48 million into Dentsu's coffers. Small wonder that there was pressure on the President to deliver World Cup 2002 to the Japanese.

The days leading up to the crucial FIFA Executive meeting in Zurich on Friday, 31 May, were, like much of the activity that has surrounded João Havelange throughout his adult life, a combination of certain elements. These ranged from farce and intrigue to betrayal, but above all there was the realisation among those members of the Executive arraigned against the President that as they had missed the Ides of March, then the last day of May was as good as any other to have done with the man they had come to regard as a tyrant.

A few days before the meeting Havelange was still playing to emerge the winner with a declaration that Japan would be the hosts of World Cup 2002. He said:

'In sport, there is always a winner and a loser. The FIFA rules do not allow co-hosting of the World Cup. As long as I am FIFA President that will not change.'

Rules of course, like Presidents, can be changed in the real world. Havelange, for perhaps the very first time since he ruthlessly conspired to remove his predecessor from office – a conspiracy that he now views as a demonstration of his great loyalty to Sir Stanley Rous – was faced with a humiliating defeat. He had not listened when those around him told him that this was one he could not win. He had not listened when Samaranch had urged him for the sake of unity in Asian sport to compromise. He had not listened when he was told that the majority of his Committee was against him. And finally, he had not listened when he was told that the two men leading their respective delegations, both former Prime Ministers, had met secretly the evening before the meeting and agreed to share the World Cup. Agreed to be co-hosts. Eventually, during the meeting itself, he finally listened. It was galling for the Japanese. Chastening for Havelange. And a triumph for the South Koreans. If the President of FIFA had bothered to conduct even the most basic research, he might well have been disinclined to consider either country. June and July, the months when the World Cup is always played, is the height of the rainy season in Korea and Japan. What Havelange has bequeathed us for 2002 is a World Cup tournament that will take place in monsoon and typhoon weather with very high humidity. Announcing that the two countries would be jointly hosting World Cup 2002, Havelange, with the chutzpah that has marked so much of his life, declared, 'My committee are fully behind me.'

Not only were his committee anywhere but behind him, they had been busy clearing the decks for June 1998. Lennart Johansson had already declared he was running. If a snap vote among FIFA's delegates had been taken in the months after the débâcle that had produced the first co-hosting in the history of the tournament, there can be little doubt that the Swede would have trounced the Brazilian. A number of times during the summer of 1996 Havelange declared that he would be there, he would be running for the highest office. He had felt the humiliation very deeply. He wanted revenge, and when through his life Havelange has sought revenge he has always obtained it. The dilemma was that the soundings he took showed that his previous support had waned. Europe would go with Johansson; so would Africa. That was virtually one hundred votes. Not enough to win on a first ballot when a two-thirds majority is needed, but more than enough on a second ballot when a simple majority would suffice.

As the summer of 1996 progressed a plan began to formulate in Havelange's mind. It was exquisite. Revenge is a dish best eaten cold and Havelange had every intention of eating well. On 6 December he was asked, shortly before a FIFA Executive meeting in Milan, about his future, and particularly his plans about another term as President. He had not ruled out another four years, he told *Gazzetta dello Sport*. 'I have always been asked to stay. This time I would be 82 and if I was asked again, I would have to consider my physical and mental condition – at my age they can change unexpectedly.'

Indeed so. Presumably his condition must have deteriorated with amazing speed because he walked from the interview into the Executive meeting and told his Committee that he would be retiring after World Cup 98 in France.

The announcement was greeted with total silence in the committee room. Among those listening was the man who was already a declared candidate: UEFA President Lennart Johansson. Also in the room was the man who Havelange had already decided would be his successor: General Secretary Sepp Blatter.

The media, when advised, promptly began playing Hunt the New President. First out of the newsroom was former German star Franz Beckenbauer. Quickly following was a man whom the media described as Havelange's personal choice to succeed him: Franco Carraro, President designate of the Italian League. Hot on his heels Pelé and then Issa

Hayatou, President of the Confederation of African Football.

Asked in January 1997 for an opinion on the 'contenders' for his title, Havelange declined to give one.

'I am not going to enter the election process.'

Which, translated, means that sooner or later Havelange was indeed going to enter the election process.

So a vacancy of an unusual nature had occurred. A job that in theory carried no salary and in practice paid a minimum of $1 million a year in non-taxable expenses. It also offered an all-expenses-paid apartment in Zurich and an office and private accommodation in the individual's normal place of residence. The successful applicant would be expected to fly to a wide variety of countries to meet the rich and powerful. He would have unlimited access to any number of tickets for any football game anywhere in the world, although neither a love of football nor a deep knowledge of the game is necessary for the job. The job carried the unusual benefit of ensuring that a number of like-minded, extremely powerful and very well-connected people were also based close to the individual's Zurich headquarters. These are the health experts and the Director General of the World Health Organisation above Lake Geneva; there is the President of the International Olympic Committee in Lausanne and, of course, there are all those Swiss bankers.

The job also means that any thought that flies into your head concerning football will be treated seriously and men who should know better will seriously consider all of your ideas. So if, like Havelange, you feel that football should no longer be a game of two halves but four quarters, then you could be what the FIFA delegates scattered around the globe are looking for.

Perhaps, again like João Havelange, you will have noted that since the end of the Second World War goalkeepers have been getting bigger and bigger while the size of the goal has remained the same. This was the explanation offered by the President of FIFA to explain the lack of goals after World Cup 90 in Italy. If you agree with Havelange that the obvious solution is to make the goals much bigger, you could be on your way. The most important thing to remember is the absolute power that goes with the job if you run the organisation along the lines so firmly laid down by your predecessor. What the President of FIFA wants, he gets.

The successful applicant will be expected to reward the loyalty of those voting for him in a suitable manner. This aspect is subject to negotiation, but assuming that you are as flexible on this aspect as the late incumbent you will walk into the FIFA Congress with at least one hundred votes in your pocket. No other qualification is necessary to become President of FIFA.

During the summer of 1997 Havelange gave a perfect example that as far as he was concerned to describe him as a man who had absolute power was to describe him accurately. Previously he had banned Brazil's most famous citizen, Pelé, from a World Cup draw. Now he threatened to ban an entire country from a World Cup because of the same man.

Pelé had been appointed Minister of Sport by President Cardoso of Brazil. In August 1997 he announced his intention of bringing a bill before the Brazilian Congress. If passed, Brazilian football would be radically restructured. It was this that had so angered Havelange. The President of FIFA was entirely happy with the state of affairs that existed within Brazilian football, but then so he should have been. Havelange and his son-in-law Ricardo Teixeira were very largely responsible for the current state of the game in Brazil.

Havelange asserted that what Pelé proposed was a

violation of FIFA rules. Not for the first time there was public comment that the President was, to use the description of him applied by both Maradona and Pelé, 'gaga'. In view of the fact that not only both former internationals but also most members of UEFA also considered that Havelange had become a dictator, a consensus appeared to be developing that believed that a mad tyrant had taken control of the kingdom of football.

Havelange and Ricardo Teixeira made repeated assertions that Brazilian football and the way that it was organised and run could not be improved. FIFA's president, fully recognising the powerful link between football and politics, also drew attention to the fact that 1998 was not only World Cup France year. Elections were due in Brazil. Repeating his threat to ban Brazil from the Finals if Pelé persisted in his attempts to reform the domestic game, Havelange asked menacingly:

'Doesn't President Cardoso want to win the elections?'

What had so angered Havelange and his son-in-law?

Pelé wanted to give players in Brazil the same freedom that the Bosman ruling had given players throughout Europe. At expiry of contract the player should be his own master. Free to go, free to negotiate with any club. What exists in Brazil is a form of modern slavery. Footballers stayed bonded to a club, even out of contract, unless someone made it worthwhile for the club to release the player. Pelé also wanted to convert Brazilian clubs into commercial enterprises which could go public and offer shares on the stock market. If that contravened FIFA rules then a great number of top European clubs were in contravention of those rules.

Pelé's bill would also allow clubs to form leagues that would not be under the direct control of Teixeira's CBF. In many countries – India is just one example – the clubs are not directly affiliated to the national association. In

England the Premier League and the Football League control the clubs, while being themselves controlled by the Football Association. Pelé envisaged something similar to this for Brazil. Of course, to do this would reduce the power and influence of Ricardo Teixeira and this went to the very heart of the matter.

What Pelé with considerable courage was attempting to do was to become a latterday Hercules. The modern equivalent of the Augean stables that he was attempting to cleanse was Brazilian football – something that has been in a putrid condition for many years.

What follows is not intended to be a comprehensive study of either the history of the game in Brazil or a definitive examination of all that ails the game in that country. Just a series of snapshots.

Brazilian football has two faces. The one that the world is familiar with is the national team. As this book has already recorded, successive generations of national squads have climbed to the very heights of football. So successful has the national team been in the past that they won the Jules Rimet trophy outright and a new World Cup had to be created. There has always been a quickening of the pulse, a heightening of expectation, when the men in yellow and green take the field. They have graced the game and on certain occasions elevated it to something quite beautiful. Then there is the other face of their game. The domestic reality.

That Jules Rimet trophy that Pelé and the team of 1970 so proudly brought back from Mexico to reside permanently in Rio was subsequently stolen from the offices of CBF. An act at once ironic and highly appropriate. Stolen from the building where first Havelange and subsequently Teixeira have played such major roles in stealing the game itself.

A great many have echoed Guido Tognoni's words to me: 'Ricardo Teixeira's most remarkable talent is that he is the son-in-law of Havelange.' In fact Teixeira and Lucia are now divorced, but the ties that bond Havelange and Teixeira are unbreakable. Ricardo – a mediocre law student with a history of unsuccessful business ventures when he married Lucia – has under the guidance and teaching of his patron, gone from strength to strength and now has so much wealth that he is constantly embroiled in legal actions that are brought by Brazil's Inland Revenue Service and the Justice Department. He is charged with tax evasion running into hundreds of thousands of dollars. The CBF, the Brazilian Football Federation that Teixeira controls, is also in constant litigation with the tax authorities, again for tax evasion and again for six-figure sums.

A similar situation involving any other president of a football association would find the association looking for a new chief, but then what would seem unbelievable in, say, European football is normal behaviour in Brazil. Teixeira is on record as paying tribute to Havelange. He said when acknowledging his debt to his father-in-law:

'He has taught me all I know about football.'

In view of the fact that after Havelange was replaced at the CBD a multi-million-dollar hole was discovered, it would seem that Havelange has also been responsible for his son-in-law's training in bookkeeping and accounts. His hand can certainly be detected in the art of gentle persuasion as practised by Teixeira.

In the run-up to World Cup 94 in the United States, Brazil, like all other countries with the exception of the host country and the defending champions West Germany, had to qualify. Again like all other nations, this meant playing a series of matches home and away. Unlike every other country attempting to qualify, Teixeira 'arranged' that Brazil would not alternate these matches. Brazil would play a series of away games against Ecuador, Bolivia,

Venezuela and Uruguay. They would then play four games one after another at home. What Teixeira paid to the respective associations for ensuring that Brazil would gain such a tremendous advantage is not known. That he did indeed pay can reasonably be deduced from what then happened.

The first game was against Ecuador on 18 July 1993. It was due to be played in the capital, Quito – a high-altitude test for the visiting Brazilians. Teixeira got busy. Talking to the chairman of Ecuador's football association he said:

'You know, you'd get a bigger crowd if you played the game down at Guayaquil. That stadium will hold a lot more people.'

The chairman pondered for a moment. 'No. I'm happy for our team to play here in Quito. Apart from anything else, our players are used to the high altitude.'

Both men knew very precisely what the real agenda was in this conversation. Ricardo Teixeira extolled the virtues of the sea port city of Guayaquil for some time without success, then poured himself another whisky.

'Look, I realise I need your co-operation in this matter. I'd like to offer you a "co-operation fee". Let's say $100,000. Is it a deal?'

'Yes, it's a deal.'

Even with the advantage of playing at sea level, Brazil only narrowly avoided defeat, the match finishing 0–0.

When the 'co-operation' arrangement leaked in Quito there was outrage. Members in the Ecuadorian Congress initiated an investigation. There was a deep suspicion that the arrangement went further than illegally changing the venue and covered a guarantee not to beat Brazil. Asked to respond to the anger in Ecuador, Teixeira affected bewilderment. 'What was the problem? If it was good for us and good for them? It is valid to break the rules if we believed that we must win.'

Discovering that the Bolivians had scheduled their match against Brazil in the capital La Paz, Teixeira reached for his wallet again. He offered $100,000 in an attempt to have the game moved to a stadium in Santa Cruz de la Sierra. The reason was the same, to escape high altitudes. Word had reached the Bolivians of the previous deal and they were not impressed with the initial offer. They also happened to fancy their chances at beating Brazil. Teixeira went up to $300,000. The Bolivians held out for $1 million, a sum that the President and his colleagues at the CBF declined to pay. The match was played at La Paz; the score Bolivia 2, Brazil 0.

In the light of the controversy that surrounds the events both before and during the recent World Cup 98 Final in Paris, Teixeira's behaviour is worthy of note. He is clearly one of those breed of football executives who without the benefit of having previously played the game at any significant level believe they know everything about the game in general and team selection in particular.

Unlike the majority of us that are in that category, Teixeira was, and indeed still is, in a position to actually influence selection and tactics and not of a village green team, but the Brazilian national squad.

Talking to the media after the Bolivian game, the head of CBF declared:

'I didn't like the game. It's not possible to spend the entire ninety minutes without scoring a goal.'

None ventured to point out to him that the Bolivians had in fact scored, twice. Teixeira continued:

'I will be complaining personally to the technical team and the players on Wednesday at their training ground.'

And complain he did. For two hours Teixeira ranted at Carlos Alberto Parreira, the manager of the squad, and at Mario Jorgo Lobo Zagalo, his deputy. He railed at them and the rest of the technical team. He told them who should be picked, he told them who should be dropped. He talked tactics and he also threatened. If Brazil did not qualify everyone would be fired. He omitted to tell his manager and his deputy that he had been talking for some time to Tele Santana with a view to getting Santana to take over. Santana had stirred the pot by telling Ricardo Teixeira what he would have done if he had been in charge against Bolivia. The president told his listeners that he wanted to see more aggression, he wanted to see more attack. The little fat man then left with his bodyguards and was driven away. His position, unlike everyone else's in the room, was not under threat. He was untouchable.

Teixeira had given thousands of dollars to the fourteen football chairmen who had voted him into office in 1989. This was to ensure in a highly dubious tactic that he obtained an extension to his presidency. He had taken thirty-three 'friends' on an all-expenses-paid first-class trip to World Cup 90 in Italy and he was planning to take over a hundred, again all expenses paid, to World Cup 94. It would be acutely embarrassing for his friends and humiliating to him, in his eyes at least, if Brazil did not qualify for the Finals in the United States. All of this largesse was of course not at Teixeira's expense. It came from CBF funds.

Like father-in-law, like son-in-law; saying hello with another man's hat obviously runs in the family. His uncle Marco Antonio had been given a job in the CBF as finance manager, an unusual career move for a teacher of biochemistry. Marco Antonio is paid in excess of $10,000 a month. Ricardo's aunt is another to benefit from his generosity. Aunt Celina is manager of purchases at the CBF.

Such a kind man. When eventually Brazil – courtesy of a last-gasp victory over Uruguay – qualified, Ricardo's joy, like his generosity, was unconfined. Everyone mentioned above, plus the rest of the staff at the CBF, got an all-expenses-paid trip to the Finals. Teixeira somehow forgot to invite any of the past heroes of Brazilian football. Perhaps it was an oversight caused by making sure that there were seats on the two planes for all of those he had actually invited. The top executives from many of Brazil's large corporations; the five members of the judiciary from Rio; the three judges of the court of appeal; the two district attorneys and many more lawyers. Most of these legal figures were involved in the at least forty lawsuits connected with the CBF which were at that time being processed. In one of the courts CBF were suing Pelé, who had alleged that there was corruption within CBF. The plane manifests read like a who's who of the legal profession. In view of the involvement that many of these men had either as judges or attorneys in cases that were being brought by or against Ricardo Teixeira's organisation, they were in direct contravention of Article 135 of the Brazilian Code of Civil Procedure, which deals with a judge's duties with regard to the acceptance of gifts either before or during a lawsuit. But who was going to sit in judgment on some of Brazil's finest legal minds?

So several hundred people had a twenty-two-day holiday and, as recorded earlier, eventually saw Brazil win World Cup 94 from a penalty shoot-out. If the journey to the States had been flamboyant, it was as nothing compared with the return.

Also on the returning planes were a number of carefully selected journalists. If a Brazilian reporter wishes to guarantee the vital press passes to venues he or she will find life much easier if a certain line is taken when writing for the press, or broadcasting on radio or television. If the writer perceives that all footballing triumphs should be credited to CBF and particularly its President, then there is never a delay in obtaining accreditation. If the same writer closes his eyes to the truth and reality in the world of Brazilian football and only writes or talks in a positive manner then, as for all good whores who perform well for their client, the rewards are great including, as they do, all-expenses-paid trips abroad.

A number of the freeloaders on the returning planes, having been given a first-class position to observe what occurred when the planes landed, appear to have suffered some curious form of collective amnesia. Given the best story of World Cup 94, they ignored it.

When Varig Airlines Flight 1035 touched down at Rio International Airport shortly before eleven o'clock on the evening of 19 July 1994 the first image that onlookers saw was a triumphant Romario holding the Brazilian national flag to a passenger window. It might have been by the penalty shoot-out lottery, but Brazil had beaten Italy in the World Cup Final and the national squad of twenty-two players had returned with the World Cup, their winners' medals and the country's fourth world title.

In the subsequent opening words from the Federal Department of Justice when they opened the government's case in the 13th Court of the Judiciary Section of Rio de Janeiro:

'The event, which should have been reason for pride and joy for the whole Brazilian nation, resulted in a series of misconducts with the aim of concealing unlawful acts consisting of the admission in national territory of foreign goods without the payment of due taxes.'

The man that they held responsible was the President of the Brazilian Football Federation and member of FIFA's Executive Committee: Ricardo Teixeira.

Between one and a half and two million people had taken to the streets of Recife and Brasilia to applaud the champions. Now touching down in Rio de Janeiro their arrival was being eagerly anticipated by over one million people lining the streets from Ilha do Governador to São Conrado.

Conscious that a huge gathering awaited the conquering heroes, the chief Customs officer on duty advised Teixeira that by prior arrangement between the Customs Secretary Osiris Lopes Filhio and CBF officials, the entire party could leave the terminal immediately with their hand luggage and return the following day to have the remaining luggage processed through Customs. Teixeira exploded with rage.

'How dare you talk to me like that? I am a world champion. I have just won the World Cup. I demand the immediate release of all the luggage. Immediately without any inspection whatsoever. We have trucks outside waiting to transport everything away. That's what we're going to do and no one is going to stop us. How dare you speak to me like that? Don't you recognise me? Don't you know who I am?'

There was a great deal more in a similar vein. It was obvious that Teixeira was showing signs of having over-indulged from the hospitality trolley – like his rages, something he has a habit of doing. By now many of the team had climbed up on a fire engine which was to be their parade vehicle.

Teixeira did not pause for a moment. Threats poured from his mouth. The Customs officer was by now being manhandled by the President of Brazilian football as he screamed abuse at the frightened official. Among the threats that came in an endless stream from his mouth was one in particular that sent a wave of terror through Customs Officer Belson Puresa.

'If you don't obey me on this there'll be no parade of the champions. Come on boys, get off that fire engine. I order you to get down from there.'

One of the team threw his winner's medal down from the fire engine onto the ground as he and the others jumped off.

This instruction from Teixeira was recounted in the sworn statements by witnesses as the moment when the real process of 'moral and physical coercion on Mr Belson started'.

Belson along with his colleagues was acutely aware that many in the crowd of more than one and a half million lining the streets had been waiting for hours for the parade. He was terrified that if Teixeira fulfilled his threat and called off the victory parade Rio would suffer very serious rioting, visions of a trashed international airport, of looting, of parts of the city going up in flames, were all seen as very likely scenarios by the airport security official.

With Ricardo Teixeira still screaming at him the Customs officer attempted to telephone his Government Minister. It was now 11.30 p.m. At that time of night Government Ministers can sometimes be difficult to locate. As the harassed, frightened Belson worked his way through various combinations of numbers, Teixeira kept up the pressure.

'This is bullshit. You had time to inspect the luggage in Recife and in Brasilia. The plane stayed in those two cities for more than eight hours. You have to release everything now.'

The 'bullshit' in fact was coming from Teixeira and he knew it. Luggage cannot be inspected unless the owner is accompanying it. At both previous stops neither Teixeira nor anyone else stayed hanging around the airports. They were off and running, accepting the plaudits of the crowds, and partying.

Incited by Teixeira, members of the national squad started to get in on the act. Branco grabbed the World Cup and called out melodramatically to Belson: 'Take it then! Confiscate the Cup!' Then he thrust it into the Customs official's hands. Romario added his voice. 'If you don't release the luggage, there'll be no parade.'

Manager Parreira and his technical co-ordinator Zagalo

began to threaten Belson. 'All right, then, if you want an inspection, let's do it out here right now. We're not worried about fines. But don't forget we're going to be spending the night out here. I'd like to know what you're going to do with all those people out there.'

When they had been struggling to qualify and had been soundly defeated by Bolivia, Teixeira had demanded more aggression from the team. He was getting it by the planeload now. Teixeira's arrogance had by now spread like a virus through almost the entire squad.

A number of Government officials in restaurants and homes down in Brasilia had, with the notable exception of Osiris Lopes Filhio, passed the buck. Filhio, the government official responsible for Customs and Excise, wanted the agreement that had been made weeks earlier adhered to. Hand luggage could leave immediately; the passengers could return the following day to have the larger, heavier items processed. In the event he was outmanoeuvred and overruled by members of the Government who were close to President Itamar Franco. Government Secretary General Mauro Durante was very revealing:

'Itamar's main concern was to release the luggage quickly. The players are national heroes. They can't return their medals. They can't protest. This would be a humiliation for the President.'

The wretched beleaguered Belson very reluctantly authorised the release of the plane's contents, without benefit of Customs inspection. By now many sections of the Brazilian media were on the story. TV cameras were in action, press photographers and journalists began to record the huge quantities of unexamined luggage that were being rapidly hustled away by the Brazilian football team and the CBF personnel. In such a manner did the President of Brazilian football and his entourage demonstrate that they were above the law. Customs regulations were not for them. They were in their collective minds very important people and João Havelange had educated Ricardo very well on this aspect of life. The best seats whether at football stadiums or on aeroplanes are only for VIPs and rules that apply to the rest of society are not for VIPs. The son-in-law had stood on the runway and screamed:

'Itamar told the boys that there would be no problems in Rio de Janeiro. If the luggage does not leave here with me I shall return to the airport with the people behind me and the parade will automatically be cancelled.

Obviously for a fleeting moment the little fat man had seen himself in the role of latterday liberator of the people. Itamar was a reference to the then President Itamar Franco.

When the implications of what had transpired at the international airport began to be considered by the general public, it became clear that Teixeira had made a serious misjudgment. The fracas had been televised live. Polls showed that over 70 per cent of the people thought that the players should pay Customs duty just like ordinary mortals.

The plane had contained an extraordinary amount of 'luggage'. Police and Justice Department investigations established irrefutably that in relation to what had gone out of the country before the World Cup, there was on the return flight an excess of nearly twelve tonnes of luggage. It had taken twenty men over two hours to unload.

After mounting public uproar, various players and CBF officials 'spontaneously' declared a variety of items, but there were still over nine tonnes of 'foreign goods'. Undeclared and unaccounted for. When the entire contents had been unloaded from the plane, it had been reloaded into five trucks that went in convoy to the Inter-Continental Hotel. Under the close supervision of five CBF officials in a discreet operation lasting several hours in a cordoned-off section of the hotel's parking lot, far removed from prying reporters' eyes, the baubles of late-twentieth-century consumerism were unloaded and given to their owners. The computers, mobile phones, colour TVs and the rest of the objects that had been considered so precious by Teixeira, his CBF colleagues and the Brazilian national squad were spirited away. Bribes to the media notwithstanding, apart from the most venal, this was a story that the press jumped on.

Teixeira remained unrepentant. He had done nothing wrong.

'If Customs charges any of the players, CBF will pay their fines and taxes. Branco's goal against Holland was worth more than a refrigerator.'

The only items that Teixeira declared after the public reaction were a horse saddle, a refrigerator and four loudspeakers.

Apart from public opinion, there was a determination in a number of official quarters that this affair could not be allowed to rest. There was much speculation in the State Prosecutor's office in Rio about the missing nine tonnes of goods. What had been brought illegally into Brazil? High on the Prosecutor's list of possibles were narcotics.

In February 1998 I interviewed State Prosecutor Dr Maria Emilia Arauto and a number of her colleagues in Rio. We discussed not only the State's case against Teixeira, but also Castor de Andrade's money-laundering and illegal narcotics. I asked Dr Arauto for her view on the possibility of these activities being linked to Brazilian football.

'I would like to say straightaway before we go any further that this department is convinced that football is indeed being used to launder drug money. Totally convinced of that. Currently we are attempting to develop the evidence on this, to gather together compelling proof. We are fully aware that in Italy, Spain and Brazil this activity has been going on for some years.'

'Do you believe that Castor de Andrade was involved in these activities?'

'Yes, we do to a certainty and not only Castor, all of the other heads of illegal gambling, the other *bicheiros*. They also used the various football clubs that they were involved with as laundries. The two running Botafogo football club for example. The *bicheiros* also used their connections with the samba schools to launder money. These represented for the *bicheiros* acceptable façades.'

'Dr Arauto. This case against Teixeira. This incident occurred nearly four years ago. You and your department have been attempting throughout that time to have these allegations judicially processed. I know the law moves exceedingly slow, but four years?'

'Every time we try to touch Teixeira he issues a writ demanding a million dollars for defamation. So every time we commence an action, the process is delayed because Teixeira sues the Government. He claims he is being morally defamed. Libelled. He always has one waiting for us.'

'So he has never apologised, attempted conciliation?'

'No, never. From Teixeira? He believes in confrontation, not conciliation. He's always suing us.'

'How is he getting away with such behaviour?'

'He is very well protected by the Tribunal of the State, the Accounts Tribunal of the State.'

'Have you made any headway in establishing what those missing nine tonnes of goods actually were?'

'Yes. We were up and running with the lawsuit during the second half of 1994. In December of that year advertisements began to appear in the newspapers announcing the opening of a new nightclub, El Turf. Investigations established that the owner was Teixeira. The publicity boasted that the club would contain very special equipment. Equipment to be used in serving drinks.

We sent people in to inspect the equipment. Teixeira then produced a pile of documents to prove that he had imported this equipment legally from Sweden. We established the documents were false. When we proved that, Teixeira said, "Oh, I've declared it incorrectly. I'll have to do it again."'

'And this equipment for the nightclub. You believe that it represents the missing nine tonnes of undeclared goods?'

'Some, not all.'

'From the evidence I have gathered during my research for this book it seems clear that Teixeira is a very wealthy man. What details do you have on this area?'

'He's being sued at present on this aspect. For three years he has not declared his revenues. We do know that all the businesses he's been involved with have eventually gone bankrupt.'

'Yet he's a multi-millionaire.'

'Well he has a very good job as a son-in-law.'

'He certainly has. When the State lost the case against Teixeira what exactly happened at the hearing?'

'Teixeira got a writ of habeas corpus, a device to stop the hearing. It was granted. The hearing was consequently immediately stopped. He produced a receipt proving that he had paid all taxes due on the goods that he had declared – the horse saddle, the refrigerator, the speakers.'

'But what did the State Tribunal say about the missing nine tonnes of goods?'

'They had nothing to say.'

Dr Arauto looked across her desk at me, then leaned forward.

'Mr Yallop, do you know how many judges, attorneys, members of the legal profession went to the World Cup as Teixeira's guests?'

'No, I don't.'

'I will make sure that you receive a copy of the passenger manifest.' She paused for a moment, reflecting. 'He doesn't have to bribe these people with actual money. A trip, all expenses paid, with World Cup match tickets ...'

When I last checked, Dr Arauto and her colleagues were still attempting to appeal the case against Teixeira and still attempting to establish exactly what he and others had smuggled into the country. Teixeira sits as supreme head of Brazilian football. He and a small group of men who control the game in the country are known as the *cartolas*: the big hats.

Eduardo Viana is a *cartola*. President of the Rio Football Federation. Confronted with the threat of legal action by an organisation dedicated to protecting the rights of the consumer, he responded:

'I detest public opinion. The people could all be shot by machine guns for all I care. I'm the son of a factory owner. The élite, and I'm a right-winger.'

The threatened legal action followed the revelation made by several referees that Viana had instructed them to rig important matches.

Viana, like the other *cartolas*, is rarely seen in public unless accompanied by a minimum of three or four bodyguards. He is equally contemptuous of that section of the public that put their money into his pocket.

'I don't give a damn for the opinion of football supporters. The only people I care about are the élite. Those who decide. That's why I care about what Ricardo Teixeira thinks.'

Eduardo Farah, another *cartola*, is President of the São Paulo Football Association and a close friend of many years' standing of João Havelange. In 1987 Farah could frequently be heard bitterly complaining about the rent he paid on the flat he was leasing. His only assets were a small studio flat in the centre of São Paulo and a small plot of land to the east of the city. A struggling lawyer, he was obliged to sell his collection of law books to pay some of his mounting debts. The rent on his business office was frequently overdue. Farah was a man in clear and desperate need of a State Lottery win. What he acquired was even more lucrative. With Havelange's assistance, he became President of the São Paulo Football Association in 1988. The position is unpaid, yet within six years Farah owned property worth in excess of $2.5 million. His assets included a penthouse flat valued in excess of $750,000. It came complete with six parking spaces, all used by Farah, with cars valued at a further $200,000. Farah has no known sources of income and dedicates himself full-time to his unpaid job. Ten months after becoming President, he bought a property valued at $500,000, shortly afterwards he bought a three-bedroom apartment valued at $100,000. During the following year he bought land valued at $400,000. In 1991 he bought a further four apartments. To have acquired all of these properties as Farah had done in less than five years would have required him to be earning more than the President of Shell Brazil. In 1993 when Farah was awarded the honorary title of 'Citizen of São Paulo' in recognition of his work as President of the Football Association, it was said of him: 'His work is an example for all involved in Brazilian football.'

Enrico Miranda, another *cartola*. Chairman of the Brazilian Football Federation – CBF. Usually referred to as 171 – the statute code number covering tax evasion and financial fraud. When elected to the chair of the CBF at a time when the Federation were about to investigate a scandal involving match-fixing by corrupt referees, one of his defeated opponents protested: 'How on earth is it possible for someone known as 171 to investigate the corruption of others?'

When filing his returns for 1979 he submitted two promissory notes. His father has signed as guarantor. His father had in fact died eight years earlier. Subsequently

Miranda submitted a series of returns that in part claimed dollar expenses covering overseas trips and stated that the reason in both instances for the trip was because a member of his family had died. Both deaths were only in Miranda's mind.

In 1990 a car dealership with which Miranda was involved appeared to make two hundred and eighty-five cars, that payments had been taken on, vanish into thin air.

Men like Miranda, Teixeira, Farah and Viana – the football 'élite' to use Viana's word – are in theory legally obligated to ensure that Brazilian football is free of corruption. To ask yet again the eternal question: 'Who guards the guards?' And if the custodians of the Brazilian game are so preoccupied with their own very lucrative activities, the rank and file are not far behind.

According to the Ministry of Employment, 80 per cent of the two hundred and thirty-nine clubs involved in the various championships at first division level are regularly evading payments of taxes and social security fund contributions for their players and staff. The average annual debt is over $100 million. But then as the Government's Tax and Revenue Departments are currently suing Ricardo Teixeira, the President of the Brazilian Football Federation, for an alleged tax debt of nearly £327,000 dollars and CBF for an alleged debt of a further $40,000, where can the clubs and their players look for an ideal role model?

This situation leaves both the clubs and the footballers vulnerable to a curious form of blackmail. 'If you don't play this exhibition match for us the IRS just might get some information on your club that could leave you with a very heavy fine to pay plus all the back taxes that you've laundered.' It's a gambit that goes back at least as far as Pelé in his playing prime. When he declined to play in the

Havelange-organised mini-cup of 1972 and again when he refused to play in World Cup 74 in Germany. He told me that he was threatened with an investigation into his earnings. His response was: 'Go ahead and investigate. I'm not playing.'

Demonstrably Pelé had nothing to hide. Others do.

The *cartolas* have a great deal to hide. Assets; kick-backs; illegal deals; illicit commission from selling the television rights of the games they control; kick-backs from sponsorship deals with Brazil's equivalent of ISL – Traffic, a company owned by Kleber Leite, who also happens to be President of Brazil's major club, Flamengo, and his partner Hawilla. These are some of the people ranged against Pelé in his attempts to clean up the cesspit of Brazilian football.

As they prepared for World Cup 98 in France, the national squad were able to take comfort that no team in the tournament had as much money to spend on their preparations as Brazil. Under Havelange's tutelage his son-in-law has created an identical monopoly situation in Brazil to that created by FIFA's President and ISL. When Pelé through his own company attempted to break this stranglehold and bid for the TV rights for the Brazilian National Championship, the Brazilian Football Federation official he was dealing with asked for a $1 million bribe to ensure that Pelé's company got the rights. Pelé refused to pay. The rival Traffic company acquired the rights for $1 million less than Pelé had offered and took 20 per cent of the gross.

When Pelé made this situation public, Havelange, as previously recorded, banned him from the draw in Los Angeles for World Cup 94.

When Kleber Leite was running for the office of President of Flamengo, he took a page in the O Globo newspaper to reproduce a letter of support from Havelange – an unusual departure for the President of FIFA who in theory retains at all times a neutral position in these matters. As has also been previously recorded, Havelange is a man who stays loyal to those he regards as good friends. Kleber Leite is ideal company to join men like Castor de Andrade, Lacoste and the others. Just before he was elected Kleber Leite was recorded discussing a variety of tactics to be used against Pelé in an attempt to destroy the former footballer's credibility.

On the recording Leite discusses a plan to invite Pelé to participate in a networked sports programme that is regularly aired on Sunday nights.

A prostitute was to be bribed to go onto the programme and say that Pelé was impotent. Asked on the tape if it was worth doing, Leite responds: 'Of course, anything is valid if you want to destroy somebody's reputation you should look for something ... If a whore says on TV that Kleber is impotent, fine, they will tease me but then forget about it. If a whore is contracted to say Pelé is impotent it will be news everywhere in the world.'

Leite's scheme also ensured that there would be maximum coverage around the world by inviting representatives from international agencies.

The sole intention of the plan, which was aborted, was to destroy Pelé's attempts to clean up Brazilian football. Many of the clubs are run as private trusts and apart from pension and personal taxes are exempt from income tax except for overseas transfers. Pelé wants to change that and also make it compulsory to publish annual accounts and run the clubs in accordance with company law. He seeks to bring transparency into the world of Brazilian football. Little wonder that those in control of what has truly become a licence to print money are using every trick in the book to destroy not only the dream, but also the dreamer.

In late 1997 João Havelange, fully preoccupied with

ensuring that his anointed successor should win the coming
FIFA presidential election, extolled not only his own
virtues, but all things Brazilian, at least in the world of
football.

'In Brazil eighteen hundred youngsters under seventeen,
some drawn from shanty towns, play in the championship.
If we could do that in every country in the world that
would be marvellous.'

That was said while the Sun King held an audience in
Marseilles. Having lobbied long and hard for many months
on behalf of the man he wished to see on the Zurich throne,
Havelange now publicly declared his deep desire that Sepp
Blatter should be elected.

'If he takes my position, I will take his hand. If he is
unsuccessful, I shall weep.'

This was four months before Blatter, ever the reluctant
suitor, announced that, yes, he was in fact going to stand
against Lennart Johansson. Havelange, both before and
after the Marseilles declaration, worked unceasingly on
behalf of Blatter. He toured the world garnering support
and he constantly used the Brazilian talisman as if in some
curious way a vote for Blatter was a vote for world football
to embrace the Brazilian way. On the pitch perhaps, and
not always then. Off the pitch – God forbid.

In Malaysia while lobbying for Blatter, Havelange again
used the lure of Brazil as bait. He declared: 'Malaysia
should send its youth players and coaches for courses and
training stints to Brazil. The sooner the better.'

He failed to explain why so many Brazilian footballers
cannot wait to leave the country. Over two thousand in the
past five years. With the state of the game as outlined in
these pages, who could possibly blame a young footballer
for wanting out?

Average attendance during the National Championship
is less than eleven thousand. Frequently attendance is

under one thousand spectators. This for Brazil's equivalent of Premier League matches. Teixeira and the *cartolas* have sold the soul of football to Globo TV. The network is not even going to consider playing around with its scheduling to accommodate football enthusiasts. Nothing must interfere with the nightly news and soap slots; consequently football matches kick off at nine-thirty in the evening. A journey home after eleven at night through often ill-lit areas with a high incidence of crime has limited appeal. During the early part of 1998 when I was in Brazil many of the matches had only one or two hundred spectators. Violence is frequent. We hear a great deal in the European press about our domestic violence. I have yet to find a detailed press report covering the criminal behaviour that frequently occurs at matches in the land of the Samba. In Brazil the players are virtually the property of the Club President. Ninety-five per cent of all professional players in Brazil earn less than $1,000 a month. To avoid large tax bills when a Brazilian star is transferred abroad, middlemen like the Uruguayan Juan Figer are used. Figer operates out of a São Paulo office. He's publicity-shy with good cause: the caller might not be a reporter but someone from the Brazilian tax authorities. What makes him highly desirable to the *cartolas* is the fact that he owns a third-rate, third-division Uruguayan side, Central Español, which serves as a letterbox company. Payments to not only the *cartolas* but also the football stars who are transferred by Figer are diverted through his club. Uruguayan football clubs do not pay income tax on profits from transfers. Central Español have numerous Brazilian players on their books. Hardly one of them has ever played for the club.

During the first half of 1997 Denilson de Oliveira, an emerging world-class talent, was going to be transferred to FC Barcelona from São Paulo club. The agreed fee was $32 million. Juan Figer was dissatisfied with his cut, which was many millions of dollars. Like all agents and middlemen, Figer is a man with a large appetite. The deal collapsed not because of Denilson's demands, but because of Figer's.

A few months later Real Betis of Spain were prepared to meet Figer's valuation of himself; terms were agreed for Denilson's transfer for the world-record fee of £22 million. Any club wishing to buy Denilson before he becomes a free agent in ten years' time will be asked to pay a figure that will perhaps finally allow for Juan Figer to receive what he considers to be his true worth. The valuation put on Denilson, which inevitably includes a cut for Figer, is £270 million. Those who the Gods wish to destroy they first drive mad.

If the transfer of players to foreign clubs is riddled with corruption, then the domestic game that these players are so anxious to leave often makes professional wrestling look positively pure by comparison.

In 1996 when the season finished in November, the two clubs relegated from the first division were Bragantino and Fluminense. Immediately officials connected with Fluminense and a number of their supporters began to agitate and seek any way possible to over-turn the relegation. Fluminense are a club with a huge following numbered in millions. They don't necessarily go to the games, but they watch them on television, creating for the network a good audience rating.

There was talk of dubious refereeing decisions in various matches that might have affected the relegation issue. Talk of one particular referee being bribed to give a penalty in a vital match. Nothing was proved and the relegation of both clubs was confirmed by the sports tribunal associated with Teixeira's CBF. The following May, shortly before the new season began, a series of tape recordings surfaced. They contained conversations between Ivens Mendes and a variety of football club Presidents. Mendes was looking for a career change; he wanted to go into politics and was looking for funds. One President talked of 'donating' $100,000; the others were equally amenable. The conversations made it clear that in the past Mendes had done a number of favours for a variety of football clubs. At the time Ivens Mendes was President of the National Refereeing Commission, which is under the control of Teixeira's CBF.

It was equally clear from the tapes that matches had been fixed. Allegations against Mendes had surfaced three or four years earlier and had been ignored by Teixeira. This time he was forced to act and what wonderful surreal actions he took.

A commission of inquiry was set up. To head the commission Teixeira appointed '171' – Enrico Miranda. Teixeira also used the scandal as an opportunity to bring both relegated teams, Bragantino and Fluminense, back into the first division. None of the taped telephone conversations had offered a scrap of evidence that the match-fixing had affected any game that remotely influenced the relegation of the two clubs, but they were brought back anyway. By doing this Teixeira was breaking his organisation's statutes, but then the CBF appear to do that on a regular basis. The rules were bent in 1990 after São Paulo were relegated. They were bent again in 1992 when Gremio were relegated. During the late 1980s when Gremio were relegated and finished twelfth in the lower division the following season, twelve teams instead of two 'won' promotion.

An indication of just how lucrative match-fixing in Brazil is can be gauged from the Ivens Mendes case. I interviewed Professor Rogerio Mascarenhas, the State Prosecutor investigating the Mendes case. He told me of a truly delightful state of affairs that exists in Brazil, delightful that is if an individual wants to defraud the IRS – the Inland Revenue.

'We asked the IRS to mount a fiscal investigation to establish if Mendes had received any monies that he had failed to declare. This they have now done. In Brazil there is an interesting law. If a person that defrauds on their tax is found out by the IRS and then pays the amount, then that absolves the individual of all criminal liability. No further action can be taken against that person. It's an absurd law which of course invites the entire nation to submit fraudulent tax returns.'

'Have they found any irregularities in this gentleman's accounts?'

'I don't know if anything has been found yet. What I do know, unofficially, is that Ivens Mendes, seeing that he was being investigated, offered to pay to the IRS $300,000.'

'The maximum rate of tax in Brazil is 26.5 per cent?'

'Yes.'

'Then if you take what Mendes if offering to pay and extend it out to a potential gross figure he must have received illegal payments of more than $1 million?'

'Yes, I believe so.'

'And has Mr Mendes offered any explanation to the Inland Revenue of how he acquired this previously undisclosed $1 million?'

'He has said that it came from selling water melons.'

It was some moments before I could continue my interview with the Professor, but eventually I asked him about the tapes that Globo TV had transmitted.

'When we asked for the tapes, Globo TV initially said that they had more than twenty hours of recordings. They have so far sent us six tapes, which contain only three to four hours of recordings. These were sent to the best laboratory here in Brazil with the facility for establishing if the tapes had been edited. They have. We believe that the material they have cut compromises either Globo TV or, far more likely, compromises Ricardo Teixeira.

Something has definitely been cut. It is our understanding that what has been cut very seriously compromises Ricardo Teixeira.'

'Do you know why Teixeira appointed Ivens Mendes to the South America Commission as President of the Referee's Board?'

'Teixeira has said he made that appointment because Mendes understands football arbitration and he, Teixeira, does not.'

'Really? Are you aware, Professor, that Teixeira is the Vice-Chairman of FIFA's Referee's Arbitration Committee?'

It was Professor Rogerio's turn to pause for laughter.

When the Generals ruled the country and thought they were immortal, they unleashed a footballing madness on Brazil that the country has yet to recover from. Not only did they build stadiums excessively and without any great forethought, a form of absurdity took over. Near Porto Alegre is the small town of Erechim. The junta built a football stadium for the population with a seating capacity in excess of the entire population of the town. The Generals had a slogan – 'Integrating the country through football'. They certainly tried. When Giulite Soutinho took over at the CBF he inherited a national championship in which ninety-four teams competed. Against tremendous opposition from the *cartolas* he whittled it down to two divisions of twenty teams per division.

Undeterred, the remaining *cartolas* increased the number of matches. The football calendar in Brazil beggars belief. In the 1998 season Vasco are scheduled to play at least ninety matches, compared with PSV Eindhoven who are due to play forty-five or Barcelona (fifty-nine) or Juventus (sixty-seven), or even Manchester United (seventy-four). And that Manchester United figure presupposes extended runs in the two domestic Cup tournaments and the

European championship, all in addition to the Premier League.

More games means more injuries, many simply caused by excessive and repetitive use of the body's muscles. Comparing two young talented players, Alexandro de Souza – Alex, who began the 98 season playing for Palmeiras – and Raul Gonzales Blanco – Raul of Real Madrid – is a salutary exercise.

Both are twenty years of age. The Brazilian began his season by playing nine games in twenty-two days. If his club's season goes according to plan, Alex will play eighty-three games averaging seven games per month. Raul played thirty-five games for his club during the 98 season. His maximum in a full calendar year would be fifty-four games.

If the two players continue throughout their careers at their current levels, the Brazilian Alex will lose 30 per cent of his playing life. Raul will still be playing at thirty-five years of age. Alex will be out of football at thirty years of age. No country in the world subjects its footballers to the number of games played at the top level in Brazil.

And in the World Cup tournament in France it showed.

Tele Santana, who played for Fluminense in the early '90s, recalls:

'When I was a player I was forbidden from training during the week to ensure that I recovered the weight I had lost during a match. I was a fragile athlete, as indeed many of the present crop are. I would lose three or four kilos in each match. Consequently the club's doctors forbade me to train mid-week. I played until I was thirty-three.'

It puts the achievements of Pelé and his colleagues into a stunning perspective. On occasions Santos played one hundred matches in a season. To ask Alex and his colleagues to match that, given the pace of the modern game, is to invite his generation of footballers to get ready for a painful crippled middle age. In view of the ten-year, $400 million deal that Teixeira and others have negotiated with Nike, that is precisely what the Brazilian Football Association is asking of today's Brazilian football talent. As the national team's sponsor, Nike have been granted a whole raft of rights. Informed observers in Brazil believe that through these various rights, Nike virtually control the Brazilian national squad. Certainly their corporate influence reaches into at the very least a significant input with regard to who is in the side and which games Brazil will play. Nike also have absolute control over the organisation of five national games per year. The inherent dangers in this deal would be demonstrated in the World Cup 98 Final.

'Football in Brazil is in the hands of the Mafia and it is the very worst kind you can imagine. Because the Mafia in Italy or anywhere else is not against the ordinary people. Here they are against the people, against the people's interests.'

These words came from Marcio Braga, former President of Flamengo, during my interview with him in Rio. Braga was part of the Brazilian Confederation of Sports for thirteen years as one of the judges adjudicating on the sports tribunal. A qualified lawyer, Federal MP, Government Secretary of Sport and a long-time bitter opponent of Havelange and Teixeira.

Marcio Braga has struggled long and hard to fight the endemic corruption within Brazilian football.

'The football structure we have was brought from Fascist Italy in 1941. It well suited the dictatorship, the Vargas dictatorship that controlled the country at that time. I and many more like me have fought for many years to change this model.'

Braga recounted to me that during his twenty-year presidency of one of Brazil's most famous and successful clubs he was continually in a state of war with successive military juntas. He painted a very vivid picture of what life was like under the rule of the military.

'I'm telling you all this to illustrate that João Havelange is the fruit of those years. He is the flower coming from this mud. According to people very close to me during my years at Flamengo I am assured that João Havelange was a member of the Brazilian Intelligence Service from the time of the military dictatorship in 1964 onwards. When he went to FIFA his role changed from being a supporter to being an informer. Particularly did he do this work for Intelligence after he became President of FIFA.'

Braga's source for this extraordinary information was a member of the Brazilian Secret Service. Subsequently through my own non-Brazilian sources, including the CIA's Latin American Desk, I was able to confirm that Braga had not been misinformed. FIFA's President for twenty-four years has been working for his country's Secret Service for even longer. It explained so many aspects of the Havelange story, not least the junta's reluctance to prosecute in him 1974–75.

Braga's reason for discussing this aspect of Havelange with me was to illustrate just how formidable were the strong ties and links that Havelange maintains with the very heart of Brazil's power structure and how difficult it was to fight such power.

'Havelange is part of this structure and it is because of that that he controlled Brazilian sports and specifically football. He managed to get his son-in-law elected. Then they became owners of Brazilian football. It's a small market and they own it all. When I was President of Flamengo I represented the real opposition to them. The truth is that I fought and fought with all my strength. I used every valid argument against them, but they are strong. Very, very strong. The maximum I could get was a draw. I could never win.'

I asked Braga about Teixeira's wealth.

'It's obvious that this money comes from football. When

he took office in the CBF he came from a very bad investment business called Minas Investimentos. It was sold for one dollar after collapsing into bankruptcy. He has no paid job. He has a farm in Pirati with a few cattle. He processes milk. The failed lawyer and bankrupt businessman now owns in Rio a Hyundai store, two nightclubs and a restaurant. With this little farm he has made a fortune reputed to be in excess of $100 million. In all of this he is protected by Havelange.'

When Teixeira, against the laws and rules of the Brazilian Football Federation, engineered a situation to give himself a further year in office, Braga in the name of his football club Flamengo went to war.

'It was in essence a fight for power. We had the very wide popular strength of Flamengo. Teixeira had the strength of politics, friendships and the money. So I took them to court. We have a system in Brazil called sports justice and another, common justice. There is a FIFA statute that forbids a football club seeking to right a wrong through common justice in certain cases. Now I know the constitution of my country quite well, in fact I drafted the section dealing with this aspect. It was abundantly clear that to seek to remove Teixeira from office I needed to go the route of common justice. This I did, at which point FIFA – which means Havelange – banned Flamengo from international competitions. It was their second mistake. If my club were to be punished then it would have to be by the Rio Federation, not FIFA and not CBF.'

At this stage it had become a national controversy. Havelange began to flail around. He declared that if he could not punish Flamengo directly he would punish the entire country. He would ban Brazil from World Cup 94 in the United States. Enormous pressure was then brought to bear on Braga and his club, by Globo TV, the press and media generally, to withdraw the case against Teixeira, which of course was precisely the object of the Havelange threat. Braga then upped the ante.

'I brought an action against FIFA. I found a Brazilian lawyer with a Zurich correspondent. Not easy, but I found one. One day before the trial in Zurich, FIFA cancelled the punishment to suspend my club indefinitely from all international football. FIFA's lawyers had warned Havelange that he was almost certainly going to lose and for FIFA this would be a very dangerous precedent. It would have been the first time that the mighty FIFA had lost to anyone in a court of law. It could have opened the floodgates.'

'A very famous victory.'

'A very short one. The following day CBF handed out precisely the same punishment to Flamengo. Banned from all international matches until I dropped the action to get rid of Teixeira. My time at Flamengo was coming to an end. I had been trying to get the Zico law through Congress. This, like Pelé's bill, was an attempt to clean up Brazilian football. So we all sat down and did a deal. I would give up the action, they would lift the suspension against Flamengo and their supporters, CBF's supporters in the Congress would not oppose the Zico bill. Now the point about that bill is that it clearly made what Teixeira had done illegal. So right, if everything goes as planned, we will get rid of this man. So sure enough I did indeed drop my action. CBF removed the ban on Flamengo. The Zico law was passed and Teixeira and his friends at CBF ignored the law. By this time I was no longer President of Flamengo and was therefore not in a position to reinstate the legal action. Teixeira continued to ignore the law. You see, David, in this country we have a democratically elected government. We pass laws that the Senate and the Congress have voted on. Those laws apply to everyone except CBF. Football in Brazil is in the hands of the Mafia.'

As this investigation in Brazil progressed, I began to realise the sheer enormity of the task that Pelé had undertaken. I was aware that a final debate on his Bill would shortly be heard in Brazil's Parliament in Brasilia. I was equally aware that Teixeira had previously hired a luxurious villa complete with in-house entertainment in Brasilia so that the deputies to Congress could be 'lobbied'. It was possible that the exercise would get repeated before the crucial vote. This time the Senators would get to sample the well-known Teixeira hospitality.

I began to need an antidote to the amount of corruption that appeared to be waiting for me on every street corner in Rio and São Paulo. Something positive, something good about the Brazilian domestic game. I found what I was looking for in Rio's Flamengo Park.

The *Nova Safra* – The New Crop School of Football – had quite an academic ring to it. The reality is an asphalt pitch full of potholes in the municipal park in the heart of Rio. At first I thought this was just a typical Sunday morning kick-about. I was wrong. It was well organised, though the players were young, a maximum of ten years of age, they were unusually disciplined. Waiting at one end was a large group of older boys, many of them towering over the diminutive figure of a little old man who in his own way is as much of an inspirational figure as Pelé.

He is sixty-six years of age and his name is José João known to most people as Jota. He is small enough to have been a jockey. In the late 1940s Jota was a young player with considerable promise. In 1951 an accident put an end to a career as a footballer. At that time he dreamed of starting a football school for young boys. Like many a working man with a dream, he put it to one side and got on with earning a living.

'Some ten or eleven years ago my sons asked me if we could all go to the park and kick a ball around. So I said,

"Sure, but get two or three of your friends to come along, it'll make it more interesting." I was playing with them, giving them a little coaching, and suddenly I thought, "Yes, this is what I want to do and now that I'm retired I can do it."

And from that simple beginning on a scruffy piece of land hardly good enough to park a car on let alone train and play football, Jota has mined pure gold. He has to beg for equipment. He asked the Secretary of Rio's Sports and Leisure Association for ten balls. He got two. Because the pitch is in such an appalling condition the life of a football is short. In 1995 the President of the Dutch club Feyenoord came to Jota's 'academy' with its stones and potholes. It was raining at the time. Raining Rio-style, Niagara is just a power shower by comparison. The boys were playing in a virtual pool. The President could not believe his eyes as, oblivious, the boys played on.

They train and play on just Saturday mornings from 7 a.m. until 1 p.m. and Sundays from 7 a.m. to 3 p.m. Because it is a public park that is the maximum allocation of time that Jota has been able to negotiate from the local authorities. Initially it was only 9 a.m. until 1 p.m. He wrote to the commander of the physical education section of the military school located in Rio asking for the use of what is a vastly superior playing field for the Sunday sessions. The answer was a brusque 'no'.

A number of former Brazilian players run football schools – Zico, Carlos Alberto, Rivelino. All of these started after Jota. All of them, unlike Jota, charge. Even the beach schools, they all charge. This of course excludes the children of the *favelas*: the shantytowns. This is where Jota and his colleagues go looking for potential talent. Boys who would never be able to afford the $120 a month at Zico's school.

The big clubs like Braga's Flamengo, Santos, Vasco,

have youth training schemes, but if the young player has not got his bus fare to get to the ground, tough, he does not get to the ground. One young player, a boy of great promise, faced precisely this problem while playing for Flamengo. He talked to the coach, whose response was, 'Tough, that's your problem.' The young man moved to a club closer to his home, São Christovao. His new club also gave him travelling expenses. The boy got better, the club got worse; they were a second-division side going nowhere. Jairzinho, the same Jairzinho who had torn England apart in Mexico in World Cup 70, saw the young boy and bought him from São Christovao. Just bought him in much the same way that men used to buy black men before the abolition of slavery. He paid $10,000 for the boy. He sold the boy to Cruzero, a club in northern Brazil. Hopefully the boy got a piece. The price was $100,000. This year the boy will earn £20.5 million. He has become the highest-paid footballer in the world. His name is Luiz Nazario de Lima, better known as Ronaldo.

Jota told me the tale of Ronaldo with a mixture of amusement and bitterness. The fact that Flamengo by their meanness and lack of vision had let a superstar slip through their fingers appealed to Jota. The fact that the big clubs are continuing to perpetuate exactly the same kind of error angers him. His passion for the game consumes him totally, dominates virtually every waking minute of his life. The young boys aged from five or six years up to their mid-teens are trained and shaped not only in the skills of football. They know that any delinquency, any truanting from school, and they are out. Jota is himself from the *favela*; his father fed the family by begging. Jota survives on a small pension. His own begging is for kit and equipment for his 'new crop'. In the last ten years since he created his 'school' many of his footballing students have graduated with honours. Twenty have gone on to

Fluminense, three to Vasco. Over one hundred have gone on to play professional football in Brazil. Another has gone to Honduras and yet another – Leonardo – is at Feyenoord in Holland. Leonardo, now fifteen years of age, is considered by many experts to be 'very special – a world-class player'.

Other potential Leonardos come to Jota's 'school', accept the free cotton shirt that Jota gives to all entrants and then never return. For the sake of a shirt worth less than a dollar. They go back to their *favelas*. Some die young involved in the cocaine trade, others stay trapped one way or another in the grinding poverty of the *favela*. Jota is not only handing out a cheap cotton shirt, he is also giving the young boys who come and stay to train, to learn and to play, a shovel, an instrument with which they can dig their way out of the *favela*.

Jota gets a pension of seven hundred dollars per month. One hundred and forty dollars are given to his own children. One hundred dollars goes on his small apartment. One hundred and ten dollars goes on private health care. Then there is the cleaner. At the end of the day there is barely enough to live on and certainly none for luxuries, which is why he has to beg for football kit.

Feyenoord donated thirty balls and several sets of kit to the school, but the need for new kit and equipment is continuous. Jota wrote last year to Ricardo Teixeira. It was a plea for help. At exactly the time of Jota's letter, Teixeira and his colleagues at CBF, the Brazilian Football Association, were putting the final touches to a deal with Nike. The deal since signed and implemented is a ten-year sponsorship deal with the sportswear corporation. It is for $400 million.

NOVA SAFRA – ESCOLINHA DE FUTEBOL
PARQUE DO FLAMENGO
Founded 13 August 1988

Rio de Janeiro, 13 May 1997

TO:
MR RICARDO TERRA TEIXEIRA
PRESIDENT OF BRAZILIAN FOOTBALL
FEDERATION
RUA DA ALFANDEGA, 70
NESTA

Dear Sir

For the sake of children and adolescents in football, on 13 August 1988 I started a project called NOVA SAFRA ESCOLINHA DE FUTEBOL with lessons entirely free of charge, and without any financial motivation, for children and adolescents ranging from 10 to 15 years.

Roja, the project in question, is a corporation in fact and in law in accordance with its foundation and statutes, registered in the CIVIL REGISTER OF LEGAL ENTITIES situated at Av. Franklin Roosevelt, No 126 – 2nd Floor, Room 205, in this city.

The lessons are held in football field No 3 of the Parque do Flamengo on Saturday and Sundays from 9:00 to 13:00 hours. This site which was granted by the Administration of the Parque do Flamengo is about 9 years old.

The work carried out by our Technical Commission, without any remuneration, began to have success beginning from 1992 with various pupils from the NOVA SAFRA ESCOLINHA DE FUTEBOL entering various clubs of the State of Rio de Janeiro in our respective categories for them.

For your further information, I list below the clubs involved. Nothing is received in return.

01 FLUMINENSE F CLUBE – 20
02 C R VASCO DA GAMA – 03
03 C R FLAMENGO – 01
04 OLARIA A CLUBE – 31
05 SAO CHRISTOVAO F R – 09
06 AMERICA F CLUBE – 04
07 A A PORTUGUESA – 02
08 BONSUCESSO P CLUBE – 04
09 PAVUNENSE F CLUBE – 05
10 A A EVEREST – 07
11 F CLUBE BAYER B ROXO – 13
12 CANTO DO RIO F CLUBE – 01
13 A A PONTE PRETA – 03 (SÃO PAULO)
14 SERRANO F CLUBE – 04 (PETROPOLIS)
15 HONDURAS – 01 (CENTRAL AMERICA)
16 FEYENOORD ROTTERDAM – 01 (HOLLAND)

TOTAL 109

At present, the ESCOLINHA DE FUTEBOL has 100 (one hundred) pupils in the age range from 10 to 15 years. The majority are natives of various shantytowns in the Municipality of Rio de Janeiro and Baixada Fluminenso [Fluminenso Valley] as well as from other districts.

In view of what I have said above, I am asking on behalf of this corporation – the senior one of Brazilian football, through the competent branch, for help in propagating this project and also for a donation of some balls.

The signatory below, the Founder, Director and Trainer,

by this letter, asks that a representative of this corporation make a visit to the above-mentioned place.

Day-time contact telephone: 225 5770, evenings: 285 0320.

Yours faithfully

JOSÉ JOÃO

CBFIAFB
INSTITUTE OF ASSISTANCE TO BRAZILIAN FOOTBALL – IAFB
OFFICIAL LETTER No 59/97

Rio de Janeiro 26 June 1997

From the Institute of Assistance to Football (IAFB)
To the Escolinha de Futebol Nova Safra

Reply to Official Letter of Mr José João

Dear Sir

We should like to inform you that unfortunately our project does not include a donation of material to schools under your project.

Although we are not at present able to comply with your request, allow us to express our admiration to you and to all in the community for the fine and humanitarian work which is being carried out.

With good wishes of encouragement to you, we remain,

Yours faithfully

Denise Cunha
Administrator

This then is a little of the situation within Brazilian football. A state of affairs with which the President of the Brazilian Federation, Ricardo Teixeira, and his former father-in-law can see no wrong. Indeed, they strained every nerve to kill Pelé's bill designed to eliminate the range of corruption recorded in this book. Both men took this issue very personally, Havelange yet again demonstrating his own sense of image:

'It's obvious that this bill is aimed at a single person. I am a person respected around the world, and yet the government of my country has turned against the organisation I direct.'

When I talked to Pelé in his São Paulo offices in early 1998, I asked him for a response to some of the wild and outrageous statements that FIFA's President had been making over the previous months as the date grew nearer for the Brazilian Senate to debate the proposed bill.

'The biggest problem with both FIFA and the CBF with both Havelange and Teixeira is that they forget to put something back in the game. They talk a great deal of how much money they have made, but for whom? What do they give back to the game at its base? At its grassroots?'

'Havelange has said that he treated you like a son. That you owe him a great deal. That you would never have been able to play in World Cup 58 in Sweden without his support. What is your reaction to all of that?'

'I have never denied that he looked after me when I was young. I have frequently expressed my gratitude for that. Yes, he did indeed look after me as if I was his son and that is what puzzles me so much now. His anger. His rage. Yes, he gave me values, just as my own father has always done. Lessons about honesty. Being decent. Never dishonest. All I am trying to do with this bill is enshrine some of those values onto the Statute Book. He should surely be pleased with what I am trying to do.'

'What of Havelange's threat to ban Brazil from World Cup 98 if your bill is passed from the Senate?'

'David, Brazil won its place at the World Cup Finals in France on the field. Not through a decision by FIFA.'

A few minutes later Pelé took a phone call. It was from Brasilia, from the Senate. He turned back to continue our conversation, the grin on his face lighting up the room.

'That was some good news. My bill has just been approved by the Senate.'

We shared his joy and I uttered a silent prayer that unlike the Zico Bill this one would bite. That Teixeira and his cronies would not be able to ignore and dismiss this legislation. That this time the stables will be cleaned.

By mid-1997 President Havelange, who had stated categorically at the beginning of that year that 'I am not going to enter the election process' was very busily engaged in electioneering on behalf of his General Secretary, Sepp Blatter. Havelange, when announcing in late 1996 that he would not serve as President of FIFA after June 1998, had talked eloquently in a personal letter to the other members of the FIFA Executive Committee of his desire to turn into a reality what Lennart Johansson had spoken of at a banquet to honour Havelange and his wife Anna Maria: 'I am referring to the unity of FIFA throughout all continents.' By mid-1997 that too was forgotten as he took every opportunity to push Blatter as his successor. With the fifty-one European block of votes committed to Johansson, to run Blatter as a candidate ensured that there would be no unity within the FIFA organisation. If Blatter should win then disunity would certainly be rife for a long time in the higher echelons of the football world.

In October 1997 FIFA invited twenty-five general secretaries and football administrators from African countries to a twelve-day training course at the University of Neuchâtel in Switzerland. It was a splendid affair.

Diplomas all round and the press invited to cocktails and lunch. The event cost over a quarter of a million dollars. The first that Johansson and his seven fellow European FIFA Executive colleagues knew about it was when they read the press release. The main purpose of this exercise was to create an opportunity for Havelange to work both the media and the delegates. The Tunisian member of the FIFA Media Commission was present when Havelange invited a group of journalists into his office and began singing the praises of Sepp Blatter and urging the press to support Blatter as his successor. Blatter of course was not a candidate and Havelange of course was not getting involved in the election.

João Havelange has over his twenty-four years' tenure of the presidency on a number of occasions made the 'over my dead body' declaration and subsequently shifted his position, or his body, when it has become clear that he has lost the argument. The Pelé Bill is a classic example. If there was one issue that from early 1997 was an 'over my dead body' issue for Havelange that would never result in a shift of position, it was the matter of who would succeed him. Havelange was determined that in defeating Johansson he would live on as President through Sepp Blatter. Continuity. That was going to be the name of the game. In Blatter, Havelange would have a living monument.

It was extraordinary to watch. One man in his eighties continued to defy the majority of his FIFA Executive Committee, virtually all of European football and a good part of the rest of the world game. The most breathtaking example of the Havelange arrogance and disregard for any form of democracy was the manner in which he dispensed the World Cup TV rights to his preferred candidates, a consortium of the German media giant Taurus Film/Kirch Gruppe and its Swiss partner, Sporis. Reference to the FIFA Finance Committee was kept to a minimum, consultation with other parties was non-existent; an earlier bid of $1 billion was simply ignored and then to top all of that the Havelange–Blatter duo sold the rights not just for World Cup 2002, but for good measure 2006. Havelange would be out of office for eight years before the rights that he had tied up would again become available. They had sold the rights for two World Cup tournaments for $2 billion. The major reason that they had extracted such a huge figure from the consortium was because the Mark McCormack organisation IMG had bid one billion for just World Cup 2002. The prospect of such vast revenue ensured that in the run-up to the election in June 1998 Havelange and Blatter would be able to be very, very generous when it came to canvassing support. A great many national associations would benefit from 'advanced payments on financial assistance'. The amount of 'benefit' given in this manner was over $1.3 million.

The Sun King and the undeclared pretender to his throne used their positions as President and General Secretary of FIFA quite shamelessly as the World Cup draw in Marseilles came and went. Still Blatter held back from declaring. The longer he could hold out, the longer he could use his official position as General Secretary in a high-profile unofficial election campaign. No one worked harder during this phoney war period for Blatter's ultimate success than Havelange. The President had embarked on a worldwide 'farewell' tour in early 1998. He came bearing gifts. In Africa, for example, it was like an eerie replay of the early 1970s. The Brazilian moved among the FIFA delegates offering 'financial inducements'. As always the range on offer from Havelange was varied. The potential to persuade FIFA delegates to vote for Blatter can be gauged from the very modest accommodation and facilities that many delegates from the Third World were obliged to function in. When he had begun his last period in office in 1994,

Havelange had talked of one of his major projects being, 'That each of the 191 FIFA members associations should have a fax machine so that all can take part in matters to be considered. This is an investment which is urgently needed.' Now, thanks to Havelange – or that is how the President would see it – there are enough fax machines to go around.

Fax machines were only a part of what the President was giving away. To each of the member associations, one million dollars. To each of the six confederations, ten million dollars. Right to the end, Havelange continued to say hello with another man's hat. In this instance it was a hat that belongs to you and me. To all of us. It was also a hat that had been made by Lennart Johansson.

Havelange remembered everyone. No one who had a vote was forgotten.

Somali Football Association
C/o Con. Afric de Football
5 Gabalaya Street
11567 El Borg
Cairo, Egypt

Zurich, 8th April 1998
JH/mmu/sk

Dear General Secretary Dr Yasin Abukar Arif

I should like to tell you how happy I was to see you on the occasion of the meeting held in Kagali, where you were able to expound your Federation's point of view, and I had the pleasure of confirming my promise to you concerning the presence of two delegates for the FIFA Congress in Paris on 7th and 8th June. The cost of travelling for one delegate will be charged to FIFA, as decided, and the other, as I promised you, will be my responsibility, as well as the cost of accommodation.

Further, I uphold my promise for the realisation of the FUTURO II course in your region, or in your country, for techniques, refereeing, sport medicine and administration. Additionally, two participants will attend the courses given in Brazil.

As to your National Association, I have had a meeting with the FIFA Deputy General Secretary, Mr Michel Zen-Ruffinen concerning your development.

Assuring you that I will be very happy to see you again in Paris, together with your President, at the FIFA Congress on 7th and 8th June, I remain, with my very best wishes and kindest regards.

Yours sincerely

João Havelange

In some instances the Havelange tour was greeted with a certain scepticism. Mustapha Fahmy, the Vice President and Secretary of CAF – the Confederation Africaine de Football – told me:

'Havelange is offering many things and he's leaving, so I don't know who can deliver these promises. During his time in office he has promised us many things and he has never kept his promises. So now who can guarantee that now when he's leaving he is going to keep his promises.'

Mustapha Fahmy's view was also influenced by the fact that the $1 million 'gift' to every association was a direct steal from UEFA President Lennart Johansson's idea expressed more than two years earlier in a document entitled Vision One. The reader may remember that when

Havelange was first given a copy he threw it across the conference room.

Of course, by presenting the idea as his own to a wide variety of associations while simultaneously urging the delegates to vote for Blatter would not affect the vote. Of course not.

With outrage in the European camp growing daily and with media comment by March 1998 finally beginning to address the situation, Blatter continued to exploit to the full his position as General Secretary. He was able to keep a global profile through his supervision of the World Cup arrangements for France 98. Regularly appearing on TV, regularly talking to the press, he was able to maintain constant contact with the executives of all 198 FIFA associations in his role of FIFA's 'foreign minister'. One aspect in particular worried Lennart Johansson and his colleagues at UEFA. Tickets for the World Cup 98 tournament. They were very aware how Havelange has over the past twenty-four years used World Cup tickets and appropriate expenses as a powerful tool of persuasion. On 18 February President Johansson wrote to Blatter:

'As always, the ticket distribution for the World Cup is a matter that is widely discussed. As Chairman of the Organising Committee, I feel obliged to take particular interest in the distribution policy. I should like to ask you to let me have a detailed and complete list of the distribution of these tickets as per today. Furthermore, I expect to be informed in writing on a weekly basis of the distribution of further contingents or any changes to previous allotments.'

Johansson was still waiting for a response to that letter over five weeks later when, with just ten days to go to the 7 April deadline for declaration, Blatter finally announced that he was going to run for the Sun King's throne.

The fact that he revealed that he was going to run with Michel Platini as some curious form of running mate, with

Platini to be given a job as Technical Director if Blatter won, gave the Europeans even greater cause for concern with regard to ticket distribution. Platini was Co-President of France 98. In the minds of the Europeans, Blatter and Platini had unlimited access to as many tickets as they desired.

That senior members of UEFA felt threatened by Blatter's link with Platini shows a quite extraordinary situation. These executives who had talked to me of how over the years Havelange had exploited his access to World Cup tickets repeatedly, now held the belief that Blatter was going to use the same tactics as one of a number of 'inducements' to voting delegates. At the very least it paints an illuminating picture of the relationship between the world's most important football confederation and FIFA's President and General Secretary. The distrust and hostility between the two camps made a mockery of FIFA unity. The first battle, one that had raged from the beginning of the year, was to force Blatter to resign his position.

Lennart Johansson's supporters were enraged that Blatter and Havelange should exploit the power and influence of high executive office while running officially for the top job. It was something that Blatter had been doing for many months. When he presided over the group draw in Marseilles in December 1997 every single FIFA delegate with a vote knew to a certainty that this man would be running against Johansson. By delaying his declaration almost to the last minute, Blatter was able to take full advantage of his position as FIFA General Secretary while preparing his campaign. On 6 February the African Association met at Burkina Faso. Blatter was in attendance in his role as General Secretary, yet he spent much of his time lobbying, making 'offers of financial inducements', as five different association members described it to me. These were not confined to plane tickets and hotel accommodation in France with match tickets thrown in. The offers included cash payments of many thousands of dollars to 'assist national associations who are in a particularly difficult economic situation at the moment'. That is Sepp Blatter's description of what he was doing. Such a kind man, just like that charming Dr Havelange who also went repeatedly to the African continent bearing gifts.

As a paid FIFA official Blatter was not allowed to conduct an electoral campaign. Apart from not campaigning at the Burkina Faso meeting, Blatter would also be restraining himself at Asunción in Paraguay. And again at the beginning of May, when he was due to attend the North and Central American Associations meeting in Guatemala, he would in the meetings at Antigua not utter a word on his prospects and so on and so on. It was to put a stop to this scenario continuing that UEFA took to the barricades after Blatter declared he would nobly carry on in his FIFA job. They eventually prevailed in early April and Blatter was forced to resign as General Secretary. It was a victory of sorts for Johansson's supporters, a moral victory, but then morals were not going to have a great deal to do with the winning of the FIFA presidency.

Sepp Blatter's critics have always seen him as President Havelange's creation. In fact he was, as previously recorded, created by Horst Dassler, and indeed, upon joining FIFA he continued to be paid by Dassler's Adidas, a situation that in any ethically run organisation would be seen as producing a clear conflict of interest.

But then no conflict has been seen in the fact that Blatter owns an apartment in Appenzell in a block owned by Emil Sutter, the man who for many years has acted as FIFA's auditor. *Independent* auditor. No conflict in the fact that Blatter's colleague, FIFA's head of finance Erwin Schmid, has been a close lifelong friend of Sutter's. In a story that is full of bizarre twists and turns the fact that for many years a small, obscure accountancy company has been responsible for the billion-dollar business accounts of FIFA topples over from the bizarre to the absurd.

Neither Blatter nor Havelange has over the years seen any problem with the fact that the real estate portfolio that Havelange so proudly boasted to me about – a portfolio worth more than $100 million – is handled by just Blatter and Schmid, and when Blatter is absent, which has been frequently, Schmid holds meetings by himself, confirms to himself that he is indeed present, takes minutes of what he says, votes on any issue that he raises and then votes to close the meeting that he alone has attended. No one in their right mind would run a sweetshop like that, let alone a multi-million dollar portfolio. Blatter also presumably sees no conflict of interest that his finance chief Schmid is also a co-director of two further property and investment companies which are owned by FIFA's accountants.

It is said that one has to get up early to put one over on Britain's Prime Minister. Someone should have told him that Havelange never sleeps. The Sun King came to 10 Downing Street on 13 March 1998. After he and Tony Blair had spun footballs for the benefit of the TV cameras, they retired with various colleagues. At a given point the President and the Prime Minister continued their discussion in French. Some in the room who understood joined in, others who were not bilingual kept quiet, nodded wisely and pretended to be deeply involved in the meeting. Among this latter category was Britain's Sports Minister, Tony Banks. He sat next to the Prime Minister, 'nodding like one of those dogs you see in the back of cars, pretending I knew what was going on.' The Prime Minister's in-house spin doctor, Alastair Campbell, a sadistic bastard at the best of times, decided that Banks should take the press conference after the meeting. Some who were bilingual

were a trifle bemused at the utterances of the Sports
Minister, who later confided: 'I think I got away with it.'

During the meeting Havelange declared that he was in
favour of England hosting the World Cup in 2006. It was
a statement that ensured headlines in every newspaper and
space on every TV and radio news programme. That much
Tony Banks had understood. At the press conference
afterwards, he pronounced himself, 'very, very encouraged
by such an endorsement from such an influential figure.'

What his Prime Minister had said in response, Banks did
not know, because the response had been in French. Cynics
might well feel that keeping the Sports Minister in the dark
was intentional. Banks does not shoot from the hip, but
from the mouth.

Blair's response would, if known, have made even bigger
headlines than the Havelange declaration. After all,
Havelange was not only offering something that was not
within his gift, it was also something that he had previously
offered at least twice: to Nelson Mandela's South Africa
and to Germany. He had also been heard singing the
praises of Brazil for the same tournament. Perhaps as
World Cup 2002 is going to be played in both Japan and
South Korea, Havelange was merely upping the bidding.
Next time four? None of this was obviously contained in
the Prime Minister's briefing before he met the FIFA
President. Consequently he was thrilled at the news. His
response to Havelange was to give a clear, unequivocal
commitment to spend 'at least one billion pounds on the
stadiums'. As this country moved inevitably into recession
in the second half of 1998, it was interesting to reflect on
the Government's priorities. Never mind health, the
elderly, the sick, the poor, the homeless and the numerous
other sections of our society crying out desperately for
greater funding. A World Cup tournament in England
during 2006, which could well be announced before the

Prime Minister is obliged to call the next election, would guarantee a Blair victory at the polls. Military juntas are not the only rulers who appreciate the importance of football.

As a demonstration of the Prime Minister's naiveté, what occurred that day in Downing Street really takes some beating. Havelange angled for a visit to Number 10 for just one reason. If through a stirring but meaningless declaration he could persuade the Prime Minister and through him the English Football Association to change their vote at the coming election in Paris, he would have driven a wedge into the solid, pro-Johansson European vote. If the English Football Association announced a day or so before the vote took place that they were switching their allegiance from Johansson to Blatter, it might bring other UEFA votes to Blatter. He did. They did. It did.

My source for what the Prime Minister said to the President of FIFA is João Havelange.

Lennart Johansson's fears that the ticket allocation for World Cup 98 might become subject to abuse had in fact become a reality even before his letter to General Secretary Blatter in February. Four weeks earlier it was clear that unauthorised dealers were selling large quantities of tickets via the Internet. The system of distribution was always going to be abused once it became known that 60 per cent of all seats were going to be allocated to the French, 20 per cent would be going to sponsors and corporate guests, a derisory 16 per cent – 8 per cent per team – would be allocated to the actual supporters and the final 4 per cent simply vanished into a Bermuda Triangle. FIFA through its Director of Communications would state after the tournament was over that all sections of the organisational infrastructure had been a resounding success, but then Keith Cooper had access to every single game.

Just seventeen travel agents around the world were authorised by FIFA to sell a mere 8 per cent of all tickets for the World Cup. The demand for tickets exceeded what was available by ratios as high as five thousand to one. With that level of odds it was inevitable that the situation would be exploited. An interesting recurring theme was that frequently the source for these illicit tickets was the United States.

In January 1998 an American agency, 24/7, based in Atlanta, claimed to have apparently unlimited quantities of tickets for any game that took the buyer's fancy. If the buyer was prepared to pay the price. Nick Harris, a reporter on the staff of *The Independent* newspaper, was offered 477 tickets covering England's three qualifying matches, the quarter- and semi-finals and the final. The tickets had a face value of £19,000. The agency in Atlanta was asking £244,000 – a profit of 1,184 per cent.

Another United States source was Murray's Tickets in Los Angeles. They also offered tickets for all games; again the mark-up was huge.

There were ticket brokers in New York, San Francisco and, it seemed, all points in between. All were offering huge numbers of tickets. The New York broker had one particular ticket source of note, if my German informants are to be believed. FIFA Vice President and Executive Committee member Jack Warner. Apart from being a very close friend of President Havelange, Warner was a man who had been at least partly instrumental in Havelange retaining power in 1994. Warner is a man of many parts. He also sits on FIFA's Emergency Committee, Finance Committee, the Organising Committee for the FIFA/ Confederations Cup, the Committee for FIFA Youth Competitions, the FIFA Technical Committee, the Players Status Committee, the Committee for Security Matters and Fair Play and the Organising Committee for World Cup

France 98. He is also President of CONCACAF – The Confederation of North and Central America and the Caribbean. If as reported he did indeed sell to the New York broker a large quantity of tickets, including one thousand tickets for the Belgium v Holland match, it is not surprising that he used the services of a broker. He would never have found the time to personally sell them on to the Hilversum travel agent that offered me a quantity of them. The face value of these tickets was $45. I was offered them at $450 a ticket. The travel agency in Hilversum is called Joscam Travel.

I discussed the ramifications of this with UEFA Press Secretary Marco Casanova. Casanova as a key member of the Johansson campaign team was very concerned with some of the implications of these illicit ticket deals.

'We [UEFA] are concerned as to how Jack Warner and Chuck Blazer [General Secretary and Treasurer of CONCACAF] are getting their hands on these tickets. We think that Blatter is involved.'

'How does Blatter get his hands on these tickets?'

'He has them. FIFA owns the tickets. So he physically has the tickets, so that means you call a President and say, I give you ten Final tickets if you want from me. And then he puts them physically in an envelope and says "Kind regards, Sepp" and sends them to somebody. There is no controlling system. No list that shows who got which tickets. Why did he choose Platini? So, he misuses the World Cup. So he has an ally in the local organising committee. So with him and Platini they have the control of one hundred per cent of the tickets. This is what happens.'

Casanova explained how a shortfall in the tickets was hidden.

'Security reasons. Media. TV camera angles. These factors would mean for example in the stadium in St Denis in Paris where they have some seventy thousand seats that up to eight thousand would not be sold or allocated through official channels. No one can go and check if they actually need to hold back so many. Those who are holding the tickets can do what they like with them.'

There is nothing like a World Cup tournament to bring out the hog that is asleep in mankind. Shady companies offering tickets for the tournament began to spring up like mushrooms after a thunderstorm all over Europe. Some had access to tickets, others did not. The latter just took the money and ran.

Supporters from virtually every country in the world were swindled out of their money. Irony is very much part of French culture. It is doubtful whether the host country appreciated what was, with regard to the ticket controversy that roared unabated from January until the World Cup Final on 12th July, the most ironic aspect of all.

FIFA's in-house marketing partner ISL became tainted by the World Cup ticket fraud. The managing director of ISL France, Marc Loison, and a consultant working for his company, Gilles Favard, masterminded a scam involving 'ghost tickets'. The amount of money that the gang acquired ran into many millions of pounds. ISL in Lucerne attempted to distance itself from the scandal, claiming that ISL France was not part of their worldwide network of associated businesses, but was run independently. This statement is totally contradicted by ISL's promotion literature that clearly shows ISL France as an integral part of the company. ISL France's offices, just a short walk from where the World Cup Final was due to be staged, was full of FIFA personnel until the scandal broke, at which point FIFA, rather like ISL's head office, appeared to suffer from collective amnesia.

'I am confident that based on what has been said to me I have at least one hundred votes.'

That was Lennart Johansson talking to me on 12 April 1998.

'I am confident that based on what has been said to me I have at least one hundred votes.'

That was Sepp Blatter talking to me a fortnight later on 27 April 1998.

Something had to give. There were fewer than two hundred eligible voters.

One of the reasons under FIFA statutes that disqualified a country's football association from voting in the presidential election was a failure over the previous four years to have participated in specific youth tournaments. Another was their financial status. If an association had failed to pay their due fees, they were disqualified. I had heard from a variety of sources that Havelange and Blatter were taking a benevolent view on this issue. UEFA's President Johansson had heard the same.

'At the most I would say there are some ten countries that are in this situation. They are of course being approached by the other party.'

'By Sepp Blatter?'

'Yes.'

'Some of these beneficiaries of Blatter's generosity are I believe African nations?'

'That is what I understand.'

'You believe you have one hundred votes. Can you break those up for me?'

'Certainly. Europe represents fifty-one votes. I am confident of virtually all of those, say forty-seven. Africa, apart from those currently disqualified, is for me. At least forty out of the forty-four associations. Asia has thirty-seven votes and I am assured that most of those are for me.'

'Well, that means victory for you on the second ballot?'

'Unless people have been lying to me.'

We talked at length of what in Lennart Johansson's mind ailed FIFA and what he planned to do if elected. He expressed astonishment at the way that Havelange and Blatter had for many years conducted negotiations when selling the TV and marketing rights.

'I have heard from many sources that there is a hidden agenda that exists between ISL and Havelange and Blatter. For myself I am astonished that the same company is being trusted time after time. I think the procedure has to be changed. FIFA should ask for offers and these offers should all be opened at the same time by an auditor and with the Executive Committee present. This would be normal business procedure. This has never happened at FIFA. That is why there are these rumours of a hidden agenda. We have heard that Havelange gets this and this and that. I don't know and I am not going to speculate. I have heard a great many things over the years, many allegations concerning both Havelange and Blatter. As far as I am concerned I will not fight this election on their ethics. If the price I have to pay to win is to behave like them, then I refrain. Then at least I will leave with my self-respect.'

Lennart Johansson's vision of the future if he won the election involved radical change. 'I don't want to read in a newspaper that FIFA has decided something ... The days when the President and his General Secretary ran FIFA to suit themselves are over ... Committees must no longer be formed by the President. The national associations, the confederations, these are where the proposals for committee members should come from. There must never again be allowed to happen what occurred in New York in 1994 ... We must have only people on these committees who are clean, who are untouchable ... They are fighting me because they are scared at what a new management will find out ... The monies that are being made, these huge amounts must be reinvested at grassroots level. We have got to give back to the game much of what we are taking out of it.'

In view of what lay waiting on 12 July at the Final of the World Cup in the Stade de France, part of my conversation with the President of UEFA was in its own way a harbinger of things to come.

'I wonder if you share my view that there is far too much football. In Brazil they sometimes play four or five games in the space of time that they should be playing at most two. While I was there even their national squad was running around the Caribbean playing a series of meaningless games. Simply to satisfy Nike.'

'We are in absolute agreement with you. You see I think that the medical expertise should have more to say. Greater input, they should be able to influence the game just like a referee can. It is almost a crime to bring a player half-fit to play. The injuries occur far too frequently in a country like Brazil where teams play approaching one hundred matches a year.'

Lennart Johansson is very much a man who falls into the 'what you see is what you get' category of mankind. He wanted to clean out FIFA to make it democratic. Make its business dealings transparently clear.

'I have, let's say, the majority of these hundred are coming from the two wings.'

Sepp Blatter reached for a table napkin and began to draw. We were in a Zurich restaurant just a short drive from FIFA headquarters. Where Johansson is serious, almost dour, Blatter is lively, ebullient, a dextrous mind. I had asked him, as I had asked his rival, to break his one hundred votes up into geographic elements.

'If Europe and Africa try to make a deal so that they can dominate world football, then the counter-attack comes from the two wings who are opposed to their plan.'

'So you have the Americas and Latin America?'

'Yes, the Americas North and South and Central and Caribbean. And Asia and Oceania. South East Asia, ten countries there. One hundred for sure.'

'As I understand it, a number are disqualified from voting because of non-payment of various monies to FIFA.'

'No, that is not a problem because at the end, one hour before Congress, they can do it and they always find the money.'

'Oh, really? How do they do that?'

'They find a sponsor who at the last minute is paying whatever is needed.'

We were interrupted at that moment by the arrival of his daughter, who was working as his campaign manager. When we returned to the presidential campaign, it was obvious that Sepp Blatter had done his homework very carefully. I was attempting to establish precisely how many delegates would at the end of the day be entitled to vote. This was at the time still very fluid. Apart from the matter of a sponsor appearing with a blank cheque book, there were other countries which, as of 27 April, the day of my meeting with Blatter, were technically disqualified because of their failure to play in at least two FIFA tournaments over the previous four years. Blatter had thought of everything.

'Yes, until recently it was indeed about one hundred and sixty-five who were eligible. Since then quite a few more have paid what was owing ... So there will be two hundred and four members in FIFA at the Congress if the candidates are accepted and therefore if you take, let's say, ten to twelve away there will in my opinion be one hundred and ninety, one hundred and ninety-two who are eligible to vote.'

In the event on the morning of 8 June Havelange announced shortly before the vote that one hundred and ninety-one countries were eligible. The 'sponsor' had indeed been very busy.

At the time of my meeting with Blatter the ticket controversy was raging as a daily lead news item, certainly throughout Europe and probably much further afield. A week earlier four million people had attempted to phone from the United Kingdom in one day in a vain attempt to get tickets. One had to admire the gall of the man who as General Secretary of FIFA was in no small part personally responsible for the mess.

'It's just a lack of communication. There are 2.5 million tickets available; there are twenty-five million demands. So if you double the quota for England, Scotland, Holland and Belgium which are the countries who have been making the noise, if you double it they will not be happy, if you triple it they will not be happy. That's all. This controversy is all because there is no major news at the moment so people are focusing on this ticket issue. It's like they say in France – the most wonderful lady in the world cannot give more than she has. We are the victims of the popularity of football.'

Blatter had a dozen reasons why the World Cup was in the middle of a monumental cock-up. None of them attributed a shred of culpability to FIFA. It was because France was in the middle of Europe. 'Paris, everyone wants to go to an attractive city like Paris ...' or, 'It was not foreseen that so many European teams would qualify. Take them all out and you would have far less noise about tickets ... Why did we give so many to France? France had to give a guarantee of SF170 million, a guarantee for the tickets, and it's obvious that half of the tickets will go to France.'

When I tackled him about the percentage that was going to sponsors and corporate elements – 20 per cent – he would not accept that figure. He could not offer an alternative one, but, 'I will organise that you are given this information.' Like Lennart Johansson's February request for detailed information on where the tickets were going, I am still waiting. Subsequently from alternative sources within ISL and FIFA I have been advised that '20 per cent to sponsors and to corporate elements is a conservative estimate'.

Before leaving the ticketing controversy I asked Blatter about the allegations that had been raised by UEFA executives that the choice of Michel Platini as a running mate was to ensure that he had unlimited access to tickets to assist his election.

'These people deserve a double yellow card, which means a red. I was asked this morning if Platini is with me because he has an influence on the French-speaking countries. I said Platini has an influence on all football-speaking countries, because he is a footballer.'

Sepp Blatter conceded that the sums of money raised for the television and marketing rights in the past and up to and including World Cup 98 were woefully undervaluing the rights. Havelange, of course, is extremely proud of these historic figures that he and Blatter jointly negotiated.

'The World Cup in France I would say is the last World Cup of the small figures.'

Blatter's version of how much the marketing rights for World Cup 98 had fetched was: 'Category One sponsors paid directly to FIFA SF110 million. The twelve sponsors, Canon, Coca-Cola, Budweiser and the others.'

An indication of the huge increase of money that is now going to pour into FIFA's coffers can be gauged from the fact that Coca-Cola alone will be paying the same gross figure – SF110 million – for World Cups 2002 and 2006. Blatter revealed that apart from the World Cup and the Confederations Cup all other FIFA tournaments 'are in the red, they are all subsidised from a central pool of money'.

Among the changes that Sepp Blatter was planning to make if he won the election was one that was destined to ensure a state of continuing warfare, not only with UEFA but other Confederations.

'I think the President should get a paid salary and also the super committee that I will create, one from each Confederation. They must be paid.'

It will be interesting to see the Executive Committee reaction to a paid super committee that will run the day-to-day business of FIFA. I asked him if he shared my belief that referees should be paid professionals.

'Most certainly. I totally agree with you and yes, they should be full time and train, just like the players.'

This, like many of Blatter's ideas, will strike a receptive chord with many who care about the game. He plans to get funds down to grass roots. 'Give them the shirts, the equipment and also something to eat, you don't need to give them the ground, they will always find a space where they can play.' These ideas came directly from Lennart Johansson's election manifesto.

I talked to him of the conditions that exist within Brazilian football. He seemed to be genuinely appalled. His plan is that Michel Platini will attempt to solve the problem of getting help to those at the bottom of the ladder.

With regard to the repeated allegations that had been made to me concerning secret bank accounts that enabled certain FIFA individuals and members of ISL to place kickbacks and bribes, Blatter too had 'heard these allegations'. His response delicately excluded everyone else.

'Yes, I am aware of these statements. Perhaps I'm too naïve to answer them, but I have only open accounts.'

He was aware of the numerous allegations concerning President Havelange, yet he claimed to have 'no knowledge'. His assertion sat oddly with his declaration that 'any corruption within football should be treated like a cancer and cut out; any allegation of corruption should be rigorously investigated.' He quoted Article 2, Clause 3 of the FIFA Statutes:

'The objects of the Federation are ...

'3 to control every type of association football by taking steps as shall be deemed necessary or advisable to prevent infringements of the Statutes or regulations of FIFA or of the Laws of the Game as laid down by the International Football Association Board, to prevent the introduction of other improper methods or practices in the game and to protect it from abuses ...'

Sepp Blatter knows the FIFA Statutes extremely well. Knowing the rules and applying them are, of course, two quite different things. Blatter is bright, intelligent and a lively companion. Unlike his rival from Sweden, what you see is most certainly not what you get. What you get with Blatter depends, in my opinion, on what you are selling.

The Havelange–Blatter election campaign continued to press every button and pull every string. On 14 April, Havelange wrote to Timothy Fok, the President of the Hong Kong Football Association:

My dear friend, President Timothy

In the last few days before I went to Africa for a meeting, I sent you a letter in which I asked you very precisely for your support for the candidature of M Blatter for the presidency of FIFA and as well as that request I would ask you also to use your influence with the Federations of Hong Kong, Macau and China as well as North Korea.

At this moment the UEFA candidate is in China and I hope that China will bring their vote to Blatter in order to continue the work and the development that is happening in the Asiatic continent ...

Two days later the President, who of course had publicly vowed not to get involved in this election, wrote yet again to a member of the African Confederation, this time to the Kenyan Association:

... The Finance Department of FIFA will send you shortly a draft for $50,000 for the running of your secretariat for a period of two years. In order to facilitate this, I would ask you to send your complete bank address to FIFA (bank, account number and name of account).

FIFA will contact you shortly to discuss the question of the computers which you want to install in your general office.

None of these payments that Havelange was making had been authorised either by the Executive or Finance Committees of FIFA.

The candidate himself was also eager to show his generosity to the electorate.

In May he wrote to every Confederation and National Association:

This information is principally addressed to those national associations which are – as is unfortunately far too often the case – less privileged than others due to a lack of money and the appropriate technical infrastructure and hence the means to run their administration efficiently at national level.

The share of the revenue from the television and marketing rights that the Havelange administration has already apportioned to each national association (one million dollars each payable in four annual instalments of US $250,000, of which US $50,000 can already be paid out this autumn) is intended to enable those who need our support to set up a permanent office, equipped with indispensable facilities, such as telephone, fax and computers with email. After FIFA technical experts have taken stock of the individual situation of the national associations on the spot, I want to make sure that these associations receive tailor-made assistance in establishing their technical, administrative and marketing programmes...

The letter was headlined 'JSB FOR PRESIDENT', as was a further letter written to the Samoa Football Association on 1 June. The letter contained four points, the third of which read:

In my programme, each national association from Oceania will receive tailor-made projects adapted to the individual needs and naturally the one million dollars for the next four years.

Blatter and Havelange were giving a continuing demonstration of the well-established fact that there's nothing like an impending election to open a candidate's wallet – or in this case our wallets, because of course at the end of the day all of this money that was being thrown at the voting delegates is our money. The people's game equals the people's money.

In early May 1998 details of a conspiracy involving bribes that had been offered to certain FIFA officials began to emerge. The sums involved were on average $50,000. The money was an attempt to influence certain decisions. The target? The referees and the players.

According to FIFA officials, the attempts to bribe players and match officials would be made by members of a bookmakers' ring. FIFA were taking no chances. More than seven hundred players and sixty-seven FIFA referees and linesmen were going to be protected by a contingent of security staff. The referees were going to be particularly well guarded: nobody without a pass would be able to gain access to their hotels. When travelling to matches outside Paris, they were going to be accompanied by FIFA officials and the announcement as to which referee would officiate at which match would be delayed until as late as was practicable. All were admirable precautions in this wicked world. Such a pity that FIFA did not take similar precautions with regard to the members of the 191 associations when they gathered in Paris for their 51st Congress.

Towards the end of May with the World Cup and the election of his successor just two weeks away, I interviewed João Havelange over a two-day period. The interviews on which I have drawn extensively throughout this book were, Havelange told me, 'the last I shall be giving as President of FIFA'. It was perhaps this factor, a time for reflection, that influenced the man. I found him extremely co-operative for much of the time we spent together. Knowing his capacity to erupt and finish interviews prematurely if his pride or self-image was offended, I had weighed carefully the moment to ask one particularly 'hard' question. The moment inevitably came.

'I am very grateful for the time you have given me, but there is one particular aspect, one set of issues, that I must put to you. Over the period of your stewardship of FIFA and indeed coming out of your earlier position as President of Brazil's CBD, a number of allegations have been made directly to me. Evidence has been produced to justify these allegations. They involve embezzlement of funds at CBD; corrupt business practices both at CBD and at FIFA; kick-backs by Horst Dassler. There is a whole range. I have the evidence and I'm fully prepared to go through it with you.

That apart, my research indicates that whenever you have
been confronted on any of these aspects, your response, if
I could summarise it, has been basically, "They can write
what they like about me," but you have never addressed
yourself to the specifics of any of these allegations. Would
you like to elaborate on that for me?'

I had warned my translator that an unusually long
statement/question was coming and I had paused several
times so that his translation into French would cover every
single word. As I spoke, Havelange had fixed me with an
unstaring gaze, then he leaned across the desk towards me,
pointing a finger.

'First of all I must say that this makes me very sad. I have
principles which I received from my father and mother and
I maintain these principles until today. And so I would like
to ask you to come to Brazil, talk to a porter at the airport
for example, a driver, go into a restaurant, talk to a major
industrialist, a doctor, a lawyer, and ask these people,
make an inquiry as to what these people would say with
regard to myself. My life has always been regular and I can
only say that I have always had problems to accomplish all
of the tasks I have set because it does cost money. I have
never asked anyone for anything. I have never asked even
for a bank loan and the few things that I've been able to
have in my life I've always given to my wife. Today if I
were to separate from my wife I would start my life from
scratch.'

'When you say that, you're talking financially?'

'Yes. The respect that I have in myself, and I have this
respect towards my wife as well.'

President Havelange then began to talk of Dassler's
1973 attempt to get Havelange as the then President of
CBD to commit to Adidas. This and the subsequent sections
of the interview are recorded earlier within this book. Thus
the response given above is his complete, verbatim answer

to an extraordinary list of charges. A response that seems
to me to be almost a plea of mitigation after a verdict has
been brought in. As will be clear to the reader, I did indeed
seek from a wide variety of people in Brazil information on
João Havelange. Their views are self-evident. His comment
that all of his assets are in his wife's name indicates that Dr
Havelange has been getting good tax-avoidance advice.
His comment that he has never asked for a bank loan
should be judged against the evidence within this book,
particularly from Dr Lobo, Havelange's business partner
for many years.

It would also appear that the curious arrangement that
he had with several banks in Nassau in the Bahamas
between 1976 and the mid-1980s has been forgotten by
João Havelange. If the regular payments of more than a
million dollars each time were not, as they were dressed up
to be, overdraft payments, then who exactly was making
regular donations to FIFA's president?

In the remaining days before the FIFA Congress, the
rival contenders for the Sun King's crown fought an
increasingly acrimonious war of words in the news media.
Profiles of Havelange began to appear in newspapers
throughout the world. The reviews of his life and times
were totally devoid of any regret that he was finally
relinquishing his position. Writers acknowledged how the
game had been transformed financially during his years as
FIFA's President, but beyond that, his actual contribution
to the game, to judge from much of the Press coverage, was
minimal. Indeed, those articles echo Havelange's own
words to me and to others. When he talks of what he has
achieved, it is confined to matters material. Of matters
spiritual, of the game's romance, its charm, drama, not a
word. The pure theatre that football at its finest represents
does not appear to Havelange to be a tangible asset. Even
Henry Kissinger was moved by Johann Cruyff's genius on

a German pitch to stand in acclamation. How appropriate
that it was Havelange pulling him back down to earth.

A FIFA Congress is not a place for any lover of football.
It is very largely populated by middle-aged and elderly
men; the majority are fat cigarette-smokers. There are very
few women and even fewer of either sex who are of the
same age as today's players.

As for Jules Rimet's view that football unifies the world
into one happy family, what was on display in the Equinox
Hall Paris on 7 and 8 June was neither unified nor happy.
Those smoke-filled rooms where the real decision-making
occurs in Republican and Democratic Conventions came
very much to mind.

In the anteroom outside the conference hall small pockets
foregathered. There was very little social intercourse
between the various groups. The Icelanders talked to each
other, as did the Estonians, Cubans, Iranians and the rest
of this Football Incorporated shareholders meeting.

The Sun King appeared. He was someone they all wanted
to talk to, if only to arrange themselves next to him for a
photographic memento. I realised for the first time that
João Havelange, whose smile on film is as rare as a virgin
in the Reeperbahn, actually sets his face in a scowl or a
grimace for the photographer, then a moment later
rearranges his face into a smile when he resumes talking. A
final word, then a moment later His Majesty is moved on
very gently by his secretary, Marie Urlacher, to the next
photo opportunity. It was more Godfather than Louis
XIV. Difficult to believe that Louis was quite so free with
his triple cheek kissing of every man he met.

When the proceedings got under way, there was a
montage of moments recorded on film of every World Cup
tournament. All showed one or other team in a moment of
triumph. Word Cup 66 did not show England winning,
but West Germany equalising – Blatter's anti-English

stance getting yet another small airing. Two days earlier the English Football Association had announced it was switching its vote from Johansson to Blatter, courtesy of Prime Minister Blair's overwhelming desire that England should host the World Cup in 2006. It was a decision that reeked of expediency and also betrayal. Johansson is an honourable man. In his mind England and Germany had some years earlier arrived at a gentleman's agreement. Germany would support England's bid to host Euro 96, which they did. England would support Germany's bid to host World Cup 2002, which they reneged on.

'... I was invited to go to London by Mr Tony Blair. He wanted to have the World Cup in England in 2006. And I think England has every right. They created football. They organised football. They set up the whole rules concerning football and the people in England are absolutely impassioned about football. Your Prime Minister told me he already had a billion pounds for the stadiums. To rebuild Wembley. Build a new stadium in Manchester. Six days after I went to Downing Street the six largest industries in the United Kingdom went to see Mr Tony Blair and they said they would support his programme to make sure that the World Cup would be held in England ...'

No one would be happier than this author to see the World Cup tournament return to the cradle of the modern game, but not at the expense of deceit and betrayal. I raised the issue of the German bid with Havelange. He dismissed the German desire to hold the tournament with, 'This has nothing to do with democracy. It's a dictatorship. It's worse than a military dictatorship. Why should Germany decide who gets the World Cup? Look, the World Cup in 2002 is divided between two countries in Asia. The vote by the Europeans in the Executive exerted a certain amount of pressure and between Seoul and Tokyo you have a flight of at least two hours. So I asked Tony Blair, "Why couldn't you have a similar set-up together with Germany? The same form of co-operation?" I pointed out to him that there is a flight time of only ninety minutes between Britain and Germany. He said, "Never." He wants it in England and he does not want to share it.'

So much for a unified Europe.

The English Football Association – Graham Kelly, Keith Wiseman and the rest of them – having reneged on an agreement made by Sir Bert Millichip, the former Chairman, then reneged on their promise to support Johansson for FIFA President, to gain some imagined advantage with Sepp Blatter. In doing so they were voting for a man who had opposed England's re-entry into European football, who has bitterly criticised the size of the Premier League, and who had condemned British football as 'being thirty years out of date'. Just three days *before* the Football Association, with their eyes firmly fixed on World Cup 2006, announced that they would be voting for him, Blatter said:

'I will not give all my programmes for Africa, but what I can promise, which will be a reality, is that if I am elected President of FIFA, I will give the 2006 World Cup to Africa.'

Blatter's commitment was greeted with acclamation in the football stadium in Monrovia, the capital of Liberia, where he was doing some last-minute shopping before the Paris Congress. Blatter's pursuit of the Francophone Africa vote had been ruthless. He obviously had to work much harder with the African countries than he had to do with England who, in voting against Lennart Johansson, rejected a man who wants to give football back to the people by building up the game at grassroots and supported Blatter, a man committed to 'continuity' – more of Havelange's policies – which, despite Blatter's remarks to me regarding his own desires on the subject, most certainly do not and never have included giving back the game to the people it belongs to.

Johansson, who had declared his candidacy in late 1995, had by May 1998 developed a momentum that was unstoppable. He had a clear run of the electoral field and had impressed many with his policies, his vision and, perhaps most of all, with his quite obvious transparent honesty. He was not seen as particularly charismatic, indeed some saw him as dull, but after twenty-four years of the charismatic Havelange, this was not necessarily a disadvantage. By early 1998 Lennart Johansson undoubtedly did have the one hundred votes that he had talked of. He had, with just a few defections, Europe's fifty-one votes. He had Africa's forty-four and at least enough from the other Associations to take him over the one hundred votes and to a certain victory.

Blatter had not declared his candidacy until a mere four months before the election, yet on the eve of the vote, the talk 'off the record' was that it was going to be a close-run thing. It spoke volumes for the persuasiveness of Havelange on his round-the-world farewell tour. It spoke eloquently of Blatter's own industry and charm. It spoke of how effective the election techniques used by Havelange in 1974 still were in 1998, but I felt that if the conventional wisdom that was whispered in my ear on the eve of the vote was accurate, there was another factor. A missing link.

The following morning there was a long, angry and bitter argument that powerfully demonstrated that there was absolutely no mutual trust as far as voting procedures went. Johansson's supporters arguing for an open ballot. Blatter's supporters arguing for, and obtaining, a secret ballot. It was the system used in 1974 when the man from Rio had won. Voting finally got under way. The odds on a first-ballot victory were very much against. Neither was likely to get a two-thirds majority. The figures stunned many, but delighted even more. Blatter 111, Johansson 90. As the election officers began to prepare for a second ballot, Lennart Johansson conceded defeat. There was not to be a Hollywood ending. The good guy lost.

Virtually the first action taken by the new President, who was staying at the Meridien, was to upgrade from a junior suite to the empty Presidential Suite at the Bristol Hotel. Shortly before the vote he had again promised 'continuity', 'more of the same', nothing was going to change if he won. The Havelange way would be the Blatter way.

Blatter could not contain himself on the podium. It was the behaviour of a man who at one level could not believe he had pulled it off. That the prize was actually his. He tried somewhat nauseatingly to pay fulsome compliments to Johansson, but rapidly gave up the attempt and contented himself in the immediate aftermath with simply wallowing in his victory.

The enduring image of the proceedings happened when Johansson graciously and gracefully declined to drag it out to a second ballot and conceded defeat. A number of delegates from African countries leapt to their feet, calling out to each other and rubbing an index finger against a thumb in that universal gesture of money.

Information that has subsequently come to hand confirms that their expectations have been realised.

Before the vote had been taken, when 'any other business' was being dealt with, among the items under discussion two in particular intrigued me. It was announced that there was to be a change of auditor for FIFA – no longer the dark-horse firm of Sutter, but a thoroughbred: KPMG Peat Marwick would be handling the auditing of the billion-dollar account of FIFA. There were a number of FIFA expenditures in Paris that would most certainly bear close examination by this internationally respected firm of accountants. The other announcement that caught my attention was that Ricardo Teixeira had been given a going-away present by his former father-in-law. He was now a FIFA Vice President. It is to be hoped that the review of FIFA's finances by KPMG which is already under way establishes whether the huge number of guests that Teixeira yet again brought to a World Cup tournament, including once more some twenty or so Brazilian judges and lawyers, was put on FIFA's bill or on that of the CBF.

One question remained unanswered after the election for the FIFA Presidency was concluded. Johansson had been categorically told not only by his UEFA election team but also by men like Issa Hayatou, President of CAF – the African Football Confederation – that the African vote was his, all or virtually all, forty-four Associations. Mustapha Fahmy, the Secretary of CAF, had confirmed to me some weeks before the election that the various associations had confirmed 'overwhelmingly' that they would be voting for Johansson. These votes plus the overwhelming majority of UEFA associations, plus more from Asia, were more than enough to sweep the man from Sweden to victory.

Hayatou is widely regarded as a man of unimpeachable integrity, yet it seemed to me clear that at least part of Johansson's Africa constituency had defected to the enemy.

During the inaugural FIFA/Confederations Cup, a ten-day tournament that took place in Saudi Arabia in December 1997, the General Secretary of FIFA went missing for at least one of those days. Blatter left Riyadh for a secret visit to neighbouring Qatar. There he met in Doha the ruler of the country, Sheikh Hamad Bin Khalifaal-Thani. The Emir had seized power three years ago after deposing his father. Khalifaal-Thani has a reputation as a moderniser, a man anxious to open his country's doors to Western investment. He has brought women into

Parliament and lifted press censorship. He has also opened trade relations with Israel. His meeting with Blatter was not to discuss innovations. The subject on the agenda was as old as man. Power and how to acquire it. The solution has been around for a while too. Buy it.

I do not know what Blatter offered the Sheikh but I would not be terribly surprised if there is a FIFA announcement in the near future that one of the many meaningless tournaments that the Havelange presidency gave birth to has been scheduled to be held in Qatar.

The General Secretary came away from the meeting with a wealthy backer who was also prepared to use his position as Head of State to activate a range of political channels. The Emir's generosity was impressive. It included putting his personal aeroplane at Blatter's disposal.

The French connection that Blatter had so assiduously been nursing also began to pay dividends early in the New Year. President Chirac, who had once threatened Havelange that he would activate French-speaking Africa against the FIFA President, now began to mobilise former French colonies to support Blatter. Chirac, like the ruler of Qatar, bypassed the various football confederations and associations and went straight to the top, to a fellow President or Head of State. It was a technique that was also used in Europe. President Chirac opened the door in Croatia for Blatter so that when he went calling, his target was not the headquarters of the Croatian Football Association in Zagreb, but the presidential residence of Dr Franjo Tudjman. It may be that they discussed Dr Tudjman's work as a historian and statesman. They may also have touched upon the fact that Tudjman has been a member of the Society of Croatian Writers since 1970. Whatever. At the end of their meeting, Blatter had the Croatian vote sewn up.

The Emir also ordered his relations who control and run

Qatar's Football Association to do everything within their power to assist Blatter's election. It developed into a two-pronged infiltration. They began to pick up votes both from the African Confederation and from Asia. Qatar's FIFA delegate, Mohamad Bin Hammam, who sits on the key FIFA Finance Committee, had an additional task. As his country's delegate to Paris he could mix freely with the other delegates without attracting undue attention.

That weekend, Paris was full of rumours. Of deals being cut, of favours being called in. The real power-centres where the ultimate vote is decided.

Blatter had a junior suite in the Meridien Hotel in Paris. It was also where a great many of the delegates were staying. In the days leading up to the FIFA Congress Hammam functioned as procurer for Blatter. Positioning himself down in the lobby of the hotel, Hammam collared the delegates as they came and went. He extolled the virtues of Sepp Blatter. If he felt the delegates' attention was wandering, Hammam talked of money. Allegedly he talked of offering $50,000 per vote. The fatigue of the day lifted and the delegates began to move towards the bar with a spring in their step. Some of Blatter's supporters had begun to panic on the Saturday prior to the Monday vote. They were convinced that Lennart Johansson still held a majority. According to the rumours, it was at this stage that money and very little else was being discussed. A number of the delegates remained sceptical. How did they know that Hammam could be trusted? Under the circumstances, an appropriate question. An undertaking was given that if Blatter was duly elected, courtesy of the Emir a plane would immediately leave Qatar with $1 million on board. First stop Paris. The delegates were assured that they could then come to Hammam and collect their fifty thousand. The figure of a million is not without significance. Between fifteen and twenty delegates were persuaded to exchange the white envelope containing their vote for another containing $50,000. If all of the Emir's million dollars went in this manner, then the missing twenty votes from Johansson's tally are accounted for.

Blatter himself would later assert that he knew nothing whatsoever about these or other arrangements. He has always vigorously and indeed furiously denied any knowledge of these various activities. The newly elected President confirmed that money had indeed changed hands, but the only payments that he was aware of concerned arrangements made earlier that year in which financial assistance had been offered to a wide variety of national Associations. The monies in question were designated for a variety of uses – to buy cars, to purchase computers, to finance competitions and other official activities. If one accepts Sepp Blatter's explanation – and there is at this time of writing no reason not to – then a quite extraordinary situation appears to have occurred that weekend in Paris.

Simultaneously with FIFA funds being officially handed out to delegates, other payments were being made to directly influence votes. The evidence that this latter activity took place has come to me from a variety of sources, including individuals within UEFA and others within the African Football Federation.

This tactic, plus the political channels that were activated, swung it for Blatter. Thus the power of the Asian and African Confederations was neutered and democracy was prostituted in the pursuit of the FIFA Presidency. Nothing had changed from the early 1970s when João Havelange bought himself the most powerful position in the world of football.

So if Rupert Murdoch or any other media baron fancies acquiring control of international football and the pot of gold that the World Cup tournament has come to represent, for a fairly modest outlay the media baron could buy a majority to ensure that his candidate was elected and he would be on course to his next billion dollars.

On Tuesday 9 June, the Presidential Suite at the Bristol Hotel was a hive of activity. So many wanted to call to congratulate the new ruler of football. The King is dead. Long live the King. Two days earlier on the Sunday the delegates had shared the Sun King's last evening before the election of his successor in highly appropriate surroundings. The gardens and the Orangerie of the Château de Versailles. If there was an absence of any latterday Racine, Molière or La Fontaine to add artistic lustre to Havelange's last World Cup as President, the continuing excesses of a number of those who were present gave this last hurrah of Havelange's a befitting brilliance that serves as an apt postscript to all that had gone before during the twenty-four-year reign.

Havelange set an example that was eagerly followed by quite a number of his FIFA Executive. He stayed at the Bristol Hotel in Paris for six weeks. The man who does not get on a plane unless he has a first-class seat or enter a hotel that is anything under four-star went out of FIFA as he had come in. General Secretary Helmut Käser had remonstrated repeatedly with Havelange from the mid-1970s onwards: 'This money from Coca-Cola is not yours. You must stop behaving as though they have donated it to you personally.' Such integrity had cost Käser his job.

Havelange's Presidential Suite in the Bristol cost £3,500 per night. Forty-two nights – £147,000. That was for starters. Then there were his eighty guests. Then there was his good, close friend from Argentina, the Senior FIFA Vice President Julio Grondona, and his forty guests. Then there was the widow of the Mexican Guillermo Cañedo, the previous Senior FIFA Vice President. Mrs Cañedo came with approximately fifteen relations and close friends. Cañedo is beyond telling us exactly who got paid how much to ensure that against all the odds Mexico was awarded its second World Cup tournament for World Cup 86. Grondona, on the other hand, may be able to help with another puzzle of far more recent times.

In the run-up to the World Cup many of the national teams welcomed a run-out in a friendly game. Aware of this, the idea occurred to a member of the Lee Dixon Testimonial Project to invite the Argentinian national team to Highbury. Dixon has given wonderful service to his club, Arsenal, and his country. A match against the 1998 League and Cup double team and one of the favourites for the World Cup in France would be a sell-out. The fans would be thrilled and Dixon would, after expenses, have a substantial amount of money. The Argentinian Football Association was contacted. The response was positive. 'It's a very good idea. Excellent. Tell me what day and I will make sure they are there to play Arsenal. Fee? There will be no fee; the players will give their services freely. However, I will require two hundred and fifty thousand dollars. Cash. In a case to be handed to me before the match begins.'

The offer was declined, but the puzzle remains as to the identity of the Argentinian. I am confident that Julio Grondona, after making the relevant inquiries, will be able to provide the name, if only 'for the good of the game'.

Far from attempting to rein in the excesses of Havelange and his entourage, Sepp Blatter appears to have regarded what was going on at the Bristol Hotel and other parts of Paris as a challenge. He had, as already recorded, upgraded himself to the Presidential Suite of the Bristol as virtually his first act after winning the presidency. That was only his opening gambit. With the World Cup getting under way Blatter, who had told me that if he won the election he would set about abolishing the 'absurdity of the job carrying no salary', set about materially improving his lot in life. The wage has yet to be established; in the meantime

FIFA has allocated £1.7 million to spend on running Blatter's office over the next four years, an increase on the profligacy of Havelange of some 70 per cent. FIFA has also earmarked a further £660,000 for travel and hospitality, a 40 per cent increase on the sum the Sun King staggered by on. FIFA has also awarded a further £1.6 million to cover the cost of 'presents'. Little items such as watches, medals, pens and pendants.

It is clear that his pre-election promise of 'continuity' is going to get kept at all costs. Thinking that he could mitigate the possible wrath of Johansson and the other anti-Blatter group on the Executive Committee – a group that is in the majority – FIFA has also decreed that they too can join the party. Five million pounds for expenses over the next four years, £240 per day as an allowance to compensate for 'loss of earnings'. The one voice that has been raised outside the paid staff within FIFA House to defend the indefensible belongs to Jack ('Who wants tickets?') Warner. Declaring that Sepp Blatter's edicts were set in stone, Warner said: 'We must move ahead, otherwise we will spend the next few years in guerrilla warfare to the detriment of FIFA.'

The final bill for FIFA from the Bristol Hotel runs to many millions of dollars. Imagine how many footballs that would buy the Jotas of this world. Imagine an injection of that money into the work being done by an organisation like SOS Children's Villages – a non-denominational organisation founded 45 years ago and now caring directly for some 200,000 disadvantaged children in 125 countries. In 1994 Havelange created a FIFA Youth Fund to help this organisation. Perhaps Sepp Blatter can be publicly shamed into matching the disgusting excesses of Paris with an equivalent amount donated to SOS Children's Villages.

The following is a verbatim extract from the current

edition of FIFA's activities report – April 1996–March
1998:

The Root of All Evil

Human nature is a fickle thing, vulnerable to the
temptations of quick and easy personal gain. There were
examples during the period of this report of those
temptations becoming too great, and of individuals falling
to them. It was a timely reminder of the constant need to
be on guard against this scourge.

In all instances, the motivation was purported to be money
– the root, as it is often described, of all evil. Indeed, there
is something very evil about corruption in football, for it
is cheating not only the players but also the innocent fans
who assume in good faith that everyone in every game is
giving nothing but his 100 per cent best. Take away that
basic trust and the whole edifice of sport collapses.

For the Good of the Game, Always ...

1   ... play to win
2   ... play fair
3   ... observe the Laws of the Game
4   ... respect opponents, team-mates, referees, officials
       and spectators
5   ... accept defeat with dignity
6   ... promote the interests of football
7   ... promote the interests of football
8   ... help others to resist corrupting pressures
9   ... denounce those who attempt to discredit our sport
10 ... honour those who defend football's good
       reputation

The reader may notice that number 6 and number 7 are
identical. This is in fact an error and FIFA have in every

sense forgotten their own edict number 7 – 'reject corruption, drugs, racism, violence and other dangers to our sport'.

Football was indeed the beautiful game – classless, colour-blind, unifying. It gave us a universal language. It offered magnificent ideals. It was in many ways an example of how life should be led. It had integrity, it had honesty, it had ethics and it had morals. Not any more. They have stolen it all away. They've stolen the game.

Epilogue

On the evening of July 12 1998 it was a time to see once again that other face of Brazilian football. The skills, the flair, the imagination, from a side that – unlike so many in this tawdry World Cup tournament – were more concerned with winning than with not losing. It was to be an evening when the spectator would be able to thankfully forget most of what had preceded it in sixty-three matches that led inexorably to the final game. And there was so much to forget.

It was time to dismiss the drunken criminals – English, German, French, Arab, whatever nationality. Time to set aside the cheating, the body-checking on the referee's blind side, the continual shirt-pulling, the cheating to get an opponent sent off, the cheating to get a free kick or a penalty. To forget that the then English manager, Glenn Hoddle, had told the boy Owen, 'Dive in the box if you get the chance, the others do it, so why shouldn't we?' To disregard how the magnificent Laurent Blanc had been cheated of his place in the Final by Slaven 'I don't deserve to be treated like a criminal' Bilic of Croatia. To overlook Belgium's Lorenzo Staelens, who continued to writhe on the ground until the referee sent Holland's Patrick Kluivert off. To ignore Argentina's Simeone also writhing in agony until he was sure that, aided by hysterical team-mates, he had got England's Beckham sent off. Time to discount matches such as Nigeria v Paraguay or Brazil v Norway, charades that were very reminiscent of Germany v Austria in 1982.

So much to forget.

So little to remember, but the Final would change that.

The best attack in the world v the best defence in the tournament. The holders v the hosts. Serie A v Serie A. Four-time winners v first-time finalists. Nike v Adidas.

Yes, particularly Nike v Adidas. The suits were everywhere. The money was wall-to-wall in the hospitality marquees. In the Coca-Cola marquee a bevy of hostesses complete with short black skirts and red tops were on £34 for twenty hours of work at £1.70 per hour. Some way short of even Prime Minister Blair's minimum wage. While the suits gorged their faces and occasionally glanced down at the match, the fans outside the Stade de France were being asked £3,000 for a ticket.

Canon, Philips, JVC and several hundred more corporates were all in full attendance. There were suits from the English National Investment Company, who either own outright, or have shares in, a very a healthy portfolio of football, including Rangers, AEK Athens, Slavia Prague and Vicenza. Suits from Mark McCormack's IMG. They own Strasbourg FC. Canal Plus, owners of Paris St Germain and Servette. There were suits from FIFA. Suits from Havelange, Blatter, Teixeira, Grondona by the hundreds, by the thousands.

It had been the same at most of the games. On top of the twenty-plus per cent that FIFA had already given to sponsors and corporate guests, vast quantities of the 60 per cent allocation to the French had found their way to the suits. It was a negative contribution to game after game. Suits don't cheer. Suits don't chant, shout or – if they are within hand's reach of Havelange – get out of their seats. Suits keep calm at all times. Even when the hosts, France, began to progress, the excitement in the stadiums when they played was non-existent. France's midfield player, Frank Leboeuf, publicly appealed before the Final for some passion from the French supporters. Lack of passion is not something normally associated with the French people and Leboeuf was not correctly identifying the problem. His fellow mid-field colleague, Didier Deschamps, knew very precisely what was wrong:

'It was like a funeral. Two-thirds of the people in there are invited by sponsors and don't really care about football. Most of the fans who love us could not afford to buy a ticket. The public fervour [in the country] is incredible but those who show up at the stadium in their suits and ties to sulk have no business being there.'

Deschamps was not talking of one specific game, but all the games that France played.

Among the missing fans were four thousand Brazilians. In the run-up to the tournament, CBF had asked for tenders to handle the commercial sale of part of the Brazilian World Cup ticket allocation. In 1994 Pelé's company had, despite the serious logistical problems of large distances to be travelled at very short notice across the United States, made a great success of the job. His company bid for the France 98 contract. When Ricardo Teixeira realised that the Pelé bid was the highest received, he telephoned one of the rival under-bidders and advised them of how much they should increase their bid by to ensure that they won the contract. The rival duly got the business and proceeded to sell thousands of air travel, accommodation and ticket packages. The result was at least four thousand customers who, having arrived in France, discovered that there were no tickets for them. Legal actions are currently in progress.

In many instances World Cup France 98 was very like the Congress that had elected Sepp Blatter. A chronic shortage of young supporters. An excess of fat old men smoking cigars and cigarettes.

On the evening of 12 July it was a time to focus on the pitch. An intriguing match was about to unfold. Brazil were odds-on favourites and very few non-French supporters gave the hosts much of a chance. 'They had no goal scoring forwards ...' 'They would be playing without the inspirational Laurent Blanc ...' There were a host of reasons given to explain why France were about to be roundly and impossibly soundly beaten. Those reasons could all be distilled into one word.

Ronaldo.

The young man who had not been able to afford the bus fare to Flamengo was the ace in coach Zagalo's hand. Currently European Player of the Year, twice voted FIFA 'Best Player in the World', his pace and power, his ability to run faster with the ball than many a player without it, was thrilling to watch. Despite carrying a leg injury he had still scored four goals during Brazil's journey to the Final. It was obvious during the earlier games that Ronaldo was not fit. Short, explosive bursts of running would be followed by an almost listless period of play by the twenty-one-year-old. But many believed that a half-fit Ronaldo was superior to any other player fully fit. It was a wantonly stupid view. Forgivable in a myopic supporter. Indefensible coming from any professional involved in the game. Too many former players now limp heavily into today's hospitality rooms after a game. Too many are in permanent, agonising, arthritic pain because they were sent on too many times with pain-killing injections to get them through the game. Twenty-one years of age and after the final game, some time soon, for Ronaldo an operation on a damaged knee.

But Ronaldo had played superbly in the semi-final against Holland. Just a few more painkillers, just one more game, then he would be able to rest that leg.

'This is the dream final. The one you'd play on a video game, or in the streets,' said French squad member, Thierry Henry.

The dream final that over one billion people sat down to watch was about to become a dreadful nightmare for one of the teams.

In January 1998, when Ronaldo was voted best player in the world for the second time, one of the also-rans was the French player Zinedine Zidane.

In July 1998, when France beat Brazil 3–0, Zidane scored two stunning goals, fellow midfield player Emmanuel Petit got the third and Ronaldo was not even an also-ran. He could barely walk. That France, the country that gave birth to the idea of the World Cup, should add a new name to the list of winners is a source of great delight. That Brazil should be defeated after such an abject performance was initially a source of mystification and subsequently the cause of deep anger.

After the game as the French jubilation spread like a forest fire throughout the entire country, the hyperbole grew more absurd by the hour. It began as 'the greatest event in French football'. Within the hour it had become 'the greatest moment since the Liberation'. An hour later it had become 'the most important occurrence since the French Revolution'. In between these flights of fantasy was wedged like a recurring fugue, 'We have beaten the great Brazil. The best footballing nation on earth.'

In 1951, on 27 October, Joe Louis, former heavyweight world champion, attempted to make a second comeback. Debts, bad tax advice, the predictable greed of those around him, plus a great deal of corruption by those he had trusted, forced the once unbeatable Louis back into the ring. The twenty-eight-year-old Rocky Marciano knocked Louis out of the ring in the eighth round. His trainer exulted, 'My boy has beaten the great Joe Louis.'

The response from Joe's own trainer was, 'No, he hasn't. That wasn't Joe Louis in the ring. It was just what was left of him.' I felt much that way about the French boasts.

Much of the answer to Brazil's performance is, I believe, contained within this book. If you surround a national squad with the seedy corruption, the lack of moral values and ethics, the false belief that all you have to do is roll up to the stadium to collect the Cup and your medals, then you are asking for trouble. If you have a president of your football association like Ricardo Teixeira, who can overcome every problem, can for example arrange that your qualifying matching are played not as FIFA lays down but in an order that takes his fancy to procure an advantage, then your team may believe that everything can be arranged. Four games away, followed by four at home? No problem. Want to play at sea level rather than at altitude? Ricardo will fix it. The double act of João and the fat man had been fixing it for so long. Strutting their stuff about how they were world champions. Look. Just watch, I'm going to smuggle into Brazil over nine tonnes of items. Nine tonnes. The nation will watch me on TV as I do it and I won't pay a dollar. How is it done? That'll be telling, but if you know a judge who wants a ticket for the game, let me know.

If you let your national squad breathe this poison there is going to a detrimental effect. I believe that this book establishes beyond reasonable doubt that there is something rotten in the state of Brazilian football. What was on show from the Brazilian team and management before, during and after the Final was a symptom of the cancer that ails what was the greatest footballing country in the world. Oh my Garrincha, Pelé, Tostao, Gerson of long ago.

The specifics of the dreadful team performance in the Stade de France fit very precisely within the framework of the innate corruption that is at the very heart of the Brazilian footballing infrastructure.

Zagalo, the coach with the famed luck, demonstrated that even he could push luck too far. Dunga, his captain, long before the Final was demonstrating that his time was over. A manager or coach with eyes and courage would have dropped him. You cannot carry a player in a World Cup Final without risking getting severely punished. Captain Dunga, the hard man, should have been confronted by a harder man. He was not, he played, he failed to deliver.

Leonardo was a boy attempting to do a man's job. Cesar Sampaio played as badly as Dunga. One can go on, if not right through the entire team, then most certainly through the majority.

Then there was Ronaldo.

In the weeks leading up to the World Cup Final, everyone wanted a piece of the boy from the Rio *favela*. At the age of eight he joined his first club, Valqueire. So little time for formal education, so little time to learn how to handle what lay waiting for him. With his remarkable abilities he had broken out of the shantytown while still a teenager. He was with his third professional club, PSV Eindhoven, before he needed to shave. Unschooled in so much, Ronaldo rapidly developed other more unusual talents. At his fourth club, Barcelona, again while still in his teens, he handled endless interviews for press, radio and television with consummate ease. Already there was a bodyguard in constant attendance. At the age of twenty he was sold and bought once more. This time by Internazionale of Milan, transfer fee £20 million. The pace was now frenetic, the demands on this young man oppressive. In 1997 he played in seventy-three matches. Then there was the string of meaningless games around the world organised by Nike.

During the Confederations Cup while Blatter was off organising football's top job with his own personal sponsor, Ronaldo began to buckle under the pressure, the demands. Zagalo, the Brazilian coach and Ronaldo's father figure, attempted, Canute-like, to keep the media at bay. The media will not be thwarted, they demand access. Ronaldo sells papers, Ronaldo sells magazines. TV commercials around items featuring Ronaldo are at a premium. It did not get better. From Ronaldo's perspective, it got worse, a lot worse. He desperately needed space, tranquillity, calm. He needed to remember his former friends in the Rio shantytown. Needed perhaps to sit down with Calango, Ze Carlos and Leonardo and remember other times.

The boy from the *favela*, the gap-toothed twenty-one-year-old footballing genius, had used his talents to escape from the shantytown but those very talents had merely transported him from one kind of hell to another. There were over one thousand journalists chasing Ronaldo at all times during the World Cup tournament. What the media had done to Princess Diana they were now doing to Ronaldo, eating the star alive. Then there was the general public – given even the suggestion of a chance they tried to get close to him. Just to see him in the flesh for a moment was enough for many. Then there were the sponsors. Oh, yes, there was always Nike. A photo opportunity here. A TV vox pop there. The stress levels rose, higher and higher. Brazil expects.

The epitaph was there before the death. 'It felt like the whole of Brazil was leaning on me,' Ronaldo was to say after the Final, but he had been feeling it for weeks, for months, before that game. Ronaldo had rented a small house near the Brazilian training camp; the incessant intrusions on his privacy forced him back into base, where he roomed with Roberto Carlos.

What precisely occurred on the Saturday and Sunday 11 and 12 July at the Brazilian base depends very much on who you talk to. Above everything else, what is irrefutable is that the lies, cover-ups, dis-information and behaviour that Machiavelli would have admired stand as the final indictment of the Havelange reign over world football and the era of Ricardo Teixeira's dominance of Brazilian football. Where is the transparency? Where is the frankness? Where is the truth?

My own sources include FIFA officials, European informants and a member of the Brazilian national squad. It would be said that during the night of Saturday Ronaldo had a convulsive fit. That the young man had an attack of some kind is unquestionable, but it occurred shortly after the team lunch on Sunday. The cause of what has been described as 'a fit' has yet to be definitely established.

The team doctor Lidio Toledo – a man who has much to answer for – has given a wide range of diagnoses. At the time, and again after hospital tests on Sunday afternoon, Toledo stated it was 'due to stress. I took him to hospital and asked for a thorough test, like electro-sonography and electro-cardiogram.' A few days later and without any further tests, Toledo said: 'It may be that Ronaldo had an epileptic fit.'

In fact it was Toledo's assistant, Dr Joaquim de Mata, who took Ronaldo by car to the Lilas clinic. He was admitted shortly before 6.00 p.m. After being subjected to a series of tests that failed to establish the cause of a convulsive attack that had been witnessed by at least two players – Carlos Alberto and Leonardo – Ronaldo left the hospital at 7.45 p.m. just seventy-five minutes before kick-off.

Perhaps in the fullness of time FIFA and the Brazilian CBF might consider the possibility that the attack that Ronaldo suffered was triggered by the pain-killing drugs that Dr Toledo administered to the player. Toledo has also said, 'My decision to say that Ronaldo was fit to play was the worst decision I have ever made in my life.' The doctor has admitted giving Ronaldo pain-killing tablets, but denied giving injections. My information is that Ronaldo was indeed given a number of injections during World Cup 98. There are a number of drugs used to mask pain which, if mixed, can induce a convulsive attack. Just as in the recent past drugs used as anti-convulsants have been subsequently discovered to cause major convulsions.

While Ronaldo was undergoing tests at the hospital, the team coach departed for the stadium. It was obvious to Zagalo and his assistants that Ronaldo could not play. On the coach Zagalo discussed the problem with his colleague Zico.

The rest of the squad were also very much preoccupied by what had happened to their star player. Roberto Carlos talked of how on the Saturday evening Ronaldo had been exceptionally quiet, distressed, close to tears. At the very least it would seem clear, based on all the available evidence, that what Ronaldo suffered on the Sunday afternoon was an acute panic/stress attack. The minimum treatment should have been total rest for a minimum of twenty-four hours.

Zagalo drafted Edmundo in to replace Ronaldo, made out his team sheet and began to revise tactics with the team.

Getting ready to depart from his hotel, Ricardo Teixeira was advised of events and told that Edmundo would be pulling on the number nine shirt. The Teixeira entourage left the Château de Grande Romaine for the stadium. On the journey Teixeira was deeply concerned about developments for a number of reasons. He had desperately wanted to make it two in a row with World Cup victories; that was understandable. He was also concerned how the team sponsor Nike would react to the fulcrum of their huge advertising campaign being absent from the game. Teixeira had been the man who more than any other had negotiated the lucrative sponsorship deal with Nike. The exact nature of the deal, the precise terms and clauses, have never been revealed. I am told that there are specific clauses relating to Ronaldo and that one of them stipulates that if fit and selected, Ronaldo must play the full ninety minutes. This cannot be confirmed until the Brazilian Football Association reveals the details of the Nike contract. Teixeira has indeed been Havelange-trained. The secrecy over commercial deals is but one of many examples of the father-in-law's teaching. In this book I have referred to the Nike deal being worth $400 million over ten years. Even that figure cannot be confirmed. Indeed, I have seen eleven different figures quoted by eleven different journalists.

The team were well into changing when, just forty minutes before kick-off, Ronaldo and Dr Mata appeared. Mata confirmed that the tests had proved nothing. Ronaldo told Zagalo that he was ready to play and all hell broke out. All of the fears, anxieties that had been simmering just below the surface of this group now exploded out of control. The team was in a moment no longer a team. It became two factions. One, led by the captain, Dunga, demanded that the team should not be changed yet again. That Edmundo should play. Zagalo was initially inclined to go along with this view. He told Ronaldo that he had changed the tactics to accommodate the selection of Edmundo. The team sheet had been printed and issued to the media. It was too late by FIFA rules to change the starting eleven. The other faction, led by Leonardo, argued for Ronaldo's inclusion. Anarchy raged.

Gilmar Rinaldi, Zagalo's assistant, was despatched to tell Teixeira the situation. The French team, meanwhile, had taken to the pitch for the warm-up period.

In the dressing room Ricardo Teixeira joined in the argument. He decreed that if Ronaldo had been declared fit by the team doctor then he should play. As for the breach of FIFA rules? 'Don't be silly, remember who I am.' Sure enough, the son-in-law rewrote that particular section of the FIFA rules in the time it takes to say 'nepotism'.

So a fundamentally divided team took to the pitch. We were not going to see that other face of Brazilian football in this Final. There was indeed that heightening of expectation when Brazil finally came out. It was followed by growing disbelief. Ronaldo was so obviously unfit. He wandered like a slow-moving sleepwalker through the entire game. The fact that it was obvious to any watcher within the first fifteen minutes that Ronaldo should be substituted and yet was not gives a terrifying credibility to what I have been told about the Nike contract. Ronaldo had been declared fit by the team doctor. Was that young man subjected to what we all saw merely to fulfil the terms of a commercial contract? If that is indeed the simple truth of this affair then the gods have indeed succeeded in driving the Havelanges and Teixeiras of the football world quite mad.

So France won the World Cup 3–0. In a stadium where the minority ordinary French football supporters succeeded in at best creating a low murmur and the suits remained absolutely silent, where empty seats in the executive boxes for the 'Hospitality Final' gave mute testimony to sponsors who would rather stand in their hospitality tents drinking champagne than actually watch the match, where other suits sat fast asleep. It had finally come to pass. Havelange and company had demonstrated that you did indeed have no need of ordinary supporters.

The medal presentation was an enduring memory. Knowing that once he had handed the Cup to President Chirac to present to Didier Deschamps his term of office as FIFA's President was definitively over, Havelange dragged out the moment. All of the winners had received their medals and were crowding the gantry when finally their captain got the Cup in his hands. By now the entire French team had climbed onto the dais, thus presenting Havelange – a man who has made an art form of pomposity – with the delightful view of a row of French arses.

The final word should be with the new incoming President, Sepp Blatter. Within forty-eight hours of the end of World Cup 98, Havelange's successor shared his thoughts on the next World Cup:

'I think the evening games, particularly the Final, should start earlier. Should start at 6.00 p.m. local time. Having a 9.00 p.m. kick-off is a bad thing. It means we cannot have a party on the day of the Final.'

A 6.00 p.m. start in Tokyo for the World Cup 2002 Final will mean sitting down in England at 9.00 a.m. Better get ready for an early morning viewing of a Far East monsoon.

My earlier comments concerning how easy it would be for Rupert Murdoch or any other media baron to buy the FIFA presidency and in doing so buy control of the World Cup tournament were written during the France 98 competition. It had seemed to me for some time that it was inevitable that Murdoch would make a major investment to gain a measure of control in the world of football. During the first week of September 1998 Murdoch duly obliged. He made an offer for Manchester United of £623 million – over $1 billion. Old Trafford would become sold-out Trafford. Another piece of the game was in danger of being irretrievably lost and notwithstanding the purchase price, stolen from its rightful owners.

So the club that earlier this year banned its supporters from standing up except 'briefly and only when there is a moment of great excitement' was eager to sell its soul to the media baron.

The journey of the soul of the young footballing fan has been reduced to a banality. If the young supporter objects to being kept sitting on the grounds that even in church you stand up to sing, he or she would now be able to get a constant supply of their Murdoch-owned Murdoch United on the Murdoch-owned BSkyB satellite TV. He or she would then be able to read highly favourable accounts of how Murdoch United played in the Murdoch-owned *Sun*, *News of the World*, *Times* and *Sunday Times* newspapers. The Murdoch United supporters would exist permanently in Murdochland. Not virtual reality. Actual reality. Difficult to experience a journey of the soul in a soulless environment.

Those difficulties are not confined to the world of football. Rugby Union supporters in this and other countries have become sickened with the arrogant intransigence of the game's administrators – men who, like their counterparts in football, are, in Will Carling's memorable phrase, 'a bunch of old farts'. The men in question promptly gave credibility to Carling's remark by suspending him from the England team until he publicly apologised. Any lover of cricket must be appalled at how the Australian Cricketing Board covered up the betting scandal involving some of their top players – behaviour just as reprehensible as the French World Cup organisers orchestrating a ticketing scandal that amounted to barefaced daylight robbery. By the end of 1998 there were also disturbing revelations of widespread corruption within the International Olympic Committee. These are, of course, the same officials that sports enthusiasts look to to ensure that the Olympic Games are kept free of drug cheats.

One wonders what the Corinthian Sir Stanley Rous would make of some of the recent events in football. What, for example, would he think of David Davies, the FA's Director of Public Affairs, writing on behalf of England

Manager Glenn Hoddle a get-paid-and-tell account, complete with dressing-room secrets, of England's participation in World Cup 98? What would Rous, former Secretary of the FA, make of the £3.2 million sweetener secretly paid to the Welsh FA by FA Chief Executive Graham Kelly and FA Chairman Keith Wiseman – money paid to further the cause of England's World Cup 2006 aspirations? Of the curious consultancy agreement that the Football Association negotiated with ex-BSkyB boss Sam Chisholm?

Attempting to justify the activities of Wiseman and Kelly, Alex McGivan, the Director of England's WC 2006 campaign, said: 'What is more natural than for them to say, is there any way you can help us? That's the real world.' This is apparently called, without any sense of irony, 'the new morality'. McGivan would do well to realise that the £10 million of our money that is being spent to further our attempts to 'acquire' the right to stage World Cup 2006 is not going to get him off the launchpad. If a £3.2 million sweetener to the Welsh FA – an organisation without any direct influence or input – is deemed necessary, then presumably the FIFA Executive Committee, the various football Federations and Confederations, the wheelers and dealers, the fixers and mixers, are going to need a great deal more than £10 million worth of sweetening. God Almighty, Havelange and his cronies spent half that amount in six weeks in the summer of 1998 in Paris.

Mr McGivan does not have to take my word for the high cost of corruption in today's world of sport. He need look no further than the recent revelations involving the IOC, whose motto 'A Healthy Spirit in a Healthy Body' has apparently been replaced with the slogan 'A Healthy Bundle in an Environmentally Friendly Envelope'. Sydney did not 'win' the rights to host the 2000 Summer Games.

They bought them. On the eve of the voting, John Coates, President of the Australian Olympic Committee, offered $35,000 a piece to the National Olympic Committees of Kenya and Uganda. The following day Sydney beat Beijing by two votes. The Australian Committee had left no stone unturned in their search for influential friends who might affect the crucial vote. Their efforts included bringing great pressure on the Australian Soccer Federation to find a job for Sepp Blatter's daughter. A source within the Australian Federation has confirmed 'It was made very clear to me that, given the football code's profile at the Olympics, it was imperative that we place her somewhere in the office after the World Youth Championships finished in 1993. Football generates a lot of cash at the Olympics. Only track and field finals drew bigger crowds at Atlanta. Clearly, having been number two to João Havelange, I believe Mr Blatter was in a position to influence IOC delegates in how they should vote in the lead-up to the vote in Monte Carlo. There was a great deal of political pressure put on Soccer Australia to keep his daughter employed, but I refused to do so. The decision to have her work for the national body was taken well above my station in life.'

At the time I met Corinne Blatter in Zurich, when she was functioning as her father's campaign manager, she was in fact still on the payroll of Soccer Australia in Sydney.

Salt Lake City did not win the 2002 Winter Games. They bought them with a sustained campaign of bribery and corruption and a multi-million-dollar slush fund.

Amsterdam made an unsuccessful bid for the 1992 Games. It was recently reported that a number of IOC delegates were wined and dined and were also escorted to exclusive brothels in the Dutch city. The delegates also allegedly demanded expensive gifts in return for their votes. Among their number was João Havelange, who has subsequently denied the published allegations that he asked for diamonds, Delft blue porcelain and paintings.

There are 110 members of the IOC. When German officials were preparing their application for the 2000 Games, utilising a wide variety of sources, they created a highly confidential document which concluded that, apart from Princess Anne, only five other IOC members were believed to be totally incorruptible.

In early February 1999 England manager Glenn Hoddle became ex-England manager. He paid the ultimate price for his religious beliefs – reincarnation, faith healing et al. – when he should have paid that ultimate price for endorsing a football philosophy that believed that practising taking penalty kicks was a complete waste of time. In view of the fact that England were knocked out of World Cup 98 after losing a penalty shoot-out against Argentina and that our manager subsequently stated that the greatest mistake he had made was his failure to take faith healer Eileen Drewery to France for the tournament, one can only hope that if reincarnation does exist, Glenn Hoddle comes back as an proficient football manager.

Now, after just one match in charge, Kevin Keegan is hailed as the new Messiah. After a victory against a Poland team who would struggle to beat my village eleven, the conventional wisdom is that Euro 2000 is already won and World Cup 2002 is a foregone conclusion. World Cup 2006, however – notwithstanding all the whistling in the dark from Alex McGivan and his colleagues – remains the elusive Holy Grail. The fact that Sepp Blatter has continued since his election regularly to state publicly his commitment to a 2006 tournament on the African continent is brushed aside by our campaign director, who appears not to understand President Blatter's very plain speaking. For example, in Nigeria during the second week of April 1999: 'I can say with more conviction than ever that Africa will have the World Cup in 2006.' In the face of statements like that, the time has surely come when we should very seriously question the activities and continuing expenditure of McGivan's campaign team. Desperate to energise a World Cup bid that is already stone dead in the water, the FA have appealed to Prince Charles to get involved in the campaign. The Prince's knowledge of the game leaves something to be desired. In 1995, while making one of his rare visits to a Cup Final, he showed little interest in the game and then attempted to present the Cup to the losers – Manchester United – rather than to the winners – Everton. His new-found conversion to the world's greatest religion is a shrewd move. Prince Charles has not had the best of Press exposure in recent years and establishing even a tenuous link with football is very good PR for the heir to the throne. It also has historic precedent. In 1914, acting on recommendations from his advisers, King George V attended the FA Cup Final – the first time that the event had been dignified by an official Royal visit. It was a move designed to increase the King's popularity within the country as he demonstrated 'the common touch'. The King watched Burnley beat Liverpool just a few months before we were at war with Germany, a country ruled by some of the King's relations. Perhaps when Prince Charles lunches with Sepp Blatter at Highgrove the day before the FA Cup Final, he might ask President Blatter – always a well-informed man – to confirm the information I have been given, namely that we currently can only rely on just three votes from the twenty-four members of the FIFA Executive Committee.

Perhaps it was a desire to throw a potential lifeline to England's aspirations to host World Cup 2006 that caused President Blatter to make what was easily the most extraordinary statement during his first year as President of FIFA, namely his pronouncement that there should be a

World Cup every two years. It was an opinion that has been greeted with universal derision, which can best be demonstrated by one particular comment from the *Guardian* journalist, David Lacey:

'Blatter has never been the same since Sophia Loren fondled his plastic balls before the 1990 World Cup Draw.'

In mid-April 1999, conventional wisdom took a good smack in the face. It had been widely believed BSkyB's attempted take-over of Manchester United would be given the nod by the Monopolies and Mergers Commission. In the event, the Commission concluded that such an acquisition would be bad for football and bad for broadcasting and therefore not in the public interest. The majority of commentators gloated at Rupert Murdoch's discomfiture, then settled down two days later to watch on Murdoch's Sky TV as Manchester United played Arsenal.

Unlike that majority of commentators, I do not believe that Sky's defeat was the end of the war, merely the end of that particular battle. The suits will come again, and they will keep on coming until they prevail. We already have a truly bizarre situation at many Premier League grounds. Many thousands of supporters earning less – often far less – than the national average regularly pay over a significant part of their weekly wage for the right to applaud on and off the pitch twenty-two millionaires. Not long ago, in the pre-all-seater age, it was somewhat different.

There was a time when pre-pubescent youth would hang from the rafters of their favourite ground, then in their mid-teens gather at a prearranged part of the terrace to watch and participate. That was the all-important thing. To participate in the game by encouragement, derision, grief and joy. By physical movement. To mourn a defeat, to celebrate a victory. Then, when a little older, late teens, early twenties perhaps, to watch the game from yet another part of the terrace, this time with just one companion. A young woman. Years later there would be other places where the game would be watched. The West Stand in a seat next to a small son. Later still, the North Stand, now as a season-ticket holder, while the pre-pubescent son was beginning unconsciously to repeat the cycle. To embark on his own personal journey of the soul as he hung from the rafters. This journey has now through the efforts of Havelange, Blatter, Murdoch and their ilk been made extinct in the modern game. The theatre of football is being systematically robbed of one of its most vital ingredients: the energy, the passion of the crowd.

Within two decades the game of football will have been transformed to pay-per-view Rollerball without the violence. People will point at Old Trafford, Highbury and the other famous grounds of England and say, 'There used to be a football club over there.'

Ah well, all good things come to an end.

Epilogue to the 2011 Edition

That was then, this is now, some eleven years later. Football has indeed undergone change, much of it of a questionable nature. The late Harold Macmillan memorably observed, 'One can only sell the family silver once.' At the time this book was written not a single Premier League club had gone into foreign hands. I predicted that for Manchester United and others it was only a matter of time. As of September 2011 nearly half of the Premier League clubs are in foreign hands.

Another prediction was that Qatar, after the 'assistance' it had given to get Blatter elected, would be rewarded with the honour of holding a 'meaningless tournament' – for as long as FIFA refuses to allow goal line technology, then the World Cup remains in that category.

Sweeteners come in all shapes and sizes, and few can rival those on offer every four years when two major events in the world of football occur. FIFA presidential elections and the prospect of hosting the World Cup have a curious effect on a wide range of people. Many an otherwise sane individual gets a rush of greed to the head. So it was in early December 2010. In the run-up to the voting, those bidding either to host World Cup 2018 or World Cup 2022 needed deep pockets, very deep pockets. The amounts spent to support a bid varied from the relatively modest amounts of around £7 million spent by Holland and Belgiumto the Qatar bid of a minimum of £70 million.

The monies from Qatar were sprayed in many directions, including proposals of financial aid to the Argentine Football Association for the recruitment of what Qatar described as 'bid Ambassadors'. This grandiosity referred to a group of ex-footballers including: Gabriel Batistuta £1.6 million, Zinedine Zidane £2.4 million, Ronald de Boer £600,000. There were other recipients including, coming in from left field, Archbishop Desmond Tutu, £60,000 would go to charities of his choice. For other non-footballing VIPs there was a budget of a quarter of a million pounds, much of which went into the pockets of journalists.

Qatar spared no effort to ensure that every corner of the world of football was covered. There was the possibility of a commercial involvement with Real Madrid, and a proposal to move the Asian Confederation headquarters from Malaysia to Qatar with various inducements, including a tower block, residential properties, limos, diplomatic status and use of a private jet – a perk that Blatter had accepted more than once. The Asian Confederation holds four priceless votes as does the African Confederation, which was also buttonholed by the men from Qatar. There was a fifty per cent discount on Qatar Airways for all European employees and the AFC president was to be granted twenty-five free trips in a private plane each year. It was BMWs all round for the AFC executives plus a complex of thirty villas in the Dafna area for AFC staff, complete with health club and swimming pool. All rent-free.

Qatar's generosity was not confined to the above, nor was it restricted to any one country. Argentinean, African and Spanish FIFA members were among the many others to benefit from Qatar's efforts to win friends and influence voters.

For Qatar to win the right to host World Cup 2022 it required the traditional level of greed on these occasions to reach previously unprecedented heights; greed duly obliged. What was also required was a collective madness to grip the majority of those voting.

The average temperature in Qatar during the summer months is 106 degrees . At the time of the vote there was not a single adequate stadium in the country. Qatar has one city, Doha; travel is by taxi, getting a beer in this overwhelmingly Muslim country, a formidable challenge. FIFA has acknowledged that holding the World Cup in Qatar is a 'potential health risk'. The required level of collective madness also duly obliged. Qatar was awarded the right to host the 2022 World Cup.

After a deliberately low profile campaign the World Cup for 2018 was awarded to Russia, which has yet to build thirteen of the sixteen stadiums required. The day before the announcements, US diplomats described Russia as a 'Mafia State'. The leaked US cables painted a picture of a rogue state replete with arms trafficking, money laundering, protection racketeering and kickbacks. This latter activity included suitcases full of bank notes being shipped to Cyprus and deposited in the local banks.

The corruption within Russia even extends to local football matches. It is estimated that between 20 and 40 per cent of the games played in Russia are subject to pre-match fixing, with scores determined by organised crime groups.

On the day of the elections a FIFA source insisted during our conversation that for at least some of the committee who were attracted to the Russian bid the answer lay in the bung, or the bribe. This was sometimes straight cash, usually US dollars, sometimes payment in kind, such as an expensive month's vacation for two, or three if they were planning to take their mistress along. These forms of 'payments' are traditional for a number of FIFA personnel. The reader will doubtless recall various incidents already recorded within this book. Other FIFA members prefer expensive jewellery. The various bribes pale into the tawdry when compared with the amount of money that the ruling Al Thani family had committed to officially spend (fifty billion on infrastructure to build or upgrade some twelve stadiums). Qatar has acknowledged that the stadiums will be of little use after the World Cup is over. They have promised to dismantle the structures and ship the material to other developing countries.

The Qatar solution to the blinding heat is to be air conditioning, which they have promised 'will be 30 to 40 degrees colder than outside'. Sepp Blatter has come up with a very typical Blatter proposal: 'I expect that it [the World Cup] will be held in winter, in January rather than June or July.' The fact that the UK football leagues do not take a winter break and are in the middle of their season in January does not apparently concern a man who as previously recorded, 'has fifty new ideas each day. And fifty-one of them are bad.'

With regard to the munificence of Qatar itemised earlier, their Football Association has stated: 'The Qatar bid played within the rules laid down by FIFA at all times.'

FIFA has its own Code of Ethics. Most recently published in 2009 it applies to all FIFA officials, including members of FIFA's executive who voted on the 2018 and 2022 World Cup bids.

The way in which the code deals with bribery is notably limited. Clause 11 of the code provides that:

> Officials may not accept bribes; in other words, any gifts or other advantages that are offered, promised or sent to them to incite breach of duty or dishonest conduct for the benefit of a third party shall be refused;

and also that Officials are forbidden from bribing third parties or from urging or inciting others to do so in order to gain an advantage for themselves or third parties.

As an article by Jeremy Summers QC in the *Law Gazette*, published in May 2011, observed:

These are not robust provisions and, in particular, fail to define the terms "bribe" and "bribing". Remarkably, there is no standalone prohibition specifically preventing executive committee members seeking an advantage.

Before going forward and exploring the events leading to the election of the FIFA President in June 2011 it is appropriate to pause and note just a few of the events that have occurred during Sepp Blatter's uninterrupted reign of thirteen years. How has the man who seized the crown way back in Paris on 8 June 1998 fared?

The controversy surrounding Blatter's initial election in 1998 is well documented within this book. His candidacy in 2002 fared little better. Allegations of financial mismanagement by no less an insider than FIFA Secretary General Michel Zen-Ruffinen in a thirty page dossier threatened to destroy Blatter's chances of re-election. The Vice President of the Somali Football Federation, Farra Ado, weighed in with the allegation that he had been offered $100,000 to vote for Blatter in 1998. The dossier alleged that the collapse of FIFA's marketing partner ISL had caused losses of up to one hundred million dollars, allegations that were supported by Lenhart Johansson. The dossier was given to the Swiss authorities. Subsequently Blatter was cleared and eventually Zen-Ruffinen found himself out of work.

In 2004 Blatter succeeded in alienating the increasing number of female footballers. He declared that women should 'wear tighter shorts and low cut shirts ... to create a more female aesthetic.'

In 2006 the President was conspicuous by his absence from the World Cup final dereliction that was roundly criticised in the international press. It was widely believed that his non-attendance was caused by his chagrin because Italy rather than France had won. Later when he eventually apologised he said that he had avoided the presentation ceremony because he was afraid of being whistled.

In 2007 and 2008 his persistent attempts to restrict the number of foreign players football clubs can field caused deep resentment. Yet again his anti-British stance was in evidence as he frequently referred to the English Premier League as one of the major problems in football. The fact that it is demonstrably the most financially successful League in the world might perhaps be the key to this particular presidential obsession.

Blatter's continuing refusal to sanction goal-line technology has inevitably led to absurd decisions on the field of play. The French striker Thierry Henry's all-important 'goal' against Ireland in 2009 was in the Maradona class of cheating. That Frank Lampard scored a vital goal against Germany in the 2010 World Cup was obvious to all, even Sepp Blatter. Unfortunately Blatter was not refereeing the game and the man who was, disallowed the goal.

It is difficult to find any change that Blatter has made to the rules that has been greeted with acclaim by football's supporters. Quite a number of the President's changes have been greeted with derision. National associations must now enforce immediate suspensions of all players sent off during a game. *Even* if television replays confirm a player's innocence.

The booking of players who remove their shirts after scoring is justified by Blatter on the grounds that football is a global sport, and thus the sensibilities of conservative nations and spectators must be respected.

In 2007, Blatter decreed that no football match would be played above 2,500 metres above sea level. The Bolivian national stadium is located more than 3,000 metres above sea level. When this was pointed out to Blatter he revised the figure to 3,000. It was again pointed out to the President that the Bolivian stadium was somewhat higher than 3,000 metres. The following day FIFA announced that the Bolivian stadium was being granted a special exemption.

One aspect that urgently needs FIFA's attention concerns the murderous attack by Angolan guerrillas on the Togo squad while travelling to the 2010 Africa Cup of Nations. Nothing about this story enhances the reputation of either FIFA or the various other governing football organisations.

The attack occurred on Friday, 8 January. It lasted for nearly thirty minutes. The coach driver was the first to be killed, the assistant team coach and the press officer were the next to die. Nine others were injured, some very seriously – among these were goalkeeper, Kodjovi Obilale and defender Serge Akapo. Among those who were relatively unscathed were Togo captain and Manchester City striker Emmanuel Adebayor.

Like the rest of the team, he was deeply traumatised and in shock. 'I don't think any of the players will sleep after this. You cannot sleep after what we have seen – one of your teammates with bullets in his body in front of you, crying and losing consciousness. It is very difficult.'

The first official response from football's hierarchy came from a spokesman of the organisers the Confederation of African Football (CAF). Souleymane Habuba stated that the tournament would proceed despite the attack: 'Our great concern is for the players, but the championship goes ahead.' From FIFA headquarters in Switzerland a statement was also issued: 'FIFA and its president Sepp Blatter, are deeply moved by today's incidents which affected Togo's national team, to who they express their utmost sympathy.'

Sympathy is well and good, practical help would have been a deal better, but it was in short supply. When the Prime Minister of Togo asked for assurances that the Togo team would be protected if they remained in Angola, CAF remain silent, prompting the Prime Minister to order the immediate return of the squad. CAF then disqualified Togo for its failure to attend the tournament, fined Togo and banned them from the next two Cup of Nations tournaments. FIFA eventually overturned these decisions.

Goalkeeper Kodjovi Obilale was left permanently disabled and has to date had seven operations. From CAF he has not received any financial help. FIFA eventually put their hands in their pockets and offered Obilale $25,000 in November 2010; this sum was subsequently increased to $100,000 but covered less than half of Obilale's medical expenses to date. To their credit, Adebayor and other members of the football fraternity have rallied around. Perhaps one day Qatar or another wealthy footballing nation or even FIFA itself can be persuaded to make adequate compensation to Obilale and his colleagues. Meanwhile the former goalkeeper is left expressing his bitterness, 'When you are on two legs, everyone's running after you. The day you fall down, there's nobody there anymore.'

In October 2010 *The Sunday Times* ran a major scoop. It was the fruits of an undercover operation by several of its reporters who had targeted two FIFA members. Posing as lobbyists working on behalf of the USA's bid to host World Cup 2022 the reporters had meetings with Nigerian FIFA delegate Amos Adamu and Tahiti's Reynald Temari, president of Oceania Football Confederation. Adamu allegedly asked for $800,000 dollars to build four artificial pitches in Nigeria. Temari was looking for £1.5 million to create a football academy and boasted that the Confederation had been offered up to $12 million from two rival bidding countries.

FIFA immediately requested full details of *The Sunday Times* investigation and a dossier containing records and videos of the reporters' meetings with the two FIFA delegates. This material was delivered to FIFA headquarters within twenty-four hours. FIFA subsequently banned Reynald Temari for a year and fined him 5,000 Swiss Francs. Amos Adamu was suspended for three years and fined 10,000 Swiss Francs.

One month later BBC's *Panorama* entered the fray. The programme alleged that three FIFA committee members – Issa Hayatou of Cameroon, Nicolas Leoz of Paraguay and Ricardo Teixeira of Brazil – had taken bribes in a corruption scandal involving a hundred million dollars. The programme detailed the alleged corruption, involving the taking of bribes in the 1990s over the distribution of FIFA's World Cup television rights. It was stated that Leoz's share of the kickback was $730,000.

The FIFA sewers flooded yet again in May 2011, less than a month before the election for President would be resolved. On 10 May Lord Treisman, the former FA chairman testified before a Parliamentary Select Committee that some of those he identified as vulnerable to a bribe have already been named but now to Lord Treisman they had come up with new demands. Leoz of Paraguay wanted a knighthood. Jack Warner president of CONCACAF (North, Central American and Caribbean Association Football), requested £3 million. Ricardo Teixeira was flexible: 'what do you have for me?' Worawi Makudi FIFA Executive Committee member from Thailand wished to acquire the television rights to a projected friendly game between England and Thailand.

Sepp Blatter declared he was shocked by these various allegations. 'If these are true, I will fight this. I am fighting for FIFA to clean FIFA. I cannot answer for individual members of our committee. I cannot say if they are all angels or if they are all devils.' His 'shock' is mystifying. Much of the evidence that supports these various alleged transgressions by FIFA members had been sent to him six months previously.

His current general secretary Jerome Valcke weighed in with his own take on the situation: 'Let us take this investigation step by step. It's like we're in an ordinary court.' Valcke has some experience of ordinary courts. He had been fired from his position as FIFA's marketing head after a New York judge had ruled he had 'lied repeatedly' to potential sponsors. The prosecution had declared that among FIFA's 'white lies, commercial lies, bluffs, pure lies, straight untruths and perjury, Mr Valcke even lied when testifying about his own lies.' Eight months later he was re-hired by Sepp Blatter. Valcke was a significant player in the run up to the Presidential election as the man charged with overseeing the campaign.

On 23 May Valcke was forced to deny that he had put pressure on Bin Hammam to withdraw from the presidential race. If against the odds Hammam should win the crown, Valcke might well find himself fired from FIFA for the second time. Blatter meanwhile got on with the serious task of ensuring the crown stayed with its current owner.

Promising to rebuild FIFA's reputation he said, "We shall find a solution how to handle the past ... in order that we can stop forever in the future all these damaging things about corruption.' Assuming that the result was a done deal, he continued: 'We have to make sure that in the next term of office immediately starting after the election, that we rebuild the image of FIFA.'

In the light of what had occurred in June 1998 – events

that the reader of this book will be familiar with – Blatter's next remarks had a strong resonance, not least because on that occasion his current opponent Bin Hammam was, courtesy of his role as postman, greatly responsible for the election of Sepp Blatter.

Now on the potential verge of a fourth consecutive victory, Blatter chose this moment to talk of a bribe he had been offered while he was acting as Secretary General under João Havelange. 'In this envelope there was an amount of money. I couldn't refuse it because he put it in my pocket.' Blatter refused to name his benefactor. 'I came home to FIFA and gave it to the finance director and he put this money on the account of the Swiss Bank Corporation.'

The cash was subsequently withdrawn by the anonymous donor. Blatter concluded, 'Then it was specifically known that please don't try to give money to somebody who's in the FIFA.'

Two days later on 25 May Blatter's idyllic picture of an ethical, honest FIFA was demolished as civil war raged and football's proclaimed headquarters threatened to self-destruct. To an outsider it might very well appear to be a case of Gucci handbags at ten paces.

Blatter, only a few days earlier, had talked of commencing to rebuild FIFA starting 'immediately after the election'. Clearly impatient for change he had now decided not to wait until there was an election result. In a classic example of getting your retaliation in first, he announced a corruption investigation into his presidential opponent, Mohamed bin Hammam, and the President of CONCACAF, Jack Warner. Was it a plot involving Warner, a pro-Blatter man for decades, switching sides to support Hammam? Was it a plot by Blatter and Warner to isolate Hammam? Why was FIFA Executive Committee member Chuck Blazer, previously a loyal Blatter ally and a close friend of Warner's, choosing this, of all times to destroy the image of cosy FIFA fraternity?

It transpired that Blazer had sent FIFA General Secretary Jerome Valcke a report that alleged that Warner and Bin Hammam had organised bribes in exchange for votes at a meeting of the Caribbean Football Union (CFU). The Blazer dossier included sworn affidavits by CFU members claiming that they were offered thousands of dollars in cash for 'development projects' at a meeting organised by Warner on Bin Hammam's behalf to discuss his candidacy.

As of Wednesday, 25 May, there were more than a third of the FIFA executive committee members suspended or under investigation for alleged corruption. The same day there was an attempt to increase the number to ten. The accuser was Bin Hammam and the man in his sights, none less than President Sepp Blatter, accused of corruption. Hammam insisted that Blatter had 'been informed of, but did not oppose, payments allegedly made to members of the Caribbean Football Union.'

The sums involved were allegedly $40,000 per bribe. Writing in his Internet column, Blatter's ramblings were very reminiscent of Eric Cantona's views on trawlers, journalists and herrings. The FIFA president's chosen metaphor was cows, Swiss cows:

> When a Swiss farmer's neighbour has a cow while he has none the less fortunate farmer will work twice as hard so that one day he can buy a cow as well. When another farmer, elsewhere has no cow but his neighbour does that farmer will kill his neighbour's cow out of sheer malice. I'd rather be a Swiss farmer, like it or not.

Hammam's contribution to the debate was succinct:

> If I'm guilty, so is Blatter.

Thank God that in the middle of this there was, on

Saturday, 28 May, the Champions League European Cup Final: Barcelona versus Manchester United. One prayed for an antidote, one's prayers were answered: Barcelona 3, Manchester United 1.

I doubt whether a single member of the FIFA executive really got it. What was unfolding on the Wembley pitch that evening was rare, very rare. No one on that pitch was concerned with Swiss cows or the rotten stench that was emanating from the FIFA executive. 'For the good of the Game' has been the derisory slogan that FIFA has touted for many years. On that May evening at Wembley those two teams did more for 'the good of the game' in ninety minutes than FIFA has achieved in the past thirty-seven years, since 1974 when João Havelange bought the presidency. Since then Havelange and Blatter have marketed football with great zeal, squeezing billions of dollars out of sponsors. It is now rarely referred to as 'football' it has become the 'FIFA Brand – our commitment'. That is how Blatter described the game in his pre-election mission statement. Presumably the current reserve pot of $1.5 billion is not enough?

Late on Saturday 28 May, Mohamed bin Hammam withdrew his candidacy to become FIFA President. Confronted with the reality that the following day he was due to face an ethics committee hearing into bribery allegations, he threw in the towel and simultaneously attempted to seize the moral high ground:

> It saddens me that standing up for the causes that I believed in has come at a great price – the degradation of FIFA's reputation. This is not what I had in mind for FIFA and this is unacceptable.

He continued.

> I cannot allow the game that I loved to be dragged more

and more in the mud because of the competition between two individuals. The game itself and the people who love it around the world must come first. It is for this reason that I announce my withdrawal from the presidential election. [end quote]

It would be splendid to believe that Hammam had been influenced by what he and the rest of us had just witnessed in those ninety minutes. But it would be naive. Sensing that Hammam had overestimated his support, the legal affidavits from those who had been offered an inducement to vote for Hammam were snowballing.

Less than twenty-four hours later after a hearing convened by FIFA's ethics committee and presided over by the Deputy Chairman Petrus Damaseb, who when not at FIFA functions as a Namibian high court judge, the ongoing scandal had its first victims.

Damaseb declared that he was confident that there was enough evidence to open an independent inquiry into claims that Hammam and Warner had offered gifts of $40,000 to members of the Caribbean Football Union (CFU) in return for supporting Hammam's bid to oust Sepp Blatter. Both men were suspended from any involvement with football. Blatter was cleared of having had prior knowledge of the bribe attempt and emerged the clear winner.

The election for the presidency had now been reduced to a coronation, unless Blatter called for a temporary suspension to allow any other potential rival to come forward. With the level of power he wielded, the Executive Committee would have acceded to his wish except that their suggestion was considered by some FIFA members to be walking in la la land.

If the suggestion had reached Sepp Blatter he would probably still be laughing. The only way for the election to be postponed was for 156 of the 208 members to vote against accepting the existing agenda for the Congress. A number of observers would declare that there was indeed a will to reform. There was talk in hotel rooms and quiet corners but those who were seriously up for radical change were never more than a minority.

On this day, Blatter's cup ran over. General Secretary Valcke announced that there was no evidence to support Lord Treisman's allegations of corruption activities by Messrs Warner, Leoz, Teixeira and Makudi. Thus it was a mixed day for Warner, a bad one for Hammam but a very good one for the others.

Listening to Blatter at a FIFA press conference on late Monday, 30 May, was to hear a man dismissing the many still unresolved issues. In his mind they no longer existed. When reporters referred to the crisis that still engulfed FIFA, Blatter responded: 'Crisis, what crisis?' This, on a day when the third and fourth of FIFA's twenty-four most senior officials had been suspended over corruption allegations, was brushed aside. Meanwhile, a number of the very biggest and most powerful sponsors expressed for the very first time concerns. Sponsors such as Coca-Cola: 'The current allegations being raised are distressing and bad for the sport.' or Adidas, declaring it was 'disappointed' with the way the organisation had become embroiled in allegations of bribery: 'The scandal is neither good for football nor for FIFA and its partners.' or Emirates airline: 'Emirates like all football fans around the world, is disappointed with the issues that are currently surrounding the administration of the sport. We hope these issues will be resolved as soon as possible and the outcome will be in the interest of the game and sport in general.'

To wave away such statements as if swatting a fly was highly dangerous. Blatter might well strut the stage in FIFA's headquarters in Switzerland but to ignore such alarm sirens was to tempt the very fabric of FIFA. Its dependence on such sponsors' good will and the millions poured into FIFA was the oil of the entire machine. Between 2006 and 2010 FIFA earned more than $1.6bn, including £1bn from its sponsors – certainly enough to concentrate the minds of every FIFA member.

On Tuesday, 31 May, the eve of the presidential election, one local Swiss newspaper published the results of a survey indicating that 86 per cent of Blatter's compatriots believe him to be 'corrupt' and an additional 7 per cent assessed him as 'a bit corrupt'. Quite a number of the 208 football federations secretly agreed with that 86 per cent but getting them to go public was quite a different matter. Just two did on 31 May, namely England and Scotland. FA Chairman David Bernstein argued that the coronation of the 75-year-old Blatter should be halted because 'FIFA is engulfed by a swirling stench of corruption.' Bernstein gave two main reasons for England's refusal to vote:

'A series of allegations relating to the FIFA executive committee members make it difficult to support the one remaining candidate. Then there is concern about the lack of transparency and accountability.

I call on FIFA to postpone the election and give credibility to this process, so any alternative reforming candidate could have the opportunity to stand for president.'

The FA Chairman also called for an independent organisation to be hired to overhaul FIFA.

Subsequently, the Scottish FA seconded David Bernstein's proposal and the Liberian Football Association also expressed support. A number of others would rally to the cause when it came to the vote but it was a long way short of the 150 votes required to stop the Blatter machine. If the

English Football Association had taken a leaf out of Sepp Blatter's book or even João Havelange's and spent a year lobbying other members, the ultimate result might have been very different. It was too little, too late.

The British Press was overwhelmingly united in their condemnation of FIFA in general and the President in particular but the rest of the world was blissfully indifferent. The result was succinctly recorded in the *Daily Mail*.

> Sleaze 186
> Football.........17

During his acceptance speech Blatter acknowledged that FIFA was in need of change. 'Reforms will be made, radical decisions will be taken. We must do something because I do not want ever again the institution of FIFA to face a situation which is undignified. Football belongs to everyone and we are the ones in charge. We will have four years.'

Blatter's constant references to the 'FIFA football family' and the need to ensure control remains for eternity in the hands of FIFA, immune from any government influence, is a regular theme. His proposals included 'a grand committee of corporate governance and compliance' and a 'committee of solutions'. A key member of the clean up FIFA committee is to be the former US Secretary of State Henry Kissinger. Another is the opera singer Plácido Domingo.

Seeking a scapegoat for the current mire and the universal contempt that FIFA is held in, Blatter very predictably fastened on the English and their chagrin at not being awarded the 2018 World Cup:

> Where does all this evil come from?' he asked. 'It has to do with the popularity of our competition, the World Cup and everything around the vote. That kicked off a wave of accusations, allegations, criticism.

It was a travesty of the truth, something which, like a decent cup of coffee, has been in very short supply in the FIFA house for many years. The President was well-supported by the speakers who followed him to the podium.

> With the English 2018 bid I said: "Let us be brief. If you give back the Falkland Islands, which belong to us, you will get my vote." They then became very sad and left … We always have attacks from the English which are mostly lies.
>
> Julio Gordona, FIFA senior vice-president, Argentina

> What a beautiful English word: allegations. Somebody stands up, says a few things in the press, then these things take … a seed in our minds, without most of the time, a single shred of truth.
>
> Costakis Koutsokoumnis, FA president, Cyprus

> The problem of some comments in the paper came from some people who may have lost in the World Cup elections. They associated us with crimes we have not committed, they insult, they attack our freedom. It's enough.
>
> Ángel María Villar Llona, FIFA
> executive committee member, Spain

There was a great deal more in similar vein. What Señor Grondona made of another current FIFA investigation into football corruption is unknown. This concerned Argentina and Nigeria and a match played on the very day that Blatter was re-elected. A betting scam had allegedly occurred, and the evidence was powerful.

The same week, Italian police made sixteen arrests in yet another betting scam, in this instance not one game but seventeen matches in Serie B. It will be interesting to see FIFA lay either of these scandals at England's door.

Doubtless Messrs Grondona, Llona, Koutsokoumnis et al. will also be able to demonstrate English links with the further developments regarding Mohamed bin Hammam. By 7 July, the FIFA investigation into the former Paris postman, – key procurer of the 2022 World Cup for Qatar, candidate for the FIFA presidency and currently the man accused of pushing yet more brown envelopes stuffed with thousands of crisp US dollars to FIFA members – had his back to the wall. There were now nine sworn affidavits from CFU members. It all sounded very familiar, and not just the brown envelopes. In Paris, May 1998, one million dollars had bought twenty votes. Now, one million dollars had been allegedly distributed to buy twenty-five votes. A meeting on 22–23 July in Zurich resolved this issue. Mohammed bin Hammam was found guilty of attempted bribery and banned for life from holding any position in the world of football.

Meanwhile, Michael Beavon, a director of Arup Associates who have been developing the solar technology that will cool the Qatar stadium in 2022 has revealed an idea that has Sepp Blatter written all over it, 'The one thing FIFA do say, although it is for guidance, is if it's 32°C they will stop the match and play three 30-minute thirds rather than two forty five minute halves.'

Anyone reading this Epilogue who takes exception to the remarks uttered by various FIFA members about the English will have a unique opportunity come the 2012 London Olympic Games, to pop into the Mayfair Hotel in Park Lane, the nearby Hilton or a wide variety of other four star hotels and indicate that they wish to have a word with one of a range of FIFA members.

In view of the fact that over 900,000 sports fans failed to get even a single ticket to an Olympic event in the recent public ballot, and quite a few of those who were more fortunate will be confronting greatly inflated hot prices, those fans will not lack for a subject of conversation.

Blatter, presumably for once controlling his anti-British tendencies, has been given an 'access all areas' pass and will have a chauffeur driven BMW at his disposal as will his secretary general Jerome Valcke. The FIFA executives will be given tickets for all the prestige events including the opening and closing ceremonies.

The FIFA executives were originally invited to stay at the Dorchester during the games. After the failure to be awarded the 2018 World Cup in such humiliating circumstances Mayor Boris Johnson withdrew the offer. Over two hundred rooms have instead been booked at the Mayfair at a heavily discounted rate. Among those expected is the Argentinean Julio Grondona, the man whose vote can be bought for the price of the Falkland Islands.

Do not line the roads leading to the various arenas in the hope of waving to your favourite FIFA members as reserved VIP Olympic roads will be made available to them. If this is how we treat a group of people who regard us with the utmost contempt and hostility, one wonders how this nation would respond to a group who showed England respect.

Three weeks after vowing to unleash a 'football tsunami' in retaliation for his suspension from FIFA, and just a few days before the ethics committee meeting, Jack Warner jumped ship and quit football to 'concentrate on his political career in Trinidad and Tobago'. He had been advised off the record that at best he was likely to be found 'an accessory to corruption'. Thus decades of ducking and diving accompanied by continuous allegations involving a raft of questionable behaviour came to an end. He remained defiant as his interview with Bloomberg demonstrates:

It's not unusual for such things to happen and gifts have been around throughout the history of FIFA. What is happening now for me, is hypocrisy. This is why I have quit football. I've been hung out to dry continually and I'm not prepared to take that.

FIFA's response to this was: 'The ethics committee procedures' against Warner 'have been closed and the presumption of innocence is maintained.' The following day it was revealed that Warner would receive a five-figure annual pension for life.

On 22 June the full report from the Ethics Committee was revealed. As predicted with regard to Jack Warner it was quite likely that he was, at the least, 'an accessory to corruption'. The Committee has found 'there is comprehensive convincing and overwhelming evidence' that the would-be President Mohamed bin Hammam tried to bribe voters, and that Warner helped facilitate this.

Damian Collins, an MP who sits on the Culture, Media and Sport Select Committee, observed, 'You've got to seriously question the judgement of Jerome Valcke and Sepp Blatter in the handling of this whole affair.' Collins expressed a very widely held view when he said, 'It all points to a cover-up.' A parliamentary report into FIFA and the World Cup bidding process is imminent as is the results of an investigation by former FBI director Louis Freeh.

The last thing FIFA wants is government involvement in its affairs, and the reasons are demonstrably obvious. Such involvement is what is needed and needed urgently. During prohibition Al Capone was prone to dismiss government attempts to intervene. What finally did for Mr Capone was just such intervention from the US Inland Revenue.

FIFA, along with a number of other organisations based in Switzerland, enjoy a tax-free status. It has also enjoyed an untroubled relationship with successive Swiss governments for many decades. Any commission examining global football would be well advised to begin their work by considering the implications of those facts. It will not happen, of course, because the game has long been stolen.

It is entirely fitting that the last words in this book should concern the man who is the central figure of so much of the story. We left him in 1999 settling down at the age of eighty-three years to enjoy his retirement. João Havelange was confident that he had left FIFA in very good hands. He had mentored his successor well, teaching him every trick in the book plus quite a few that cannot be found in any book. It was time to enjoy the fruits of his career.

Seeing him at this year's FIFA conference was to look at a man now into his ninety-fifth year who was apparently indestructible. Less than a month later, Havelange was making the front page again – for the wrong reasons: 'Havelange faces ICO inquiry into "bung" claim'. Yet another fire had broken out in the FIFA forest.

Havelange, Honorary President of FIFA and a member of the International Olympic Committee, has been accused in a BBC exposé of taking bribes. The alleged corruption concerns a time when he was still football supremo, but Blatter has so far refused to open his own investigation – nothing new there. Within the programme the BBC claimed, 'Mr Havelange got a one million dollar bung in 1997. Sepp Blatter knew about it. He did nothing.'

Several FIFA insiders have assured me that 'this time they have got the old man.' Really? Don't hold your breath.

David A Yallop
London
September 2011